RISKS, REPUTATIONS, AND REWARDS

Risks, Reputations, and Rewards

*Contingency Fee Legal Practice
in the United States*

HERBERT M. KRITZER

STANFORD LAW AND POLITICS
An imprint of Stanford University Press
Stanford, California
2004

Stanford University Press

Stanford, California

www.sup.org

© 2004 by the Board of Trustees of the Leland Stanford Junior University.
All rights reserved.

Library of Congress Cataloging-in-Publication Data

Kritzer, Herbert M., 1947–
    Risks, reputations, and rewards : contingency fee legal practice in the United
States / Herbert M. Kritzer.
        p.   cm.
    Includes bibliographical references and index.
    ISBN 0-8047-4967-1
    1. Lawyers—Fees—United States.   2. Law offices—United States.   I. Title.
KF310.C6K75 2004
338.4'334'00973—dc22   2004006008

Printed in the United States of America on acid-free, archival-quality paper.

Original Printing 2004

Last figure below indicates year of this printing:
13   12   11   10   09   08   07   06   05   04

Designed and typeset at Stanford University Press in 10 / 12.5 Palatino.

Contents

Tables

Figures

Preface

IN THE SPRING of 1994, I got together with Frances Zemans, then the executive director of the American Judicature Society, for lunch in Chicago. In collaboration with Lawrence Marshall at Northwestern University Law School, Frances and I had recently completed a study of Rule 11, and I was finishing up the research for what was to become my book *Legal Advocacy: Lawyers and Nonlawyers at Work*. We spent a good part of our time together talking about possible future research projects. In the course of the conversation, I said that I had long wanted to do a small-scale study of the case screening practices of contingency fee lawyers. As Frances prodded me to spell out this idea in more detail, I starting talking about other questions concerning contingency fee practice that interested me, and at some point I made the observation that contingency fee practice really seemed to me like a kind of portfolio management.

It was one of those "lightbulb" moments. As soon as I made that statement, I sat back and thought, "My god, that's really the way to look at this issue." A number of different themes started rushing through my mind. I remembered some of the comments made by lawyers I had spoken to in the course of observation of social security disability hearings. I began listing in my mind, and to Frances, some of the myriad risks involved in contingency fee practice. I thought about the recently published proposal from the Manhattan Institute to strictly limit contingency fees in many cases. Frances encouraged me to pursue this thickening thread of an idea.

In the next few months, I began formulating what a research project to get at some of these many themes might look like. I was invited by Warren Schwartz to present a paper at the Conference on the Law and Economics of Litigation Reform, sponsored by the Georgetown Law Center in October 1994. With the excellent assistance of Nancy Paul of the University of Wisconsin Law Library, I took advantage of that invitation to pull together all of the empirical materials that I could locate on contingency fees. The resulting paper, "Rhetoric and Reality . . . Uses and Abuses . . . Contingencies and Certainties: The Political Economy of the American Contingent Fee," served as the key building block for the research. That winter I sought funding from the National Science Foundation to support a multifaceted research project to begin in the summer of 1995 to be coordinated with a sabbatical during the 1995–96 academic year. Ultimately, I did receive the necessary funding and was able to devote all of 1995–96 to the various aspects of the data collection.

Over the several years after the data collection, analysis and writing was slowed by a three-year term as chair of the Political Science Department; I was able to publish several articles reporting key findings during that time, but I never had the sustained time necessary to pull together the materials to frame the central argument. A leave after my term as chair allowed me to start on the book manuscript. Between family crises and other professional commitments, it took another three years to complete a draft to be circulated for comment.

The debts I owe for this project are huge.

By far the largest are to "Steve Clarke," "Chuck Brown," and "Bob Adams," the three lawyers who opened their practices to me and allowed me to spend a month with them as they went about their day-to-day work. The insights I obtained from this intimate look at contingency fee practice could not have been obtained in any other way. I have expressed my thanks to Steve, Chuck, and Bob privately; here I do so publicly, although my pledge of confidentiality means that only they will really know who is being thanked.

Several graduate students, one law student, and one undergraduate have assisted me in data collection, preparation, and analysis over the years. These include Lisa Nelson, Mitch Pickerill, Jay Krishnan, Catherine Weaver, Mark Brown, Steve Yonish, Kathryn Scanlan, and Ian Crichton.

A variety of people have assisted me in gaining access to various data sets, and at times, in working with those data. Several organizations have made available to me various data sets for additional analysis; these include the University of Wisconsin Business School, the Institute for Civil Justice at the RAND Corporation, the State Bar of Wisconsin, the Wisconsin Board of Attorneys Professional Responsibility (BAPR), the Administrative Office of the United States Courts, and the Applied Statistics Laboratory. Individuals who helped get me access to these data or assisted me in working with the data include Lawrence Stiffman (Applied Statistics Laboratory), George Brown and Rebecca Murray (State Bar of Wisconsin), Nicholas Pace (RAND), James Kakalik (RAND), Deborah Hensler (RAND, now at Stanford Law School), Mark Browne (University of Wisconsin Business School), and Gerald C. Sternberg (BAPR).

In addition to gaining access to data, this project required access to people. Ralph Cagle of the University of Wisconsin Law School and George Brown of the State Bar of Wisconsin were instrumental at various stages of the project in helping me make some key contacts. I am particularly indebted to George for helping me make contact with one of the lawyers I observed (even George does not know exactly to whom I am referring).

The core survey data were collected by the University of Wisconsin Survey Center (UWSC). The work was overseen by Bob Lee. In addition the director of UWSC, Professor James Sweet, helped me in working with data collected for BAPR. I also worked with Barbara Burrell at the Wisconsin Survey Research Laboratory (WSRL) in designing questions for a statewide public opinion survey conducted by WSRL.

Additional data collected by the RAND Corporation from its study of compensation for injury were made available through the Interuniversity Consortium for Political and Social Research, as was a data set collected by Terance D. Miethe at the University of Nevada on "Public Attitudes Toward Lawyers and Legal Disputes." Unpublished summary statistics from data collected by the Alaska Judicial Council were shared with me by Teresa Carns and Susanne Di Pietro. Stephen Daniels and Joanne Martin of the American Bar Foundation kindly made available to me some unpublished summary statistics from their survey of Texas plaintiffs' lawyers. Terisa Chaw, executive director of the National Employment Lawyers Association (NELA), made available some original tallies from a survey NELA conducted of its membership.

Over the years, I have had many opportunities to talk about my research. These include several occasions at the Georgetown Law Center (my thanks to Carrie Menkel-Meadow and Warren Schwartz), the Wisconsin chapter of the Inns of Court, DePaul Law School's annual Clifford Symposium (my thanks to Steve Landsman for inviting me to participate and to Robert Clifford for his generous funding of the symposium series), a conference organized by the Institute for Law and Economic Policy (my thanks to Steve Burbank, University of Pennsylvania Law School), William Mitchell College of Law (where I spent my 1999–2000 sabbatical year), the University of Wisconsin Law School, the University of Wisconsin Sociology Department's Law and Deviance Colloquium series, the Institute for Advanced Legal Studies (London), and Oxford University.

Neil Vidmar, Stephen Landsman, and Malcolm Feeley read and commented on a complete draft of the manuscript. Lynn Mather read and commented on Chapter 7. The final product is much improved by their critical readings. I remain the buck stopper and bear all responsibilities for any residual errors. My neighbor Eric Thompson prepared the graphic for Figure 5.2.

My colleagues in the law and society community at the University of Wisconsin have provided the environment that made this research intellectually possible. I am particularly indebted to my law school colleague Marc Galanter, who has provided encouragement to pursue this line of inquiry over the years. I am also deeply in debt to my colleagues of more than twenty years ago from the Civil Litigation Research Project (CLRP), which launched me in this research direction: William L. F. Felstiner, Joel B. Grossman, Austin Sarat, and David M. Trubek. While we have all gone our separate directions in our research endeavors, the questions and issues we debated for long hours during the brief life of CLRP have been an important part of my research agenda over most of my career.

Primary funding for this project came from the National Science Foundation, Law and Social Science Program (grant no. SBR-9510976). Additional funding was provided by the Research Committee of the University of Wisconsin Graduate School.

As mentioned above, I have previously published several articles based on this research. I have drawn on those prior publications in a number of places in this book. I gratefully acknowledge permission to reuse material from the following:

> In Chapters 3, 6, and 8: "Seven Dogged Myths Concerning Contingency Fees," *Washington University Law Quarterly* 80 (2002): 739–94. Reprinted with permission.

In Chapter 1: "Stories from the Field: Collecting Data Outside Over There," in *Practicing Ethnography in Law: New Dialogues, Enduring Methods*, ed. June Starr and Mark Goodale, 143–59 (New York: Palgrave / St. Martin's Press, 2002). © June Starr and Mark Goodale. Reprinted with permission of Palgrave Macmillan.

In Chapter 3: "Lawyers Seeking Clients, Clients Seeking Lawyers: Sources of Contingency Fee Cases and Their Implications for Case Handling," *Law and Policy* 21 (1999): 347–75 (coauthored with Jayanth Krishnan).

In Chapters 4 and 5: "Contingent-Fee Lawyers and Their Clients: Settlement Expectations and Settlement Realities," *Law and Social Inquiry* 23 (1998): 795–821. © 1998 American Bar Foundation, published by University of Chicago Press. All rights reserved.

In Chapter 6: "The Wages of Risk: The Returns of Contingency Fee Legal Practice," *DePaul University Law Review* 47 (1998): 267–319. A short version of this article appeared as "Investing in Justice: Can You Profit from Contingency Fee Work?" *The Wisconsin Lawyer* 70 (August 1997): 10–13, 44–45. Reprinted with permission of the August 1997 *Wisconsin Lawyer*, the official publication of the State Bar of Wisconsin.

In Chapter 3: "Contingency Fee Lawyers as Gatekeepers in the American Civil Justice System," *Judicature* (the Journal of the American Judicature Society) 81 (1997): 22–29. A short version of this article appeared as "Holding Back the Flood Tide: The Real Role of Contingent Fee Lawyers?" *The Wisconsin Lawyer* 70 (March 1997): 10–13, 62–64. Reprinted with permission of the March 1997 *Wisconsin Lawyer*, the official publication of the State Bar of Wisconsin.

Finally, I owe the deepest gratitude to my wife, Amy, who has seen me through several of these projects and has always been a source of support and encouragement. The data collection came at a time when I was the sole resident parent to our then high school son Nate; the need to maintain confidentiality made it necessary to work out some complex arrangements should emergency arise, but we were able to do so, and fortunately, no emergencies arose. One of the joys of parenthood is to think back over the now nine years this project has gone on to realize that the son who was just starting high school as I started this research project is now an aspiring professional trumpet player having completed his bachelor of music degree; my daughter Naomi, who had just finished college, has become a published novelist and the mother of my two wonderful granddaughters, and my daughter Abi, who was just beginning college, has launched a career as a chemist. It is to my always supportive family that I dedicate this book.

CHAPTER 1

The Political Economy of the American Contingency Fee

Introduction

Contingency fees are praised as the average person's "key to the courthouse" and attacked as the cause of excessive litigiousness, frivolous lawsuits, and greedy trial lawyers finding new ways to bring corporate America to its knees. But what do we know about the actual working of the contingency fee and the actual work of contingency fee lawyers? In this book, I describe and explain the routine work of lawyers who rely upon "no win, no fee" payment structures.

In recent years, trial lawyers, also known as "plaintiffs' lawyers," "injury lawyers," or "ambulance chasers," have been the subject of criticism and attack. Trial lawyers are blamed for contributing to, if not causing, the supposed "endless tide of litigation" referred to in the 1994 "Contract with America" (see *New York Times*, November 11, 1994, p. A26). They encourage the "blame game," whereby individuals do not take responsibility for their own lives but look to others for undue compensation and thereby increase insurance and other costs to everyone (Howard 1994; O'Connell and Kelly 1987). These lawyers continue to enrich themselves through windfall fees in cases such as tobacco litigation (see Brickman 1999). They engage in activities that contort the justice system to advance their own interests, contributing to excessive adversarialism (Glendon 1994, 81; Kagan 2001, 133–35; Olson 2003, 5). And they take advantage of naive injury victims, charging high fees to compensate for the risk they are undertaking when there is no doubt that the victim will recover damages (Brickman, Horowitz, and O'Connell 1994).

Critics, often backed by corporate interests, have advocated major changes in the existing contingency fee structure in the United States. These critics have advanced legislation and referenda and have sought to change ethical rules by petitioning state bar associations and state supreme courts.[1] Typically, these proposals rely upon a variety of assertions about contingency fees—fees are virtually standardized at 33 percent, or much contingency fee work involves little or no risk—that this book will show lack a basis in fact. The advocates of the proposals will refer to windfall fees in areas such as the tobacco litigation or describe cases where lawyers have won awards for persons who were themselves, allegedly, responsible for the injury they sustained.

Imagine what comes to mind when the subject of "contingency fee lawyers," as I will label them throughout this book, comes up at a social gathering. It is probably that of a man standing before a jury in a courtroom explaining how it is that his poor client was injured because of the recklessness of some large corporation or some doctor, and justifying some huge award for all of his client's pain and suffering. The specific image will undoubtedly depend on recently reported unusual cases reported in the media; if this were the mid-1990s, the image might well be that of the lawyer in the McDonald's hot coffee case, arguing that McDonald's should be punished for injuring his little old lady client, who was burned as she tried to open her coffee while pulling out from the drive-up window in her sports car.[2]

While contingency fee lawyers do appear in court, and do argue damages in front of juries, the day-to-day work of most of these lawyers is quite distant from such activities. What might you see if you actually spent a day as a fly on the wall in the office of a contingency fee lawyer?

Let's visit the office of "Steve Clarke" (a pseudonym—except for discussions of cases reported in the media, all names in what follows are pseudonyms). Clarke works in a small firm that largely specializes in personal injury cases, including workers' compensation. This firm handles routine, run-of-the-mill type cases, most of which are under $50,000; as of the time of my research, no one in the firm had ever handled a case that led to a judgment or settlement of over $500,000, and the two senior lawyers had been in practice for over fifteen years.

At 7:00 A.M. Steve Clarke calls to say that he isn't going to his gym this morning and wants to get in to the office early. On the ride in, Steve talks about having worked on a brief (for a case he is appealing) the night before for four hours; he had sat down to do one paragraph and ended up revising one subsection.

Upon arrival at the office (about 8:00 A.M.), Steve immediately goes to work on the brief. He dictates changes. This takes thirty to forty minutes, during which he declines to take one or two phone calls. He gives the dictation tape to his paralegal / secretary, Jim Allen, at 8:55.

At 9:00 he turns to the mail and telephone messages. In the mail are a police report for the accident of one new client, medical records for another couple of cases (including one which prompts Steve to make an observation about the high charge for copying a bill), and a motion (and accompanying brief) from the opposing lawyer in a non-PI (personal injury) case he is handling as cocounsel with another attorney.

In reaction to one of these bills, Steve comments on a $55,000 medical bill in a workers' compensation case. The medical insurer in that case has agreed to pay Steve a fee (20 percent) if he can recover the medical costs from the workers' compensation carrier. The case was referred to Steve by the medical insurer; it would not have been worth his while to pursue the case just for the benefits that would come to the client. Steve notes the potential for conflicts of interest between the insurer and the client in cases like this. The client comes first.

At 9:30, Steve calls Bob Strong, a client for whom he had been negotiating a settlement the day before. He gets some additional information on Strong's work situation, work duties, and prior medical treatment. Strong tells Steve that he had no related symptoms prior to the auto accident; his former job (he had been dismissed for absenteeism last month) was on a limited-term basis (meaning that he received no benefits), even though it had lasted three or four years. Steve has Strong describe his job duties; this produces a somewhat confused discussion, but the thrust is that most of the work was light duty such as sorting mail, with occasional assignments (perhaps two to three times a month) that involved moderate to heavy over-the-head lifting (getting this information from Strong is not easy, but Steve does eventually get it). Strong missed virtually no work before surgery. Steve explains the adjuster's concern (to me): "It is just as likely that the client's problem with his neck is related to work as to the accident." Steve observes to Strong, "It's not clear what happened here." Steve tells him that the situation is difficult, repeatedly explaining that the issue is whether the surgery is really related to the auto accident and the difficulty of establishing proof. "This is a very iffy case in terms of litigation. I'm concerned whether this is provable in a court of law." During this conversation, Steve discusses with Strong the option of filing for bankruptcy to avoid paying other outstanding debts which would absorb most or all of any settlement Strong might receive.

The call ends at 10:00 A.M. (having lasted thirty minutes). Steve comments, "This case is going to be a tough one." He adds that Strong mentioned some leg problems that aren't in the record; Steve's view is that Strong does not have good recall on this. He mulls over the bankruptcy issue; under Wisconsin law, you can keep up to $25,000 of an injury settlement. Steve is very skeptical about this case; clearly he doesn't want to take it to litigation. Steve says that if the adjuster makes a low offer and Strong rejects it, Steve will encourage Strong to get another lawyer.

Jim, the paralegal, comes in with the revised brief. Steve spends fifteen minutes or so reviewing it.

Steve's partner comes in with a question about whether there can be multiple independent medical examinations (IMEs) when there are multiple insurance carriers. After responding, Steve discusses a drunk driving case with his partner, wondering about whether the facts of the case might restrict the availability of punitive damages. Steve decides he needs to check the statutes; there is also the question of who is responsible. A few minutes later, he checks the statute and finds a clear answer to his question.

At 10:30, Steve calls Carl Hopkins, a client in another workers' compensation case, to check in. Hopkins's employer has no available work that complies with the restrictions on what Hopkins can do given his injuries. Steve mentions he has another client from the same employer (but at a different location). Hopkins comments that "it's rough work." Hopkins has a question about a recruitment bonus he got for finding another employee; he is supposed to get a bonus of $500 if the new employee stays six months. The employer is hedging on whether he will pay this bonus because Hopkins is not currently working. Steve tells Hopkins that he is probably entitled to the bonus but that Steve can't really do anything about it; he advises Hopkins to go to small claims court if it becomes necessary.

Hopkins is concerned about problems he might encounter if he goes back to work for the employer. Steve strongly warns him not to quit. Steve tells Hopkins about a case he had settled earlier in the week in which the employee had quit and the problems quitting created. Steve tells Hopkins, "Don't do anything without talking to me." He mentions the upcoming IME, and Hopkins asks, "What should I expect?" Steve describes how the company that will do the IME operates, stating that "the doctor is looking for ways to save the company money." Steve tells Hopkins that he needs to emphasize *how* the injury happened. About the specific doctor who will do the IME, Steve comments, "there are worse doctors around. . . . He's on the conservative side. . . . I'm not looking for great things from him. . . . Be polite. . . . Show him deference." The call lasts about thirty minutes.

Steve calls back the adjuster, Stan Davis, in Bob Strong's auto accident. Steve gives Davis some information that Davis had requested (Strong's work history, medical treatment, work situation). Steve explains that his client does not have health insurance because of his LTE (limited-term employee) status. Steve emphasizes that he has no independent information but is simply taking what Strong has said at face value. Steve offers, "If you want to interview him, I'm willing to make him available." Davis mentions that he is looking through his notes. Steve says, "There is nothing I am aware of [that explains the injury other than the accident]. I've asked him eyeball to eyeball. There's nothing I'm aware of that would be an intervening cause." Davis responds that "it's a hard one to swallow . . . that the auto accident is the sole cause."

Davis is clearly having difficulty coming to a decision about what to offer, and Steve is not doing anything here to push him. Steve is holding back to see what he will say. Davis offers $30,000 "to get rid of this one." Steve is stunned; he was expecting $5,000 or $10,000 as an opening offer (and he would have been happy to get it and get out of the case). Steve does not hesitate in leaping to it: "Let's probe this one. . . . If causation was not an issue, is my demand of $50,000 appropriate?" Davis concedes that if there were no causation issue, the $50,000 demand would be reasonable, but he goes on to say that he still has a problem with the case. Steve says, "I appreciate the problem you have, but here is my problem." Steve describes Strong's outstanding $17,000 medical bill and the problem of getting medical providers, as opposed to health insurers, to take a reduction. Steve adds, "I know where you are coming from." The call ends at 11:05, having lasted twenty-five minutes.

Steve thinks again that Strong needs to seriously consider the bankruptcy option. He then immediately calls Strong and tells him about the offer, commenting that it is "double what I thought he would offer . . . a neck surgery with a good result is worth about $50,000 [if there is no causation problem]. We would have serious problems proving the case [at trial]." Steve relates his conversation with the adjuster in detail (including the adjuster's reluctance to come up with a number). Steve recommends a counter at $42,500 and hopes for a $35,000 settlement. He then goes on to tell Strong, "I think you've got to make some tough decisions." Steve goes through various options, mostly related to bankruptcy. He offers to take a fee reduction (rather than one-third of the total, he will take half of what's left after paying the outstanding medical bills and expenses; this would probably be about $9,000 rather than $12,000 if the settlement is $35,000). Steve comments to Strong that he wants to be sure that he (Strong) gets at least as much as Steve gets. Steve goes on to brag a bit: "I've done a fine piece of work on this case. I handled the adjuster the right way."

Steve again talks about the bankruptcy option, which would avoid payment to the medical providers, adding, "I hate to write off the doctor's bill, because he made the case for you . . . but business is business and the doctor probably makes at least $400,000 a year." Steve asks Strong about other debts. He then suggests some other options, such as talking to the medical providers to see if they would reduce their bills to avoid getting nothing at all if Strong filed bankruptcy. Steve asks for authority to demand $42,500 and to settle for whatever he can get, and Strong grants him this authority. He again emphasizes the problems with the case, concluding that "it's not a good risk at all." Steve mentions the downside of bankruptcy. The call lasts about fifteen minutes. Steve decides to wait until Monday to call Davis back, because he wants Davis to think that Strong really had to think about the offer and perhaps that Strong had some reluctance.[3]

At 11:40, Steve receives a call from a chiropractor; a couple of days earlier Steve had a rather heated conversation with the receptionist at the chiropractor's office. Steve describes what happened. He had called the office to ensure that medical records pertaining to his client would be sent to him before being sent to a third-party insurer, in order to check that there were no errors in the records. He describes an example of an error he recently discovered in the records of another medical provider. Overall, the conversation with the chiropractor goes very well; the chiropractor has no problem sending records to Steve for review before sending them to the insurer but will not erase records, only note corrections. That is fine with Steve. The chiropractor says that he normally sends a draft of his report to the lawyer before doing the final version; Steve is delighted. Overall, it is a very good conversation. Steve comments to himself, "wasn't he great." The call lasts twelve minutes. Steve tells Jim, the paralegal, to call the client to let her know that things are smoothed over and that her husband doesn't need to straighten out the situation with the chiropractor.

At 11:55 another client, Sue Edwards, calls. Steve had been waiting for the doctor's report, which finally has come in. Steve tells Edwards that on first glance the report looks good. Edwards has a notice from DILHR (the agency responsible for workers' compensation); Steve tells her to send the notice to him and he will deal with it. They discuss the case a bit; Edwards is concerned that her postinjury wage potential is reduced. Steve explains that because she is back at work at her former employer he can't do anything about the larger labor market, even though Edwards is concerned about what might happen if the employer were to close up the local operation. The call lasts eight minutes.

For about fifteen minutes, Steve works on miscellaneous tasks such as looking at his mail, sorting through and balancing a checking account, and the like.

At 12:22, adjuster Bob Fox calls regarding a claim. Steve had demanded $75,000; Fox had previously acknowledged that the case was in a range of $50,000 to $75,000. Fox offers $62,500 on a take-it-or-leave-it basis, saying that he will not budge. When Steve indicates that he "would like to counter it," Fox essentially says that he would be wasting his time. Steve talks about the problems of getting the subrogation claims reduced,[4] but he gets no encouragement from Fox. This is an underinsured motorist claim, so if they can't agree on a settlement the case will go to arbitration; Steve raises that possibility, but Fox says that going to arbitration is no problem as far as he is concerned. The call ends at 12:27, having lasted five minutes. Steve notes that the "offer is eminently fair" (there were two accidents, and there is some uncertainty about which accident caused what), and he considers the likelihood that Fox might be serious that $62,500 is all there is (i.e., take it or leave it), but Steve decides that he will test it.[5]

From 12:30 to 1:35 Steve leaves the office for lunch.

When he gets back at 1:35, his partner is on the phone with an adjuster. The adjuster would like to talk to Steve. It turns out that the adjuster wants status reports on several cases, which Steve provides.

Steve had tried calling Sarah James, a potential client involved in an accident caused by a drunk driver, several times before lunch, and he tries again now; the line was busy earlier and is still busy.

Steve has a call from another lawyer on the "lawyer-to-lawyer hotline." Steve is listed as knowledgeable in a particular area. The conversation lasts about ten minutes.

Steve looks at the opposing brief in the non-PI case for which he is serving as cocounsel. The defendant has moved for dismissal on several bases. Steve does not think the other side has a strong argument.

At 2:00 P.M., Steve calls another lawyer to discuss the brief he had worked on the previous evening. The lawyer has little to say: "I think it [the second argument] is splendid. . . . I think it's a darn good job." He has no substantive comments. The call ends at 2:10.

Steve returns a call from Larry Gavin, the other driver in a case he is handling as an uninsured motorist (UM) claim. Gavin wants to know what's happening. He specifically asks about the injuries suffered by Steve's client, information which Steve does not want to provide. Gavin asks for the name of Steve's client's insurer, which Steve is reluctant to give out because he is concerned Gavin might make a claim against his client (Gavin ran a stop sign, but Steve's client might have been speeding). It turns out that Gavin needs to get documents from the insurer in order to get his driver's license back under Wisconsin's financial responsibility law. Steve explains that his client cannot sign a release, because that would jeopardize the client's UM claim. Steve agrees to call his client's insurer to explain that Gavin wants to get in touch, and then the insurer can contact Gavin.

Steve and his partner talk about letters from doctors. Steve notes that a doctor he met with a few days earlier charged $87.50 for a ten-minute conference. His partner tells of a $187 bill from a doctor for a fifteen-minute conference. Neither is really complaining, because in these cases the doctors' letters were central for making the case.

At 2:30, Steve finally gets through to Sarah James (the potential client injured by a drunk driver). Steve tries to explain something about one of the possible issues in the case; James gets confused and thinks Steve is telling her that no damages are available. Steve clarifies. James had expected to be downtown in connection with the arraignment of the drunk driver, but it turns out she doesn't need to come. Steve had suggested that would be a good time to meet (and he had hoped to get a signed retainer at that time). Steve offers to come out to James's home (which is just outside of town). James says that if the doctor on Monday says she can get out, she would just as soon come downtown. They leave it that they will talk on Monday or Tuesday after the doctor's appointment. James asks about a crime victimization form which she has filled out and returned; Steve tells her that it raises no problems. The call lasts about twelve minutes.

At 2:48, Steve takes a call from a doctor to whom Steve has written for a report (Steve is not at first sure who the doctor is). The doctor is sympathetic, but not sure what to say. Steve coaches him on the "magic language," the words dealing with injury causation and the degree of recovery that insurers and others look for in evaluating a claim. Steve is careful not to push the doctor on the substance of opinion but on *how* to say it. Steve emphasizes that the magic words are that the accident was "a substantial factor"; the doctor says, "I think I'm willing to say that." The call ends at 2:52. Steve comments after the call, "That's a surprise"; he had not expected to get a favorable opinion from the doctor.

Steve tries calling his cocounsel in the non-PI case; the other lawyer is not in, so Steve leaves a message asking him to call back.

Steve calls another lawyer to talk about the bankruptcy issue confronting his client Bob Strong. The discussion suggests that it might be best for Strong to file bankruptcy before consummating the settlement. Steve says he will try to call Strong immediately and make it a conference call. There is no answer at Strong's number.

At 3:45 Steve gets another call from a lawyer on the lawyer-to-lawyer hotline. The other lawyer has a question having to do with the claim of an adult child; the case is complicated by the fact that the accident happened out of state. Steve is clearly thinking stuff through as he goes. Steve talks about some cases he's had involving recovery by adult children in wrongful death claims. The call lasts about thirteen minutes.

Steve makes notes on his extensive to-do list.

Jim brings in the completed brief, which is ready for printing.

Steve reviews the status of medical bills in a couple of cases, and then at about 4:30 he cleans off his desk. This is a bit earlier than his usual 5:30 departure, but he arrived at the office about an hour earlier than usual.

He goes over to Econoprint to drop off the brief to be printed.

While this day's activities differ in some ways from other days' work—more time was spent on settlement discussions than is usually the case, and less time was spent on client intake activities—the overall pattern is reasonably typical. In the course of the day, Steve Clarke dealt with at least twenty different cases, often moving quickly from one matter to another; for Clarke to keep anything resembling accurate time records would have been virtually impossible. A very large portion of the day was spent on the telephone, with incoming calls often disrupting the activity that Clarke was working on. Clarke had conversations with clients, potential clients, adjusters, medical providers, and other lawyers. No clients actually came in to the office; generally, most clients come in only for the intake interview and then to receive the settlement check, with most contact taking place via telephone.

In a day's happenings in Steve Clarke's office, one can see a variety of issues that challenge stereotypes about contingency fee lawyers and that call out for systematic theoretical and empirical analyses. Embedded in these many issues are three central themes that structure the analysis to follow:

1. *Risks*: Contingency fee legal practice involves significant risks and uncertainties which go well beyond the simple win-lose dichotomy that dominates general discussion of the fee structure.
2. *Reputations*: The contingency fee practitioner's reputation is a crucial element in achieving and maintaining a successful practice; reputation is important for both obtaining and resolving cases.
3. *Rewards*: Contingency fee legal practice can yield significant rewards to the successful practitioner, but these rewards are generally achieved over a set, or *portfolio*, of cases which involve varying risks and payoffs.

These three Rs of contingency fee legal practice can be integrated theoretically through the construct of the portfolio and ideas drawn from "portfolio theory."

Understanding Contingency Fee Legal Practice

The American Contingency Fee

The standard description of the contingency fee is "no win, no pay." That is, a litigant has to pay his or her attorney only if the litigant in some sense wins the case. In practice, contingency fees apply almost exclusively to matters involving the payment of money (although this need not be the case).

The commonly discussed American contingency fee is a particular type of "no win, no pay" arrangement. Specifically, the attorney receives a percentage of the amount recovered from the other side. Thus, the most widely used contingency fee in the United States is actually a commission or percentage fee (Grady 1976), much like the commission paid to a real estate broker who receives no fee if the property does not sell. It becomes a "no win, no pay" fee as a result of the simple calculation that any percentage of nothing is nothing.

While the contingency fee in the United States is associated with plaintiffs' lawyers receiving a percentage of whatever is recovered for the client, subject to some specific statutory limitations, the contingency fee system is actually very flexible. As a result, there are a wide variety of payment structures that are entirely or partially contingent on successful outcomes. Still, most contingency fee contracts in the United States do specify a percentage basis fee; that percentage can be either fixed or variable, depending on factors such as the amount recovered or how far through the litigation process the case progresses. Those contingency fees not based on a strict percentage include such structures as an hourly fee computed at an enhanced rate with no fee due unless there is a recovery, or an hourly fee plus a percentage with no fee due unless there is a recovery, or some mixture of a reduced hourly fee payable regardless of outcome plus a bonus for recovery.

Moreover, contingency fees in the United States are not limited to the plaintiffs' side of litigation. Contingency arrangements of various sorts have been employed by defense lawyers in certain kinds of civil cases (see Litan and Salop 1994, 195–96). For example, the lawyer in consultation with the client might devise some target result, with the lawyer receiving a percentage of any amount less than the target that the defendant-client ultimately has to pay to resolve the case (i.e., the lawyer shares in whatever is saved for the client). In principle, a defense lawyer could contract with the client on terms that no fee is payable unless the lawyer wins the case for the client, either at trial or by a motion decided by the judge in the client's favor.

While these other forms of contingency fee practice raise interesting questions, I have restricted the analysis in this book to lawyers representing plaintiffs. While I do not limit my data to cases in which the lawyer is being paid on a percentage basis, such cases make up the overwhelming proportion of work done on a contingency basis in the United States.

Contingency Fee Legal Practice as Portfolio Management

While various economic approaches have been suggested for understanding the working of the contingency fee (Clermont and Currivan 1978; Danzon 1983; Dover 1986; Gravelle and Waterson 1993; Hay 1996a, 1997a, 1997b; Johnson 1980–81; Micelli and Segerson 1991; Miller 1987; Rubinfeld and Scotchmer 1993; Schwartz and Mitchell 1970), they all focus on the individual case. Contingency fee lawyers work in a legal practice, which involves dealing with numbers of cases, both at any given time and over a career. The typical focus on single cases in analyses of the contingency fee ignores the context of practice.

The work of the contingency fee lawyer can best be viewed as the management of a *portfolio* of cases. From the viewpoint of the contingency fee lawyer, a single case represents an investment of the lawyer's time and resources in the hopes of a return. The lawyer makes that investment under conditions of uncertainty. While the lawyer's goal is to achieve a positive return on every "investment," the reality is that some investments yield positive returns while others don't. The contingency fee lawyer is thus much like any other manager of a portfolio of risky investments.

The lawyer's management of the portfolio of cases involves several aspects:

- Choosing an investment strategy (i.e., what types of cases does the lawyer want to handle? to what degree does the lawyer want to specialize? etc.)
- Given that strategy, establishing criteria for implementing the strategy (i.e., minimum damages, degrees of uncertainty, etc.)
- Implementing those criteria by selecting cases into the portfolio (i.e., screening potential cases)
- Deciding how much to invest in specific cases (i.e., whether and when to initiate a lawsuit; what type of discovery to undertake, etc.)
- Seeking to enhance the value of cases in the portfolio
- Deciding when and how to dispose of cases (i.e., liquidating investments through write-offs, settlements, trials, appeals, etc.)
- Assessing the returns from specific cases (i.e., analyzing the return on time investment by computing an effective hourly rate achieved)

While much of the management of the portfolio focuses on individual cases, the portfolio perspective emphasizes thinking about individual cases within the context of the broader portfolio strategy. The portfolio perspective suggests the need to understand how lawyers might go about dealing with the problem of managing risk, and *portfolio theory* provides a starting point for ideas about how we might understand what lawyers do regarding risk.

Modern Portfolio Theory

Nobel Prize–winning economist Harry Markowitz is the father of "modern portfolio theory" (Brainard and Tobin 1968; Markowitz 1952,

1959, 1991; see also Tobin 1965). As originally developed, modern portfolio theory focuses on the stock investor, although it has been applied to other types of investments (Bhattacharya and Mookherjee 1986; Reinbach 1993). The key argument of this theory is that investors (should) desire to balance expected return and uncertainty; that is, the utility investors seek to maximize is a combination of expected return and uncertainty. Investors face a variety of risks (Hagin 1979, 95–103): interest rate risk, liquidity risk, inflation risk, overall market risk, business risk (i.e., the risk associated with a particular type of company), company risk (the risk associated with a particular company). While some of these risks are unavoidable to the individual investor (e.g., inflation risk, overall market risk), portfolio diversification can mitigate other types of risk.

Much of portfolio theory has to do with measuring expected return and risk. For example, Markowitz argues that the risk associated with a particular stock can be measured by using the over-time variability of return (i.e., the variation or standard deviation of the annual return over a period of years). Given an assessment of expected return and risk, one can design a portfolio that maximizes the expected return for a preferred level of risk.

As noted above, the key argument of portfolio theory is the value of diversification. The idea is that while some investments will perform below expectation, others will perform above. Of course, if the entire market suffers a decline, diversification will have little impact, but diversification can mitigate the risk associated with segments of the market (by investing across segments) and with particular companies within segments (by investing in several companies in a particular segment). A second issue considered in discussions of modern portfolio theory is the problem of correlation across investments. That is, the return and risk of one investment may be related to that of another investment. The presence of such a correlation has implications for assessing the likely performance of the portfolio. A manager of a portfolio must take such correlations into consideration in constructing and assessing the portfolio.

The Contingency Fee Lawyer as Portfolio Manager

While few contingency fee lawyers have heard of modern portfolio theory, or even think of themselves as managing a portfolio, lawyers who have had it described to them frequently comment on how it seemed to describe their situations. Lawyers, when asked to describe their practice, often provide a description that sounds very much like managing a portfolio. For example, a lawyer participating in a study of Social Security disability cases (Kritzer 1998a) described his practice in the following way: "I make enough on Social Security cases to pay my fixed costs, and to make a reasonable profit; it's how I do with my personal injury cases that makes the difference between a so-so year and a good year." A personal injury lawyer interviewed by Jerry Van Hoy (1999, 359) described his practice as combining a large flow of small cases obtained by extensive advertising as generating the cash flow to "pay the bills," while his partner focuses on a small number of high-labor, high-value medical malpractice cases which generate most of the firm's profits.

But what are the implications of the portfolio perspective for theoretical and empirical research on contingency fees? Modern portfolio theory suggests several key points that are important in helping to understand the nature of contingency fee practice (as opposed to the incentives working in individual cases). The first is the need to analyze the various types of risk inherent in contingency fee practice, and how that risk can be spread across cases through something similar to diversification (see Coffee 1986, 703–5; Hadfield 2000, 978–80). I discuss this in the next section.

A second issue suggested by portfolio theory is the need to understand the relationship among cases in the portfolio; in portfolio theory this is the issue of "correlation." While researchers have occasionally observed that contingency fee lawyers may approach cases as packages for settlement (Carlin 1962, 72; Ross 1980, 82), little has been done to thoroughly develop the implications of sets of cases. Marc Galanter (1990) considered what he called "case congregations"—sets of substantively related cases (e.g., asbestos cases, Dalkon Shield cases, silicon breast implant cases)—which create incentives for lawyers to invest heavily in early cases to facilitate later cases; however, most of these congregations are relatively short-lived.

There are at least two ways in which cases interrelate. The first is similar to Galanter's case congregation notion: cases may be substantively similar. Lawyers can use what they learn in handling one type of case to advantage in another case. This may be represented in the lawyer's own substantive expertise, or it may be represented in something like the knowledge of who is an effective expert witness.

A second way cases may be related is reputationally. That is, the lawyer may rely upon a reputation developed in one case to create expectations on the part of the defendant. The reputation may concern any of a variety of things. The lawyer may be known as someone who is a hard bargainer (see Genn 1988, 164–67). The lawyer may be known for thoroughly preparing cases. The lawyer may be regarded as someone who is very selective in the cases accepted for representation. A lawyer may have the opposite reputation on any of these dimensions. Reputations have important implications for how the defense deals with the case. For example, the fact that a lawyer with a reputation for selectivity takes a case can signal to the defendant that this is a good case from the plaintiff's perspective, and the defendant is likely to be more willing to engage in early serious settlement discussions than would be true if the lawyer handling the case did not have a reputation for selectivity. Similarly, defendants may assess the value of a case depending on who the lawyer handling it is; if a case is being handled by a multilawyer plaintiffs' firm, the defendant's perception of the value of the case may change as that case moves among lawyers within the firm (i.e., if the senior partner passes the case off to a junior, the defense will reduce its evaluation of the case).

Reputation is important for a second reason as well. Unlike the typical investor, who may turn to the public market to acquire elements for his or her portfolio, the contingency fee lawyer must attract potential cases. As I will show in later chapters, a lawyer's reputation is central for attracting clients, either directly or through referrals. Thus, a lawyer may choose to do something in a particular case, such as go to trial (Gross and Syverud 1991, 351), if the lawyer believes such an action will enhance his or her reputation in a way that will attract future clients. Alternatively, a lawyer might accept work that is not highly remunerative but that attracts substantial publicity (e.g., some highly visible criminal case) for the reputational gains the case might offer. While the O. J. Simpson trial was under way, I had the opportunity to speak with a prominent contingency fee lawyer. At that time there were wide expectations of a hung jury, which prompted the lawyer to comment that he would gladly represent Simpson in a retrial on an arrangement whereby he would be paid his fee only if Simpson were to be found *guilty*. The lawyer's rationale was that if he won the case, the value of the publicity would more than cover any fee that he might be paid.

A third issue raised by portfolio theory relates back to the types of uncertainty confronting the contingency fee lawyer: How does the lawyer select cases for inclusion in the portfolio? There are a variety of possibilities. First, the lawyer can make the decision to minimize uncertainty by being extremely selective in the types of cases handled. This extreme selectivity does not mean that the lawyer necessarily screens out most cases. Rather the lawyer might choose to focus on routine cases which have little uncertainty about the investment and achievable returns. Second, the lawyer can engage in a kind of hedging (Hadfield 2000, 978) or diversification. This entails handling a mix of cases. Some cases have relatively low but certain payoffs. Other cases entail much more risk, but success results in high payoffs. Third, the lawyer can be relatively nonselective. Under this approach, the lawyer may want to minimize the investment in most cases. The goal is to achieve lots of small recoveries, with relatively little investment. The portfolio perspective does not suggest a preference for any one of these, but views them within the context of risk-return trade-offs. That is, case screening strategies represent ways of managing the various types of uncertainty inherent in contingency fee practice.

One final issue raised by portfolio theory has to do with managing risk or uncertainty. One difference between a portfolio of contingency fee cases and a portfolio of stocks is that the investment at risk in the latter is determined up front in the purchase price paid while in the former the investment cannot be known with certainty until a case terminates. The result is that contingency fee practitioners strive to control investment as a means of limiting what is at risk. As I will discuss in Chapter 4, a key way of controlling investment is to adopt routines and procedures for efficient case processing.

One possible challenge to the portfolio perspective is that the individual client seems to get lost because the lawyer is looking at aggregates rather than the needs of individual clients. There is some truth to this. In his study of insurance claim settlements, Laurence Ross observed that the lawyer's "goal of maximizing the return from any given case may conflict with the goal of maximizing returns from the total series of cases he [sic] represents" (Ross 1980, 82). The lawyer may find it advantageous to not press one case either in return for a better result in another case or to maintain an ongoing relationship that will produce returns in the future. More generally, some critics have asserted that it is a fundamental violation of professional ethics to cross-subsidize among cases (Horowitz 1995, 181–82), even though such cross-subsidization is lauded with regard to the pro bono work lawyers are called on to perform.[6]

Balanced against the ethical issues is the fact is that contingency fee lawyers provide more than legal services to their clients; they also function as financier and insurer. In the words of one commentator at the time England implemented legal changes to permit a form of contingency fee, "solicitors [offering 'no win, no pay' fees] must realize that their role will no longer simply be that of a lawyer, but also that of investment banker and risk manager" (Balen 1995).

In some ways, the most important role may be that of a risk manager. The standard problem for the individual involved in litigation against a large organization such as an insurance company is that the latter is a repeat player while the former is a one-shot player (Galanter 1974). The repeat player can afford to play the odds, accepting losses in some cases, knowing that in the long run it can expect a certain frequency of success. Furthermore the legal costs associated with losses can be balanced against the gains achieved in wins. On the other hand, the one-shot player is at a distinct disadvantage, particularly if he or she must face the prospect of covering legal costs in the event of losing. As a repeat player, the contingency fee lawyer can afford to take on the risks of losing, allowing the one-shot player both to pursue the claim in the first place and potentially to hold out for better settlement terms or even an adjudicated outcome. That is, the risk manager functions of the contingency fee lawyer serve to level the playing field between the institutional litigant (such as an insurance company) and the individual litigant.

Thus, by its fundamental nature, the insurance function of the contingency fee intermixes the interests of clients because it allows the lawyer to spread all of the various kinds of risk across a number of clients. Where a one-shot client might be very reluctant to proceed if required to bear all of this uncertainty, the lawyer is less concerned about the loss in any individual case and more concerned about outcomes across a portfolio of cases. While lawyers have a fiduciary duty to their clients, in risky situations this must be looked at beyond just the interests of the individual client because if the lawyer did not have the ability to spread the risk of client A across clients B through Z, the lawyer would never take client A's case, and client A would be unable to obtain representation or unable to bear the risks and costs of hiring a lawyer on a "pay, win or lose" basis.

Once one accepts that contingency lawyers are providing a risk-sharing service, it becomes paramount to incorporate into the analysis of contingency fee practice frameworks that explicitly consider this element of risk sharing. The portfolio perspective does precisely this.

The Multiple Risks in Contingency Practice

As noted above, the nature of the risks involved in a portfolio of contingency fee cases differs substantially from the risks inherent in most of the types of investments considered in discussions of portfolio theory. Discussions of the contingency fee typically speak of risk as the possibility that the lawyer will receive no fee; thus the traditional idea of the contingency in the American contingency fee is whether a client has to pay a fee: "no win, no pay." For both the lawyer and the client, this is in fact only part of the concern; the other part is how much the fee will be. The American contingency fee system, by relying on a percentage of recovery calculation, assuages concerns of clients about both whether they will have to pay the lawyer and how much they will have to pay. It does this by incorporating the other major contingencies or risks.

While in many cases the contingency fee lawyer can be confident of obtaining some recovery, the size of that recovery may be much less clear. While much of the literature speaks of going rates and what cases are worth, evidence suggests that case worth is very slippery (Kritzer 1991, 58–59); it is not even clear that, given complete case files, experts can always agree to an order of magnitude on what a given case is worth (Rosenthal 1974, 204–5; Williams 1983, 5–6). It may be clear that a case involving permanent paralysis is worth much more than one involving a broken ankle, but knowing what each is worth, plus or minus 25 percent or even 50 percent, may be extremely difficult. This uncertainty involves at least two components in most jurisdictions: the valuation of the damages and the apportionment of responsibility. Thus, while a lawyer takes a case with little doubt that some fee will result, the lawyer cannot be sure whether that fee will be $5,000 or $20,000.

Another element of uncertainty concerns the size of the investment the lawyer will make. With certain very specific exceptions, a lawyer can seldom know in advance how much time and effort a particular case will require, because that is largely out of his or her control. It is the actions of the opposing party that largely determine the effort of a lawyer in litigation, although factors such as stakes and case complexity are important as well (Kritzer 1990, 115–16). In effect, at each decision point (whether to take a deposition, file a motion, respond to a brief, etc.), the lawyer must decide whether and how much to invest, and in doing so, the lawyer almost certainly considers the potential return from the case. Each decision to invest additional effort will then influence the defense side, which in turn may make investments that require further investment by the plaintiff's side.

In summary, the contingency fee lawyer must deal with the uncertainty of achieving any recovery, the size of that recovery, and the size of the investment needed to obtain that recovery. One way of thinking about this set of uncertainties is in terms of a kind of investment return, where the measure of expected return is "expected effective hourly rate," $E(EHR)$. This in turn is a function of whether *any* recovery is obtained, $P(R)$ for probability of recovery, or "liability risk"; the expected amount or quantum of damages, $E(D\$)$, or "quantum risk"; and the expected number of hours the lawyer invests in the case, $E(\#H)$, or "investment risk."[7]

$$E(EHR) = \frac{P(R) \times E(D\$)}{E(\#H)}$$

All three elements of the right-hand side involve contingencies (i.e., risk). Even if there is little or no uncertainty about whether there is liability—that is, $P(R)$ is equal to or approaches 1.0—uncertainty almost always remains with regard to damages ($D\$$), lawyer effort ($\#H$), or both. These uncertainties reflect that both of these variables take the form of distributions rather than a known specific value at the time a case is accepted, and continuing up until the time it is resolved.

Liability, quantum, and investment do not exhaust the set of risks that contingency fee lawyers have to deal with. There are at least two more: how long the lawyer will have to wait until any fee is actually received ("delay risk") and whether the lawyer will be able to collect the fee ("collection risk"). While neither of these risks is unique to contingency fee practice, and the latter does not exist for some classes of cases, the nature of these risks differs from the comparable risks facing the hourly fee lawyer, who often expects payments to be made as the case progresses and who can discontinue work if payment is not forthcoming.

Simplistic statements, such as "how can a lawyer charge a contingency fee in an airline accident case when the lawyer knows that there is no contingency because someone will pay damages," ignore the contingencies associated with uncertainty over the cost of obtaining those damages or the amount of damages that will eventually be obtained. In other words, it is misleading to think of the American contingency fee simply in terms of "no win, no pay." Moreover, while the level of one type of risk might decrease (e.g., the probability of recovery might go up in a particular type of case over time), that might well be accompanied by increases in other types of risk (the uncertainty about the amount of effort a case will require could well be greater as the sophistication of the defense side increases).

Study Design and Data

To understand the working of the contingency fee and to assess the validity of the portfolio perspective outlined above requires a variety of types of data. Consequently, I designed a research project that involved collecting data through a combination of structured surveys, observation in lawyers' offices, and semistructured interviews. For reasons of convenience and access, the geographical focus of my research is the state of Wisconsin, with the observation conducted in or near Madison and interviews within a three-hour drive of Madison. Where possible I sought to draw upon data collected by others to assess whether my findings are in any ways peculiar to Wisconsin. While the focus of my analysis is on these data, I also draw on data and research to demonstrate that my findings are reasonably generalizable to contingency fee practice throughout the United States.

Mail Survey of Practitioners

My initial data collection was a survey of Wisconsin contingency fee practitioners (see Appendix B for a copy of the survey instrument), conducted in the fall of 1995 and administered by the University of Wisconsin Survey Center. The survey resulted in 511 usable responses representing an estimated response rate of 47.7 percent. The response rate is only an estimate because the survey was mailed to a sample that included many lawyers not involved in contingency fee practice. The sampling frame was the Litigation Section of the State Bar of Wisconsin. The mailing list provided by the State Bar included 2,011 names and addresses, 161 of which clearly involved lawyers not in private practice (e.g., government lawyers, in-house counsel for corporations, etc.); the removal of these resulted in the final sample size of 1,850. Included in the mailing that went to these 1,850 lawyers was a postcard which respondents could return indicating that they did not do any contingent fee work; 1,192 of the lawyers provided some kind of response. In order to estimate the number of contingency fee practitioners among the 658 who did not respond, a research assistant called about 200 law offices and asked whether the lawyer handled cases on a contingency fee basis. Putting this all together, provided an estimate that 1,072 of the 1,850 (58 percent) lawyers receiving the questionnaire did at least some contingency fee work.

To obtain information on a sample of contingency fee cases, the survey instrument asked lawyers for data on up to three cases: the case closed most recently after a trial had at least begun, the case closed most recently after filing but before the start of trial, and the case closed most recently before filing. The "most recent" strategy provides an approximation to random sampling, and asking about the three different disposition stages provides for stratification along the key dimension of when a case is closed. Without this kind of stratification, little if any information about cases that actually went to trial would be available for analysis. To further frame the sample of cases, the survey asked only about cases that the lawyer had closed during the preceding twelve months (or fiscal year, if that was easier). Respondents were also asked to provide information on the number of cases they had closed in each of those categories during the time period, making possible the development of a weighting scheme to adjust for the relative frequency of different types of dispositions and the lawyer's practice volume. Overall, lawyers provided information on 989 cases (332 unfiled, 390 filed but not tried, and 267 that went to trial).

Observation

Between January and April 1996, I observed each of three different legal practices for one month. In each practice, I focused on the work of a single attorney, literally sitting in his office watching him work regardless of whether that work involved interviewing a client, talking on the telephone, reading documents, writing a brief. Only one lawyer who was approached about participating in the research declined. The three lawyers who did participate were extremely cooperative. Very little was excluded from the observation, and most of what was excluded was not related to the contingency fee focus of the study (a firm "business meeting" in one practice, a trip to talk to an expert in another, and a number of noncontingency-fee related events in the third).

The three settings were very different. One was a specialist plaintiffs' firm; one was a contingency fee plaintiffs' specialist in a relatively large firm, and one was the "litigation" (broadly defined to include criminal and family as well as civil) specialist in a small general practice firm. In each of the firms, the observational process involved extensive note taking while onsite, followed by several hours of transcription and elaboration each evening. I did not attempt to tape-record any of the activities. Follow-ups with the lawyers continued for a number of months after the observation in order to obtain information on subsequent events relating to cases that came up during the observation.

To deal with issues of attorney-client confidentiality, I was formally employed as a one-dollar-per-month paralegal in each of the practices. In each practice I did complete a small number of tasks involving legal research, preparation of briefs, and the like. All of the observation was conducted with a pledge of confidentiality, and the lawyers have had the opportunity to review the book manuscript in order to identify any discussions that might reveal confidences or identities. In order to protect those confidences, a variety of specific details have been altered in some of the narrative materials.

Semistructured Interviews

The goal of the interviews was to determine the generalizability of what was seen during the observation and to further supplement the observational data. The specific questions used in the interviews were developed after a review of the observational field notes. The sample of respondents, from around southern and central Wisconsin, was drawn using a combination of legal directories and yellow page advertisements. A total of twenty-eight in-person interviews were conducted with contingency fee practitioners; the interviews averaged about one hour in length, and all were tape-recorded and transcribed. An additional nineteen persons who typically work opposite contingency fee lawyers were interviewed; thirteen were litigation defense lawyers, and six were former and current claims adjusters. These respondents were identified in the course of interviews with other respondents; during the interviews with contingency fee practitioners, names of defense lawyers and adjusters were solicited, and additional names of adjusters were solicited from the defense lawyers, focusing on individuals who had recently retired, on the assumption that they would feel less constraint than would individuals currently employed by insurance companies. The interviews with defense-side actors were conducted by telephone, were tape-recorded, and averaged about thirty minutes in length.

Telephone Survey of Accident Victims

In 1996, as part of its consideration of whether or not to impose a rule banning unsolicited mailings being sent to injury victims within the first thirty days following the injury, the Wisconsin Board of Attorneys Professional Responsibility (BAPR) commissioned a survey of recipients of direct mail. The survey was conducted by the University of Wisconsin Survey Center (UWSC). Using lists of names filed with BAPR by lawyers using direct mail, UWSC's interviewers completed telephone interviews with 503 persons who BAPR's records indicated had received one or more mailings from attorneys; at least twenty-one different law firms were involved (Sweet 1997, 2–3). The survey was carried out in the fall of 1996. Both the report prepared by UWSC (Sweet 1997) and the original data that were collected were available for analysis.

General Population Survey of Wisconsin Residents

On a quarterly basis during the mid-1990s, the Wisconsin Survey Research Laboratory conducted a periodic statewide poll it called the Wisconsin Opinions Survey. This omnibus public opinion survey employed a sample drawn using standard random digit dial (RDD) sampling techniques. The spring 1997 edition of the survey included several questions concerning the visibility of prominent contingency fee practitioners and whether the respondents had predefined notions of lawyers they might turn to in case of injury producing accidents. The survey provided data from 409 respondents for analysis.

Plan of the Book

Throughout the following chapters, I will develop the central themes suggested by portfolio theory: contingency fee practice involves balancing risks and rewards through the major vehicles of reputation maintenance and practice routines. The realities of day-to-day contingency fee practice diverge sharply from the stereotypes critics of the plaintiffs' bar have relied upon in their attacks and their proposals for reform.

In Chapter 2, I present a profile of contingency fee practice and contingency fee practitioners. The chapter opens with a brief discussion of the experience the lawyers bring to their work and the nature of the firms within which they practice. I then turn to a discussion of the degree of specialization and expertise involved among lawyers handling contingency fee cases, including the proportion of contingency fee cases handled by those specializing in contingency fee work, and whether this is a firm-level specialty or simply that of the individual practitioner. The chapter concludes with a discussion of the wide variety of cases handled on a contingency basis, including personal injury, workers' compensation, social security, discrimination, and contract issues.

Chapter 3 focuses on case acquisition. Where do lawyers get clients? How do potential clients find lawyers? As the analysis will show, a key element here is lawyer reputation. The modern methods of advertising play a surprisingly small role for most lawyers handling contingency fee cases and for most individuals seeking a lawyer. The second major theme in this chapter is case screening: What proportion of cases do lawyers accept? What are the considerations in making those decisions? What differences are there in case selection strategies?

Chapter 4 turns to the broad theme of case management and processing. What is involved in handling a case? What is the nature of the work involved in activities such as investigation, interacting with medical providers, and the like? What is the role of documentation? How do the lawyers handle client contacts during the processing period? Several themes emerge here. Lawyers often counsel their clients vis-à-vis treatment; two concerns are evident: a need to document injuries and to ensure that the client has achieved some finality in his or her recovery. The lawyer often has to deal with a client's inclination to quit treatment because it's not helping rather than seeking alternative treatment modalities. In addition to documenting the loss, the lawyer wants to involve the client in documenting the incident and the recovery; this can include photographing lacerations, damage to vehicles, keeping a pain diary, and the like. Finally, the lawyer is centrally concerned with managing the client's expectations about likely outcomes of the case; the lawyer does not want a client to expect compensation substantially above what is likely to be achievable, because that will both make clients less willing to accept settlements and rebound negatively to the lawyer's reputation in the community of potential clients. How does the lawyer manage the relations with the opposing side, and what types of expectations vis-à-vis the case does the lawyer establish for the opposing side? As the analysis will show, many of the issues here are central to the lawyer's maintenance of his or her reputation. A second central concern is cost management, and the role of staff support and routinization becomes very important; here the lawyer is essentially trying to manage the level of investment devoted to the case, and hence control the level of investment risk.

Chapter 5 focuses on case resolution. What is the nature of the settlement process? What strategies of negotiating do lawyers adopt, and what difference does a strategy make? What role does the lawyer's reputation play in the settlement process? What are the variations in dealing with different opposing parties? How does the specific nature of the fee structure influence the settlement process? How does the lawyer communicate the settlement offer to a client and manage the client's decision regarding whether to accept or decline a specific offer? How does the lawyer's concern about future clients influence the settlement process?

Chapter 6 deals with the rewards or returns contingency fee lawyers achieve. The particular focus is on a measure of effective hourly rate (i.e., what is the return per hour of effort that the lawyer invests in the case?). This chapter will return to the earlier concern with efficiency and the need of the contingency fee lawyer to control investment. It will show that contingency fee work, viewed across a portfolio of cases, is "profitable"; however, it will also show that for most lawyers, significant profits come from a very small proportion of the cases that they handle.

Chapter 7 draws together the themes of reputation and reputation management, which will have been touched on in several of the prior chapters. The focus here is on different elements of lawyers' reputations. The vehicle for much of the discussion and analysis in this chapter is game theory. One of the key themes of this discussion is that the importance of reputation, particularly reputation within the community of potential clients, serves to counteract some of the "agency" problems identified by past economic analyses of the American contingency fee.

The concluding chapter will return to the portfolio perspective to assess its strengths and weaknesses for understanding contingency fees.

The chapter will also offer some thoughts on the "agency" / "conflict" of interest debate and the legal ethic issues raised by the risk-pooling aspects of contingency fees. The chapter will conclude by coming back to the ongoing debate over litigiousness, adversarialism, and the role played by contingency fee legal practice; in this final discussion, I will also consider developments around the world vis-à-vis contingency fees.

CHAPTER 2

A Profile of Wisconsin's Contingency Fee
Practitioners and Their Cases

Introduction

This brief chapter is descriptive. It provides a profile of contingency fee practitioners, contingency fee cases, and contingency fee practice. A number of studies have profiled lawyers who work in various types of settings in the United States: small and solo practice (Carlin 1962; Seron 1996), criminal practice (Flemming, Nardulli, and Eisenstein 1992; Mann 1985; McIntyre 1987), divorce practice (Mather, McEwen, and Maiman 2001), or large corporate practices (Nelson 1988; Smigel 1964). Other books and articles, such as Jonathan Harr's *A Civil Action* or Gerald Stern's *Buffalo Creek Disaster* or John Jenkins's *The Litigators*, have profiled individual lawyers who have been particularly successful or have been involved in cases that have captured the public's attention. Popular fiction also provides images of litigators, whether it is the down-and-out lawyer played by Paul Newman in the film version of Barry Reed's *The Verdict*, the plaintiff's lawyer in John Grisham's *The Runaway Jury*, or the corrupt personal injury lawyer in Scott Turow's *Personal Injuries*. Popular portrayals tend to capture extremes, of the rich, the noble, or the corrupt. This chapter describes the real world of everyday contingency fee lawyers and contingency fee practice.

The primary source of data for the discussion that follows is my survey of 511 Wisconsin practitioners and 989 Wisconsin contingency fee cases that they described. The survey provides a slightly distorted image of lawyers who do work on a contingency fee basis because the sample is based on the State Bar of Wisconsin Litigation Section mailing list. Lawyers who have a "general practice," or who do contingency fee cases either rarely or occasionally, are underrepresented in the sample, and hence the profile that follows overemphasizes the role of specialists. I will draw on other data concerning the makeup of the Wisconsin Bar to put the patterns in better perspective.[1]

The Lawyers

Specialization

While contingency fees are most closely associated with personal injury cases and the lawyers who specialize in handling such cases, prior research has shown that contingency fees are probably best associated with individuals seeking to recover money in virtually any type of case other than those arising in connection with divorce (Kritzer 1990, 58–59). Consequently, it should not be surprising that many lawyers are, at least partially, compensated through contingency fees. The 1998 Economic Survey of the Wisconsin Bar (State Bar of Wisconsin 1999) found that six in ten Wisconsin attorneys reported at least some billing on a contingency basis. However, 52 percent of those using contingency fees said that less than 15 percent of their work was performed on a contingency fee basis (State Bar of Wisconsin 1999); only 19 percent said that 50 percent or more of their work was done on a contingency basis (Gene Kroupa & Associates 1999, 15). This is consistent with the 1992 Economics of Practice report, which found that only 11 percent of private practice attorneys in Wisconsin reported that the contingency fee was their "primary billing method" (Weiner 1993, 6).

My survey of Wisconsin contingency fee practitioners asked lawyers to describe the primary nature of their practices as personal injury plaintiffs, personal injury defense, business litigation, other or general litigation, general practice, or "other." No single response dominated: 33 percent described their practices as "personal injury plaintiffs," 21 percent as general practice, 17 percent as personal injury defense, 18 percent as other or general litigation, 7 percent as business litigation, and 5 percent as "other." Looking at the "other" responses, another 1 percent were in contingency-fee-based practices other than personal injury (e.g., workers' compensation, social security disability), and 2 percent had what could be called "general court practices" (handling a mix of civil litigation, family matters, and criminal cases). A 1998 survey of the Wisconsin bar asked as an open-ended question, "What is your primary area of practice? (e.g., business law, general practice)?" "Personal injury" and / or "workers' compensation" were the reply of only 2 percent of the respondents, compared to 27 percent who responded "general practice"; another 10 percent replied "civil litigation," 1 percent "business litigation," and 2 percent "insurance." The 1998 Economics of Practice Survey did not include a question asking lawyers to characterize their practices; rather, the survey asked the lawyers to estimate the number of hours devoted to each of forty-five specific areas of practice; the list of areas included "general practice," "personal injury / torts," "social security," "workers' compensation," "business litigation," "antitrust," and "insurance." The survey also asked whether the lawyer "ever use[d] contingent fee billing," and for those who do use it, "what percentage of your work is performed on a contingent fee basis?" Using this information, and some arbitrary definitions, I estimated that 5 percent of the respondents could be described as having practices best characterized as personal injury plaintiffs,[2] and 22 percent of the respondents had practices best represented as "general practice."[3]

The importance of contingency fees as sources of income varies sharply depending on the type of practice. The typical (median) personal injury plaintiffs' lawyer reports receiving 90 percent of his or her practice income from contingency fee work, while the median for the other areas ranges from 10 percent to 25 percent. In describing my survey in Chapter 1, I noted that an estimated 58 percent of members of the State Bar's litigation section in private practice obtain some of their incomes from contingency fee work. The median general practitioner who belongs to the litigation section and who does some work on a contingency fee basis obtains 20 percent of his or her income from that contingency fee work. Personal injury defense lawyers who do at least some plaintiffs' work typically obtain only 10 percent of their incomes from contingency fees. Of those lawyers who describe their practices as "general litigation," at least some of which is contingency fee work, the median lawyer obtains 25 percent of his or her income from contingency fee work. Of those business litigators who do some contingency fee work, contingency fees generate only 15 percent of the median lawyer's income. Another way to look at it is that overall among the survey respondents 42 percent reported that half or more of their income came from contingency fees. This was true of 95 percent of the lawyers who described their practice as specializing in a field associated with contingency fees (i.e., plaintiffs' personal injury, social security disability, or workers' compensation), but only about 15 percent of those lawyers who described their practice as specializing in something else.

Practice Setting

John Heinz and Edward Laumann's (1982) seminal work on the Chicago Bar described two hemispheres of legal practice: corporate services and personal plight. Despite some efforts by corporations to move toward various contingency arrangements with their outside lawyers (see Richert 1994), often under the euphemism "value billing," contingency fee work is largely to be found in the realm of personal plight practice. What this means is that the large firm practices described by scholars such as Robert Nelson (1988), Marc Galanter and Thomas Palay (1991), and Jeffrey Slovak (1980) simply do not capture the world of contingency fee practice.[4] At the other end of the practice spectrum, there may be a temptation to associate contingency fee work with the solo practitioner (Hadfield 2000, 979) and the kinds of marginality that is sometimes connected with solo practice (Carlin 1962); however, contingency fee work is not largely the province of solo practitioners, although more lawyers who do contingency fee work are to be found in such practices as compared to large firm settings.

The size of practices represented in my survey ranged from lawyers practicing alone to a firm with 485 lawyers. Fifteen percent of the lawyers responding to the survey practiced alone, compared to 5 percent in firms of fifty or more.[5] These numbers mirror the pattern found over twenty years ago for litigators more generally, when a study of lawyers who had litigated a random sample of cases in state and federal courts in five judicial districts around 1980 reported that 18 percent of the lawyers were in solo practice and 5 percent were in firms of fifty or more (Kritzer 1990, 44). In 1980, the median lawyer handling litigation was in a firm of four lawyers (Kritzer 1990); the median lawyer in my survey of Wisconsin contingency fee practitioners works in a firm with six lawyers. In contrast, in Wisconsin in 1995 (about the same time as my survey was conducted), 43 percent of private practitioners were in solo practice, and the median private practitioner worked in a two-lawyer firm; at the other end of the spectrum, 14 percent of private practitioners in Wisconsin worked in firms of more than fifty lawyers (Carson 1999, 229).[6]

Firm size does tend to vary somewhat depending on the lawyer's specialization. Lawyers doing business litigation or general litigation tend to be in larger firms (medians 13.5 and 10 respectively); the median size firm for lawyers who describe themselves as specializing in personal injury defense work is eight lawyers; the median for plaintiffs' personal injury specialists is five lawyers; and for general practitioners, the median is three lawyers. General practitioners are most likely to be in solo practice (26 percent), business litigators and personal injury defense lawyers are least likely (2–3 percent), while plaintiffs' personal injury specialists and general litigators fall in the middle vis-à-vis the prevalence of solo practice (17 percent and 15 percent respectively).

About 30 percent of the respondents worked in firms that specialized in "plaintiffs' work." This was true of 72 percent of the lawyers who described their own practice as "primarily" personal injury plaintiffs; it was also the case for 16 percent of those who characterized their own practice as "general practice" and 14 percent of the other respondents. Of those who worked in firms specializing in plaintiffs' work, only 70 percent described their own practice as primarily personal injury plaintiffs; most of the rest had either a general litigation practice (12 percent) or general practice (10 percent). A smattering of the lawyers who described their firm as specializing in "plaintiffs' work" described their own practice primarily as either personal injury defense (3 percent) or business litigation (2 percent).

Finally, of those respondents not in solo practice, most (78 percent) characterized their positions as "partners" (or "owners" or "shareholders") within their firms. Most of the rest (19 percent) were associates, with a small number describing themselves as either "of counsel" or as an "employee."

Personal Characteristics

Law School Attended.   Wisconsin has two law schools, one at the University of Wisconsin–Madison and one at Marquette University in Milwaukee. Among the respondents, 43 percent graduated from UW-Madison, 33 percent from Marquette, and 24 percent from law schools outside Wisconsin. The 1998 Economic Survey found a very similar pattern: 46 percent UW-Madison, 25 percent Marquette, and 28 percent out-of-state (Gene Kroupa & Associates 1999, 35).

Years of Practice.   My survey of contingency fee practitioners did not specifically ask the respondents' age. It did ask how long the lawyers had been in practice (i.e., the lawyers' professional age). Lawyers ranged in experience from a year or less to one lawyer who reported having been in practice for sixty-seven years! The median lawyer in the sample had been practicing seventeen years,[7] with the first and third quartiles at ten and twenty-three years respectively. While this may appear to suggest that the sample was biased toward more experienced lawyers, the 1998 Economic Survey found that the median years of practice was twenty years (Gene Kroupa & Associates 1999, 33). There is little variation in typical experience depending on how the lawyer described the primary nature of his or her practice: general practitioners had a median of nineteen years of experience, personal injury plaintiff specialists seventeen years, and the other groups sixteen years.

Gender. Women appear to be underrepresented among contingency fee practitioners. Only 13 percent of the respondents to the survey were women;[8] this compares to 20 percent among Wisconsin private practitioners according to the *Lawyer Statistical Report* for 1995 (Carson 1999, 226). This gap is too large to simply reflect sampling variation.[9] However, this pattern is not a surprise, because the underrepresentation of women among litigators has been observed by other researchers and commentators (e.g., Hyman et al. 1995, 20).

The women differed from the men in the sample in two respects. First, the median woman had been in practice for only ten years compared to eighteen for the median man. Second, men were more likely to be partners (or owners or shareholders) in firms than were women (70 percent versus 51 percent); women in turn were more likely to be either solo practitioners (20 percent versus 14 percent of men) or an employee of a firm (29 percent versus 17 percent of men). The primary nature of practice did not differ significantly between men and women in the sample: identical percentages (32 percent) of men and women described their practices as personal injury plaintiffs. Men were slightly more likely to describe their practice as a "general practice" (21 percent of men versus 15 percent of women), but this difference was well within sampling error.

Location. About one-third (34 percent) of the contingency fee practitioners in the sample were located in Milwaukee or the Milwaukee suburbs; 16 percent were in communities with fewer than 25,000 residents, and the remaining 50 percent were in communities from 25,000 through about 400,000 (the Madison area). The likelihood of describing one's practice as "personal injury plaintiffs" decreased slightly as the community size decreased: 37 percent in the Milwaukee area, 31 percent in the medium-sized communities, and 28 percent in the smaller communities. The major difference related to community size was in the percentage describing themselves as having a general practice: 14 percent in the Milwaukee area, 17 percent in the medium-sized communities, and 45 percent in the smallest communities. More general types of litigation practices were common in both Milwaukee and the medium communities (48 percent and 52 percent respectively) but much less common in the smaller communities (27 percent). Not surprisingly, there was a higher incidence of solo practice in the smallest communities (23 percent) than in the larger communities (11–15 percent), and a higher incidence of working as an employee in the Milwaukee area (26 percent) than in either medium (16 percent) or small (11 percent) communities.

Income.   My survey employed a set of bracketed response categories for responses to a question on the lawyers' income for 1994. The median respondent fell in the category $75,000 to $99,999; applying standard statistical methods (Blalock 1979, 61–66), the best point estimate of the median is $88,861. This is consistent with private practitioners in the Wisconsin Bar as a group, although perhaps slightly on the high side. The 1992 economic survey done by the State Bar of Wisconsin reported a median income of $64,838 (Weiner 1993, 33); the 1998 Economic Survey reported median for 1998 income of $100,000 (Gene Kroupa & Associates 1999, 21).

Income varies significantly by gender and position, somewhat by nature of practice, and not at all by size of community. Starting with the latter, the median in all three categories of communities (Milwaukee area, 25,000 to 400,000 population, and under 25,000) fell in the range of $75,000 to $99,999. By type of practice, all categories except personal injury plaintiffs' lawyers fell in the $75,000-to-$99,999 category; personal injury plaintiffs' lawyers had a median in the next-higher category ($100,000 to $124,999). The estimated medians for lawyers in plaintiffs' personal injury practice, general practice, and other practice are $109,920, $77,243, and $85,950 respectively. Another way to see the income differential is in the percentage of lawyers in each group who report incomes exceeding $200,000: 24 percent of those with personal injury plaintiff practices, 10 percent of those with a general practice, and 9 percent of those describing their practices as something else.

It should not be surprising that whether one is a partner or an em-

TABLE 2.1

Median Annual Income by Gender and Position

	Men ($)	Women ($)
Partner / owner / shareholder	105,800	91,637
Employee	59,931	52,518
Solo practitioner	82,513	56,231
All positions	92,146	67,492
Controlling for Experience		
Partner / owner / shareholder, 20 or fewer years of experience	95,648	87,500
Partner / owner / shareholder, 15 or fewer years of experience	84,065	81,154
Employee, 8 or fewer years of experience	53,125	52,753
Solo practitioner, 16 or fewer years of experience	54,114	50,000

ployee, or working solo, has an impact on income: the median for partners / owners / shareholders is $103,099, for employees $58,424, and for
those in solo practice $77,060. Given these differences and the differ-
ences in the positions held by women, the significant difference in median incomes of men and women in the sample should also not be surprising: $92,146 for men but only $67,492 for women. However, as
shown in Table 2.1, even if one holds the position constant, a consistent
income gap remains. It is particularly striking in the case of solo practitioners, where women's median income is only 73 percent of that of
men; some of this gap in turn reflects years of experience: the median
years of experience for male solo practitioners is eighteen years versus
only eleven years for women. The lower part of Table 2.1 adds controls
for years of experience to the gender by position analysis of income.
Comparing only solo practitioners with sixteen or fewer years of experience (33 percent of the men but 85 percent of the women), the medians are $54,114 for men and $50,000 for the women. Similarly, if one
compares employees with eight or fewer years of experience (62 percent of men, 90 percent of women), there is virtually no difference in the

medians of men and women. There are enough partners (including "owners" and "shareholders") to allow introducing experience controls in stages. I first looked at those with twenty or fewer years of experience (60 percent of men and 82 percent of women); where looking at all partners, the median for women was 87 percent of that for men, for this group it is 91 percent. Restricting the comparison to partners with fifteen or fewer years of experience (31 percent of men but 70 percent of women), the median for women grows to 97 percent of that for men.

Contingency Fee Cases

One important question is what percentage of contingency fee cases are handled by the lawyers who specialize in such cases. My survey of Wisconsin practitioners included questions on the number of cases the respondent had closed in the prior twelve months before starting a lawsuit, after starting suit but before trial, and after the case went to trial. The lawyers in the sample report disposing of 14,081 cases during the prior twelve months; 73 percent of these cases were handled by lawyers in practices specializing in contingency fee work. Most of the cases handled by these lawyers were personal injury (tort) cases, but they also included workers' compensation, social security disability, and plaintiffs' civil rights cases.

These figures exaggerate the role of contingency fee specialists in contingency fee work, because of the underrepresentation of general practitioners in the sample—only 21 percent of the respondents described themselves as general practitioners. The General Practice section of the State Bar of Wisconsin has about 2,000 members, approximately equal in size to the entire Litigation section. From my sample, I estimate that about 400 of the members of the Litigation Section of the state bar specialize in contingency fee work. If one assumes that general practitioners join the General Practice section at the same rate that contingency fee specialists join the Litigation section, then the true ratio of general practice lawyers to contingency fee specialists is 5 to 1 rather than the approximately 2 to 3 in my sample. If one makes the further assumption that the general practitioners in the Litigation Section are representative of all general practitioners in their volume of contingency fee cases, my sample would have needed to have 855 general practitioners to be representative, and this would have reduced the share of cases handled by contingency fee specialists to 46 percent. If one assumed that general practitioners in the litigation section handled more contingency fee cases than the average general practitioner, this figure would go up; for example, if the average general practitioner handled half the number of cases of those general practitioners in my sample (the average general practitioner reported about eleven cases per year), the estimate of the share of contingency fee cases handled by contingency fee specialists would be 58 percent. Given the uncertainties inherent in this analysis, my best estimate is that contingency fee specialists handle somewhere between 50 and 60 percent of contingency fee cases.

As noted above, despite the strong association between the contingency fee and personal injury claims, lawyers handle a wide variety of types of cases on a contingency fee basis. The survey asked lawyers for information on up to three cases closed within the last twelve months:[10] their most recently closed unfiled case, their most recently closed filed but untried case, and their most recently closed case that went to trial. For each of the cases, lawyers classified the case based upon one of twelve broad categories (auto-related injury, products liability, medical malpractice, other personal injury, workers' compensation, social security, discrimination, other employment, securities, non-personal injury torts, contract and other business, and other professional malpractice) plus an "other" category. As one would expect, personal injury was the dominant type of case; of the 978 cases for which lawyers provided the information, 83 percent involved personal injury (including wrongful death) and 60 percent involved personal injury claims arising from automobile accidents. However, lawyers also reported handling on a contingency basis cases such as workers' compensation, social security, non-personal injury torts, professional malpractice, discrimination and employment, contract and other business disputes, and securities. Among the unspecified "other" category, lawyers listed collections, probate disputes, libel, copyright, and fiduciary duty issues.

Because different types of cases are filed and tried at different rates, the simple tabulation may misrepresent the true distribution. To adjust for this, I applied a weighting scheme based upon an estimate of the relative proportion of cases handled without filing, with filing but without trial, and going to trial (see Appendix A for a description of the derivation of the weights). Applying this weighting scheme actually produces only small changes in the overall distribution, although there are some notable shifts (a decrease in medical malpractice cases and an in-

TABLE 2.2

Types of Cases Handled by Contingency Fees

	Unweighted (%)	Weighted (%)
Auto accident injuries	60.4	65.7
Medical malpractice	4.3	3.3
Products liability	2.0	1.5
Other personal injury	16.6	16.5
Workers' compensation	6.2	5.5
Non–personal injury torts	2.0	1.4
Social security disability	1.0	0.6
Other professional malpractice	1.1	0.8
Discrimination and civil rights	3.0	2.7
Other employment	1.0	0.9
Contract and other business	4.1	3.1
Securities litigation	0.4	0.4
Other	1.5	1.3
All cases[a]	103.8	103.6

[a] Adds to more than 100 percent owing to multiple responses.

crease in auto accident cases). Table 2.2 shows both the weighted and unweighted distributions.

Comparing the distribution of cases handled by lawyers with different types of practices shows that the only type that stands out with an appreciably different profile of cases is the group of lawyers who described their practices as specializing in "business litigation"; a much lower proportion of their cases is personal injury–related, and a much higher proportion is contract and discrimination / civil rights. General practitioners and lawyers who describe their practices as "general litigation" have a slightly higher proportion of non-personal injury cases than do personal injury plaintiffs and personal injury defense lawyers. The sample may slightly underrepresent non-personal injury cases because of the underrepresentation of general practitioners, but the bias is not sufficient to significantly misrepresent the population of cases handled on contingency fees.

Assessing what cases are worth, particularly in personal injury cases, is fraught with uncertainty. Two experienced litigators or claims evaluators can look at the same case and arrive at very different assessments of what the case is worth (see Williams 1983, 5–6; Rosenthal 1974, 204–5). In my survey, I asked the lawyers the following question about each of the cases the lawyers described in order to try to assess the potential value of each individual case:

At the time you accepted the case, or when you first valued it, what did you think was the likely range of recovery?

$ _____ low; $ _____ high

Lawyers provided estimates for 94 percent of the 989 cases in the sample. The low valuation ranged from zero to $10 million, and the high value ranged up to $90 million. Not surprisingly, as Table 2.3a shows, the median low and high values varied depending on whether the case was tried, filed, or unfiled. Consequently, as with the nature of the issue discussed above, the cases must be weighted to arrive at an overall estimate. Table 2.3a shows the overall weighted medians for both the low and high values. The typical case handled on a contingency basis appears to involve potential recoveries somewhere between $10,000 and $30,000.[11] Table 2.3b shows that the amount at stake is typically much higher for cases involving medical malpractice and for products liability cases. These differences are not surprising given the greater uncertainty involved in such cases and the costs of preparing the cases.

The median fee earned, after weighting for type of disposition, is $5,000. This median includes cases resulting in no recovery, but 92 percent of the cases in the sample (after weighting) result in some recovery for the client, from a low of 48 percent in medical malpractice cases to a high of 99 percent in injury cases arising from automobile accidents. The median case requires thirty hours of the lawyer's time. As one would expect, the median varies by stage of disposition, with unfiled cases requiring a median of twenty hours, filed cases fifty hours, and tried cases 100 hours.

Characteristics of Contingency Fees

The number "one-third" typically comes to mind when the topic of contingency fees comes up. One can readily find reports of fees exceeding one-third (Meier 1997), and it is also true that for some types of

TABLE 2.3

Value of Cases Handled by Contingency Fees

(a) By Stage of Disposition

	Median of High Valuation ($)	Median of Low Valuation ($)
Cases going to trial	55,000	17,500
Cases filed but not going to trial	40,000	15,000
Cases not filed	20,000	6,000
All cases weighted by disposition	30,000	10,000

(b) By Substance of Case

	Median of High Valuation ($)	Median of Low Valuation ($)	Weighted N
All torts	30,000	10,000	823
All personal injury	30,000	10,000	804
Auto accident injuries	25,000	10,000	610
Medical malpractice	500,000	200,000	31
Products liability	175,000	51,337	14
Other torts	30,000	10,000	151
Workers' compensation	25,000	7,500	48
Contract cases	15,000	7,000	31
Other cases	41,288	6,771	40

cases fees below this are either dictated by law (e.g., social security disability cases, workers' compensation cases in many states, and, in Wisconsin, medical malpractice cases) or appear to reflect market forces (see Kakalik et al. 1988, 44–45). Critics of the current contingency fee system have asserted that one-third (or more) is the "standard" contingency fee figure (Brickman 1996a, 248), or that contingency fees "sel-

TABLE 2.4

Fee Percentages

Fee Percentage	Percentage of Cases
Flat one-third	60
Flat 25%	3
Other flat percentage	1
Variable percentage	31
Other contingency arrangement	5
Weighted N	822

dom amount to less than one third" (Brickman, Horowitz, and O'Connell 1994, 13), or that "a flat rate of 33% is almost uniform" (Common Good 2003). They are not alone in associating the contingency fee with the figure one-third; the Association of Trial Lawyers of America, the national organization of lawyers who work on a contingency fee basis, states in one of its publications that the contingency fee is "usually one-third" (Association of Trial Lawyers of America 1994, 3). Is "one-third" a "standard" or a "usual" or virtually a "uniform" contingency fee?

One of the questions asked on my survey was the exact nature of the contingency fee specified in the retainer agreement.[12] Excluding those types of cases for which fees are specifically governed by statutes or regulations, 64 percent of the cases in my sample involved retainers specifying a fee as a flat percentage of the recovery, 31 percent employed a variable percentage, and 5 percent employed some other type of contingency arrangement (see Table 2.4). Of those with a fixed percentage, one-third was by far most common, accounting for 93 percent of the fixed percentage fees; 5 percent called for fees of 25 percent or less, 1 percent for fees around 30 percent, and 1 percent for fees exceeding one-third. Thus only about 60 percent of the cases employed the "standard" one-third contingency fee, and this figure is based only on those cases in which the attorney had the leeway to charge a one-third (or greater) fee. At least in Wisconsin, the assertion by contingency fee critics that there is a uniform contingency fee is clearly false. Before addressing the question of whether the absence of a uniform or standard contingency fee is peculiar to Wisconsin, let's look in more detail at how Wisconsin fees do vary.

The most common pattern for those cases employing a variable percentage called for a fee of 25 percent if the case did not involve substantial trial preparation (or, in some cases, did not get to trial), and one-third if it got beyond this point, perhaps rising to 40 percent or more if the case resulted in an appeal. For cases not involving a lawsuit, the percentage could be as low as 15 percent or as high as one-third; the range for those cases involving a suit but not trial was 20 percent to 43 percent; and for those going to trial 25 percent to as high as 50 percent. One of the lawyers I observed told me that he would consider taking certain types of risky cases which he saw as having a high likelihood of going to trial only if the contingency percentage was 50 percent if the case did go to trial. Another of the lawyers I observed explained that he would consider quoting a fee that might involve a percentage as high as 50 percent for cases in which the potential client came in with an offer in hand; in these cases, the fee would be based only on any recovery over and above the offer in hand, with the fee being the lesser of 50 percent of the additional recovery or 33 percent of the total recovery. Interestingly, these types of variable fees can work to both the client's and lawyer's advantage. For the client, it means keeping more of the recovery. For the lawyer, it can provide a powerful tool to convince a client to accept a settlement, because the client can actually net more on a smaller settlement where the fee is only 25 percent and which avoids incurring costs associated with experts (e.g., pretrial depositions, trial preparation, and actual appearance at trial); this issue is considered in more detail in Chapter 5.

Five percent (weighted) of the cases involved a fee with a contingency element that did not rely entirely or at all on a percentage fee arrangement. The variations included the following:

- An hourly fee up until an initial settlement offer is obtained, and then 50 percent of anything over and above that offer
- Hourly capped at one-third of the recovery
- A flat retainer plus a percentage
- An hourly retainer, plus a percentage once that time is exhausted
- Hourly up to a set maximum, with a percentage if that is exceeded
- Premium hourly rate, with no fee if there is no recovery
- Reduced hourly rate plus a bonus based on recovery
- Reduced hourly rate plus a reduced percentage
- Capped hourly plus a percentage

In my interviews, it was clear that some lawyers were open to negotiating individualized retainer agreements, while others were very firm in offering only a specific type of arrangement. Some lawyers expressed a willingness to negotiate with the client to get a case that they viewed as good; others rejected any idea of such negotiations. Others told me that they specifically laid out the choice of an hourly versus a contingency fee, and during my observation in one of the offices I specifically saw the lawyer do this on one or two occasions. Another lawyer, whose practice was exclusively contingency fee, told me that in a case of clear liability, severe injury, and a relatively low policy limit, he would charge 5 percent or less (e.g., $5,000 on a $100,000 recovery) if he was able to get the insurer quickly to tender its policy limits.[13]

While the fee is usually described as being based on the gross recovery (i.e., before the lawyer is reimbursed for expenses), some lawyers in Wisconsin treat the gross recovery for fee computational purposes as the recovery after deducting any payments to subrogated interests. Even when they do not do this, lawyers will typically seek to get the subrogated parties to take a reduced payment, which serves as a way of netting more for the client (or as a way of having the subrogated party pay a share of the attorney's fee).

It is not at all uncommon for lawyers to collect fees that are less than what the retainer agreement entitles them to. In the survey, I asked lawyers if the final fee differed from the fee specified in the retainer. In 18 percent of the cases for which the respondents obtained some recovery for their clients, the final fee was less than what they could have taken under the terms of the contingency fee agreement.

The survey did not include questions as to why these reductions occurred. My follow-up interviews suggest that two primary elements drove the decision to take a lower fee. First was a perception on the part of the lawyer that taking a smaller fee would facilitate a settlement. For example, a lawyer might feel that the client would be more likely to go along if the legal fee was cut from one-third to 30 or 25 or even 20 percent. A large proportion of the reductions were from one "round" figure (e.g., one-third or 25 percent) to another (e.g., 30 percent or 25 percent or 20 percent). Second, some lawyers expressed the view that the lawyer should not walk away with more than the client; in cases in which substantial payments had to be made to subrogated parties, lawyers often reduced their fee to a level that they split with the client what was left after paying the subrogated claims. Occasionally when the case yields a minimal payoff, the lawyer will simply waive any fee. Sometimes a lawyer will waive a fee on a small case as a means of generating good will, particularly if the client is in a good position to refer future potential clients to the lawyer.[14]

What this survey shows, particularly when combined with my observations and my follow-up interviews, is that there is substantial variation in the contingency fee system vis-à-vis the fees charged, although I have no evidence that indicates that the variation reflects market competition. Still, clients potentially have a range of options to choose from. This does not mean that potential clients have any idea that there may be alternatives available or that they "shop" for the best arrangement. It also does not necessarily mean that the "cheapest" is the best; a client clearly would do better to pay a lawyer who can get a $100,000 settlement a one-third fee than to pay 25 percent to a lawyer who gets only a $50,000 settlement. There was no appreciable evidence, however, that the lower percentages were charged by lawyers who were less successful.[15]

Given the assertions about standard or uniform contingency fees, it is important to know whether the patterns described above are peculiar to contingency fee practice in Wisconsin. A partial answer to this question can be derived from three sources, although none of these sources provides the level of detail found in the Wisconsin survey. The first is data from a survey of lawyers handling cases in the federal district courts conducted by the RAND Corporation as part of its evaluation of the Civil Justice Reform Act. RAND's survey question ask respondents what percentage they charged; lawyers were not given the opportunity to describe a fee that varied depending on the stage of disposition or that involved alternative types of contingency arrangements. Of the cases handled under a contingency fee in the RAND survey, 55 percent involved a one-third contingency fee, 25 percent involved a contingency fee of less than one-third of the recovery, and 20 percent involved a contingency fee of more than one-third of the recovery. This pattern is both similar to and different from the Wisconsin pattern. It is similar in the percentage of cases that involved a one-third fee; it is different in that a substantially larger proportion of cases involved a contingency fee of more than one-third of the recovery. Despite these differences, it is clear that while the average contingency fee may be on the order of one-third, there is significant variation in the fees that are charged.

The second source is data collected by the Alaska Judicial Council. In Alaska, lawyers are required to file a form ("Information About the Resolution of Civil Cases") upon the resolution of all cases (whether by dismissal, settlement, or final judgment).[16] One item on this form asks about fee arrangement, and for contingency fees, the responding lawyer is asked the "percent of judgment."[17] For the period September 1997 through December 2000, information was available for 938 non-debt cases; 71 percent of cases involved fees of one-third of the recovery; 17 percent were less than one-third, and 12 percent were more than one-third.[18]

The third source is a 1988–89 survey of injury victims also conducted by the RAND Corporation (Hensler et al. 1991, 135–36). That study found that of those who hired lawyers on a contingency basis, 77 percent contracted for a fixed percentage and 23 percent contracted for a percentage adjusted "according to circumstances." Only 87 percent of the injury victims who hired lawyers reported using a contingency fee: 4 percent had flat fee arrangements, something less than 1 percent an hourly arrangement, and 8 percent some "other" fee arrangement; I suspect that this "other" category actually included a number of mixed arrangements that included contingency elements. For the fixed percentage fees, only 49 percent were set at 33 percent, with 41 percent less and 10 percent more (Hensler et al. 2001, 230).[19]

Clearly, while a fixed 33^1/3 percent (one-third) of the recovery is the single most common contingency fee arrangement, there is substantial variation in the kinds of fees charged.[20] Moreover, this variation is by no means unique to Wisconsin. The repeated assertions of contingency fee critics that there is a uniform or standard contingency fee does not reflect the reality of contingency fee practice either in Wisconsin or around the country.

Summary

This chapter has provided an overview of some of the key characteristics of lawyers working on a contingency fee basis, the practice situation of those lawyers, the nature of cases handled on a contingency fee basis, and the structure of the contingency fees that the lawyers charge. If there is any single theme to be extracted from this overview, it is that of variety: the lawyers who work on a contingency fee basis work in a variety of practice settings, handle a wide variety of cases, and charge contingency fees that follow a variety of formulas. There are some patterns that are noteworthy:

1. Lawyers who work on a contingency fee basis tend to have substantial practice experience (75 percent have ten or more years of experience).
2. Women are underrepresented among contingency fee practitioners (13 percent) as compared to the proportion of women comprising private practitioners in Wisconsin (20 percent).
3. Only a small percentage of contingency fee lawyers work in firms of fifty or more (5 percent compared to 14 percent of Wisconsin private practitioners generally).
4. Contingency fee practitioners are less likely to be solo practitioners (18 percent) than are Wisconsin private practitioners more generally (43 percent).
5. Personal injury cases make up the dominant proportion of cases (83 percent) handled on a contingency basis.
6. The most common contingency fee arrangement (60 percent of cases) is for the lawyer to receive one-third of the amount recovered.

While this portrait is specific to Wisconsin, I have been able to draw comparisons to other settings along a number of the dimensions that I have discussed. Overall, there is nothing here that suggests that contingency practitioners in Wisconsin, the cases handled on contingency fees by lawyers in Wisconsin, or the nature of the contingency fees charged are particularly unusual. While there are undoubtedly some differences elsewhere, they are unlikely to change the general shape of the overall picture.

CHAPTER 3

Clients Seeking Lawyers, Lawyers Seeking Clients

Finding and Screening Potential Cases

Introduction

Thinking about contingency fee cases as a form of investment by lawyers presents the questions of where the investments come from and how lawyers choose among the possible investments. There are two contrasting images of how lawyers get contingency fee cases. One is that of the "ambulance chaser" who seeks out clients in the immediate wake of an accident or other injurious experience (Bergstrom 1992, 92–93; Karsten 1998). This image is reflected in both popular culture, such as the character of Frank Galvin played by Paul Newman in the 1982 film *The Verdict*, who is shown trying to find clients by handing out business cards at wakes and funerals, and in news accounts of the aftermath of major accidents and disasters where lawyers are reported to be rushing to the scene of the event or to be contacting the families of victims (Biederman 1996; Lyons and Blum 1996; Blum 1987; Davis 1995; MacLachlan 1993; Stanley 1991; Taylor 1986). The second image is that of the lawyer inundated by potential clients seeking to get rich in the wake of injuries. Scott Turow's 1999 novel, *Personal Injuries*, captures this in a dialogue between one of the novel's characters and a potential client: the client was injured when she was thrown out of a window in her apartment by her boyfriend. She knows that nothing is to be gained by suing her boyfriend because he is broke and in jail. She wants to sue her landlord because there were no screens on the window. The lawyer declines the case explaining that if the potential client "weighed more than Tinker Bell, I don't think a jury anywhere in America would believe a window screen would have offered her any protection" (p. 65).

While both client solicitation and calls from potential clients with dollar signs dancing before their eyes do occur, they are not the day-to-day reality for most lawyers handling contingency fee cases. In this chapter I discuss both how lawyers attract potential clients to contact them and how lawyers handle the resulting contacts. Central to the following discussion is the lawyer's need to attract a stream of potential clients while at the same time declining to represent a large proportion of those clients. A lawyer must constantly look beyond the risks and rewards of a single potential case to the implications of a case for the lawyer's continuing portfolio of cases. At one level, this need to attract future cases is not news. Lawyers will capitalize on high-visibility cases, either civil or criminal, as a way of making themselves known to future potential clients. For example, in 2000 Johnny Cochran, of O. J. Simpson fame, ran a series of television advertisements in New York City touting his firm's personal injury practice (Rohde 2000).

For most lawyers, however, the need to generate an ongoing stream of contingency fee cases is a much more humdrum activity. With or without advertising, Johnny Cochran will be attracting clients for as long as he wants to practice, barring some major error or scandal. Similarly, lawyers in the "corporate hemisphere" of legal practice (Heinz and Laumann 1982) depend heavily on continuing business from clients. Even many lawyers in the personal services sector of the bar generate much of their business from ongoing or repeat clients with property, divorce, and estate matters. In contrast, the contingency fee client is the archetypical one-shot player (Galanter 1974). Although the analysis I present below indicates that this may be less the case than is typically presumed, lawyers relying upon contingency fee representation do have a constant need to find new clients in whose cases the lawyers can invest their time and skill.

Yet, while the client acquisition problem may be an especially prominent one for contingency fee practitioners, it is a problem that extends widely through the bar.[1] Even if a lawyer comes to rely significantly upon continuing clients, that lawyer must somehow initially obtain those clients and ensure that they come back when future legal needs arise. As the analysis will show, most contingency fee practitioners rely upon the tried and true method of building and fostering a reputation within the community where they work. Very few lawyers rely primarily upon modern solicitation or advertising techniques; moreover, even large users of such techniques do not generally find solicitation and advertising to be their most productive sources of cases.

The percentage nature of the American contingency fee leads to the expectation that lawyers will be interested in cases with significant fee potential and low risk. While these characteristics represent the ideal case, the reality of securing a portfolio of cases means that most lawyers cannot limit themselves to low-risk, high-fee cases. At the same time, lawyers must take into account both the level of investment a potential case will require and the nature of the potential return in relationship to that likely level of investment. While Jan Schlichtman, the lawyer described in *A Civil Action* (Harr 1995), seemed willing to put all of his chips on a single relatively high-risk case that had the potential for a very high return, most lawyers must pay much more attention to balancing risks and returns. The result is that many lawyers try to construct portfolios of cases that involve a mix of risk and return.

The empirical presentation in this chapter is divided into two parts. In the first part, I discuss how potential clients find their way to particular lawyers; or, to put it the other way around, what do lawyers do to try to get potential clients to contact them?[2] In the second part of the chapter, I discuss how lawyers decide which potential clients to represent and which to turn away. Two major elements link these two aspects of creating case portfolios. First, the more aggressively lawyers seek out clients, the more aggressively they must turn away potential clients. Second, lawyers rely heavily on their reputations to attract potential clients, and they are very cognizant of the impact on their reputation of decisions to accept or decline potential clients.

Where Do Clients Come From?

An Overview

Wisconsin Patterns.   As part of my survey of Wisconsin lawyers, I asked the respondents what percentage of their contingency fee cases came from each of the following: referrals from other lawyers, referrals from other clients, Yellow Pages, other advertising (television, etc.), existing clients, community contacts and word of mouth, direct mail advertising, other, and unknown.[3] A total of 471 lawyers provided usable

TABLE 3.1

Sources of Cases

	All Respondents (%)	Personal Injury Specialists (%)	General Practitioners (%)	Others (%)
Lawyer referrals	19	19	10	24
Client referrals	25	26	29	23
Existing client	19	11	27	21
Yellow Pages ad	11	16	10	7
Other advertising	3	8	< 1	< 1
Direct mail	< 1	< 1	< 1	< 1
Community contacts	15	14	18	17
Other and unknown	7	6	5	8
N	471	154	99	318

NOTE: Cell entries are the mean percentage reported for the source.

responses to this question. To summarize this information, I computed the mean percentage for each source. Table 3.1 shows these means for four different groups of respondents: all of the lawyers in the sample, those who identify themselves as personal injury plaintiffs' specialists, those who identify themselves as general practitioners, and those who identify themselves as neither personal injury plaintiffs' specialists or general practitioners. Recall from the discussion in Chapter 2, that general practitioners are underrepresented in my sample, both in terms of the proportion of lawyers who do contingency fee work and in terms of the proportion of contingency fee cases handled by general practitioners.

Given the public debate about lawyer advertising and direct mail solicitation of potential clients, one might think that these constitute major sources of clients for most lawyers. However, the clearest pattern in the table is the relative unimportance of these two controversial sources: direct mail accounts for an average of less than 1 percent, and advertising other than Yellow Pages for only about 3 percent for all lawyers and 8 percent for personal injury specialists;[4] of the modern ad-

TABLE 3.2

Dominance of Case Sources

Percentage of Cases from Lawyer's Largest Source	All Respondents (%)	Personal Injury Specialists (%)	General Practitioners (%)	Others (%)
20–35	23	27	19	23
36–49	19	26	19	15
50–65	37	31	46	37
66–100	21	16	15	25
Mean %	51	48	50	53
Median %	50	44	50	50
N	471	154	99	218

$\chi^2 = 16.40$; d.f. = 6; $p = .012$

vertising-based sources of clients, only the Yellow Pages accounts for as much as 10 percent (16 percent for personal injury specialists). The dominant source of clients is the combination of those traditional sources that private practice lawyers have long employed to secure clients, including client referrals, lawyer referrals, existing clients, and community contacts. One intriguing element here is the significance of "existing clients." For those lawyers who are not personal injury specialists, one might expect that a sizable proportion of their contingency fee clients would have previously retained the lawyer for some other type of matter; this is most true for general practitioners, for whom existing clients constitute an average of about 27 percent of their contingency fee clients. However, even for the personal injury specialists, more clients on average come as "existing clients"—who for personal injury specialists usually are repeat rather than existing clients—than come from the combination of media advertising and direct mail.

The pattern shown in Table 3.1 obscures the lawyer-to-lawyer variation in client sources. One way to try to see the variation is to look at each lawyer's largest source of contingency fee clients. First, to what degree do individual lawyers tend to have a clearly dominant source of clients? Table 3.2 shows the percentage of clients coming from whichever source produces the lawyer's largest proportion of clients;

the table shows this separately for all respondents, for those respondents who are personal injury plaintiffs' specialists, for those who are general practitioners, and for those who are neither personal injury plaintiffs' specialists nor general practitioners. Because this table is displaying percentages about percentages, it might be useful to use an example to make clear what it is saying: among personal injury plaintiffs' specialists, 27 percent of the lawyers get between 20 and 35 percent of their clients from the largest single source while 31 percent get between 50 and 65 percent from their largest source.

Table 3.2 contains several interesting patterns. First, the mean percent from the largest source is 51, and 58 percent of the respondents obtained half or more of their cases from just one of the sources shown in Table 3.1. However, both general practitioners and other non-personal injury specialists were more likely to have a dominant source of cases—that is, half or more of their cases coming from a single source—than were personal injury specialists (61 or 62 percent versus 47 percent).

Table 3.3 shows information on the nature of the client sources that the lawyers identified as producing the most clients. The pattern in this table confirms the dominance of traditional sources of clients. Overall, only 21 percent of the respondents report that the largest source of clients included Yellow Pages advertising, direct mail, or other advertising;[5] only one lawyer in the sample reported direct mail contacts as the largest source of cases. Among those for whom a source provided at least half of their contingency fee clients, less than 10 percent relied upon one of these sources. Even among personal injury specialists, less than 17 percent reported that half or more of their clients came from one of the advertising-based sources. If Yellow Pages, direct mail, and other advertising are combined into a single "advertising" category, this still does not constitute a dominant source for a major proportion of the lawyers: among the full sample, only 6 percent obtain half or more of their contingency fee clients through advertising, and just over 50 percent of the respondents obtain *none* of their contingency fee clients through advertising.[6] Only 14 percent of personal injury plaintiffs' specialists obtain half or more of their contingency fee clients through advertising, and only 2 to 3 percent of general practitioners and other lawyers rely on advertising for half of more of their clients.

The dominance of traditional client sources is also evident from my semistructured interviews. I asked the lawyers about the contingency fee case that the lawyer had most recently closed. In most interviews

TABLE 3.3

Largest Sources of Cases

Largest Source	All Respondents				Respondents with a Dominant Source[a]			
	All (%)	Personal Injury Specialists (%)	General Practitioners (%)	Others (%)	All (%)	Personal Injury Specialists (%)	General Practitioners (%)	Others (%)
Other lawyers	25[b]	24	11	32	24	22	5	33
Yellow Pages	16	26	14	9	8	12	8	6
Existing or prior client	24	9	35	29	25	8	38	28
Direct mail	< 1	1	—	—	< 1	1	—	—
Referred by prior client	38	38	34	35	34	40	43	26
Other advertising	5	14	1	1	1	3	—	—
Community contact	19	12	23	22	13	8	16	12
N	471	154	99	218	270	73	61	136

[a]Includes only lawyers reporting 50 percent or more of cases from a single source.
[b]Percentages may sum to more than 100 owing to equal percentages from multiple sources.

(twenty out of twenty-seven) the lawyer reported the source of the case as follows:

Referral from a prior client	8
Referral from friends	3
Referral from lawyers outside the firm	3
Referral from medical providers	2
"Cold call" (source not otherwise reported)	2
Referral from another lawyer in the firm	1
Yellow Pages	1

As I will discuss in some detail in the sections that follow, the observational data are also consistent with this pattern. All three of the lawyers in whose practices I observed rely mostly on referrals from satisfied clients and other contacts in the community; this was true even for one lawyer who was a heavy user of media and Yellow Pages.

Two Comparisons.   These patterns are roughly consistent with those reported in a study based on a survey of accident injury victims conducted by the RAND Institute for Civil Justice in 1988–89 (Hensler et al. 1991, 134). The RAND study found that 78 percent of those who consulted an attorney identified that attorney through personal contacts including prior use, recommendation by an acquaintance, or the lawyer was him or herself an acquaintance. Only 20 percent had relied upon advertising: 8 percent media advertising and 13 percent Yellow Pages advertising.

These patterns are also consistent with results from a study of plaintiffs' lawyers in Texas (Daniels and Martin 2002; see also Daniels and Martin 1999). This study involved both semistructured interviews and a mail survey (conducted in the fall of 1999 and winter of 2000). Based on ninety-five semistructured interviews, the authors found that only 10 percent of the respondents obtained more than half of their clients through "direct marketing," which included all forms of advertising (Yellow Pages, television, radio, newspaper, billboards, direct mail, etc.). In contrast, 27 percent obtained more than half of their clients through client referrals and 51 percent obtained more than half through lawyer referrals.[7] The mail survey produced responses from 552 plaintiffs' lawyers practicing in Texas. The authors split the respondents into four groups depending on the types of cases the lawyers handled: Bread and Butter 1 (handling the most routine cases), Bread and Butter 2, Heavy Hitters 1, and Heavy Hitters 2 (handling the largest, most complex cases). Table 3.4 shows the average percentage of clients from each source listed in the survey questionnaire. Advertising in general accounts for about 12 percent of cases, and two-thirds of this is generally from Yellow Pages advertising. Advertising is least important for those at the top end of practice and most important for those toward the bottom; however, even for those in the group most dependent on advertising, only an average of about 20 percent of clients are obtained in this way, and about three-quarters of those come from Yellow Pages. Thus, even for the group most dependent on advertising, no more than about 6 percent of clients come from a combination of television and direct mail.

TABLE 3.4

Sources of Contingency Fee Cases, Texas

	All (%)	Bread & Butter 1 (Mean %)	Bread & Butter 2 (Mean %)	Heavy Hitter 1 (Mean %)	Heavy Hitter 2 (Mean %)
Referrals from other plaintiffs' lawyers	18.3	10.0	14.2	21.5	27.5
Referrals from other lawyers	19.1	10.0	17.7	20.7	27.8
Referrals from former clients	28.9	36.4	34.1	26.2	18.2
Other referrals	12.8	13.8	11.8	14.4	11.3
All advertising	12.3	20.0	13.0	9.2	6.9
Yellow Pages	8.4	14.8	9.3	6.0	3.2
TV advertising	2.6	3.8	2.2	1.8	2.8
Direct mail	0.3	0.2	0.2	0.2	0.5
Other media	1.1	1.2	1.3	1.2	0.4
Other sources	6.3	6.9	5.7	5.4	6.9
N	540	138	141	134	139

SOURCE: Stephen Daniels and Joanne Martin, "It Was the Best of Times, It Was the Worst of Times: The Precarious Nature of Plaintiff's Practice in Texas," *Texas Law Review* 80 (2002): 1794. Some of the detail was provided to the author by Stephen Daniels (personal correspondence).
NOTE: Cell entries are the mean percentages reported for the sources.

Summary. These patterns are not surprising. Other recent analyses of personal plight legal practice (Seron 1996, 48–66; Van Hoy 1997b, 1999) generally reported that relatively few lawyers rely upon advertising techniques, although it is not unusual for a lawyer to experiment with advertising or to use advertising as a secondary source; only one study reports heavy reliance on advertising, and that dealt specifically with franchise, storefront law firms (Van Hoy 1997a, 12–14). Overall, the reliance on referrals and community contacts reported by the lawyers in my survey does not differ from patterns reported thirty to forty years ago (see, e.g., Reed 1969, 71).

Specific Sources

I now turn to look in more detail at each of the types of client sources.

Direct Mail.   Direct mail solicitation of injury victims is controversial.[8] A number of states have tried to ban any such contacts, but in 1988 the Supreme Court in *Shapero v. Kentucky Bar Association* (486 US 466 [1988]) ruled that states could not do so. In a later case, *Florida Bar v. Went-For-It* (515 US 618 [1995]), the Court ruled that states could bar lawyers from sending such solicitations for thirty days.

In Wisconsin, lawyers are permitted to send letters to persons injured in accidents; no waiting period is required. In the letters they send, lawyers can provide information about themselves and the tort compensation system, and they can offer their services to the recipient. The rules established by the Wisconsin Board of Attorneys Professional Responsibility (BAPR) require lawyers contacting potential personal injury clients by mail to file copies of their mailings and lists of recipients with BAPR.[9] The number of law firms actively using direct mail at any one time is small, so it is not necessarily surprising that the average proportion of clients coming from direct mail is low. Only 8 of the 471 respondents in the practitioner survey reported that they were currently using direct mail. Moreover, even among those using direct mail, most report that direct mail accounts for a very small proportion of their cases; one lawyer reported the figure to be 50 percent, two reported 15 percent, four reported 5 percent, and one reported only 1 percent. Several lawyers participating in the semistructured interviews were aggressive users of direct mail, but they reported that only a small proportion of their clients (under 20 percent) actually came from that source.

In 1996, BAPR commissioned a survey of recipients of direct mail as part of its consideration of whether to impose a rule banning such mailings for thirty days following the injury. The survey produced data from 503 respondents. Among those respondents who recalled receiving one or more letters from lawyers, only about 5 percent actually contacted one of those firms (computed from Sweet 1997, 11–12). Of those persons who eventually hired a lawyer, 11 percent reported that they hired someone from a firm that had sent the injured person a solicitation after the accident. Given that less than 50 percent of the respondents reported hiring a lawyer (Sweet 1997, 17), and that the average respondent who recalled receiving at least one letter reported receiving about five letters (Sweet 1997, 13), I estimate that the yield rate from the letters was only about 2 percent.[10] Clearly, whether one adopts the perspective of all attorneys doing contingency fee work, attorneys who use direct mail as a source of contingency fee clients, or persons injured in accidents who receive direct mail solicitation, direct mail appears to play a relatively small role in connecting lawyers with potential clients.[11]

Media Advertising.   *Bates v. Arizona* (433 US 350 [1977]) eliminated state bans on advertising by lawyers. In the years since 1977, lawyers have tried a variety of ways to use television and radio to draw clients to their doors (Bowen 1995a). Most lawyers who have tried media advertising have abandoned it as too expensive and relatively ineffective, at least at the level of advertising that they could afford.[12] My survey shows that advertising does not play a large role overall, but it is important for those lawyers who use it. Across the sample of lawyers, an average of 3 percent of clients come from advertising other than the Yellow Pages;[13] this is almost exclusively owing to personal injury specialists, who on average obtain 8 percent of clients from such advertising, compared to an average of less than 1 percent for both general practice and other practitioners. Among the respondents to the BAPR survey of direct mail recipients, only 3.5 percent of those hiring lawyers reported that they chose their lawyer on the basis of television advertising (Sweet 1997, 18).[14] Advertising other than the Yellow Pages is used by relatively few lawyers who handle contingency fee cases but who are not personal injury specialists; only 4 percent of the general practitioners and other lawyers reported obtaining any clients as a result of such advertising, compared to 36 percent of personal injury specialists. Among the personal injury specialists who do advertise, an average of 21 percent of the clients come as a direct result of the advertising; only two of the personal injury specialist respondents reported obtaining half or more of their clients from advertising.

One of the reasons that more lawyers do not rely on aggressive television (or radio) advertising is that it can generate very large numbers of telephone calls from persons with weak or nonexistent cases (or cases entirely outside the area of the lawyer's or firm's expertise). As I discuss later in this chapter, the result is that firms that advertise heavily must set up systems to handle the influx of calls, systems that can add substantially to office overhead (compare to Daniels and Martin 1999, 390; Van Hoy 1997b, 19).[15] A number of the lawyers interviewed reported that they use radio as an advertising medium. There are obvious reasons for this: it is much less costly than television, and it is easier to reach a specific target audience, both geographically and need-based (drive time is an effective time to reach people with potential workers' compensation claims or auto accident injury claims).[16] Also, radio may not carry the stigma of television advertising. However, at least some lawyers see radio as having the same disadvantages as television; one lawyer who had run radio spot advertisements for a period of time reported that "they gained us some notoriety but not a lot of clients."

One of the problems for potential advertisers in Wisconsin is the dominant media position that has been established by one statewide firm, Habush Habush & Rottier (Habush, Habush, Davis & Rottier at the time the research was conducted).[17] The Habush firm is an aggressive user of advertising, including television, radio, Yellow Pages (the firm has the back cover on many telephone books around the state), and billboards.[18] While the Habush firm has the reputation of being very selective in accepting cases, the firm nonetheless generates a very large volume of telephone calls and has an elaborate system for screening those calls. To assess the impact of large advertisers, I asked the following question in a statewide survey conducted in Wisconsin in 1997: "If you were injured in an accident and decided to contact a lawyer to possibly represent you, can you think of the names of any lawyers or law firms that you would likely call? What are the names of those lawyers or law firms?"[19] About 50 percent of the respondents said yes to the first question, and of those who then specifically did name a lawyer or firm, 15 percent named Habush; the next highest figure was 4 percent (for a Milwaukee-based firm). Since the question required respondents to recall the names of law firms, the 15 percent who could recall Habush is undoubtedly less than the percentage who would have recognized the Habush firm's name if it had been on a list that was read to the respondents. Habush has effectively established a brand name and aggressively defends it by increasing its use of media advertising in response to advertising campaigns by firms it views as potential competitors. Importantly, Habush's successful use of advertising is closely tied to its reputation for successfully handling large, complex cases;[20] Habush's advertising is successful because the firm has a reputation of delivering a high-quality "product." One of the cases listed among the *National Law Journal*'s top verdicts of 2000 was a $99 million dollar award arising from a construction accident at a new baseball park in Milwaukee—Robert Habush was the lawyer who won that award (*National Law Journal*, July 16, 2001, C9);[21] a report about that case related that one of the victims of the accident had specifically told his wife some days before his death, "If anything ever happens to me, I want you to call Bob Habush."

Taken together this suggests the difficulty that most lawyers face in considering the "television alternative." First, a firm has to be prepared to handle an influx of calls, most of which will not be from clients the firm wants. Second, the firm has to be prepared to use advertising over the long haul.[22] Third, a firm probably has to tie media visibility to visibility in other arenas (e.g., the Yellow Pages). Fourth, the firm must deliver results or the flow of clients will disappear as word spreads regarding the firm's lack of success. Finally, the cases that come in from aggressive advertising may not be particularly strong; several lawyers who are aggressive advertisers commented during interviews that their best cases come not from the advertising but from word-of-mouth referrals or repeat clients.[23]

The Yellow Pages.   Open any telephone book with a Yellow Pages section and the largest group of advertisers will almost certainly be attorneys. It is not altogether clear how much attorneys have in fact benefited from Yellow Pages advertising (although I have no doubt the companies that market the Yellow Pages would fight to the bitter end should a constitutional amendment be introduced to allow such advertising to be banned); a large proportion of lawyers employ Yellow Pages advertising in an attempt to attract contingency fee clients: 68 percent of personal injury specialists, 52 percent of general practitioners, and 32 percent of other lawyers. As a form of explicit advertising, the Yellow Pages are clearly the most important media, with lawyers estimating that an average of 11 percent of clients (16 percent for personal injury specialists, 10 percent for general practitioners, and 7 percent for other lawyers) come through this source. Interestingly, lawyers may overestimate the role of Yellow Pages advertising as a source of clients; in the BAPR survey of direct mail recipients, only 3.5 percent of the respondents named the Yellow Pages as how they chose the lawyer whom they hired (Sweet 1997, 18); only one of the twenty cases described by lawyers during the semistructured interviews involved clients known to have found the lawyer through the Yellow Pages.[24]

This suggests that potential clients may not be as naive as some lawyers would like to believe. Any lawyer with enough money may purchase a full-page Yellow Pages advertisement stating his or her availability to handle personal injury or other contingency fee cases; it may be a lawyer with a long record of success with such cases (such as the Habush firm) or it can be J. Q. Lawyer who just graduated from law school (near the bottom of his or her class) but who happens to have access to the finances needed for such advertising. One of the lawyers I observed asked a potential client who had identified the lawyer from a small listing under specialized areas of legal practice why he had not called one of the law firms with a full-page ad in the Yellow Pages; the potential client replied, "The full pagers are just blowing their own horns." On more than one occasion, I heard lawyers talk disparagingly about some of their competitors who are prominent users of the Yellow Pages (e.g., "this guy couldn't try a simple rear-end collision case"). It appears that the potential clients do not find the large Yellow Pages ads all that helpful; persons seeking a lawyer do not rely upon the Yellow Pages as much as the lawyers spending large amounts of money on such ads appear to believe.

One final caveat about the Yellow Pages: it may be that they are a very useful device for assisting potential clients with name recognition. For example, recall that only about 7 or 8 percent of the respondents in the statewide Wisconsin Opinions survey spontaneously named the Habush firm as the one they would call if they were seeking representation after a significant injury. Habush has very prominent advertisements in the Yellow Pages (as do other firms that have established reputations and / or that use a lot of television advertising). These ads may serve to help potential clients recall the name of a firm when those clients find themselves in possible need of a lawyer. I have no way of assessing this secondary, albeit potentially important, role of Yellow Pages advertising.

Referrals from Other Lawyers.   The lawyers in the Wisconsin survey estimate that almost 20 percent of their clients come as referrals from other lawyers.[25] Not surprisingly, referrals from other lawyers are least important for general practitioners (an average of 10 percent), although it is the other lawyers (an average of 24 percent) rather than personal injury specialists (an average of 19 percent) who rely most heavily on such referrals.[26] Referrals from other lawyers can come either on a fee-sharing basis or on a nonsharing basis.[27] In some situations, paid referrals are an extremely important part of a lawyer's business (see Daniels and Martin 1999, 386–87; Parikh 2001, 158–60), and the "referral fee" may range as high as 50 percent of the overall fee that is eventually collected. Unfortunately, my survey did not specifically distinguish between paid and unpaid referrals, in part because of an initial assumption, based on existing literature (e.g., Carlin 1962, 82, 162), that most lawyer-to-lawyer referrals involved some fee splitting.

The observational phase of the research revealed that many, perhaps even most, referrals do not involve payments, but rather simply reflect one lawyer's desire to direct potential clients to another lawyer who might be able to handle the matter in question.[28] In two of the three observed offices there was at least some work handled on a referral fee basis (in one office this included both cases referred in and cases referred out). However, many more cases were referred elsewhere because the lawyer did not handle that type of work; typically these referrals involved the lawyer (or the lawyer's receptionist) giving the caller the name of one or more other firms to contact. For example, Bob Adams, one of the lawyers I observed, did not handle workers' compensation cases; when a former client called regarding a friend who had been injured on the job using a particular type of machine, the lawyer referred the caller to another Madison lawyer who had a reputation for handling injuries involving that type of machine. Adams received at least one new client during the observational period as a referral from another lawyer because Adams handled a particular type of case that relatively few lawyers were willing to handle. Neither of these referrals involved fee sharing. The prevalence of referrals not involving referral fees came out again in the interviews following the observational phase of the research; while some lawyers did refer or receive cases on a fee-sharing basis, much more common were referrals with no expectation of compensation. There is at least some cross-referral going on, where lawyer A refers certain types of cases to lawyer B, and B other types of cases to A with no referral fees given or expected.

While probably the most common reason that lawyers referred cases elsewhere was that they simply did not handle a particular type of case, another very frequent reason for referring a caller to a different lawyer was a conflict of interest. In my practitioner survey, I asked lawyers what percentage of potential clients they referred to more specialized lawyers, to less specialized lawyers, or to another lawyer because of a conflict of interest. I estimate that over half of referrals are to a more specialized lawyer, while about a third of the referrals reflect conflicts; general practitioners are least likely to make referrals owing to conflicts (25 percent versus 36 and 38 percent for personal injury specialists and other lawyers) and most likely to make referrals to more specialized lawyers (72 percent versus 46 and 50 percent of referrals). It is easy to see how the conflicts might arise. One type of conflict situation is common among the significant number of lawyers in the survey who handled insurance defense work; if a potential contingency fee client has a claim against an insurer that the lawyer had represented, the lawyer has to decline representation. Frequently, the lawyer refers the caller to another defense lawyer who has not represented that particular insurer. Another conflict situation arises for contingency fee specialists who are members of relatively large general practice firms; those lawyers have a measurable probability of having partners who have represented or do represent a potential defendant (particularly in a premises liability case or a professional malpractice case). For personal injury specialists, conflicts can arise when several persons have claims arising from the same incident and there is a limited pool of insurance money available for compensation; in these situations it would be a conflict of interest for the lawyer to represent all of the claimants. When conflicts like these arise, lawyers can simply decline representation, or suggest other lawyers; the latter course of action appears common among the lawyers in Wisconsin.

As it turns out, there are relatively few lawyers or firms in Wisconsin that depend heavily on paid referrals.[29] There is at least one firm that I identified which describes itself as primarily depending on referrals from other lawyers ("we rarely take cases that don't come from other lawyers") and which usually pays a referral fee. That firm jealously guards its relationships with referring lawyers, to the point that if a client previously referred by another lawyer directly contacts the firm about a new case, the firm will ask the client to go back through the original lawyer. As part of the practitioner survey, I asked lawyers to name the lawyers who had been the recipients of the respondent's two most recent referrals, and this firm showed up most often (constituting almost 10 percent of the names provided). Three other firms combine to constitute another 10 percent of the referrals mentioned; two of those firms are well known for handling large cases, and the third has a reputation for expertise in some very specific types of cases. However, 45 percent of the mentions appeared only once.[30]

Some lawyers report specific activities aimed at obtaining referrals from other lawyers. Some lawyers advertise specific specialties (e.g., legal malpractice) in periodicals aimed at other lawyers. Others seek out opportunities to speak before bar groups about developments in their specialty (compare to Daniels and Martin 1999, 387). Some lawyers emphasize mutual referral networks, where they received referrals from lawyers who do not handle personal injury or social security or workers' compensation and refer other cases back to those same lawyers.

Paid referrals are controversial, and some states consider them a violation of professional rules of ethics. However, there is a strong argument that referrals work largely to the client's benefit because the referring lawyer can serve as the client's expert alter ego (see Hay 1996b; Parikh 2001, 146–51; see also Spurr 1988). If one presumes that the client's interest is to maximize the settlement, this same interest accrues to the referring lawyer, who is to receive a percentage of the ultimate fee. Note that on a single-case basis, this may not be the profit-maximizing outcome for the lawyer actually handling the case ("working the case"); as economic analyses have shown (Johnson 1980–81; Kritzer 1991, 63–64; Miller 1987; Rosenthal 1974), the rational lawyer working the case, and thinking only about the instant case, wants to maximize his or her hourly return, and this often happens at a point that is not optimal for the client paying on a percentage basis. The problem for the typical client is that the client lacks the information to assess a proposed settlement. This problem is much less the case for a referring lawyer who is not investing his or her own time and hence prefers the same outcome as the client rather than the outcome preferred by the lawyer working the case. While the referring lawyer may not be formally included in the decision to settle, that lawyer will be aware of the payment ultimately received. If the lawyer working the case wants future referrals from the referring lawyer, the former wants to be sure that the referring lawyer is satisfied with the outcome, with the result that the lawyer handling the case will not want to underperform. This need to satisfy the relatively knowledgeable referring lawyer serves as one check on the potential conflict of interest between the lawyer working the case and the client.

Existing (and Repeat) Clients. Overall, in my Wisconsin survey, the lawyers report that an average of 19 percent of their contingency fee clients are "existing clients." The category of "existing clients" captures two very different situations, one for contingency fee specialists outside a broader firm structure and one for mixed practice lawyers and contingency fee specialists within a general practice firm. The idea that a firm offering a range of services to its clients would potentially service contingency fee cases for existing clients is not surprising, particularly in smaller communities where firms have to offer a range of services to survive. In Madison, and no doubt elsewhere, there are twenty to fifty lawyer firms that have significant business / corporate clienteles and at the same time include small groups of lawyers who are contingency fee specialists. Often these specialists rely very heavily on what amounts to an internal referral network for many of their clients. Those lawyers who are not personal injury plaintiffs' specialists report that an average of 23 percent of their contingency fee clients are "existing clients," 27 percent for general practitioners and 21 percent for other lawyers.

Lawyers who describe themselves as specializing in personal injury plaintiffs' work report that only an average of 11 percent of their cases come from "existing clients." For these lawyers, this usually means that the clients are repeaters; that is, the lawyer had previously represented the client (or a member of the client's immediate family) on a personal injury matter. The general image of personal injury lawyers is that they represent a succession of one-shot clients. The reality appears to be that for most of these lawyers the repeat client is a measurable part of their work. In two of the firms included in the observational part of the research, at least one of the contingency fee cases resolved during the month involved a repeat client.[31] In both cases, while the claims were quite small, the lawyer greatly valued working on behalf of the repeat client because the lawyer believed that the repeat client was particularly likely to be a source of future work, either from the client him- or herself or from persons referred by the repeat client. One of the interviewees summed up the role of repeat clients: "Clients come back. I just had a client come back. I settled his auto case, and now he got hit by a car as a pedestrian. You find, and this seems very odd, but you find that the same people have accidents over and over; I don't know if they are looking for trouble, or if they are accident prone, but it happens." Not surprisingly, lawyers want to facilitate this type of repeat business. Beyond delivering a good result and creating a positive impression, lawyers do many of the standard types of things businesses do to maintain client-customer contact: mail out Christmas cards, send newsletters, notify clients of developments that may be of interest to them, and the like (see also Daniels and Martin 2001, 177).

Client Referrals.   Besides returning when a new matter arises, satisfied clients produce additional cases by referring others in need of legal services to the lawyers they have previously used. As shown in Table 3.1, referrals from prior or existing clients tend to be the largest single source of new clients for Wisconsin personal injury specialists (26 percent); for general practitioners, referrals are also the largest source (29 percent), although existing clients is a close second (27 percent); for other lawyers, three sources produce virtually identical proportions, and one of these is referrals from prior or existing clients (23 percent with 24 percent from lawyer referrals and 21 percent from existing clients). Of the twenty cases described during the semistructured interviews, eight (40 percent) came as client referrals.

The importance of client referrals came up repeatedly during the observation and during the interviews. For example, Steve Clarke, one of the lawyers I observed, repeatedly stated how much he valued receiving clients via referrals from prior clients, taking an extra close look at potential clients who came as referrals before declining their cases; on occasion this led Clarke to accept some marginal cases he might otherwise have declined. Whenever Clarke was contacted by someone referred by a prior client, he made an effort to communicate his appreciation to the referrer. Clarke's view was that a former client who has made one referral is likely to make future referrals, and whatever he can do to encourage this—taking the referred case even if it is marginal, expressing his appreciation, and the like—he will try to do. The importance of referrals to Clarke was nicely illustrated by his "exit procedure": after handing the client a check from a decision or settlement, Clarke would then hand the client one of his cards and say, "Hopefully you won't need me again, . . . [but] if you know someone who does, please send them in."

Community Contacts.   Perhaps the most traditional way for lawyers serving the "personal plight" (Heinz and Laumann 1982) sector of the legal marketplace is by building up community contacts (Seron 1996, 52–56; Van Hoy 1997b, 1999). At the simplest level, this starts with friends and family who find that they need legal services. At the other extreme, it may be a lawyer who has achieved local prominence, often by having served in a visible public office such as district attorney or as a member of the state legislature (Barber 1965, 67–115; Van Hoy 1999).

Table 3.1 shows, based on the survey of Wisconsin practitioners, that only about 15 percent of clients come directly through community contacts, and this does not vary appreciably depending on the lawyer's type of practice.[32] Both the observation and the interviews show that lawyers see community visibility and the resulting community contacts as important sources of clients. One of the lawyers I observed made a special effort to develop contacts through labor organizations, offering to speak to various labor groups, and willingly accepting telephone calls on very marginal matters from members of union organizations. Over the month of observation, the lawyer remarked several times that he "gives out a lot of free advice" to union members; he typically made such a comment after an extended telephone conversation that he had realized almost immediately would not lead to a fee-generating case. Nevertheless, he continued to devote significant time to these calls in the hopes that someone from one of the unions would call him should a large claim come up.

Both of the other two lawyers I observed were very active in community and local service organizations. One served as an officer of one such organization. The other made a very specific effort to be seen in the community by circulating among various local restaurants (he was based in a town outside Madison) for lunch. He stated very explicitly that he did this to be seen so that should someone have a case they would be more likely to think of him.

These kinds of contacts were frequently mentioned by interview respondents: speaking before unions and community groups, serving on boards of directors of service organizations, giving scholarships, sponsoring Little League teams, and the like. In one sense these activities are a form of advertising, but they are more of an institutional ad rather than an ad targeted to a specific market or clientele. The idea, as expressed by one interview respondent, is to have the lawyer's or firm's name associated with positives in the community with the hope that the effort will pay off over time. One lawyer described a senior partner who was very active in a variety of community settings as "a schmoozy sort of guy" who makes a lot of very good contacts for the firm. Another lawyer commented, "I have a lot of activities that have nothing to do with practicing law, but [they expose] me to a lot of contacts who hopefully see me as a person to come to when they need a lawyer."

Community contacts include a variety of other types of sources: referrals from medical providers, public officials, and law enforcement personnel. Bob Adams, the lawyer I observed who, as I will describe in more detail below, had a mixed-court practice, received a number of referrals from political and legal officials, particularly from the contacts he had cultivated in the courthouse setting. During the month of observation, one of the personal injury clients who came to Bob had obtained his name from a local prosecutor; another new personal injury client obtained his name from a local judge; and one of his new criminal clients was given his name by a local political figure.

Another potential referral source is medical providers (see Daniels and Martin 1999, 390–91). Lawyers may try to initiate contacts with medical providers who might be good referral sources. Some lawyers report contacts from medical providers who are interested in a mutual referral system because the medical provider frequently comes in contact with accident victims. Even without mutual referrals, medical providers can be a source of clients; two of the twenty cases described during the semistructured interviews came from such referrals; several respondents to the structured survey specifically mentioned medical providers under the "other" category of client sources.

Other Sources.   There are a variety of other sources from which clients might come. Referrals from members of the lawyer's family or social friends is one such source. Occasionally a client might obtain the lawyer's name from a referral service operated by the state or local bar association, or from a lawyer referral service operated by some other type of organization (e.g., a labor union, an employer, or a social service agency). A few clients might find the lawyer's name in a specialized directory, such as Martindale-Hubbell or a state bar directory. No one of these appears to be a major source of clients.

There is also the likelihood that at least some lawyers engage in practices pejoratively labeled ambulance chasing. Such practices did not come up, either in my observations or in my interviews. Other research (Parikh 2001, 200–202) suggests that a small number of lawyers in some communities probably do seek out clients in ways that violate ethical, and possibly legal, strictures, and that while the number of such lawyers is small, such activity does put competitive pressure on other lawyers. Still, the fact that no one brought it up in the course of my observation or interviews, even to complain about the economic pressures of contingency fee practice, suggests that it is probably rare in Wisconsin.

Systematic Variation in Client Sources

Clearly there is substantial variety in how contingency fee clients find their way into a particular lawyer's office. Lawyers specializing in personal injury plaintiffs' work are slightly more likely to rely upon nontraditional, advertising-based sources, while other lawyers are slightly more likely to draw from an existing client base. However, all three of the groups I looked at are most likely to draw on sources such as referrals from prior clients and from other lawyers and from community-based contacts. Are there other variables that might account for systematic variation in client sources? I explored the possible influence of several variables: years in practice, size of community, gender, and firm versus solo practice.

The details of my analysis are discussed in Appendix 1 at the end of this chapter. While I found a number of relationships that served to specify lawyers' sources of cases to some degree (some of the relationships are as one would expect, while others are more difficult to explain), none of the relationships is strong enough to substantially modify the thrust of the patterns discussed above: lawyers rely most heavily upon word-of-mouth referrals and existing or prior clients for their contingency fee cases. Few lawyers obtain more than a relatively small fraction of their contingency fee clients primarily as a result of advertising in the Yellow Pages, direct mail, or media.

The Role of Reputation in Client and Case Acquisition

One theme binds a number of the sources of contingency fee clients together: the importance of a lawyer's reputation (see also Daniels and Martin 1999, 382; Van Hoy 1999). In order for a lawyer to secure clients through referrals from other lawyers, prior clients, and community contacts or through repeat business from existing or prior clients, a lawyer must have a reputation that he or she will provide a good service to the client. Good service can involve any of a variety of elements: responding positively to client contacts, returning telephone calls, keeping the client abreast of developments, interacting positively and effectively with the client, and delivering a result that the client sees as satisfactory and continues to see as satisfactory over time. In a case involving the payment of money damages, which by necessity is almost always the case when the lawyer is paid on a contingency fee basis, the result is gauged in terms of the payment the client receives and possibly how long it took to secure that payment.

It is easy to imagine that the lawyers who make these referrals are able to distinguish between their colleagues who deliver for their clients and those who are more concerned about their own interests. How is this the case for former contingency fee clients (who might be recommending the lawyer to friends, family members, or coworkers, or coming back with a new case themselves)? Very simply, clients talk about their experiences and compare their experiences with those of their friends. A client who obtained a settlement of $2,000 or $3,000 for a serious injury such as a broken leg is likely to hear things from others that suggest that the injury was substantially undercompensated. Contingency fee lawyers want their clients to leave satisfied with the result the lawyer obtained on their behalf; more important, the lawyers want the clients to *stay* satisfied. A lawyer who settles cases too cheaply will have trouble maintaining the reputation necessary to create the flow of potential clients that is in the lawyer's long-term interest.

As the discussion in the second half of this chapter as well as that to come in Chapter 7 will show, the concern for reputation is important in how the lawyer works with clients and disposes of cases.

Screening and Selecting Cases

Introduction

Getting potential clients to make contact is only half of the problem of lawyers seeking contingency fee clients. Once presented with investment opportunities in the form of potential clients contacting their offices, the lawyers must decide which investments to make and which to decline. In this way lawyers serve as gatekeepers to the legal system while at the same time trying to choose potentially profitable investment opportunities. Commentators have long noted the gatekeeping role played by lawyers; Elihu Root is said to have observed that "about half of the practice of the decent lawyer consists in telling would-be clients that they are damned fools and should stop" (quoted in Jessup 1938, 133).[33] More recently, Pierre Bourdieu (1987, 835) posited that "legal qualifications comprise a specific power that allows control over entry into the juridical field by deciding which conflicts deserve entry." One image of lawyers that seems particularly popular in contemporary United States is that they stir up trouble, and do this more today than in prior times (see, for example, Glendon 1994, quoting Root *twice*, 37 and 75). I cannot provide any evidence on whether lawyers have changed in their tendency to encourage or discourage potential litigants compared to some supposed golden era, but my survey, along with a survey from Texas, does provide some of the first systematic evidence on the screening of potential cases by contingency fee lawyers.

The contingency logic suggests that contingency fee lawyers should reject a large number of cases that potential clients bring to them. Thinking in terms of the portfolio model, lawyers should evaluate potential cases in terms of the risks involved and the potential returns associated with those risks. An attorney will reject cases which do not satisfy the attorney's to return criteria. As the following discussion will make clear, the third of my Rs is also important: lawyers have an eye on their reputations as will as on the risk and rewards of particular cases.

There is little prior research to build on in understanding lawyers' screening practices and decisions. There have been occasional articles in the legal press that describe case screening practices of top-end law firms (e.g., Crane 1988), as well as prescriptive articles in periodicals targeted to the legal profession that discuss what should be considered in screening cases (e.g., Trine and Luvera 1994). I have been able to identify only two reported studies, both focusing on a narrow range of cases. One, conducted about thirty years ago, focused on medical malpractice and found that attorneys accepted only about one in eight potential medical malpractice clients who contacted them with possible claims (Dietz, Baird, and Berul 1973, 95–101). The second was a survey conducted by the National Employment Lawyers Association (NELA) of its membership in 1991 (National Employment Lawyers Association 1991); NELA found that "44 percent of the lawyers responding to [the] survey decline to represent more than 90 percent of the individuals who seek their assistance" (p. 4; see also Holmes 1991). NELA provided me with their raw hand tallies of the survey results; from the tallies, I estimated that the mean percentage of cases declined was 79 percent; that is, the average NELA lawyer accepted just over 21 percent of the potential discrimination cases that came to him or her.

Both employment discrimination and medical malpractice present somewhat unique situations. Let me now turn to my survey, which provides a much broader, and much more up-to-date, view of the screening practices of contingency fee lawyers. I will then report some data from the survey done in Texas by Stephen Daniels and Joanne Martin (2002).

Contact Volume

The first question is how many potential clients contact contingency fee practitioners. Not surprisingly, the volume of contacts varied widely among the lawyers. My survey included the question, "During the past

12 months, approximately how many potential contingent fee clients made initial contacts with you/your firm?" followed by "How many of those clients did you/your firm accept?" Four hundred fifty-five survey respondents provided usable responses.[34] The number of potential clients contacting the respondents or their firms ranged from 1 to 5,000, with the number of clients accepted ranging from 0 to 600. Table 3.5a summarizes the volume of contacts. Overall, these lawyers had contacts from 53,584 potential clients. Seven respondents reported more than 1,000 contacts, which represents an average of at least twenty contacts a week, or four per day; at the other extreme, almost half (47 percent) report about two or fewer contacts per month (twenty-five or less over the year).

One problem with the figures above is that some lawyers (about 10 percent of the 455 respondents) work in firms where case screening is handled on a firmwide basis, while other lawyers handle screening on an individual basis either in a firm or as solo practitioners. Preliminary analyses indicated that the general pattern in the results is the same regardless of whether the "firm-level" screeners are included or excluded. Consequently, because I want to take into account individual characteristics later in the discussion, the right two columns of Table 3.5a show information for lawyers where case screening is not a firm-level function. For these lawyers, the range of contacts is from 1 to 2,500; aggregating across all of these respondents, there were 40,518 contacts.

One further problem with the patterns shown in Table 3.5a is that they do not take into account the structure of the sample. Specifically, recall that the sample underrepresents general practitioners. In Chapter 2, I attempted to come up with an estimate of the true ratio of general practitioners to personal injury specialists. In the sample, the ratio of general practitioners to personal injury specialists is about 2 to 3; I estimated that in the overall population of Wisconsin lawyers it might be as high as 5 to 1. In order to try to better estimate population patterns, I reestimated Table 3.5a applying a weight factor to adjust the ratio to be closer to the true figure. The reestimated figures are shown in Table 3.5b. What these adjusted figures suggest is that if I had kept the number of nongeneral practitioner respondents fixed at the number I actually had but had increased the number of general practitioners to represent more accurately the population of lawyers doing contingency fee work, the total number of contacts would have been close to 70,000 and the number of contacts to individual screeners only would have been

TABLE 3.5

Contact Volume

(a) Unweighted

Number of Contacts	All Respondents				Individual Screeners Only			
	Number of Respondents		Total Number of Contacts		Number of Respondents		Total Number of Contacts	
	%	N	%	N	%	N	%	N
1–10	23	106	1	683	22	87	1	571
11–25	24	109	4	2,058	25	99	5	1,874
26–75	24	111	10	5,155	26	103	12	4,815
76–200	18	80	20	10,657	18	72	23	9,477
201–1,000	9	42	34	18,331	9	37	39	15,781
Over 1,000	2	7	31	16,700	1	4	20	8,000
All	100	455	100	53,584	101	402	100	40,518

(b) Weighted to Adjust for Sample Properties

Number of Contacts	All Respondents				Individual Screeners Only			
	Number of Respondents		Total Number of Contacts		Number of Respondents		Total Number of Contacts	
	%	N	%	N	%	N	%	N
1–10	25	236	8	1,513	24	197	8	1,256
11–25	30	279	29	5,403	30	254	31	4,894
26–75	27	251	59	10,830	27	228	63	9,915
76–200	13	125	86	15,707	13	112	89	14,027
201–1,000	5	47	108	19,831	5	42	110	17,281
Over 1,000	1	7	91	16,700	1	4	51	8,000
All	101	945	382	69,984	100	837	351	55,373

NOTE: Totals may not add to 100 owing to rounding.

over 55,000. More important, the share of contacts received by higher-volume firms (more than 200 contacts per year) would be slightly over half of the total contacts (52 percent, computed from Table 3.5b) rather than close to two-thirds (65 percent, computed from Table 3.5a).

Selectivity in Taking Cases

How many of the potential cases do lawyers accept? As stated above, the number of clients accepted ranged from 0 to 600. There are at least two ways to convert the number accepted into acceptance rates. First, one can look at it from the perspective of the lawyer by asking, what is the typical proportion of potential cases lawyers accept? This involves looking at mean or median acceptance rates across the sample of lawyers. Alternatively, from the viewpoint of the potential client, one can ask, what is the likelihood that a randomly selected client calling a randomly selected lawyer will have his or her case accepted by that lawyer? The best estimate involves aggregating across lawyers: adding up the number of cases accepted across all of the lawyers and the number of contacts received across all of the lawyers and dividing the two figures. In the discussion that follows, I present both types of estimates. Also, in the following discussion I rely on estimates based on data weighted to adjust for the underrepresentation of general practitioners in the sample.

Overall, lawyers reported accepting cases from a mean of 49 percent (median 50 percent) of the potential clients who contacted them; the "midspread" is 23 percent to 67 percent.[35] Aggregating across the lawyers, they accepted 23,614 (of 69,984) cases for an acceptance rate of 34 percent.[36] Eliminating the seven respondents reporting 1,000 or more contacts, the aggregate acceptance rate is 42 percent. As shown in Table 3.6a, there appears to be a fairly clear linkage between volume and selectivity. For those lawyers or firms receiving about one and a half or fewer contacts per week (seventy-five or fewer contacts per year), the acceptance rate tends to be on the order of just over 50 percent; for those with more than one and a half and up to about twenty contacts per week (up to 1,000 cases per year), the acceptance rate is under 40 percent; for the very high-volume practices with more than twenty contacts per week, the acceptance rate drops off sharply to around 10 percent or less. Table 3.6b eliminates those respondents who work in firms which screen at the firm level. Other than reducing the number of higher-volume respondents, the general pattern is essentially the same.

TABLE 3.6

Acceptance Rates by Case Volume

(a) All Respondents

Number of Contacts	Number of Respondents	Mean % Accepted	Total Number of Contacts	Total Number of Cases Accepted	% of Total Number of Contacts Accepted
1–10	236	51	1,513	764	50
11–25	279	54	5,403	2,868	53
26–75	251	53	10,830	5,602	52
76–200	125	35	15,707	5,469	35
201–1,000	47	37	19,831	7,616	38
Over 1,000	7	7	16,700	1,295	8
All	945	49	69,984	23,614	34

(b) Individual Screeners Only

Number of Contacts	Number of Respondents	Mean % Accepted	Total Number of Contacts	Total Number of Cases Accepted	% of Total Number of Contacts Accepted
1–10	197	48	1,256	610	49
11–25	254	50	4,894	2,641	54
26–75	228	51	9,915	4,930	50
76–200	112	38	14,027	5,129	37
201–1,000	42	36	17,281	6,491	38
Over 1,000	4	12	8,000	855	11
All	837	46	55,373	20,656	35

NOTE: Results are based on weighted data.

One question this analysis raises is whether potential clients seeking lawyers can find a lawyer to take their case if one or more lawyers initially declines. Quantifying this is not easy based on a survey of lawyers. I did ask the lawyers, "What percentage of the potential contingent fee clients you talk to have 'lawyer shopped' by contacting other lawyers in addition to you?" This question is ambiguous in its use of "lawyer shopping"; some respondents might take it to mean "comparison shopping" while others might understand it to refer to "searching for a lawyer who will take the case." In response to this question, about 10 percent of the lawyers claimed that more than half of their potential clients were engaged in lawyer shopping, although the median respondent reported that this was true of only 25 percent of the potential clients who contacted them; 30 percent reported that 10 percent or fewer of the potential clients had lawyer shopped. Interestingly, the small number of high-volume respondents reported much lower incidents of lawyer shopping (median of 10 percent) than did low- (median of 25 percent) or medium-volume (median of 20 percent) respondents. Personal injury plaintiffs' specialists reported a slightly lower incidence of lawyer shopping (median of 20 percent) than did general practitioners or other practitioners (median of 25 percent), perhaps reflecting something of a pattern that some lawyer shoppers turned to nonspecialists after being declined by specialists.

During the observational phase of the research, I saw a number of examples of clients who had contacted multiple lawyers in a search to find one to take a case. One case that was declined in the first practice I observed turned up in another of the practices. A number of potential clients explicitly stated that they had previously contacted a highly visible but highly selective firm and been turned down. One client, the daughter of an elderly man who had been "dropped" by personnel in a local hospital, was told by the lawyer that he "wouldn't consider pursuing the hospital unless there was significant injury"; in ending the call, she responded, "You are only about the twelfth lawyer who is not interested." Generally, the lawyers I observed, as well as those I interviewed, were more cautious when they realized that the potential client had been calling around looking for a lawyer to handle the case. However, some of the lawyers also prided themselves on taking cases turned down by other lawyers and getting a very good result; for example, one lawyer mentioned several times during the interview a case that had been declined by four other firms in which the firm obtained a seven-figure verdict.

In a notable proportion of potential client calls I observed, the lawyer specifically told the caller that he did not think there was a case (i.e., no liability) or that the damages were simply not sufficient to get a lawyer involved; one lawyer suggested that a potential client who was getting nowhere with an adjuster ask to speak to the adjuster's supervisor and tell the supervisor, "I've consulted with an attorney. Do you want to resolve this or do I need to go to court?" If that did not move things along, he advised the potential client to take the case to small claims court. In another case with doubtful damages, which had initially looked promising enough to have the client come in for a meeting, the lawyer told the potential client, "I can't think of a lawyer who would take this case at the present time."[37] In a case in which a potential client wanted to sue a psychologist who had lost her records, necessitating that she go through the psychological exam a second time, the lawyer declined the case, explaining that he saw no significant damages that could be recovered and closing with "I suspect that any other personal injury attorney would give you the same opinion." Overall, it was fairly common for the lawyer to explain why he was not interested in taking the case, usually attributing it to dubious liability or a lack of damages. Sometimes, if the liability was clear but the damages were low, the lawyer would suggest bargaining strategies with the insurance company combined with the option of small claims court.

My data cannot answer questions such as what proportion of potential clients keep calling other lawyers either after not getting past the person who answers the telephone in the lawyers' offices or after speaking to a lawyer who gives a reason for not accepting the case; the only way to answer such questions would be to conduct a survey of injury victims, and this would have to extend to persons with various types of injuries. One study that did survey accident injury victims was conducted by the RAND Institute for Civil Justice in 1988–89. That study found accident victims reporting a higher rate of acceptance of their cases by lawyers than I find based on my survey of lawyers (only 22 percent of the injury victims who reported contacting an attorney reported being turned away); 69 percent reported contacting a single lawyer, 26 percent reported contacting two or three lawyers, and 5 percent reported contacting more than three (Hensler et al. 1991, 133–34).

Correlates of Selectivity

As with methods of attracting clients, there are a variety of variables which might influence acceptance rates: lawyer's gender, experience, specialized nature of practice or firm, size of community. I looked at relationships between acceptance rates and ten different control variables; because of the already documented relationship between contact volume and acceptance rates, I controlled for this variable in looking at the possible relationships.[38] I did find a number of statistically significant differences (a total of six out of twenty comparisons that I made), although none of the relationships were particularly strong—the largest percentage difference in acceptance rate was about 10 percent.

The only discernible pattern I could find was an apparent inverse relationship between selectivity and dependence on contingency fee (particularly personal injury) work: for lawyers handling a relatively low volume of contingency fee inquiries, selectivity decreases as dependence on contingency fee cases increases. That is, lawyers who have substantial work that is not contingency fee–based are able to be more selective in the cases they accept. An established lawyer whose practice is largely noncontingency fee work can afford to be more selective. For these lawyers, the question is, why take contingency fee cases that will be less lucrative than hourly fee work? One lawyer I talked to put it bluntly: "I'm in contingency fee cases to beat my hourly rate." This relationship disappears for lawyers with a medium volume of contacts by potential contingency fee clients. All of those with a very high volume (more than 1,000 contacts per year) are almost exclusively dependent upon contingency fee work; they are all plaintiffs' personal injury specialists. They are in fact the most dependent on contingency fees, and at the same time the most selective, as shown in Table 3.6; the most extreme example in my sample is the lawyer who reported that his or her firm as had 5,000 contacts per year but accepted only 200 cases (an acceptance rate of 4 percent). However, most lawyers with substantial dependence upon contingency fee cases do not run high-volume operations and are not able to be as selective as those lawyers or firms who cherry-pick among potential cases or those who combine contingency fee work with hourly fee work.

One other pattern is worth noting. I looked at a total of fifty different overlapping categories of lawyers. I found no identifiable group that accepted "most" of the cases that lawyers in the group screened. The highest acceptance rate I found for any category of lawyers was 60 percent, and most of the groups were at around 50 percent or less. Simply stated, contingency fee lawyers generally turn down at least as many cases as they accept, and often turn down considerably more than they accept.

Screening Patterns Among Texas and Illinois Plaintiffs' Lawyers

Daniels and Martin's study of Texas plaintiffs' lawyers and Sara Parikh's study of Chicago plaintiffs' lawyers allow some comparisons that show that Wisconsin contingency fee practitioners are probably reasonably representative. Parikh asked her respondents, "Roughly what percent of the personal injury cases you screen do you actually end up taking?" The mean for her "low-end" practitioners (who she estimates constitute about 80 percent of plaintiffs' practitioners) is 49 percent. For "high-end" (19 percent of practitioners) and "elite" (1 percent of practitioners), the mean acceptance rates are 36 percent and 24 percent respectively (Parikh 2001, 78).

Daniels and Martin asked the lawyers to estimate the percentage of calls from potential personal injury clients that lead to a signed contingency fee agreement. Table 3.7 shows the pattern both for all respondents and broken down by the same four categories of lawyers discussed previously. Overall, the typical respondent reports that about one-quarter (considerably less using the median) of calls lead to representation. For lawyers handling the most routine cases, this figure rises to about one-third, and for those lawyers handling the biggest cases, the figure drops to under 20 percent.

Based on these two comparisons, Wisconsin lawyers do not stand out as atypical in the results of their screening of potential cases. If anything, if we use Texas as the primary comparison, Wisconsin lawyers may be less selective than are lawyers in other states.

The Process of Screening Cases

Three Examples

While there is no single process that attorneys use to screen cases, there appear to be certain common elements, particularly the use of initial telephone calls to screen out large numbers of cases.[39] This was evident

TABLE 3.7

Acceptance Rates, Texas

	All (%)	Bread & Butter 1	Bread & Butter 2	Heavy Hitter 1	Heavy Hitter 2
Calls/Month, Firm					
Mean	36.2	37.8	35.3	38.6	33.6
Median	15	18	20	20	20
Calls/Month, Respondent					
Mean	18.9	21.9	18.3	18.5	16.8
Median	10	12.5	10	10	8
Percent Accepted, Firm					
Mean	25.4	35.1	26.7	24.2	16.6
Median	15	30	15	15	10
Percent Accepted, Respondent					
Mean	27.2	35.1	27.0	26.8	17.9
Median	20	30	20	20	10
N	552	138	141	134	139

SOURCE: Stephen Daniels and Joanne Martin, "It Was the Best of Times, It Was the Worst of Times: The Precarious Nature of Plaintiff's Practice in Texas," *Texas Law Review* 80 (2002):1789.

in the three practices I observed. Over the course of my three months of observation, I counted a total of forty-seven potential clients speaking with the lawyers; in one of the practices, substantial numbers were screened out by the secretary-paralegal who answered the telephone and who turned away cases that she knew by their nature the lawyer did not handle. Only six of the lawyers' conversations led to appointments to come in to the lawyers' offices, and only four resulted in signed fee agreements. In several cases, the lawyers asked the potential clients to obtain some additional information and get back in touch, although recontacts did not occur during my period of observation, and follow-up checks with the lawyers did not indicate that any of these contacts matured into cases. The following brief sketches of practices in the three offices provide a context for the survey results which follow.

Steve Clarke.   In Steve Clarke's firm, Barbara, the person who routinely answers the telephone, had been trained to do a first-level screening (this office probably receives between 500 and 1,000 calls from potential clients a year—ten to twenty calls per week, two to four per day). Barbara knows the general parameters of the cases Steve and his partner are interested in handling. A large proportion of the calls clearly fall outside the spectrum of interest, and Barbara will tell the caller that the firm does not handle that type of case and possibly suggest a firm whose practice is more in line with the caller's need.

If a case sounds like it might be of interest to the firm, Barbara does one of two things. If the attorney designated to handle intake that day is available, she puts the caller on hold and briefly describes the caller's case to the attorney; either the attorney decides immediately that he is not interested in the case, in which case Barbara so informs the caller, or the attorney takes the call to obtain more information and make a decision whether to schedule a time for the caller to come in to the office. If the attorney is not available, Barbara puts the basic information into a brief memo and tells the caller that someone will call back; the attorney then reviews the memo and either calls the potential client back if he wants more information or tells Barbara that he is not interested, in which case Barbara calls the potential client back and reports the lawyer's decision.

There is one major exception to this process. If a caller asks for one of the lawyers in the firm by name, Barbara tries to ascertain how the caller got the name. If the caller has been referred by someone or is a prior client, the lawyer almost always will at least talk to the caller. Steve and his partners know that their best source of new clients is referrals, and they take particular care in reviewing referrals.

Bob Adams.   Bob Adams practices in a modest-size firm which handles the full range of legal work. His own practice includes a variety of court-oriented cases: criminal and family cases along with personal injury and other contingency fee work. While other lawyers in the firm also do court-oriented work, Bob is the only partner who handles cases on a contingency fee basis. The result is that he tries to handle all of the screening of potential contingency fee cases himself. The person who answers the telephone at the firm transfers the call either to Bob, if he is available, or to Bob's paralegal if he is not available. The paralegal creates a brief memo, and Bob calls the potential client back unless it is clearly a case he is not interested in; in the latter situation, he has the paralegal call the potential client back. When Bob takes the call, he first tries to assess whether the case is in the range that he handles; if it is not (e.g., workers' compensation), Bob informs the caller of that fact and typically suggests another firm the caller might contact.

Assuming that the case is of potential interest, Bob next ascertains enough facts to make an initial judgment on whether there is a good case on liability; if the case is weak or nonexistent, he informs the potential client. For example, Bob received a call from a farmer who was injured when he tripped over some construction debris chasing a cow that had gotten loose. The debris had been left by a contractor who was doing some work on one of the farmer's buildings. Bob asked whether he had asked the contractor to clean up the debris; no, he hadn't. Bob asked whether the contract had a clause requiring the contractor to keep the work site clear of debris; no, there wasn't. Bob told the farmer that he would not consider handling the case, on either a contingent or hourly fee basis: "I think you are fighting an uphill battle. . . . I wouldn't let it get to a jury if I were the judge. . . . Chalk it up to bad luck and farming."

The amount of damages does not seem to be a major issue for the potential cases Bob received calls about. The exception is possible medical malpractice cases. These cases typically present issues of both liability and damages. Even if liability is relatively clear, which it usually is not, most of the potential clients contacting Bob had not experienced permanent disability or lasting problems, and that meant that the potential damages would not be adequate to make pursuing a malpractice claim worthwhile.

Chuck Brown.   Chuck Brown is in a medium-sized general practice firm. The firm includes a small group of lawyers who do contingency fee work; however, while these lawyers have their offices situated next to each other, they practice more or less independently of one another except for occasional informal consultation. Chuck does a range of contingency fee work but particularly likes challenging, high-risk, high-payoff cases. Chuck has not generally employed advertising, other than a small Yellow Pages ad. Instead, Chuck sought to facilitate referrals; these referrals come from other lawyers in the firm, from other lawyers in the community who are unwilling to handle the kinds of risky cases that are Chuck's forte, from former clients, and from other community contacts that Chuck works hard to cultivate.

Chuck's firm does not receive many cold calls. Those that are received come primarily from persons who found the firm listed in the Yellow Pages and from referrals. The three or so cold calls that do come in each month are screened by a paralegal shared among the lawyers doing contingency fee work. If the paralegal judges the case to be at all promising, she distributes the cases on a rotating basis among the lawyers in the contingency fee group. The paralegal logs the cold calls; over a thirty-month period about 100 calls had come in, but only five resulted in cases pursued by one of the lawyers in the contingency fee group.

In contrast, if a call is a referral to Chuck, he tries to handle the initial contact himself. The volume of calls is not large. During the month I observed in Chuck's office, I saw him handle seven potential client calls. Only one turned into actual representation during that month, although for two others Chuck asked the potential client to get some additional information and get back in touch.

Chuck will spend a significant amount of time on the phone with a potential client even when he has quickly determined that the case is not one he wants to handle. This is particularly true with callers referred by one of the community contacts he has tried to cultivate; his view is that even though he is declining the case, he wants the caller to go away happy, with the hope that should the caller have occasion to suggest a lawyer to someone else, good memories of the contact with Chuck will lead to a recommendation. As with the other lawyers I observed, the first issue for Chuck was getting a handle on the question of liability. At one point, he commented to me that he gets a lot of calls where "there is no liability, only an injury." He cited an example of a tree trimmer who had a tree he was cutting fall the wrong way and hit him; he called to determine whether he could sue the homeowner for the injuries resulting from his own negligence.

Some Broader Patterns

While a structured survey cannot capture the variety and texture of screening processes, I did obtain some very basic information. Lawyers responded to the following survey items:

[For lawyers working in a firm:] Is the screening of potential contingent fee clients handled primarily on a firm-wide basis or does each lawyer do his or her own screening?

Who handles the initial telephone contacts (nonlawyers, lawyers, both)?

Who makes the decision whether or not to pursue a case (I do, I do subject to review, a more senior lawyer, a committee)?

Screening is largely handled by individual lawyers; 84 percent of the respondents working in firms reported that individual lawyers had responsibility for screening cases. However, only 73 percent could decide to accept a case entirely on their own; another 17 percent could accept cases subject to review by a more senior attorney. For 3 percent of the respondents a decision to accept a case was the responsibility of a more senior attorney, and for 4 percent a decision to accept a case was made by a committee. Individual lawyers appear to have less autonomy in the high-volume firms, where only 58 percent report being able to make decisions to accept a case entirely on their own, compared to 75 percent and 80 percent in low- and medium-volume firms respectively.[40]

As I will discuss below, a great deal of the screening process relies upon telephone conversations, particularly the initial telephone contact. While lawyers dominate in handling these initial contacts, nonlawyers play a significant role. Ten percent of the respondents indicated that nonlawyers handle the initial telephone contacts, and another 22 percent said that a combination of lawyers and nonlawyers handle the calls; 68 percent of the respondents reported that initial calls are handled exclusively by lawyers. It should not be surprising that the exclusive reliance on lawyers is strongly dependent on the volume of calls: 72 percent of respondents with a low volume of contacts rely exclusively on lawyers, compared to 59 percent of those with a medium volume of contacts, and only 25 percent of those with a high volume of contacts. Interestingly, the shift is found not in exclusive reliance on nonlawyers (around 10 percent for all three groups), but in reliance on a combination of lawyers and nonlawyers: 18 percent, 30 percent, and 67 percent going from low to medium to high volume. One way to read this is that in most firms lawyers try to handle initial calls, but as the volume increases there is a tendency for calls to be handled by whoever is available when the call comes in.

Lawyers are very cognizant of the impression they make during the screening process. Some lawyers spoke of wanting to always speak to the potential client, by which they did not mean *all* potential clients but rather all clients with the generic kinds of cases the lawyer handles. For example, several lawyers told me that as soon as the person answering the phone determines that the call is in relation to a potential personal injury case, the office practice is to get a lawyer on the line, and others sought to get every potential personal injury client in to the office to actually meet with a lawyer. Part of this was to best assess the caller's case, but another part was to show interest in the potential case or to impress the caller with the quality of the lawyers in the firm. Clearly, part of what goes on is not only screening the current case but establishing a reputation for being interested in potential clients and being willing to listen to them. In the words of one interviewee: "I don't want people to say I called Jones and he wouldn't give me the time of day, or that he blew me off, or whatever. I want to get people in. I want them to feel that we've looked at their case. We might not take the case, but we want them to understand that we had a reason for not taking it." What this indicates is that at least some lawyers address the reputational issues involved in obtaining clients even as they decide which clients to turn down; they want the rejected clients to go away with a positive view in the hopes that they will speak positively of the firm and consider contacting the firm in the future should an appropriate occasion arise.

When Are Cases Declined?

Almost always the first contact between lawyer and client comes in a phone call initiated by the potential client.[41] As should be clear by now, the initial telephone calls are extremely important because they form the basis of the lawyers' decisions to decline the cases for a large proportion of the cases eventually declined. The survey data may actually *underestimate* somewhat the importance of the telephone contacts if the patterns in the three offices where I spent time were typical. The average lawyer in the survey estimated declining almost half (47 percent) of all eventually declined cases based solely on telephone conversations with potential clients (see Table 3.8a). Of those who contacted lawyers and were declined, 62 percent never made it to the lawyer's office (Table 3.8b); telephone contacts alone formed the basis of the lawyers' decisions. As Table 3.8b makes clear, the rate of decline based on telephone contacts alone increases as call volume goes up, with the low-volume lawyers declining 51 percent of the total declined based solely on one or more telephone conversations, medium-volume 59 percent,

TABLE 3.8

When Cases Are Declined

(a) Mean Percentages

	All Cases (Mean %)	Low Volume (Mean %)	Medium Volume (Mean %)
Based solely on one or more telephone calls	47	45	55
Client did not appear for first appointment	7	7	6
After first appointment	33	35	23
After additional investigation	15	14	16

(b) Aggregate Percentages

	All Cases (%)	All Cases Without High Volume (%)	Low Volume (%)	Medium Volume (%)	High Volume (%)
Based solely on one or more telephone calls	62	57	51	59	83
Client did not appear for first appointment	5	5	7	5	5
After first appointment	20	24	28	23	6
After additional investigation	12	14	14	14	6

NOTES: Results based on weighted data.

The percentages in table (b) were computed by aggregating across lawyers; that is, by adding up all of the cases declined, all of the cases declined at each of the four stages (telephone contact only, failure to make the first meeting, etc.), and then dividing the sum for each of the four stages by the total number declined.

Percentages may not add to 100 due to rounding.

and high-volume 83 percent. Lawyers report dropping about 5 percent of the declined cases after a potential client fails to keep a first appointment. Most of the rest of the cases declined were declined after the first in-person meeting. Clearly, lawyers make relatively quick decisions on most potential contingency fee cases.

Why Are Cases Declined?

Why do lawyers decline cases? In the survey, I asked lawyers to estimate the percentage of cases declined owing to each of the following factors:

- Lack of liability
- Low damages or inadequate fee potential[42]
- Both lack of liability and low damages
- Outside the area of the lawyer's practice
- Other reasons

Table 3.9a shows the aggregated figures for all lawyers, for all lawyers omitting the four high-volume lawyers, low-volume lawyers, and medium-volume lawyers. As the table shows, lack of liability and inadequate damages (singly or together) are the dominant reasons for declining cases, accounting for about 80 percent. Lack of liability alone accounts for the largest proportion of cases declined, particularly for those lawyers with a higher volume of contacts from potential clients. Excluding the high-volume lawyers, something less than a quarter of the declined cases were rejected solely because of low damages.[43] Table 3.9b shows the mean percentages declined for each reason; because of the dominance in numbers of respondents by those handling low volumes of cases, the pattern looks more like the aggregate pattern for the low-volume lawyers shown in Table 3.9a.

One might expect personal injury specialists to differ from general practitioners and other lawyers in the reasons for declining cases. However, if I remove from the comparison the small number of very-high-volume personal injury practitioners, the pattern for the remaining (i.e., the majority of) personal injury plaintiff specialists does not differ appreciably from the other two groups of lawyers. In fact, the patterns for personal injury plaintiff specialists and for general practitioners are virtually identical.

The observation and interviews provide insights into the other rea-

TABLE 3.9

Reasons for Declining Cases

(a) Aggregate Percentages

	All Cases (%)	All Cases Without High Volume (%)	Low Volume (%)	Medium Volume (%)
Lack of liability	47	41	35	43
Inadequate damages	19	22	23	22
Both lack of liability and inadequate damages	13	15	20	13
Outside lawyer's area of practice	11	10	12	10
Other reasons	11	12	11	12

(b) Mean Percentages

	All Cases (%)	All Cases Without High Volume (Mean %)	Low Volume (Mean %)	Medium Volume (Mean %)
Lack of liability	36	36	34	44
Inadequate damages	18	18	17	20
Both lack of liability and inadequate damages	20	20	21	13
Outside lawyer's area of practice	10	10	10	9
Other reasons	13	13	13	14

NOTE: Results based on weighted data.
    Percentages in (a) may not add to 100 due to rounding.

sons for declining cases. The lawyers occasionally expressed concerns about what it would be like working with a particular client.[44] For example, one lawyer expressed concerns about working with "high-maintenance clients"; another lawyer explained that he tries to get almost every personal injury caller in to the office except for those where there is an obvious conflict or the "ones who sound completely nuts." Other lawyers expressed concerns about potential clients who engage in lawyer shopping. Lawyers did not always decline cases because of difficult clients. One lawyer was handling a complicated case with a difficult client who had had a previous accident claim handled by another lawyer; the current lawyer told me that the previous lawyer was delighted when he heard that the client had chosen a different lawyer this time.

As discussed earlier, conflicts of interest can also lead to decisions to decline cases. Whenever there is a conflict, ethical rules mandate that the lawyer decline the case, although there are some circumstances under which conflicts can be waived by the consent of all those involved. The result is that the lawyer will often refer the potential client to another lawyer, or at least suggest other lawyers who might handle the case.

The lawyers I observed sometime accepted cases "for purposes of obtaining a settlement." Typically these were cases where liability was relatively straightforward, but there were problems with damages. For example, one case involved a victim of a rear-end collision who had a number of preexisting medical conditions that made it difficult to sort out what resulted from the accident and what did not. This particular case was referred to the lawyer by another lawyer, and that pushed the receiving lawyer toward finding a way to handle the case in part to encourage future referrals from the referring lawyer. The receiving lawyer also had some concerns about whether the client would make emotional demands in their relationship. In the end, the lawyer agreed to accept the case but with the understanding that he would not continue with the case if it got to the point that it was necessary to file suit.

A final question addressed by the survey was the degree to which lawyers have explicit criteria vis-à-vis the amount of damages for accepting cases. I asked the respondents whether there was a minimum damage figure for each of three types of cases: auto accidents, medical malpractice, and products liability. Most lawyers (94 percent) provided a response for auto accidents, but only 43 percent stated that there was a minimum for such cases (the median minimum $5,000). Substantially fewer responded regarding medical malpractice (61 percent) or products liability (69 percent), reflecting that many lawyers did not handle these kinds of cases. Of those who did respond, a higher percentage reported a minimum damage figure: 61 percent for medical malpractice (median $100,000) and 60 percent for products liability (median $75,000).

While my survey data do show variations among lawyers in selectiveness, they do not provide direct information on variations among types of cases. My observations, however, make it clear that lawyers are more selective in some types of cases than in others. To some degree this reflects the fact that injury victims are more knowledgeable about whether they are entitled to compensation for some types of injuries (auto accidents) than for others (falls, medical malpractice, etc.). One of my months of observation was in the middle of a typical Wisconsin winter; during that time, there were several significant snowfalls, and I listened in on several calls from persons who had slipped on snow or ice. Most of these cases were turned away simply because Wisconsin law allows property owners a period of time to remove snow or ice from sidewalks before they become liable for injuries arising from falls on their property.

Medical malpractice is one of the areas most talked about as needing reform to provide relief to medical providers from increasing numbers of lawsuits. During three months of observation in three different law practices, I saw lawyers deal with contacts from fourteen potential medical malpractice clients. *None* of these cases led to a retainer being signed to pursue a medical malpractice claim.[45] In several cases the lawyer asked the potential client to send in a copy of the medical records, but later follow-ups with those lawyers revealed that none of these contacts matured into cases. Lawyers are extremely cautious in accepting medical malpractice cases, and the lawyers I observed spent a lot of time explaining to these potential clients why their negative medical outcome did not constitute malpractice, or the difficulty in establishing that it did arise from malpractice, or that even if it was malpractice, the ultimate medical outcome was probably not affected by the error (and the interim consequences did not give rise to sufficient damages to make pursuing the matter financially attractive).

For example, one potential client had gone in for a surgical procedure to correct a swallowing problem that involved insertion of an instrument down his esophagus. During the procedure the esophagus was injured, necessitating surgery through the chest. The potential client was upset because (1) he had been in substantial pain in the recovery room and there was a delay in realizing the problem with the esophagus, and (2) the recovery from the more major surgery was several months longer than it would have been from the simpler procedure. As it turned out, a torn esophagus was a known risk of the simpler procedure, and the client had been warned of that risk as indicated by a signed informed consent. Furthermore, there was a significant chance that a more invasive, through-the-chest procedure would have been needed even without the injury to the esophagus, because the simpler procedure was substantially less than 100 percent effective. In this case, the lawyer explained to the potential client that the physician who conducted the original procedure probably had not committed medical malpractice, even if the recovery room staff had been slow to realize that there was a problem, and that there would be questions about damages because the final result was very good (i.e., the original problem had been corrected) and there were no residual problems from the chest surgery.

Even if it is clear that a medical error occurred, lawyers almost never take cases that involve limited damages. One lawyer who receives a lot of medical malpractice referrals described a case of clear error. A man had surgery on his nose. In the days immediately after the surgery he had trouble breathing; this continued for almost a week. He repeatedly called the doctor who performed the surgery, who told him that everything was fine and to stop worrying about it. He bumped into a friend who is an emergency room physician and told him about the problem he had been having since the surgery; the friend had him sit down, checked his nose, and discovered that the surgeon had left some packing in the nasal cavity. From the viewpoint of the lawyer, while there is clear negligence, there are minimal recoverable damages: what is a week's worth of breathing difficulty worth in pain and suffering damages? The potential recovery would not even begin to cover the cost of bringing a claim.

Discussion

One question that this analysis cannot answer is whether lawyers turn away too many or too few cases, or whether they turn away the right cases. Many people have lamented the supposed growth in "litigiousness" among the American population (Bok 1983; Kagan 2001; Manning 1977; Olson 2003), but it is not necessarily self-evident that Americans are too eager to seek compensation when under our law compensation is due (Abel 1987). One might use Elihu Root's injunction, "about half of the practice of the decent lawyer consists in telling would-be clients that they are damned fools and should stop," as one possible measure. If one takes "half of the practice" to refer to the proportion of potential cases accepted, then most contingency fee lawyers achieve this measure of decency.

What this analysis does make clear is that the process of seeking and screening cases is driven by a combination of the three "R" factors: risk, rewards, and reputations. Lawyers are constantly balancing the risks and rewards of particular cases with the reputational implications of how they make decisions about which cases to accept. What the lawyers know is that they must keep one eye on the immediate portfolio, which is defined by the risks and potential rewards of current cases, and the potential case being presented to them, and another eye on the future portfolio. The latter concern affects both how lawyers deal with potential clients and, at least at the margins, actual decisions to accept or decline cases. Lawyers will take time with potential clients, even ones they have already decided to decline, if those clients are important for building and maintaining the lawyer's desired reputation among the world of potential clients.

Appendix 1. Systematic Variation in Client Sources

I examined in some detail four variables that might be expected to account for variation in client sources: years of practice, type of community, gender, and type of practice (firm versus solo). As the following discussion shows, while some of the variables did relate to client sources in ways one might expect, other variables had either no relationship or a relationship that was not readily explainable. More important, none of the relationships was particular strong.

Years of Practice

Conversations with several lawyers suggested the hypothesis that reliance on advertising might decrease as a lawyer built up his or her reputation and a client referral network comprising prior clients, community contacts, and other lawyers. The logic of this was simply that one could buy name exposure through advertising and that this could be a useful way to get a practice started. However, I could find no evidence that those who relied heavily upon advertising for clients differed in years of experience from those who did not.

In fact, I could find little evidence of any impact of years in practice. There did seem to be a break at around ten years of practice; those with less than ten years reported an average of about 20 percent of clients coming as referrals from other clients, compared to 27 percent for those in practice for more than ten years. Further analysis showed that there was no such difference for personal injury specialists or general practitioners; for lawyers who were neither personal injury specialists nor general practitioners, those with less than ten years' experience obtained an average of 17 percent of clients as referrals from prior clients, while the comparable figure for those in practice at least ten years was 26 percent.[46]

Size of Community

Research has shown that the nature of legal practice differs between large urban and rural communities (Landon 1985, 1988, 1990). Does this translate into differences in sources of contingency fee clients? Surprisingly, and to some degree in contrast to the situation in Indiana (Van Hoy 1999) and Texas (Daniels and Martin 1999), the answer is that it does so only in relatively small ways. For example, one might expect that lawyers in large urban communities would be more likely to rely upon impersonal sources such as advertising. However, overall among the lawyers in the survey, there are no statistically significant differences in the use of advertising based on community size, varying between 11 and 17 percent across four categories of community size.[47] More interesting, adding a control for the lawyer's type of practice produces a statistically significant difference only for those who are neither personal injury specialists nor general practitioners, and it is the lawyers in smaller communities who rely more on advertising (11 to 14 percent of contingency fee clients versus about 5 to 7 percent for those in larger communities).[48]

The one other difference that showed up clearly related to community size is that as community size decreased, the average percentage of contingency fee clients coming as referrals from other lawyers decreased, although controlling for type of practice showed that this was true only of personal injury specialists.[49] This probably reflects varying degrees of specialization in the bar by size of community, which I discussed in Chapter 2. More lawyers in smaller communities engage in general practice and hence are less likely to refer out clients generally (and contingency fee clients more specifically);[50] in fact, in communities of 100,000 or larger (including Milwaukee and its suburbs), only 15 percent of the respondents described themselves as in general practice, compared to 47 percent of the respondents from communities under 25,000. Also, in smaller communities, relatively few attorneys do insurance defense work (because insurance companies tend to retain firms in larger cities, even to handle cases coming from smaller, outlying communities), and hence the problem of conflicts of interest that lead some attorneys to refer cases to other lawyers is less common.[51]

Gender

Only about 13 percent of the practitioner survey respondents were women.[52] Women appear somewhat more likely than men to obtain contingency fee clients as referrals from other lawyers or as preexisting (or prior) clients, while obtaining fewer clients as referrals from other clients or from community contacts.[53] Advertising plays essentially the same role as a source of clients for both men and women. The pattern remains the same controlling for the lawyer's type of practice.[54] A part of these gender-based patterns might be attributable to the fact that, as noted in Chapter 2, the women in the sample have tended to be in practice for shorter periods than the men (80 percent of the men have been in practice ten or more years, compared to only 59 percent of the women), but recall that years in practice related only to referrals from other clients. In light of this, I do not have an explanation for this gender-related pattern.

Practice Setting

As discussed in Chapter 2, only about 15 percent of the respondents reported being in solo practice. Solo practitioners are more likely than firm practitioners to obtain contingency fee clients as referrals from other clients or as existing clients; firm practitioners are more likely than solo practitioners to obtain clients as referrals from other lawyers and through community connections.[55] There is no difference in the role of advertising depending on practice setting.

Some shifts in these patterns occur when I control for type of practice. There are no significant differences between firm and solo general practitioners, and all of the actual differences are smaller than for the sample as a whole. Among personal injury specialists, the pattern described above holds up (solo practitioners obtain more clients through client referrals and existing clients and fewer from lawyer referrals and community contacts); although not all of the statistical tests remain significant, the differences are at least as large, with the exception of referrals from other lawyers. Among lawyers who are neither personal injury specialists nor general practitioners, the pattern is again consistent with that for all lawyers, with the magnitude of the differences about the same but with fewer statistically significant differences. Also, while the role of advertising did not differ previously, it differs with the controls, and in diverging ways. A larger proportion of the clients of personal injury specialists in firms come in response to advertising than for solo practitioners; however, among general practitioners and those in other types of practices, advertising is a more important source of clients among solo practitioners than among firm practitioners, although the difference approaches statistical significance only for those in other types of practices.

Appendix 2.   Systematic Variation in Acceptance Rates

I examined ten variables which might be expected to account for variation in acceptance rate: the four I looked at for contact volume (years of practice, type of community, gender, and firm versus solo practice), plus general content of practice, percent of income from contingency fees, whether the respondent's firm specialized in plaintiffs' work, percentage of cases involving medical malpractice, percentage of cases involving products liability, percentage of contingency fee work that was not related to personal injury. Because these might be correlated with contact volume, which the analysis above shows is clearly related to acceptance rate, I controlled for volume using two categories: low (seventy-five or fewer contacts over the year) and medium (76 to 1,000 contacts). Eliminating the respondents in firms where screening is a firm-level function (which is necessary to look at any types of attorney characteristics), there are only four high-volume (over 1,000 cases per year) respondents; I report the characteristics of those four respondents in the right-most column of Table 3.10. The analysis was carried out using the data in their unweighted form.

The table shows acceptance rates controlling for the ten variables listed above; statistically significant (at the .05 level of better) differences are indicated set in bold type.[56] Of the twenty comparisons shown in the table (ten comparisons done separately for low- and medium-volume practices), only six achieve statistical significance. Five of these are for the low-volume lawyers:

1. Women are more selective than men.
2. Lawyers with more than twenty years' experience are *less* selective than those with twenty or fewer years of experience.
3. Lawyers describing their practice as primarily personal injury plaintiffs or general practice are *less* selective than are those who are primarily personal injury defense or other types of litigation.
4. Lawyers whose contingency fee caseload is predominantly (50 percent or more) personal injury are *less* selective than are those whose contingency fee caseloads are not dominated by personal injury cases.
5. Selectivity *decreases* as the lawyer's dependence (in terms of income) on contingency fee work goes up.

The only statistically significant difference among the medium-volume lawyers is that those whose caseloads involve 10 percent or more medical malpractice work are more selective than are those with little or no medical malpractice work. The absence of statistically significant patterns for medium-volume respondents probably reflects the smaller number of such respondents compared to the low-volume respondents; the directional patterns for some of the variables mentioned above were similar for medium-volume lawyers, even though the differences did not achieve statistical significance (e.g., the percent of cases accepted by men was higher than that by women, selectivity decreased as dependence on contingency work increased, and selectivity increased as non-personal injury contingency fee work increased).

TABLE 3.10

Acceptance Rates by Practice and Lawyer Factors

	Low Contact Volume			Medium Contact Volume			High Contact Volume
	Mean %	Aggre-gate %	N	Mean %	Aggre-gate %	N	
Gender							
Male	50*	50	245	40	39	89	All
Female	42*	40	35	34	36	18	
Type of Practice							
Personal injury (PI) plaintiffs	55*	54	52	41	39	79	
PI defense	45*	42	63	—	—	3	All
Other litigation	45*	48	88	35	46	13	
General practice	54*	52	78	32	30	9	
Percentage of Income from Contingency Fees							
0–19%	44*	42	116	—	—	(4)	
20–49%	52*	49	94	34	43	12	
50–89%	54*	55	58	40	38	34	
90–100%	60*	55	20	43	39	57	All
Firm Specializes in Plaintiffs' Work							
Yes	53	54	54	40	40	64	All
No	49	48	213	40	36	36	
Medical Malpractice Cases							
10% or more	47	50	29	28*	27	25	
Less than 10%	50	50	260	42*	42	84	All
Products Cases							
10% or more	51	47	36	45	48	26	
Less than 10%	49	50	253	37	36	83	All

TABLE 3.10 (*continued*)

	Low Contact Volume			Medium Contact Volume			High Contact Volume
	Mean %	Aggre-gate %	N	Mean %	Aggre-gate %	N	
Non–PI Contingent-Fee Work							
50% or more	41*	46	50	31	50	7	
11–49%	51*	51	60	44	45	17	
10% or less	50*	51	136	37	36	69	All
Position in Firm							
Solo	50	50	49	45	41	18	—
Partner / owner	50	50	183	40	41	73	2
Nonpartner	46	47	50	30	27	16	2
City Size							
Milwaukee	50	49	86	35	34	35	All
100,000 & up	45	48	54	33	36	22	
50,000–99,999	49	49	62	42	39	27	
Under 50,000	53	53	79	44	43	22	
Years of Experience							
10 or less	45*	43	73	42	37	26	2
11–20	47*	46	117	36	35	46	2
21 or more	56*	59	96	41	42	36	—

NOTE: Results are based on unweighted data.

* Difference statistically significant at .05 level or better.

CHAPTER 4

The Work of the Contingency Fee Lawyer

Introduction

Those who have studied the criminal justice system often speak of two contrasting models or images of the system (e.g., Packer 1964). One model, the adversary, or due process, model, views the system as operating in an adversary mode with the twin goals of arriving at the truth and protecting the rights of the accused; the core presumption of the system is that defendants are presumed innocent until proven guilty. The other model, variously called the "crime control model" or the "dispositional model," views the system as operating in a processing mode where defendants are presumed guilty and the goal is determining appropriate sanctions given a defendant's record and the current offense. These two models coexist side by side, with lawyers sometimes acting in terms of one model and sometimes in terms of the other model; some actors tend to lean more toward one model than the other, although the dispositional model is probably dominant.

While these models do not translate directly to the civil justice system, or apply specifically to contingency fee legal practice, my observation makes it clear that there are two very different approaches to handling the work of contingency fee cases that have some parallels to the to criminal justice models. I label these the "litigational" approach and the "case-processing" or "dispositional" approach. Under the former, the lawyer, while recognizing that most cases will settle, presumes that cases should be prepared as if they were going to go into suit and will eventually be tried. Under the latter, the lawyer works from the presumption that cases should be prepared for settlement, given that virtually all cases will settle, most without a lawsuit ever being filed.[1] Just as with the criminal justice system dispositional model's assumption that most defendants are guilty, the case-processing approach assumes that liability is not the major issue. As with the dispositional model's focus on finding an appropriate sanction, the case-processing model of civil justice focuses heavily on determining an appropriate settlement amount. In the criminal justice system the adversary and dispositional models exist side by side, and the same is true of the litigational and case-processing models in the civil justice system. Lawyers sometimes pursue one approach and at other times the second approach, and the approach can change within a given case. While I suspect that the case-processing approach is the more dominant of the two, at least for relatively routine cases, my research does not provide any systematic evidence on that question. Moreover, in some types of cases—medical malpractice, products liability, mass torts, discrimination, and large-stakes business cases (securities, business torts, antitrust, etc.)—the litigational approach probably dominates.[2]

Some lawyers intentionally intermix the two types of approaches in a way that directly reflects the portfolio nature of contingency fee practice. For example, one lawyer I interviewed, who is a highly regarded trial attorney, disposed of as many as 200 cases per year. Most of these cases were handled, *processed*, entirely by his staff, none of whom were attorneys. These cases served to cover the overhead of the practice and to attract a large number of clients, a small number of whom had significant cases that the lawyer himself handled in a litigational mode. He estimated that two-thirds of his gross fees come from perhaps a dozen of these cases; in other words, 5 percent of his cases produce two-thirds of his revenue. In addition to covering the firm's overhead, the large number of cases were needed in order to produce a flow of potential clients from which he could find the small number of cases that produced significant fees and established relationships that led to both repeat representation and referrals. To handle the high volume of cases that are processed, his large staff is organized by task—people who specialize in dealing with medical records, others who obtain police reports and the like, still others who draft demand letters and actually negotiate with insurance adjusters. While many of these cases are best described as "processed" rather than litigated, about 20 percent of cases lead to a lawsuit being filed, and the lawyer tries five to ten cases a year.

I spoke with lawyers at several high-volume firms. While those firms tend to be oriented toward case processing, they are also structured to handle litigation. This may involve a division of labor, with some lawyers overseeing cases as long as they are in the processing mode and other lawyers handling cases that have moved into the litigational mode. These firms typically rely heavily on staff to handle many of the processing aspects, such as collecting and reviewing medical records, obtaining and reviewing police reports, initial case screening, and the like. The most processing-oriented volume firms are structured so that the modest cases do more than simply cover overhead costs; this is accomplished by creating procedures that provide efficiencies which in turn keep costs low.

What little we know about how lawyers handle contingency fee cases comes in the form of personal accounts of lawyers handling cases (Keen and Goldberg 1998; Stern 1976) and the occasional journalistic retelling (Harr 1995). Moreover, the accounts that do make it into print almost always focus on the spectacular or unusual case, not the day-to-day routine case that constitutes perhaps as much as 99 percent of the cases lawyers handle on a contingency fee basis. Not surprisingly, these published accounts portray the litigational approach, not the case-processing approach. In part, this is because the cases meriting journalistic attention, or looming large enough in lawyers' memories to be discussed in memoirs, are precisely the types that get litigated rather than just processed for settlement.

In this chapter I look at how contingency fee lawyers handle cases, except for the settlement process itself, which is the topic of the next chapter. As will be clear from the discussion that follows, the three lawyers I observed differ in where they fall in the litigation–case-processing continuum. While all three lawyers at times process and at times litigate, the balance differs sharply. Chuck Brown is very litigation-oriented, Steve Clarke is very case-processing-oriented, and Bob Adams falls somewhere in between. To some degree, this reflects the kinds of cases each of the lawyers handles. Brown handles mostly larger cases involving significant damages; he prides himself on taking and winning large recoveries in cases that other firms decline as too risky. Adams and Clarke handle a lot of very routine cases, most of which would not be economical to take to trial; in some proportion of the cases they accept, they have explicit understandings with the client that they will handle the case for purposes of obtaining a settlement only.

I will focus on three general tasks that lawyers must deal with after they have accepted a case: obtaining and managing information, managing the relationship with the client, and managing the relationship with the opponent. As the discussion that follows will show, whether the lawyer is case-processing-oriented or litigation-oriented appears to be linked to how the lawyers handle each of these tasks. For lawyers taking both approaches, there is a concern about the amount of time being invested in a case. That is, in line with portfolio theory, the lawyer must be constantly thinking about the size of the investment in relation to both the likelihood of a return and the likely size of the return; in addition to the instant case, the lawyer must keep in mind the implications of how he or she handles the case for the reputation that will have long-term impacts for future cases.

Information: Investigation and Research

Regardless of whether the lawyer is processing or litigating cases, civil litigation of the type handled by contingency fee lawyers is fundamentally about information. The rules of civil procedure devote substantial attention to the formalized "discovery" processes for obtaining and exchanging information. More generally, the rules of procedure structure the information process by requiring the parties to define claims and issues about which information will be needed.

Factual Investigation and Research, Outside Formal Discovery

A large proportion of cases, particularly routine personal injury cases, involve relatively little factual investigation. Over the three months I spent observing in lawyers' offices, there was not a single occasion on which a lawyer went out to inspect an accident scene or to collect evidence. The lawyers went out of the office for court and hearing appearances, for depositions, and meetings with experts (e.g., on one occasion one of the lawyers went to the office of a medical provider to discuss the report the physician had been asked to prepare). Most of the investigation that did occur took place over the telephone and often involved more background work than anything else.

    1. In a workers' compensation case involving an employer's unwillingness to accommodate a work restriction, the lawyer had an extensive discussion with a union representative over whether the employer had in the

past made accommodations for other employees and whether the union contract contained any restrictions that might have made it difficult to make accommodations.

2. In a case involving a claim that arose because of delays in medical treatment owing to the failure of a shipping container used to transport biological materials, the lawyer contacted several companies to obtain background information about the type of container that was used and the shipping process involved in handling certain types of biological materials; the lawyer also obtained additional information from industry literature on shipping containers.

3. In a case involving an injury resulting from involvement in a medical study at an institution in another state, the lawyer contacted various people trying to determine who were the key people on the research project. He later looked at information available online at a site at the National Institutes of Health that had information on grants.

4. In a case involving an injury at a construction site, the lawyer spoke to people in the industry about the standard procedures used at similar sites and to other workers at the site where the injury occurred to determine whether particular procedures had been followed. Both the lawyer and his paralegal reviewed a number of industry safety publications trying to find material that might be useful to challenge opposing testimony about the standard of care expected on construction sites.

On a couple of occasions, the lawyer making the phone call did not reveal the true purpose of the call or that he was a lawyer; usually this was because of a concern that if the caller revealed that he was a lawyer, the person at the other end of the call would immediately be suspicious and would be reluctant to provide even the most routine information. For example, in one case, the lawyer needed information about a key piece of equipment that was crucial to his client's claim. One point concerned the weight of the equipment when crated for shipment. To get this information, he called the manufacturer and pretended to work for a company involved in a billing dispute with a common carrier that had transported a piece of that equipment and hence needed to know what the normal shipping weight was.[3]

The closest any of the lawyers came to engaging in field investigation during my observation involved a slip-and-fall case. The client claimed to have fallen walking into a store in a nearby town because gravel was scattered across the walkway. The lawyer had determined that the landscaping around the establishment used decorative gravel and considered having a law clerk who doubled as an investigator make the rounds of the landscaping companies in the town to see if any had recently done any work at the store. Before this was actually done, the case settled for a modest payment. In another case, involving a slip and fall on ice, this same lawyer did have his law clerk speak to someone at a building inspection office about whether there had been complaints regarding sump pump discharge onto the site that would have created unusual and excessive ice buildups, although this investigation was done before my observation began.

That none of the lawyers I observed personally undertook any field investigation during my time in their offices does not mean that they never did such investigations. One of the lawyers related going to the site of the accident in one of the cases he was working on while I was in the office, but this field investigation occurred prior to my period of observation. This same lawyer described to me doing field observation in other cases he had handled. While neither of the other two lawyers described any field investigation they had done, they both had at least some cases where I would be surprised if they had done no field investigation. My point is not that contingency fee lawyers do not undertake field investigation, but rather that it is not a significant part of their day-to-day work in terms of the amount of time devoted to such investigation.[4]

The only other factual research, outside of formal discovery, that I saw involved reviewing various kinds of literature.[5] For example, in a medical malpractice case, the lawyer handling the case had amassed an extensive collection of more than 170 articles from medical journals relating to various aspects of the case.[6] He spent time both reviewing those articles and identifying additional articles he thought might be relevant. Most of this effort was background research rather than trying to answer specific questions related to the case. Similarly, while reviewing files from a workers' compensation case in which the claim involved repetitive stress syndrome, the lawyer at some point consulted an electronic "medical adviser" for information on repetitive stress. In the construction accident case mentioned above, the lawyer had obtained copies of company brochures and the like for the general contractor on the site and reviewed these for ideas about potential witnesses and experts.

In retrospect, the sparseness of active factual research should not have been surprising. In most routine cases, the lawyer obtains an account of what transpired from the client, plus any reports on the incident that might have been prepared by or filed with government authorities. Little investigation is necessary because what happened is often not in dispute, or in the case of workers' compensation claims, fault is not at issue. Early in the case, often at the first meeting with the client, the lawyer will collect names of witnesses to be prepared to contact them if there is a dispute over what happened; some lawyers will contact witnesses regardless in order to obtain their account of what happened before it fades into memory, although potential witnesses may not be lined up until just before trial (or hearings in workers' compensation).

In one of the offices, the lawyer was scheduled to try a case the month following my observation and was engaged in a combination of preparing for trial and trying to settle the case during my time in his office. Part of his preparation, at this late date, involved trying to line up witnesses who could testify to the psychological trauma experienced by his client in the wake of the incident precipitating the case. From the telephone conversations with the potential witnesses, it was clear that these were not simply calls checking back with persons who had previously been contacted, but rather initial contacts with persons suggested by the client.

One fact-related issue that the lawyers did address early in handling the case involved preserving, or even creating, evidence. Most often this involved photographs of damage and injuries, particularly lacerations. The lawyer may instruct the client to take photographs or possibly have someone from the firm or an investigator take photographs. For small routine cases, the lawyers I observed relied upon the clients to handle this task. One other way in which the lawyer may instruct the client to create evidence is by having the client keep a diary of what normal activities the client could not engage in and any pain or discomfort the client experienced. Several of the lawyers I interviewed reported that their firms had investigators on staff who would routinely take photographs of damaged vehicles, injuries, and accident sites; however, this was true only of firms that had high-volume personal injury practices. In one of the firms where I observed, a paralegal would be sent out to take photographs in substantial cases.

The nature of the investigation depends upon the type of case and whether the lawyer is handling the case in a litigational or case-processing mode. As noted earlier, medical malpractice cases are generally handled in a litigational mode; this is because lawyers perceive defendants in "med mal" cases as always resisting the claim regardless of how meritorious and clear-cut it is. In these cases the lawyer will conduct much of the investigation through formalized discovery procedures, such as taking depositions of hospital staff persons.

Formal Discovery

By definition, formal discovery occurs after the lawyer has initiated a lawsuit. In most offices, only a minority of cases end up in suit, and thus formal discovery may be infrequent. There are several types of exceptions to this. The first is workers' compensation claims, which are always filed with the state agency responsible for adjudicating workers' compensation disputes. The discovery in workers' compensation typically involves medical examinations by physicians retained by the workers' compensation insurance carrier and vocational assessments by specialists retained by the insurer.[7] The second exception can involve medical examinations conducted on behalf of the defending insurance company in cases other than workers' compensation claims before a formal action is initiated, although this is relatively rare. A final exception would be the taking of a sworn statement before a court reporter, something that was suggested by one of the lawyers in connection with a case he hoped to settle without filing suit.

In all three offices I attended at least one deposition. In Steve Clarke's only one deposition occurred the entire month I was there. In Bob Adams's office I attended two depositions, although both involved cases in which Adams was being paid by the hour rather than on a contingency basis; in one case he was defense counsel, and in the other, a dispute over remodeling of a home, he was representing the plaintiff.[8] In Chuck Brown's office, I observed five depositions, three of which involved the same case and were done back-to-back. Only one of the depositions I observed was initiated by Brown. None of the depositions was very long, all lasting less than an hour. The approach to depositions varied by office; it was clear that in Brown's office they were both more routine and more important than in the other offices.

In Steve Clarke's office, depositions were relatively rare simply because very few of Clarke's cases were ever filed in court. The one court filing that happened the entire month I was in the office involved a case in which the statute of limitation was fast approaching and it was evident that the case would not be ready for settlement because the client was still receiving medical treatment. Clarke did not view the filing as anything more than a pro forma move to protect the claim, and he spoke of the opposing side as seeing it in the same way. A significant portion of Clarke's time was spent on workers' compensation cases, which do not normally involve formal depositions because the rules governing the process do not allow for discovery (other than medical examinations and assessments by occupational specialists) except in rare instances where a physician needed for a hearing is unavailable.[9] The one deposition that did occur during my month with Clarke involved a tort claim arising from a workplace accident; the deponent was Clarke's client. The day before the deposition, Clarke had the client come in for preparation. Both the preparation and the deposition itself were unusual because the client could remember virtually nothing about what had caused his head injury; Clarke focused the preparation on things the client should avoid saying and on the importance of taking his time and being sure that he understood the question. At the start of the deposition, the opposing lawyer, who was conducting the questioning, did not realize the problem he was encountering. After about thirty minutes, the lawyer realized the deposition was not yielding any information and asked Clarke what was going on. When Clarke explained the situation, the deposition was adjourned.

As noted previously, depositions were much more a part of the routine for Chuck Brown. He went into the depositions very well prepared. As I previously noted, three of the depositions involved a single case dealing with third-party liability in an injury that occurred in the workplace. The three deponents, all of whom were Brown's witnesses concerning the circumstances of the accident, had previously given depositions, and Brown had unsuccessfully tried to block the opposing party's request to take another deposition; the judge overseeing the case had issued an order that the new depositions not be repetitive, but Brown was expecting them to be repetitive, given a communication he received from opposing counsel. He went into the depositions with detailed knowledge of the previous depositions and with the transcripts of the prior depositions available on a laptop computer he brought along. As the first deposition proceeded, Brown began pointing out to opposing counsel that he was asking questions covered in the previous deposition, giving the exact text of the question that he located on his laptop. Essentially the same thing happened in the second deposition, which started soon after the first one concluded. Brown had previously told me that rather than instructing the witness not to reply to repetitive questions, he might simply state an objection and then later move to have the entire deposition deemed inadmissible as in violation of the judge's order.

The importance of depositions to Brown's litigation-oriented practice was also evident in a deposition involving one of his clients. That client had been injured in an auto accident in which several passengers had filed suit against the driver and the driver's employer; the client was to be deposed by the lawyer for one of the other passengers as a witness in that passenger's lawsuit. While the information that his client was likely to provide was not particularly important, Brown saw the deposition as extremely important because it was the first look the lawyer for the common defendant would get at the client as a potential witness at trial. Brown met with the client several days before the deposition, both to go over some interrogatories and to discuss the upcoming deposition. Brown advised the client that his physical appearance at the deposition would be important (the client was a bit "artsy" in his appearance, with a long ponytail down his back); Brown explained to the client that it would be good if he would come to the deposition dressed to reflect his professional occupation. When the client arrived at Brown's office thirty minutes before the scheduled deposition, he was sporting a neat haircut and was dressed in a jacket and tie. The brief preparation session itself involved helping the client recall such things as times and distances; Brown used a stopwatch to help the client think about how long certain colloquies might have taken. The deposition itself proved to be uneventful, reviewing the events of the accident with Brown remaining largely silent, breaking in only when his client expressed an answer as a "guess" or in terms of "probably."

The importance of depositions to Brown was further evident in another case in which he wanted the court to strike one of the opposing party's proposed witnesses. In preparing the motion to strike the witness, he drew upon the witness's deposition testimony. One afternoon, I sat and watched as Brown devoted a substantial block of time to editing the draft motion, most of which involved searching through the electronic version of the witness's deposition to find citations from the deposition to insert. The next day, he devoted another block of time to working on the motion, much of which was spent creating an extract from the deposition to attach to the motion.

It is possible that the three practices where I observed were atypical vis-à-vis depositions. I think not; if anything, the discussion above may suggest that there is more deposition-related activity than is in fact the case in most practices. In my follow-up semistructured interviews, I asked each of the contingency fee lawyers, "Walk me through what you did yesterday. . . . What would I have seen if I had sat in this office from the time you got here until you left for the day?" Not a single lawyer even made reference to a deposition; only two made any reference to formal discovery, one about needing to plan who was going to do what concerning discovery in one case, and the other about the failure of the opposing party to conduct any discovery in a case scheduled to go to trial in two weeks. This pattern is generally consistent with other empirical research that has shown that most civil cases involve only modest amounts of formal discovery, if there is any formal discovery at all (Connolly, Holleman, and Kuhlman 1978; McKenna and Wiggins 1998; Mullenix 1994a, 1994b; Trubek et al. 1983; Willging et al. 1998). At the same time, one must be cautious in not dismissing the importance of discovery in some subset of cases. For Chuck Brown discovery was crucial to his practice and to many of the cases he handled, and he was constantly thinking in terms of how a client or witness would perform in a deposition and how particular deposition responses might help or hinder a case. However, Brown's practice was far from typical.

Medical Records

By far the biggest factual issue in the cases I observed concerned damages and the related issue of causation—whether the medical condition associated with the claim for damages was caused by the defendant or, in workers' compensation cases, was attributable to the claimant's employment. Most of the cases involved personal injury, the result of which was that damages turned on a set of interrelated questions: What was the nature of the claimed injury? What evidence was there of preexisting conditions related to the injury or the client's current condition? What evidence was there that the injury was caused by the accident? A significant amount of effort goes into obtaining and reviewing medical records. In all three offices where I observed, much of this work was handled by paralegals. From the interviews with other practitioners, it was clear that delegating this task to staff was common and perhaps typical.

The detail in medical records can be extremely important. Lawyers and their staffs closely review records with a variety of issues in mind. An incident from a case handled by Steve Clarke illustrates this. The issue dealt with a single letter, the letter *s*, in a medical provider's case notes. This case involved a soft tissue injury; in noting the source of the injury, the physician had at one point referred to the "accidents" rather than to the "accident." If the injury had resulted from more than one accident, that fact would raise questions about whether the accident which led to the claim was the cause of any of the injuries, or the degree to which the client's condition was attributable to preexisting conditions. There was only a single accident, and the lawyer was able to get the medical provider to correct the record before it was forwarded to the insurance company's claims adjuster. While this is the kind of error the lawyer wants to catch, this particular error was actually identified by the client when he reviewed the records.

In part for this reason, most lawyers insist on reviewing medical records before they are sent to the opposing party. Clarke had a sharp exchange with the office of a medical provider that had sent records directly to an insurer without having received a release to do so; Clarke discovered the problem only when the adjuster with whom he was dealing sent copies to Clarke. The medical provider's office manager, who explained that the records had been sent because the third-party insurer would not demand a fee reduction as would the patient / client's HMO, became extremely upset when Clarke demanded that this not be done in the future and explained his concern about errors in the medical records, citing the case discussed above.

One of the first things all three of the lawyers I observed did upon being retained by a new client was to revoke any releases the client might have previously signed at the request of the opposing party's insurer. Again, this was usually to allow the lawyer to review the records for errors and for extraneous information which could be used to damage the client's claim. However, Bob Adams's practice differed somewhat; he allowed medical records to be sent directly to insurers but made sure that the provider was acting on a restricted release that he drafted rather than the kind of blanket release that the insurer typically used. This was also true of several of the lawyers I interviewed, although the dominant practice was that the lawyer would review records before forwarding them on to the insurer.

All of the foregoing involves the handling of medical records prior to a suit being filed. Once a suit is in progress, the rules concerning discovery govern access to medical records. Opposing lawyers can then obtain any medical records that they can argue are potentially relevant to any aspect of the case. Some of the lawyers I interviewed reported that they had encountered insurance companies that insisted upon direct access to medical records before discussing a settlement; the lawyers varied in how they responded to such demands, some allowing access because the insurer would get access through formal discovery if the case got into suit, while others refused such demands, telling the insurer that if that was the way the insurer wanted to play it, the lawyer would simply go ahead and file suit and start taking depositions.

While records of medical treatment are important in assessing damages, such records are probably even more important concerning issues of causation. Given the nature of the injury, how does it relate to the precipitating incident? What other conditions preexisting the incident, or other factors coexisting with the incident, might account for the client's injury or disability? A client may be claiming back injury but have a history of back complaints. The lawyer will often try to ascertain during intake or soon thereafter directly from the client whether there are complications lurking in the medical records by simply asking about the client's health history or prior injuries.

Alternatively, a client may have a number of preexisting medical conditions that make it difficult to sort out what is and is not related to an accident. For example, Steve Clarke agreed to represent a woman who had been in an auto accident in which her car was rear-ended. While there was little issue over liability, the woman had a host of preexisting medical conditions, including chronic fatigue syndrome. Clarke explained to the client that "this is not going to be easy to sort out"; he went on to say that "while there is a claim here, given the complexities, [he could] handle the case only to obtain a settlement, because the preexisting conditions would complicate things in a way that it would be very expensive to bring in all of [the client's] doctors to testify to try to sort things out."

Medical records can also reveal other types of facts about clients that make it difficult to pursue a case. For example, one lawyer I interviewed had accepted a client who claimed she was injured in a fall from a stairway in her apartment house. Allegedly this occurred because of poor lighting and a low railing, and the lawyer contemplated a negligence claim against the landlord. During the intake interview, the lawyer had asked the client whether she had had anything to drink, and the client reported a single beer. When the lawyer obtained the client's hospital record, the lawyer discovered an unrelated visit to the emergency room around the time of the injury when the client had told the hospital staff she had consumed two beers, but the hospital laboratory reported a blood-alcohol level of .26. The lawyer withdrew from representing the client.

As noted above, the lawyers differ somewhat in how they process medical records. Some lawyers delegate the responsibility largely to paralegals. Of the lawyers I observed, this was most true of Steve Clarke. Other lawyers distinguish between their routine cases and their nonroutine cases, with paralegals handling the former and lawyers the latter; this tended to be the case with Chuck Brown. Others, particularly those who do not have practices specializing in personal injury (and hence do not have paralegals with significant experience in reviewing medical records), do much of the review of the records themselves. One important distinction is between medical records and medical bills; some lawyers handle the records review themselves but leave the sorting out of medical bills, between those related to the injury and those unrelated, to a paralegal or secretary. High-volume practices depend the most on staff to process and review medical records. Some lawyers have staff members prepare a treatment chronology to be used both in arriving at a valuation for an initial demand and as the basis of the damages portion of a demand letter or brochure; other lawyers prepare summaries or chronologies themselves in order to become familiar with the records.

Lawyers often need to have medical providers prepare reports that speak directly to issues of causation and long-term impact, issues that are frequently unclear in the medical records that are produced in the normal course of medical treatment. Medical providers differ in their willingness to cooperate in preparing such reports. Some do not want to be bothered; some provide the reports grudgingly, often in a form or language that is not as helpful as the lawyer would like; and some want to be as helpful as possible. Sometimes there are very specific issues that the lawyer needs to have addressed, such as allocating causation among several sources, the implications of which the medical provider does not understand. A lawyer may try to educate the provider about why this is necessary and how best, from the client's perspective, to approach it. Often the issue turns on whether the report contains the "magic words," referring to a specific turn of phrase or some specific statement of degree of certainty.

The importance of having a "good report" from the treating physician was clearly illustrated throughout my research. One example involved an auto accident one of the lawyers I interviewed had recently closed. The client had suffered a soft tissue neck injury when another driver pulled out in front of him and struck the car the client was driving. The client had medical bills totaling $2,500 and lost wages of $3,200; if the client had no lasting effects from the injury, one might expect this case to settle in the range of $10,000 to $15,000. However, the treating physician's report stated that the client-patient had suffered injuries that would result in lifelong pain and consequent limitations on his activities, which lowered the client's work life expectancy. When the lawyer received the doctor's report describing the permanency, he contacted the insurance adjuster, explained that "we have permanency," and asked for a certified copy of the insurance policy in order to ascertain what the limit was. The adjuster refused,[10] and the lawyer sent a letter demanding $75,000, attaching the report; the adjuster responded with an offer of $20,000. The case settled for $35,000.

Lawyers will do what they can to get physicians to write reports that use terminology that is favorable to a client. One lawyer I spoke to went so far as to state that he would draft reports for physicians because physicians did not understand what needed to be in the report. This was exceptional. Most lawyers will try to explain the importance of certain types of statements; in a sense they will try to put words in the physicians' mouths but they do not try to manipulate the physicians' medical conclusions. Words like "permanency" or "continuing pain" or "permanent restrictions" do more to bolster the case than do words such as "possible limitations" or "uncertain prognosis." For the lawyer, the good medical provider is one who will both provide good treatment for the lawyer's client and use the "magic words" in their reports on the treatment and condition of the client that trigger desired responses from insurance adjusters and defense lawyers. I accompanied Steve Clarke on a visit to a doctor's office to discuss the situation of a workers' compensation client who had preexisting medical conditions that complicated the case. Clarke explained to the physician that the issue was whether an upcoming surgery was connected to a work injury; he told the physician that the independent medical examination had concluded that while the work accident had temporarily aggravated the client's condition, the current situation was not due to the work accident. The physician immediately stated that while there is no definitive way to determine whether the client's current condition was due to the accident, the client had been stable before the incident and had definitely worsened after the accident. The upcoming surgery was specifically to deal with that worsened condition. The physician then proceeded to pick up his recorder and dictate a letter to the lawyer giving his opinion that the current condition necessitated surgery, that the client's current condition was a result of an aggravation of the client's preexisting medical condition, and that the aggravation was due to the work injury.

Information: Summary

Litigation centers on information. Much of the work of litigators, including those working on a contingency fee basis, involves collecting, sorting, and evaluating information. However, in most cases handled on a contingency fee basis, little of this information processing involves "investigation" in the sense of on-scene assessments, digging for details or obscure facts, or interviewing witnesses. Most of the information is available directly from the client or in documents generated through routine processes by medical providers and law enforcement personnel.

Where possible, lawyers seek to manage the information that the opposing side receives. Lawyers are most able to manage information prior to the initiation of formal litigation because once a lawsuit is filed, the rules of formal discovery limit the lawyer's information management capability. Much of the information involved in personal injury claims is very routine and is frequently not in dispute. Lawyers, particularly those in specialized personal injury practices, often rely on staff to collect, sort, and manage the information that forms the basis of the eventual settlement demand (or trial, in the few cases where trials occur).

Managing the Client

Organizing Client Management

Managing the relationship with the client is an important part of the lawyer's work, both to handle the instant case and to further the client's likelihood of recommending the lawyer to others in the future. In my observation, I saw examples of two distinct approaches to this part of the practice.

Steve Clarke (relatively high-volume, routine cases, processing-oriented) handles almost all of the client contact himself. Calls that came in from clients were routed to him unless he was unavailable. His paralegal would handle calls from clients only when Clarke was unavailable; I never saw him refer a call to his paralegal. Clarke had organized himself to be able to respond to calls from current clients efficiently. He used an entirely paper-based filing system and maintained the files of current cases in lateral files which he could access without getting out of his chair. If a client called in and he needed a bit of information he did not have in his head, he could grab the file and talk intelligently about the case, such as telling the client what he was still waiting for. Clarke also initiated a lot of status calls to his clients. If he had not heard from someone for a while, he would call the person. While he did not have a formal tickler system to maintain client contact, he did regularly review his pending files to see if it was time to check in with the client. Clarke had a high volume of calls in the course of most days, and he was able to move among clients and cases with ease, partly because of his filing system and partly because of his memory of cases. On several occasions he was able to remember off the top of his head details about clients' injuries and treatment that the client did not recall. Clarke also went beyond strictly business interactions; one client who called in to report on his postsurgery progress expressed his thanks to Clarke for the plant Clarke had sent to cheer him up.

Chuck Brown (low-volume, focus on high-value cases, litigation-oriented) bifurcated his client contact between routine cases and high-value cases. His paralegal handled most of the client contact in the routine cases, and he handled much, if not most, of the contact in high-value cases. His paralegal would often be present at the client intake meeting, and she would handle the completion of routine forms such as releases and the like at the conclusion of that meeting. This served to introduce the client to the paralegal and create the image of there being a team working on the case. For routine cases such as workers' compensation or soft tissue injuries, the paralegal would handle most of the work, sometimes even drafting the demand letter. On the rare occasion when a call from a client in a routine case got through to Brown, he was not particularly conversant with the status of the case because he was not involved in the day-to-day work of handling it. He and his paralegal did maintain an online case status log, which he could, and did, consult from the computer workstation next to his desk. After telephone calls from clients, he would assiduously update the information in the online system to record the call and note any changes to the status of the case. Brown did handle client contact in larger or more complex cases, particularly when significant events such as hearings or depositions were approaching. The combination of lower volume and delegation meant that Brown's office was a much quieter place than was Clarke's; where Clarke might receive or make twenty-five or more telephone calls in the course of a day, a busy telephone day for Brown would involve half a dozen calls.

The interviews showed that both approaches to client contact were common. In very high-volume offices, delegation was the norm, although many smaller offices also delegated routine contacts to support staff. Part of the rationale for this was that it was more cost-efficient for staff to handle calls (hence helping to control the lawyers' time investment in each case), but lawyers also commented that it made it easier for the client to get through immediately to someone knowledgeable about the case. Lawyers would often be tied up in meetings with other clients, or be out of the office, and have to try to return calls. Other lawyers try to handle the client contact as much as possible themselves. Still others distinguish between routine and nonroutine contacts or cases.

One general point to be distilled from both my observations and interviews: relatively little client contact involves face-to-face meetings. For many, possibly most, cases, the lawyer and client meet only twice: to establish the lawyer-client relationship by signing a retainer agreement and to end the immediate relationship with the delivery of a settlement check. The rest of the contact between lawyer and client is conducted either over the telephone or by written communication from the lawyer to the client. The key exceptions to the pattern of minimal face-to-face contact come in either high-value, complex cases or cases that get at least to the stage of formal processes such as the taking of depositions; for most lawyers, a minority of cases meet either of these criteria.[11]

Signing the Retainer

The first aspect of client management is establishing the formal attorney-client relationship by signing the retainer agreement. While some lawyers seek to do this as quickly as possible, others see the process as somewhat more of a transition. The survey included the question, "When do you normally ask a potential client to sign a retainer agreement?" The response options and the resulting percentages are as follows:

At the first in-person meeting	43%
After the first meeting but before any independent investigation	22
After some minimal independent investigation	24
After more than minimal independent investigation	6
Other (including volunteered responses that "it varies")	5

The last of these responses typically came from lawyers who distinguished between routine cases such as auto accidents, when the lawyer asked the client to sign a retainer before obtaining accident reports or conducting any independent investigation, and more complex cases such as medical malpractice, when the lawyer wanted to do some significant preliminary evaluation such as reviewing medical records and seeking the opinion of an independent expert.

Not only is there considerable variation in when lawyers have clients sign contingency fee retainer agreements, but there is a systematic pattern to that variation, as shown in Table 4.1. Personal injury specialists are much more likely to have clients sign a retainer at the first in-person meeting (65 percent) than either general practitioners (36 percent) or other lawyers (31 percent). Some of this difference may reflect the fact that for the personal injury specialists there is no ongoing relationship with the potential client, while for the other lawyers, particularly the general practitioners, there often is an existing attorney-client relationship and the retainer agreement serves primarily as a fee agreement rather than to establish the relationship. However, it also reflects the importance to contingency fee lawyers of getting clients "signed up."

Some lawyers have a client sign what effectively is an option for the lawyer to handle the case, which gives the lawyer the authority to conduct investigatory activities but allows the lawyer to decide to drop the case depending on the result of that investigation. Others simply have the client sign a regular retainer agreement but make clear that the results of the lawyer's investigation may result in a decision not to pursue the case. Still others undertake investigatory activities with no retainer in place and then have the client sign the retainer once the lawyer has made the decision to pursue the case.

Treatment Counseling

The perceived linkage between medical expenses and compensation for pain and suffering raises the possibility that treatment is undertaken for nonmedical reasons. In some states with no-fault systems, which is not

TABLE 4.1

When the Retainer Agreement Is Normally Signed

	All Respondents (%)	Personal Injury Specialists (%)	General Practitioners (%)	Others (%)
At the first in-person meeting	43	65	36	31
After the first meeting but before any independent investigation	22	12	32	24
After some minimal independent investigation	25	14	24	33
After more than minimal independent investigation	6	2	3	9
Other (including volunteered responses that "it varies")	5	8	5	4
N	494	161	102	231

$\chi^2 = 27.27$ (8 df, $p < .001$)

the case for Wisconsin, payments for pain and suffering will be made only if the medical expenses exceed some threshold amount; this creates an incentive to get above that threshold. A number of studies provide evidence that in at least some situations accident victims receive "unneeded" or "excess" medical services (Abrahamse and Carroll 1999; Carroll, Abrahamse, and Vaiana 1995; Insurance Research Council 1996). The assumption underlying the supposed excess medical service is that insurance companies use the amount of the medical bills as a guide to deciding on compensation for pain and suffering; "three times specials" is sometimes quoted as a rule of thumb (Ross 1980, 100; Wolfram 1986, 528n21). The logic of maximizing medical treatment to maximize compensation is clear, assuming that insurance companies do use simple rules of thumb or view medical expenses as a simple surrogate for amount of pain and suffering.

I would not expect the lawyers I observed or interviewed to admit to counseling clients to get medical treatment purely for the purposes of increasing the value of a claim.[12] While I have little doubt that some lawyers do engage in activities that lead to questionable medical services, what I saw and heard raises some important questions about what critics have labeled "excess" treatment. The lawyers confronted several issues with regard to advising clients about obtaining medical services, all of which might legitimately lead to clients obtaining more medical services than they would obtain without the advice of a lawyer. These issues include the need to document that an injury has occurred, the reluctance of some clients to obtain medical treatment—or the inclination to simply grin and bear it—and the desire to have the client find an effective treatment modality. The lawyers also recognize that some treatment modalities raise more questions with insurers than do others.

A frequent theme I heard, both as I observed and in my interviews, is that clients need to have an injury documented by a physician. In the words of two of my respondents:

I usually tell my clients that I don't necessarily encourage them to go to the doctor just because I am handling the case. But I do tell them the facts of life: insurance companies do not take cases seriously unless the claimant has received medical treatment. . . . I have clients [who] I know are legitimately hurt, but when I talk to the insurance adjuster, all the adjuster wants to know is how many times the client has been to the doctor.

I have to have the medical testimony of a doctor; it doesn't do much good for the client to sit there and tell me about all of the things that resulted from the accident. I tell the client to go to a doctor and tell the doctor, because the doctor is the person who has to provide a report and possibly testify.

A somewhat similar situation arises with a client whose injury lingers but who does not continue in medical treatment. In the words of one lawyer,

If I've got a client in shortly after an accident, within a week or two, they may ask me about treatment. I will tell them, if you continue to have problems, seek medical care, because what's going to happen if you don't is either you're going to have a lapse in treatment or you're going to have no treatment, and then there's going to be no documentation of the injuries. If, when it comes time to settle, you come into my office and tell me that you've been suffering for six months but you've got only one month's worth of medical records showing treatment, I will tell you that your case is worth one month's worth of treatment. The last thing I want to encourage is for the client to try to milk up the claim a little bit, but they need to have the treatment indicated by the injury.

A third problem with documentation can arise if a treating physician simply does not want to prepare reports or go to court if necessary. My sense is that most treating physicians will provide support for their patients, but lawyers did remark on the need to have clients go to a different physician if the treating doctor was known as someone who would not be supportive in the claims process.

While a lawyer could try to steer a client to providers who would overtreat and thus build up medical expenses, I did not see any clear evidence of this, nor would I expect to. I saw a lot that clearly went in the opposite direction. For example, during my observation in Steve Clarke's office, one potential client called in about a minor accident she had been involved in several days earlier. Clarke asked if she had obtained any medical treatment; the caller said she had not but that she had a prior appointment scheduled with her doctor later in the week (the call came in on Tuesday). Clarke suggested that she might not want to wait until Friday to get medical treatment. He went on to tell her that if she was feeling fine by Friday, she might want to just call the insurer and that they might pay her a few hundred dollars; no lawyer would be needed. However, if the problem did not clear up by Friday, she should get back in touch.

The concern about avoiding clearly unnecessary treatment was also evident in the frequent comments about excessive treatment by chiropractors. Generally the lawyers were wary of chiropractic treatment because they knew that insurance companies tend to be skeptical of such treatment, and hence often heavily discount chiropractic fees in assessing the significance of the injury. Lawyers are careful to avoid blanket characterizations, but several lawyers had stories about chiropractors contacting them about mutual referral arrangements. One lawyer I interviewed did report initiating contacts with chiropractors to obtain referrals. Lawyers did not rule out chiropractic treatment, but they were concerned about the issues such treatment raised in the settlement process. Some of the lawyers saw chiropractic treatment as having more credibility with juries than with insurance adjusters.

Lawyers try to make it clear to their clients that once the case is settled there is no second bite at the apple. If a client indicates that she is still experiencing symptoms related to the injury caused by the accident, it is important that she go back to her doctor, to obtain additional treatment, to document a condition that is likely to continue, or to assess the client's current medical status. Lawyers appear to be concerned that their clients obtain the medical treatment they genuinely need, even when the client is inclined to "grin and bear it." This can mean referring the client to a different type of medical provider—a neurologist, an orthopedic surgeon, a pain management clinic, a physical therapist, or in some circumstances a chiropractor. Clients will sometime ask the lawyer for advice either on what type of provider to see or for a specific recommendation of an individual provider; some lawyers will refer to an individual physician, while others provide the client with a list of possibilities, and some decline to name names.

Most of the "delay" in resolving cases I became aware of was related to medical treatment issues. The lawyers were extremely sensitive to the need for clients either to recover fully from their injuries or to reach a "healing plateau"—that is, to recover as much as they are going to recover. If lawyers believed that further recovery was possible, they would counsel clients not to settle yet and to seek additional treatment that might help the client's condition. If the client seemed to have reached a healing plateau, then the lawyer would seek to have the treating physician provide a report stating that a plateau had been reached and giving a prognosis concerning the possibilities of future improvement.

Managing Client Behaviors

One issue that lawyers confront is that a client can do things that jeopardize the client's claim. The lawyer needs to manage aspects of the client's behavior to keep this from happening. Two common issues came up during the observation.

The first related specifically to workers' compensation cases. When a workers' compensation claim involves a permanent partial disability, it is common that the current employer will no longer have work that the claimant is able to do. It is much better for the claim for an employer to inform the claimant that the employer has no work that the claimant is able to do than for the claimant to quit his or her job with the employer. Many claimants are tempted to quit, and employers may do things to try to encourage them to quit. The lawyers advise clients not to quit because doing so can jeopardize the claim or reduce its value. Quitting creates problems because employers have the option of accommodating an employee who becomes disabled, and if the employer can find an accommodation that does not significantly reduce the employee's wage rate, the employer avoids having to compensate the employee for lost potential income.[13] The employee quitting makes it easier for the employer to argue that an accommodation would have been made if the employee had stayed.

A second way that a client's claim can be jeopardized is if the opposing party documents behaviors inconsistent with the claim. In particular, if a client is claiming a disability that prevents something like heavy lifting, catching the claimant engaged in activities such as shoveling snow, or vigorous recreation such as touch football or basketball, will call into question the claimed disability. It does not matter whether the client realizes afterward that he pays with significant pain or discomfort for having engaged in the activity. When one lawyer warned a new client of the consequences of being caught engaging in such activities, the client reported that he had done a little snow shoveling . . . but had then "paid for it." Being captured on a surveillance tape only a single time will be sufficient to damage the claim. Surveillance is undertaken by workers' compensation insurers because of concerns about fraud, and these concerns are not entirely without a basis, as reflected in one exchange I observed between a lawyer and a client:

> During one conversation, the client mentions the possibility of working under the table. The lawyer immediately says, "I don't want to hear about it," and goes on to warn the client that if he does do something like that, the insurer is very likely to find out about it and even might catch the client on video. If the insurer finds out, the client will lose the workers' compensation case. The client acknowledged that he is very fearful of surveillance; he has heard of it happening to people he knows and won't even do stuff around the house because of this concern.

On the other hand, workers' compensation cases often involve claimants who are used to a high level of physical activity, and controlling the urge to get out and do things, even if there is a cost in pain to be paid later, can often be very difficult. While the issue of surveillance seemed to come up most often in the workers' compensation context, it can arise in any situation where a client is claiming a permanent disability.[14]

Managing Client Expectations

Many if not most clients know that relatively few cases ever get to trial. Even so, the process of settling cases takes place in the shadow of what might happen should the case go to trial; unfortunately, the only way to know for sure what would happen at trial is to go to trial. Lawyers believe that they have some idea of what would happen, both from their own direct experience and from the attention they pay to the trials in which they are not directly involved (either by word of mouth or from sources such as jury verdict reporters). The only sources of information for most clients are news reports, which are wildly biased toward the largest cases (see Bailis and MacCoun 1996; Chase 1995), word of mouth from their social circle (which is likely to be based largely on the biased media reports), and the assessments of their lawyers. This provides the lawyers with a substantial measure of control over the client's expectations, and in this section I discuss how the lawyers go about managing the clients' expectations.[15] I leave the issue of how the lawyers use those expectations, and how they deal with conflicting expectations, during the settlement process, to the next chapter.

Managing the client's expectations about the likely case outcome typically begins at the very first contact and involves three key strategies by the lawyer: avoiding creating expectations, deflating expectations, and emphasizing uncertainty. Exactly how and when lawyers deploy these strategies depends in part on when the client first contacts the lawyer. That is, if the client contacts the lawyer very soon after the accident, it is easy to avoid answering specific questions because the client is just beginning his or her recovery period; on the other hand, if the client waits some months until recovery is complete, the situation presented to the lawyer may be more clear with regard to injuries, although it may be less clear with regard to other factors relevant to resolving the case.

Avoiding Creating Expectations.   While a number of the lawyers I spoke with remarked that they knew of lawyers who would create expectations of substantial recoveries early in a case, the lawyers I observed and spoke to generally avoided talking about specific amounts of potential compensation during initial interviews or early in the case. Surprisingly, given the popular image of the litigious American, in few of the initial lawyer-client discussions that I observed did the client (or potential client) specifically ask the lawyer how much they might be able to recover. Furthermore, the lawyers were generally careful to avoid bringing up the subject of what the case was worth. When it did come up, it was likely to be in the context of some limitation on damages, such as the schedule of damages under workers' compensation or the damage cap that applies to governmental defendants in Wisconsin.

This pattern was also clear from the interviews. In response to my question, "What do you do to try to establish a client's expectation [regarding amount of compensation]?" lawyers told me things like the following:

I try to avoid the subject as much as possible because I never really know until the end how much a case is worth. It depends on a lot of factors. A lot of my clients try to pin me down.

At the outset I don't promise or guarantee them anything.

I don't want to get clients thinking at the initial conference that somehow or another we are talking about boxcar figures, because then it is very difficult to talk settlement when you want them to be reasonable.

When I see people, I first tell them that I do not know what your case is worth. Anybody who tells you that they know is just making it up, because your bills are not in, we don't know how long your treatment will take, we don't know how well you will recover. We don't know all of these things.

I probably do stuff specifically not to establish expectations. . . . I try not to build up any expectations. [If they ask,] I tell them that I'm not going to be able to give them that information. I can only give them my version of what goes into how the decision is made.

I don't give [clients] any numbers right off the bat because you have no idea. You don't have enough [information] at the first meeting. If you say any number, it sticks in their head and then that's what their expectation is forever. So, I always try to keep their expectations down.

Lawyers might try to find out if a client has some amount in mind, but the goal here is primarily to determine whether there is a need to head off unrealistic expectations. "You have to start feeling them out from the beginning to find out if all of a sudden they have an inflated value of the case. You have to find out where they are at."

Deflating Expectations.   As noted previously, the nature of the news coverage of jury verdicts and compensation for injuries creates a biased image of the outcomes of compensation claims. This does not stop potential clients from taking news reports as indicators of what their claims might be worth. One lawyer reported that "some clients bring in clippings of somebody who was malpracticed upon" and won a large jury verdict. Another lawyer commented, "It is amazing how many clients come in and say that they are not trying to get rich off this case but think they should get $100,000 for a whiplash or a slip-and-fall." Still another described the situation of a woman with some questionable soft tissue injuries who insisted that her case was worth $700,000.

An unrelated national survey I conducted in 2000–2001 (Kritzer 2001c) included the following open-ended question: "In addition to deciding guilt and innocence in criminal trials, juries are used in the U.S.

to determine liability and the amount of money to be paid in compensation for damages in noncriminal cases. From what you know, can you give me an estimate of the typical or average amount of money that juries award as compensation in a personal injury case of the type that arises from auto accidents, injuries from defective products, medical negligence, and the like?" A total of 1,524 respondents answered this question in some way, with *40 percent replying that they did not know what the typical or average amount was*. The median for those who did respond was $100,000, and 23 percent gave estimates of $1 million or more. In comparison, an analysis of jury verdicts in tort cases from the seventy-five largest counties in 1996 found that the median verdict was $31,000 and that only 6 percent were $1 million or more (DeFrances and Litras 1999, 8).

If the client comes in with inflated expectations, it is important for the lawyer to try to shift the client to a more realistic perspective. Sometimes the context of the injury provides a way for the lawyer to lower expectations. For example, under workers' compensation statutes, there are strict limits on the amount of compensation available to persons injured on the job when there is no third party involved. Lawyers can use the limits imposed by those statutes to make clear the range of compensation that is likely to be available. In effect, the workers' compensation limitations themselves tend to lower expectations. One of the lawyers I observed frequently commented to a new client that his or her injury would have been "worth a lot more" if the case was not limited by the workers' compensation statute.

While the caps under the workers' compensation statutes tend to lower expectations, other types of damage caps, or debates about caps, actually tend to increase expectations. While very few injury claims result in compensation payments of $250,000 or more, this is a common figure for caps for various types of damages.[16] The existence of such caps can create expectations, particularly when the lawyer needs to advise the client of the limits of recovery. This kind of "anchoring" effect is well documented in social psychological research (Kahneman, Slovic, and Tversky 1982; Plous 1993; Tversky and Kahneman 1974, 1128–30), including research applied specifically to the legal system (see, e.g., Babcock and Pogarsky 1999; Guthrie, Rachlingski, and Wistrich 2001, 787–94; Hastie, Schkade, and Payne 1999, 463–65; Hinsz and Indahl 1995, 1013–15; Pogarsky and Babcock 2001; Robbennolt and Studebaker 1999). In Wisconsin, anchoring can happen in a variety of contexts, but, as noted above, it is most common in cases involving a governmental unit as the defendant (e.g., an auto accident caused by the negligence of a governmental employee operating a government-owned vehicle).

When a cap of $250,000 applies to a case, it can be necessary for the lawyer both to advise the client of the limit and then to immediately move to prevent that from anchoring an expectation. For example, I sat in on discussions with one potential client who had been seriously injured ("I'm lucky to be alive") in an auto accident involving a state car, where the driver of that car was unambiguously at fault for the accident; the injuries involved broken ribs and other internal trauma and resulted in seven days of hospitalization including three days in intensive care. In the course of the discussion, the lawyer explained that because the other driver was a state employee operating the vehicle in the course of his employment, the claim against the state was capped by statute at $250,000. The problem, of course, was that as soon as the lawyer mentioned the $250,000 cap, that had the likely effect of getting the client thinking in terms of that amount. To counteract this, the lawyer engaged in what I came to recognize as a common method of deflating a client's expectations; the lawyer said to the client, "Hopefully, you don't have a $250,000 claim, because that would mean that you had some serious *permanent* injuries; for your sake, I hope this claim is *not* worth $250,000." One of my interviewees described this strategy very clearly: "I always start out explaining that if, for example, their child had suffered a broken leg, the case would be worth a lot more if instead the child had been left crippled by the accident. . . . Isn't it better that the child is not crippled, because it's far better to have a healthy child than to have a big case. You try to get them thinking about things in perspective. . . . If the child had two broken legs, the case would be worth more, but aren't you glad it's only one?"

The many-year campaign of the insurance industry to portray the tort system as in crisis and out of control (see Daniels 1989; Daniels and Martin 1995; Galanter 1993; Sanders and Joyce 1990) has, in some ways, made the situation of unrealistic expectations worse. As one lawyer described his experience: "It is not unusual that somebody comes in and says, 'Well, I won't take a dime less than $500,000.' We say, 'Well, that's interesting, but the last one we tried that we had that involved these injuries and these similar facts, we got an initial offer of $5,000. We were delighted that we were able to eventually get $16,000.' It is a constant problem because people really believe the insurance industry propaganda that you get $500,000 for showing up."

A final way for a lawyer to deflate a client's expectation is to quote what the lawyer knows is likely to be a lowball figure. That is, a lawyer may simply tell the client that a case is worth less than the lawyer thinks will eventually be recovered. In the words of one lawyer, "I always tell them that it is worth less than what I think I'm going to get, and then when I get the settlement they are ecstatic, I look good, and everybody is happy. Now is that honest? Probably a little tinge there of not being totally honest with the client. Does it work? Yes!"

Emphasizing Uncertainty.   As I noted previously, neither lawyers nor clients tend to bring up the question of specific valuing of a case during the initial meetings. The lawyers tend to emphasize to the client the need to get through the recovery period in order to determine the nature of treatment the client needs and whether the injury has any continuing consequences. When the client does raise the question of how much the compensation might be, the lawyer usually explains that the amount will depend upon how well the client recovers from the injury and whether any complications come up. The lawyer also explains that the amount the client will end up with depends upon how much will have to be paid to medical insurers to satisfy subrogation claims.[17] Typically the most that the lawyer will say is that "we should be able to get you some money." If a client presses the question, the lawyer may go through a list of the elements that will ultimately determine the amount of compensation, with the emphasis on whether there is any permanent impact.

Assessing Who's in Charge

The discussion above raises the specter of extensive manipulation of clients for the lawyers' benefits. The issue of control in the lawyer-client relationship is important, both from the perspective of those who study the legal profession and from the practical perspective of the fairness of the legal system. In the mid-1970s, Douglas Rosenthal (1974) published a book focusing on lawyer-client relations in personal injury cases; the title of that book, *Lawyer and Client: Who's in Charge?* states the issue directly: Do lawyers use their knowledge and position to manipulate their clients, or are clients able to exert control over their lawyers to ensure that the work carried out on their behalf genuinely reflects their needs and interests? Law and economics scholars typically express this issue in terms of the "agency problem" (Hay 1996a; Miller 1987), while sociologists of law focus on the issue of "power" in the lawyer-client relationship (Felstiner and Sarat 1992). Underlying all of the discussions is the observation that the interests and needs of lawyers and clients often conflict, and consequently a fully autonomous, self-interested lawyer will make decisions that a fully informed client would reject (Clermont and Currivan 1978; Johnson 1980–81; Schwartz and Mitchell 1970).

Empirical studies of lawyers and their clients differ in their answers as to the locus and nature of control. Some find that the clients, at least in some situations, exercise a reasonable amount of control:

- John Heinz and Edward Laumann (1982, 360–74) found that corporate lawyers are quite responsive to their corporate clients but largely autonomous of their personal services clients.
- Maureen Cain (1979, 334–35) found that most of the solicitors she observed had their objectives defined by their clients and that the solicitors generally provided the service the client requested.
- Jerry Van Hoy (1995, 705) found that, because of the high level of routinization in franchise law firms, lawyers (and secretarial staff) do dominate clients, but the standardization imposed by management "helps to protect clients with basic problems who might otherwise be subject to unscrupulous practices."

However, many more studies report that lawyers dominate the relationship:

- Roger Bryant Hunting and Gloria Neuwirth (1962, 107–9) found that accident clients had little say in the settlement of their accident claims; Rosenthal (1974) found that lawyers were more responsive to active clients but that largely it was the lawyer who was in charge.
- Carl Hosticka (1979, 604) found that, in the legal services setting, lawyers seldom even asked their clients what the client wanted the lawyer to do.
- In criminal justice cases, studies have repeatedly found that defense lawyers see themselves as moving guilty clients through the system rather than seeking to get the clients' input and defining goals and strategies in terms of those inputs (see Blumberg 1967; Casper 1972; Flemming 1986; McConville et al. 1994; McIntyre 1987, 153–62; Nardulli 1986) and that to do otherwise can produce problems for the client (see Mann 1985; Simon 1991).
- In consumer bankruptcy, lawyers generally sell what amounts to a product (a Chapter 7 filing, or a Chapter 13 filing), often on a take-it-or-leave-it basis, while doing relatively little to determine what is best for the individual client (Neustadter 1986).
- Lynn Mather, Richard Maiman, and Craig McEwen (1995; see also Mather, McEwen, and Maiman 2001, 87–109) found that divorce

lawyers reported that they largely controlled the direction of their cases and the best way to handle them. The researchers found that lawyers try to avoid taking cases in which the client insists on things that the lawyer views as unrealistic or undesirable. They use the metaphor of passenger and driver, arguing that the driver (the lawyer) largely determines both the destination and the route to that destination, with the passenger (the client) at best being allowed to do a little backseat driving.

Still other studies find more ambiguous patterns:

- Ann Southworth (1996) reported that lawyers in civil rights and poverty practice vary substantially in the degree to which they respond to and defer to clients and that these variations depend upon certain character-istics of the lawyers.
- John Flood (1987, 386–90) found that corporate lawyers are more re-sponsive to those clients who are seen as having substantial long-term fee potential.
- Drawing on extensive observation of divorce lawyers interacting with their clients, William Felstiner and Austin Sarat (1992, 1495–98) found a great deal of ambiguity in the power relationship, with issues of domi-nance and control constantly in flux and subject to implicit renegotia-tion.

My research makes it clear that there is not a simple answer to the question of control in the lawyer-client relationship (see also Felstiner 2001). While lawyers may try to manage the relationship in a number of ways (Reed 1969), both professionalism and long-term concerns about a continuing portfolio of contingency fee cases create the conditions for lawyer deferral to clients. The answer to the question of how lawyers use the potential for control described in part above must be left for later in the book, until the settlement process itself is considered.

Law Talk

A second important question in the way lawyers and clients interact is the image of the legal system that lawyers present to their clients. Sarat and Felstiner (1989) coined the term "law talk" to describe divorce lawyers' routine portrayal of the legal system to their clients as "rele-gating rules [and other formalisms] to the background" and as "stress-ing instead the peculiar patterns of individual legal actors" (pp. 1684–85). To what degree do contingency fee lawyers engage in similar pat-terns of law talk with their clients?

At one level there are certainly parallels between Sarat and Felstiner's divorce lawyers and the contingency fee lawyers I observed and interviewed: both groups of lawyers emphasized indeterminacy and uncertainty in the process. As I will describe further in the next chapter, contingency fee lawyers portray the formal adjudication process as highly risky, and this portrayal is used as one argument to convince balky clients to accept a settlement offer rather than going to trial. However, a major difference is that divorce clients come into the legal process from a different position than do contingency fee clients; divorce clients would like to preserve the financial position and their parent-child relationships that existed prior to the initiation of the divorce proceedings, something that is extremely unlikely to occur. In contrast, many contingency fee clients can expect to achieve something akin to the status quo ante; if the client achieves a full medical recovery by the time settlement looms on the horizon, the payment received to settle the claim becomes something of a future benefit as much as compensation for prior economic and noneconomic loss. Furthermore, the relationship between the claimant and the defendant is impersonal in most cases, particularly when the defendant is for all practical purposes an insurance company, and the emotionality inherent in the divorce proceeding and the resulting need for formal vindication is usually absent.

The reality is that, unlike all divorce clients, the majority of contingency fee clients do not become involved in formal legal processes. Most cases are settled before a lawsuit is filed, and even when a lawsuit is filed, many if not most of those cases settle relatively early in the process, either because the filing of the suit was simply to protect a claim against a looming statute of limitation, or because an opponent was not revealing key information such as the name of the insurance company that would have to pay any damages, or because the filing was primarily to make clear to the opposing party or insurance company that the claim was serious.[18] Furthermore, the lawyers are able to focus their discussions of uncertainties on juries, which do not exist in divorce cases and which clients easily accept as involving a high degree of chance.

There were very few occasions when I heard the lawyers speak critically of court officials or officials who adjudicated workers' compensation claims. At the same time, the lawyers did express frustration at times about not being able to deliver some benefit more quickly to a client. For example, Wisconsin's workers' compensation system provides for some interim payments; however, these payments must be or-

dered by an administrative law judge. Consider the following telephone interaction with a workers' compensation client who had had a
prehearing the previous week:

The client explained to the lawyer that he is in a major financial crunch; there is
a lot of tension with his wife, who is working much overtime to bring in money.
The lawyer responded, "I kind of don't know what to tell you," and went on to
explain that there was nothing the lawyer could do for a while because they
had to give the opposing party a chance to do its thing. "The administrative law
judge is not going to make them pay until they have an opportunity to complete an independent medical examination. . . . That's the way the system
works." The lawyer went on to acknowledge that "they [the opposing party]
are stalling. . . . That's the way they play the game. . . . This [opposing] lawyer
does it on every case. . . . They aren't going to do anything for you." The lawyer
was clearly frustrated and commented that "maybe it will get to the point that
the workers' compensation department is ready to throw the book at them."

To the degree that there is something like law talk going on here, it is directed to the opposing side and how the opposing side uses the rules either for its own benefit or to the client's detriment. During my observation, it was not uncommon for the lawyer I was shadowing to make a
disparaging comment about an opposing lawyer, but there were few
such comments in the presence of, or to, clients.

Lawyers do make statements about the uncertainty of the legal
process to their clients. Lawyers bring up these uncertainties most often
in discussing the pros and cons of accepting a settlement offer. As I will
discuss in the next chapter, it is likely that lawyers devote more emphasis to uncertainty when they want a client to accept a settlement
that is on the table. Lawyers also regularly tell prospective clients who
call with dubious cases that the legal system does not offer the kinds of
remedies that the client might think he or she is entitled to. However,
this is not so much a matter of "law talk" as it is a problem of dealing
with the misperceptions created by a combination of popular culture
and the sustained campaign of insurers and other advocates of so-
called tort reform to convince the American public that redress through
the tort system needs to be sharply limited.

Overall, "law talk," as conceptualized by Sarat and Felstiner, does
not appear to be a major part of the interaction between contingency fee
lawyers and their clients.[19] The interesting question is whether the relative lack of law talk indicates that contingency fee practice (particularly
personal injury plaintiffs' work) is fundamentally different from other
types of legal practice in terms of the way lawyers talk about the legal

system to their clients. Alternatively, it may be that law talk is largely a phenomenon that is specific to the divorce setting, reflecting the particular problems lawyers and clients confront in divorce cases.

Working with Opposing Parties

The third major element in the day-to-day of contingency fee work is dealing with opposing parties. Mostly this means interacting with and responding to defense lawyers and insurance adjusters.[20] Many of these interactions take place within the context of ongoing relationships where the contingency fee lawyer has repeated contacts over a number of cases.

Defense Lawyers

A central theme both in the observations and in the interviews was reciprocity: "what goes around comes around" (compare to Mather, McEwen, and Maiman 2001, 127–30). While recognizing that the litigation process is designed to be adversarial, the lawyers clearly preferred positive working relationships with their adversaries. This is not surprising given (1) a human inclination to have a pleasant work environment and (2) the expectation of repeat contact with opposing actors. While the amount of repeat contact in the general civil arena is much less than in criminal court work groups (Eisenstein and Jacob 1977) or criminal court communities (Eisenstein, Flemming, and Nardulli 1988), there is still enough, particularly in a moderate-sized legal community such as Madison, that there is an incentive and a desire to maintain positive relations. In the larger community of Milwaukee, the higher volume of cases handled by many firms creates incentives to maintain positive relationships as a means of facilitating case processing.

One can overstate the importance of reciprocity. It does not mean rolling over and playing dead in the face of a demand. It does mean (1) playing relatively straight and (2) not engaging in activities that are simply intended to hassle the other side. The lawyers I observed and spoke with did express concerns about opponents who engaged in activities simply to delay; in reference to one opposing lawyer, Steve Clarke commented, "This lawyer is a jerk. He could care less about my client. . . . If he can stall off in paying benefits, he will." While the overall norm appears to be one of reciprocity, some defense lawyers and adjusters had reputations as being difficult to work with, or in some cases, even as untrustworthy. An extreme example of this was described by one interviewee:

I had one particularly bad experience with an attorney. It wasn't so much being jerked around, the guy was just a liar, could not trust a word that he said. He was very friendly, at first. And as time went on it became clear that you could not trust a word that he said, and to the point where you couldn't trust a settlement offer that he would give me on the phone: "My clients gave me authority to $50,000." "OK, I'll take it." "I didn't mean I wanted to settle it for that, I was giving you, I mean, I meant . . . or something along those lines." So it got to, actually at that point in the negotiations we were getting ready to go to trial.

This was about two or three years ago that I was dealing with this guy. He has this reputation with other lawyers. In fact I've gotten a couple of calls from people who said, "I've dealt with this guy; he does some weird stuff—I heard that you had dealt with him in this case, what was your experience?" I tell, "My experience is, get everything in writing. If he wants to extend a deadline, you put it in writing. Because he will tell you later that he didn't agree to it."

At that point, we were trying to settle this age discrimination case, so I was still doing it with him, three years ago, I guess. He said, $50,000, and I asked, "Is that a firm offer, is that a settlement offer of $50,000?" He said, "Yes." "OK," I said. I take it to my client. This was like on a Saturday before a Monday trial; we are preparing for trial, and the client was here, so I said OK. We go to appear before the judge for the pretrial—actually a magistrate, it was $50,000 at the time over here—and I said my clients are going to accept that offer. And he says, "Well I have to check with my. . . . " I said, "Wait a minute. You gave us an offer, and we are accepting it." Fortunately I hadn't already stopped preparing, because I didn't trust the guy, but that is the kind of person that he was. So, in dealing with that kind of thing, I mean, that kind of situation, I was just calling the guy a liar to his face. I said, "I can't trust you."

Contingency fee lawyers expected defense lawyers to engage in a vigorous defense on behalf of their clients. It was only those lawyers who behaved in an untrustworthy manner or engaged in scorched earth tactics that generated wrath from the contingency fee practitioners.

With this said, there was a common view among contingency fee practitioners that once a defense lawyer had a case, that case would not settle until the opposing lawyer had put in some minimum quantity of time that the defense lawyer had to bill to his or her client. That is, while the contingency fee lawyer's incentive was toward efficiency (i.e., only put in time that is productive in achieving a result), the contingency fee lawyers saw the defense bar as having a very different set of incentives which led to patterns of behavior that served neither the interests of the contingency practitioners nor the defense bar's own insurance company clients. The lawyers I observed and spoke with viewed this as a normal part of what defense lawyers did, although there seemed to be a some animosity for those defense lawyers who did this to an extreme, which the plaintiffs' lawyers referred to as "churning." For example, one lawyer commented that the opposing lawyer in a particular case worked for a firm which had recently opened a Madison office. In order to attract insurance company clients, the firm cut deals with insurers at rock-bottom rates, but then "had to churn their files to generate adequate fees." Another lawyer I spoke with described a particular defense lawyer as the "queen of churn." A lawyer whom I interviewed in his role as a defense lawyer, but who did handle some plaintiffs' cases on a contingency basis, commented that "the Milwaukee [defense] firms need to churn their files a little more."

There were some exceptions to the expectations that formal filing inevitably meant a defense lawyer wanting to run the meter for some minimum period of time. Typically these involved situations in which a plaintiffs' lawyer had to file a case to avoid problems with statutes of limitations. This happens when a client is still in treatment as the statute's deadline approaches. The claimant's lawyer will make it clear to the adjuster that the filing does not represent any effort to escalate the case. In Wisconsin state court, the plaintiff has ninety days to serve the complaint on the defendant; a plaintiff's lawyer may send a copy of the complaint to the adjuster after filing and tell the adjuster that the copy is for information purposes only and that he will hold off on service in the hope that the case can be settled within the ninety-day period required for service. One lawyer told me about a case in which the ninety-day period was ending and so service had to be completed; in that case, the lawyer notified both the defending insurance company and the judge to whom the case was assigned that the plaintiff was waiving the forty-five-day limit on time for the defendant to file a response, explaining that the plaintiff was still in treatment and that the case should settle once treatment was completed. In all of these situations, the goal of the plaintiff's attorney is to avoid the case being referred to an outside defense lawyer who will want to start "running the meter."

Insurance Companies

For most contingency fee lawyers, dealing with insurance companies through the adjusters (see Ross 1980) who work for those companies constitutes a large part of their work. For personal injury claims, the adjusters both evaluate cases and negotiate settlements for those cases that do not get into formal litigation. As one would expect, the contingency fee lawyers want to influence how the adjusters evaluate cases because that evaluation influences the amount of money the company is going to be willing to put on the table when settlement is discussed. In a sense, the lawyer wants to "help" the adjuster dispose of the case in a favorable way, and this involves doing whatever the lawyer can to get the adjuster to see the case in the same way the lawyer sees it. An important part of this involves giving the adjuster the information he or she needs to justify a settlement to supervisory personnel (see Ross 1980, 61–63).

One example of "helping" the adjuster involves the practice in insurance companies of setting a "reserve" when a claim is lodged. The reserve is the adjuster's estimate of the likely case payout. For the lawyers it is important to get the reserve set at an appropriate amount for several related reasons. First, adjusters work within a hierarchical setting, with the level of settlement authority depending on a particular adjuster's experience and position. Second, adjusters are evaluated at least in part based on their judgment in setting reserves; it does not look good for an adjuster to set a reserve at a relatively low amount, only to find later that a case settles for a much higher amount. Finally, once an adjuster has a reserve amount in his or her head, that is the general framework within which the adjuster will be thinking about the case. It takes some effort to move an adjuster significantly once the mind-set is established. This latter point has essentially the same type of "anchoring effect" discussed earlier in this chapter with regard to client expectations. While for the client the lawyer wants to avoid unrealistically high expectations, with the adjuster, the lawyer is concerned about an assessment that is too low. Not surprisingly, most lawyers typically are more than happy to help the adjuster justify setting a high reserve, although at least one lawyer I spoke with viewed the issue of reserves as the insurance company's problem and not his.

The need to be cognizant of the reserve setting process influenced other aspects of how the lawyer processed a case. This was nicely illustrated by one of the lawyers I observed after a telephone conversation with an adjuster:

For a long time I followed the practice of not requesting medical records until the client was more or less finished treating, because I had noticed a pattern where the style / content of records changed once [the] doctor knew a lawyer was involved; often the doctor seemed less sympathetic. To avoid this, I would not ask for records while treatment was ongoing. However, this practice created problems when I submitted cases for settlement. The adjuster had no idea what was going on and had set a small reserve on the case. When he got hit with large specials [medical expenses and wage loss], he would be thrown for a loop. Now I ask for medicals as a case progresses, and I keep the adjuster informed of the case progress and treatment my client is receiving.

Even with this approach, the lawyer found himself at times making demands that greatly exceeded the reserve the adjuster had established. In one case, the lawyer demanded the policy limits of $300,000, when the adjuster had reserved only $120,000. Before submitting the demand, the lawyer had observed to me that the adjuster probably had underreserved the case, and in a phone conversation after the demand was received, the adjuster commented, "I have it underreserved."

Adjusters have differing styles in their interactions with the lawyers. Some of the differences appear to be individual, while others reflect company cultures. At the individual level, some adjusters are easier to work with and more accommodating than are others. As Steve Clarke commented after a lengthy conversation with one adjuster with whom Clarke had had a lot of dealings, "He doesn't jerk you around a lot"; in regard to another adjuster, Clarke commented, "He's a good guy. . . . A lot of people think he's a cheap jerk, but I've found that he's quite reasonable if you deal with him straight."

An example of how adjusters can be accommodating came up while I was observing in Clarke's practice. This involved a case submitted for settlement near the time that the statute of limitations was due to run; the delay reflected a long period of recovery on the part of the client. The adjuster handling the case called Clarke's office to tell him that they would not be able to complete their review and evaluation before the statute ran out; he went on to say that they would waive the statute for one month should it turn out that, after they completed their evaluation, no settlement could be reached within that extra month and Clarke had to file suit.

Of course, there are other adjusters with negative reputations. This was reflected in a variety of comments during the observation and interviews:

There's an adjuster that I deal with who is a stupid jerk if I talk to him on the phone or negotiate with him on the phone. If I correspond with him, they are nasty, short, snippy letters.

Some adjusters are just jerks, and there's a couple of them that I won't even deal with. I'll talk to them a couple of times and if they prove themselves as living up to my past experience, I'll put it into suit. There's one guy from [insurance company]; . . . I deal with other people in [insurance company] and I have no problem. Some of them are tough, but this guy's such a jerk, and he said personal things about my clients. I will not listen to this stuff; I put it into suit.

Overall the tenor of the observation and interviews was that most people on the other side were reasonable people to deal with, given an understanding that they were there to oppose you.

Apart from the individual adjusters, some insurance companies have long-standing reputations as being difficult to deal with: refusing to make settlement offers, making clearly lowball offers, and the like. These variations are more problematic for lawyers who are oriented toward processing cases than for lawyers who are more oriented toward litigation. For the latter group, needing to file suit and use the formalized processes of litigation is more a part of their day-to-day routine. For example, Chuck Brown, whose practice is litigation-oriented, described the problems he had with one large insurer which for a period of time was giving only "lowball offers"; Brown said that at one point he just put all of his cases involving this insurer into suit and advised the other personal injury lawyers in his firm to do the same. Eventually, he got a call from one of the adjusters at the insurance company; the adjuster wanted to know why Brown was putting all of the cases into suit. Brown responded that he did not like the offers he was getting. The offers then seemed to get better, at least for a while, and Brown backed off from putting all of the cases with that insurer into suit; however, Brown reported also that the offers may have shifted back toward lowball again. This lawyer's experience with this particular insurer was by no means unique; a number of the lawyers I interviewed specifically mentioned this same company as one that was difficult to deal with, although at least one lawyer I spoke to described this company as "good to deal with," identifying one other large national company as much harder to deal with ("traditionally been cheap, and they still are").

Another way that contingency fee lawyers routinely interact with insurers involves what are called "independent medical examinations" (IMEs). Such examinations are more or less standard practice in workers' compensation cases and frequently occur in other kinds of personal injury cases that get into suit. These examinations of the lawyer's client are conducted by a physician chosen by the insurance company that is liable for the claim.

Lawyers view these examinations not as "independent" medical examinations but as "adverse" medical examinations. They view the primary purpose of the exam, particularly in workers' compensation cases, as to find reasons not to pay compensation or to dispute the level of disability found by the client's own physician. Lawyers explain to their clients that the insurer is entitled to have such examinations done and that the examination is done in aid of the insurer's case, not the client's case. One of the lawyers told me about a skit that was performed at a meeting of workers' compensation practitioners.

A reporter has come to interview the doctor, but the doctor mistakenly thinks the reporter is a patient who has come for an IME. The doctor tells the patient to strip to the waist. Without looking at the reporter, the doctor starts dictating a report about this and that. After completing the dictation, the doctor takes the tape out of the recorder, places it in a microwave oven sitting on a counter near his desk, presses a few buttons, waits ten seconds, and then pulls out a thirty-page report.

While one might mark this skit up to the cynicism of the contingency fee practitioners handling workers' compensation cases, it is noteworthy that the skit was performed by *defense* lawyers who represent workers' compensation insurers.

The lawyers are particularly skeptical of physicians working for companies that specialize in providing medical examinations for insurance companies, believing that these companies are hostile to the lawyers' clients because the companies believe that findings of their doctors will affect whether the company will continue to receive business from the insurer. While not all doctors doing independent medical examinations work for such companies, the lawyers still see the incentives of future business as affecting the doctors' conclusions. One lawyer told me that he tried to neutralize doctors working independently by actually having them on occasion do examinations for his side of the case; he remarked that one such doctor had just done an IME for an insurer in one of his cases and that the doctor had "just given an incredibly fair IME" in that case.

Is the generally cooperative approach described above peculiar to contingency fee lawyers in Wisconsin? Would I have found similar patterns had I conducted this research in New York City or Chicago or Dallas or Los Angeles? Older studies that focus on, or at least touch on, practice in such areas (Carlin 1962; Ross 1980), as well as studies of settlement negotiation (Hyman et al. 1995; Kritzer 1991), are not inconsistent with an emphasis on cooperation, at least when such cooperation is reciprocated. Moreover, the investment image of contingency fee practice provides a theoretical expectation that contingency fee lawyers should prefer to find ways of resolving cases that allow them to control the amount of time they are investing in those cases; controlling time investment is facilitated by cooperation. None of this says that highly competitive, conflictual cases are necessarily rare, and many of the lawyers I interacted with could tell stories about cases that involve little or no cooperation from the opposing side, its insurer, or its lawyer.

What Is Missing Here?

In reading this chapter, one might naturally ask, where are activities such as legal research, or drafting legal documents such as briefs, motions, and pleadings? From my observations, these activities consume small portions of the time of contingency fee lawyers. Chuck Brown, whose practice is the most litigation-oriented of the three I observed, did devote roughly the equivalent of one day during the month I was in his office to drafting motions in connection with two of the cases he was working on. Steve Clarke, whose practice is the most case-processing-oriented of the three lawyers, also spent about that amount of time, or perhaps a bit more (he reported to me having spent one evening working on a brief), drafting a brief in connection with a case he was appealing and drafting a complaint in connection with a case that he had to file because the statute of limitation deadline was coming up. Each of the two lawyers did do some legal research, half a day's worth at most, in connection with these and other cases. For Chuck Brown this involved working from electronic search tools his firm licensed; for Steve Clarke, the primary research tool he used was the telephone, calling individuals who could quickly answer technical questions concerning very specific legal and procedural issues.[21] For these two lawyers, at most 10 percent, and probably closer to 5 percent, of their time during the month was devoted to legal research and drafting. The third lawyer I observed, Bob Adams, undertook neither drafting nor legal research himself; several drafting and research tasks did come up during the month, but in every instance he delegated those tasks to his paralegal.

The distinction between litigational and case-processing styles of practice points to some important differences in what contingency fee lawyers do in their day-to-day work. A practice dominated by the litigational style is likely to involve more formal discovery activities, while a lawyer whose practice is dominated by the case-processing style will try to handle fact gathering in less formalized ways. In part this is because lawyers employing the litigational style are more likely to file cases and thus bring into play the rules of civil procedure. However, the differences between the two styles of practice is less in what the lawyers actually do than it is in the mind-set of how the lawyers see what they do and in the ways they imagine their opponents understanding what it is that they are doing. Regardless of which style the practice takes, the lawyer's time is largely consumed by gathering and processing information, managing the relationship with the client, and managing the relationship with the opposing party.

My interviews suggest certain types of exceptions to these generalizations. In some types of high-volume practices, there are lawyers who focus specifically on immediate trial preparation and trial itself. The three primary tasks I focused on in this chapter may be delegated to staff, or there may be lawyers within the firm who handle those activities. For example, one lawyer I interviewed, who disposes of approximately 200 cases per year, focuses his personal attention on perhaps ten to fifteen of those cases. These are the cases that get close to trial or are among the five to ten that he actually tries in a given year. Most of the work for most of his cases is handled by staff, leaving the lawyer to focus on trial work and motions practice. Alternatively, a lawyer may specialize in cases with a relatively high probability of filing and trial (i.e., medical malpractice cases), where motions practice and trial preparation are much more central to the typical case.

Regardless of the type of practice a lawyer has or the style of practice a lawyer adopts, the investment nature of contingency fee practice puts a premium on efficiency. Lawyers want to run their practices efficiently because they profit from efficiency. This stands in contrast to lawyers working on an hourly basis, where one could argue that inefficiency, to the extent that clients will tolerate it, leads to increased profit. This emphasis on efficiency is evident in high-volume, case-processing-oriented practices where tasks are routinized and assigned to staff whenever possible. It is also evident in litigational style practices. In the words of one lawyer in a litigational style practice, "We pride ourselves on being really cost-efficient. We think about every penny we spend." During my observations, the lawyers I was with frequently expressed frustration with costs they incurred in handling cases; while these costs would largely be passed on to the clients, this would not be true if a case did not yield a recovery. It was in the lawyer's own economic interest to be careful about the costs being incurred.

One of the problems for the contingency fee lawyer is that the incentives of lawyers on the other side run directly counter to their own. Defense lawyers billing by the hour increase their revenue by engaging in precisely those activities which effectively reduce the return to contingency fee lawyers. This flows logically from the investment nature of contingency fee practice and the fact that the contingency fee lawyer wants to control the size of the investment. One of the reasons that settlement before filing is so attractive to contingency fee lawyers is that adjusters, unlike defense counsel, have a significant concern about efficiently disposing of cases, because they are evaluated in part on the basis of how quickly they close files (Ross 1980, 59–61).

The need to control investment, both in terms of time and in terms of expenses, is a central aspect of contingency fee practice. Those lawyers who specialize in contingency fee work tend to be very sensitive to the issues of efficiency. A constant concern for the lawyers is finding the balance between controlling costs and doing what is necessary to get a good result, both from the client's perspective and from the lawyer's perspective.

CHAPTER 5

Understanding Settlement Negotiations

Introduction

The contingency fee lawyer must resolve a case in order to collect on the time invested in the case. The resolution can come either through an adjudication or through a negotiated settlement. During my observation in the three offices, I saw the lawyers work on only one case that was ultimately definitively resolved by an adjudicatory decision, and this was a workers' compensation case decided by an administrative law judge. One of the lawyers told me about a case that did go to trial the previous year which he had lost, and another lawyer told me about a case he had taken to trial a year or two earlier but that settled immediately after the defense's key witness testified. In fact, Chuck Brown, the lawyer most oriented toward litigation of the three whom I observed, tried only one case to verdict between the time I observed in his office in the winter of 1996 through the summer of 2000.

While only a very small fraction of cases end as a result of definitive adjudication, adjudication of parts of a case or of procedural disputes can and does influence the settlement of cases (see Kritzer 1986). One of the cases being handled by Chuck Brown while I was observing in his office involved precisely this kind of process. The case involved a number of claims, and one issue was whether Wisconsin's or another state's law governed some or all of the claims. A second issue was whether either state's law allowed for a particular category of damages. The trial court ruled that the other state's law controlled, a decision which reduced the amount of damages that could potentially be awarded.

Brown appealed the case but lost on key points: the appeals court found that Wisconsin law did control but that neither state permitted recovery of damages for the high value claim in the case. In the end, he settled the remaining claim for a very modest amount, and the fee he received did not even cover his disbursements (which he did not try to collect from the client).

Given the dominant place of settlement, what is the best framework for understanding how it proceeds? There is an extensive literature on bargaining and a substantial specialized literature on bargaining in the context of litigation, a literature to which I have previously contributed (Kritzer 1991). The current study was not designed with a focus on negotiation, and the survey instrument asked only a small number of questions about the settlement process. Nonetheless, the data I collected do shed light on the key questions of how the settlement process works in the context of contingency fee practice and whether the portfolio perspective informs our understanding of that process.

We do know from my earlier research that the contingency fee structure serves to constrain and focus negotiation on money for the simple reason that contingency fee lawyers have to collect money for their clients in order to be paid (Kritzer 1987). To quote a respondent from Jonathan Hyman et al.'s (1995, 77) study of negotiation and settlement in New Jersey, "In negotiations, [the] plaintiff's attorney always asks for money, and if he can't get $1/3$ of it [the settlement], he's not interested in it."

Other research and analyses have raised the possibility that the contingency fee lawyer's stake in the outcome creates a conflict of interest between the lawyer and client, with the lawyers more concerned about turning cases over in a way that maximizes fees per hour worked than providing a reasonable service to the client (Johnson 1980–81; Miller 1987; Rosenthal 1974). One problem with these analyses is that the conflict can work both ways, with the client wanting the lawyer to devote an unreasonable amount of time to a small case when there is no way the client would consider paying a lawyer on an hourly basis to do that amount of work even if there was absolutely no risk of losing the case (see Shapiro 2002, 244n18).[1]

The literature on bargaining in litigation has a heavy focus on different modes of bargaining which have been variously labeled integrative versus distributional (Raiffa 1982), problem solving versus adversarial (Hyman et al. 1995; Menkel-Meadow 1984), competitive versus cooperative (Williams 1983), or concessions-oriented (maximal result) versus consensus-oriented (appropriate result) versus pro forma (Kritzer 1991). Much of the literature is prescriptive, arguing that one form or another of negotiation is "more effective." In my earlier work, I found that much of the negotiation in "ordinary litigation" was either simply pro forma (demand, offer, compromise) or consensus-oriented, by which I meant that the lawyers sought to determine an appropriate result given some belief about "going rates." In consensus-oriented bargaining, demands and offers were pitched within the actual range of an expected settlement; while initial demands were higher than the expected settlement and initial offers were lower, they were not out of line with what would be a reasonable settlement.

The image of the settlement process that underlies most of the theoretical and empirical work is fairly simple: there are two sides to the dispute, and the lawyers serve as the alter egos of their clients. The sides exchange demands and offers until a settlement is reached, the case goes to adjudication, or the plaintiff / claimant abandons the case. While analysts recognize that the simple alter ego model of the relationship between lawyers and clients is too simplistic (Johnson 1980–81; Kritzer 1991, 63–65; Miller 1987), relatively little empirical analysis shows how this relationship actually works in the settlement process. The reality for the contingency fee lawyer is that there are multiple parties with whom to negotiate: the opposing party or its representative, the lawyer's own client, and third parties who have a claim against any recovery obtained on behalf of the client. All of this negotiation takes place in the context of the lawyer's own self-interest in the outcome *and* in what is required in terms of the lawyer's time and expense to obtain that outcome.

In my earlier study of lawyers' work in ordinary litigation, I characterized the lawyer's role as that of a broker, "a person hired to act as an intermediary" (Kritzer 1990, 12). Central to the conception I developed is that the broker "has a set of interests that intervenes on, or even conflicts with, the goal of pure service" (Kritzer 1990). This conception fits nicely with the problems the contingency fee lawyer faces in representing the client's interest while negotiating with the other parties and the client, all the time recognizing the lawyer's own costs and the gains of settling or not settling at any given time.

In this chapter I do not try to develop a general theory of negotiation, nor do I even seek a comprehensive understanding of the negotiations engaged in by contingency fee lawyers. Rather I seek to describe the variations I observed and understand the implications of those variations for the lawyer's need to close cases with an eye to the implications of settlements for the portfolio of cases the lawyer currently has and hopes to obtain in the future. In the next section, I present some patterns from the survey of contingency fee practitioners drawing on the limited questions regarding settlement included in the survey. The following sections discuss in order: negotiations with opposing parties, negotiations with third parties, and finally "negotiations" with the lawyers' own clients.

Negotiating with the Other Side

Typical Negotiations

What do negotiations with opposing parties look like in ordinary cases? It is difficult to come up with anything that could be described as the archetypical case, but it is still worthwhile to look at the negotiations in some specific cases to get the flavor of what actually transpires in the day-to-day world of contingency fee lawyers.

For most of the contingency fee lawyers, the start of negotiation with the opposing party, which for practical purposes is usually an insurance company, comes once the lawyer has concluded that the client has fully recovered from any injuries or has reached a plateau in the recovery process that reflects the maximum recovery the client is likely to obtain. Once the case is "ripe" for settlement, the lawyer or a paralegal prepares a formal demand to go out over the lawyer's signature. This is typically in the form of a letter or a brochure, with the elaborateness reflecting the size of the demand. The brochure may include photographs of injuries or even a videotape showing the recovery process or the residual effect of the trauma. The demand letter will detail the medical treatment and other losses the client suffered, plus any special circumstances which might justify a higher-than-normal level of compensation. After the letter is sent, the lawyer will wait for a call from the adjuster (or opposing lawyer), and if none is forthcoming within a reasonable amount of time, the lawyer will call the opposing party's representative.

Typically, the opposing party's representative will make a counteroffer that is lower than the demand, and the two sides will then work toward a compromise somewhere in between. Not infrequently, there is a fair amount of haggling over the last bit of difference between the two sides. Sometimes, one side or the other will stand firm with its initial offer, but usually there is some movement on both sides. Most commonly there is no written offer or demand after the initial demand letter; most of the negotiation takes place over the telephone, with exchanges of documentation sometimes supplementing the conversations.

Some Examples

What follows are synopses of the negotiation I observed in three cases, two involving attorney Steve Clarke and one involving Chuck Brown. These synopses give a fairly good idea of the nature of the give and take that goes on, along with a sense of the range of negotiation that I saw during my observation.

Case A, Steve Clarke. This case involved a personal friend of Steve Clarke's. The client had been in a minor auto accident in which her car had been totaled; there was no issue of fault. After the accident, she had not initially gone to the hospital. When she went to an urgent care center the day after the accident complaining of neck and back pain, she was transported by ambulance to the emergency room. No major problems such as a ruptured disk or other "hard tissue" injuries were found, but even as the case was being settled, she continued to complain of some occasional discomfort. The case was being settled without waiting longer because the client had specifically directed Clarke to go ahead and settle it. The total special damages (medical bills, lost wages) were $1,900, much of it in diagnostic procedures.

In his demand letter, Clarke asked for $6,000. The adjuster called Clarke and offered to settle for $2,000 for general damages (pain and suffering), plus the special damages of $1,900, rounding up to $4,000. Clarke responded, "Could I push you up to $5,000?" The adjuster said that this case is more like a $3,000 case, explaining that in her view the special damages seemed high. Clarke explained that the specials are not high; "I know this client," he said, explaining that she was reluctant to seek treatment after the accident and was still experiencing some discomfort but didn't want to go through more treatment. Clarke told the adjuster that he did have authority to settle the case. The adjuster offered $4,500, and they agreed to settle at that amount.

Case B, Steve Clarke. The client in Case B had suffered a broken vertebra in an auto accident that occurred while he was on the job. The injury occurred shortly before the client was to get married. The client had made a full recovery. The wedding did go ahead as scheduled, but the client had to wear a brace and the honeymoon had to be deferred. Special damages totaled $7,500; workers' compensation had a $5,600 lien on any settlement. Steve Clarke sent a demand letter requesting $32,500.

Clarke had initiated a call to the adjuster because he had not heard anything in response to his demand. The adjuster told Clarke that she had just sent a letter proposing a counteroffer of $22,000. Clarke asked if she had any room to move; the adjuster responded, "I like to make a fair offer. . . . I don't like to go back and forth. . . . If you can convince me that the offer is low. . . . " Clarke brought up the disrupted wedding, acknowledging that it is "hard to quantify," but going on to state, "I think there is some value there." The adjuster came back with the observation that the client had experienced no permanent disability. Clarke told the adjuster that he would call his client for instructions. The adjuster concluded the call by thanking Clarke "for presenting the case so well; it made it easier for me."

An hour or two later Clarke reached the client. He described the offer to the client and suggested that $25,000 to $27,000 was as good as one could expect if the case went to trial. Clarke went on to explain that the client would actually net more with a $25,000 settlement than with a $32,000 verdict, reflecting the costs of going to trial and the fact that Clarke's fee would be paid at a higher percentage. Clarke said of the adjuster, "she made a pretty fair opening offer, so she won't move as much." The client gave Clarke authority to settle for as much as he could get.

About ten minutes later, Clarke was able to speak to the adjuster: "I spoke to my client; we think you are low, but we are willing to move." He explained the rationale for his demand, $7,500 for the special damages, $15,000 for usual pain and suffering, plus an extra $10,000 because the accident occurred shortly before the client's wedding. He went on to comment that given the wedding/honeymoon angle, "this would be a fun case to try; I think the jury would be sympathetic to it." Nonetheless, Clarke went on to explain, he was willing to reduce this part of the demand by $3,000 and stated that he had "authority to offer to settle at 29.5."

The adjuster responded, "This will be my final offer . . . $25,000." Clarke told the adjuster that he would call his client: "I never say never . . . maybe I can push him toward your figure." About two hours later, without having spoken again to his client, Clarke tried to call the adjuster back. He left a message, and about thirty minutes the adjuster returned the call. Clarke told the adjuster, "I spoke to my client and he's willing to accept 27.5." The adjuster reiterated her offer of twenty-five. Clarke described the workers' compensation line, emphasizing that he was not likely to be able to get a reduction from the workers' compensation insurer. The adjuster offered $26,000. Clarke proposed $26,500, telling the adjuster that if she would accept that figure he would close the case. He went on to explain that this would net the client about $14,000, which was what the client wanted. The adjuster then agreed to $26,500. There followed about five minutes of discussion of the mechanics of executing the settlement agreement, given that the workers' compensation carrier had to sign off and that it was necessary to get a signature from an administrative law judge from the state agency that adjudicated workers' compensation claims.

Case C, Chuck Brown.   This case was scheduled for trial during the month I was observing in Chuck Brown's office. It was a premises liability case that arose out of a robbery. The claim was against the owner of the property where the robbery had occurred. At one time, Brown had made a demand for $300,000; the lack of a response to this demand led Brown to file suit. There had been no negotiations other than this unanswered demand very early in the case (perhaps two years prior to when the negotiations described below took place).

Brown decided to make what he referred to as a "statutory" demand of $90,000. Under Wisconsin law, if he could better this statutory demand at trial, his client would be entitled to recover prejudgment interest at a higher rate and some additional costs.[2] He described this demand as "on the low side" so that he could have a good shot at getting more at trial. He viewed the case as worth more.

About a week after the statutory demand was filed, the opposing lawyer called to request some documents related to the case in preparation for trial. In the course of the conversation, the lawyer made an offer to settle at $56,000. Brown explained to the lawyer that his lower demand (for $90,000) did not reflect any discounting owing to concerns about a pending summary judgment motion, stating that he did not expect to lose on that motion and that if he did lose, he would appeal.[3] He went on to explain that the $90,000 demand reflected not uncertainty about liability but his reevaluation of damages. He told the lawyer that he thought the case would be easy to try, and given the amount of time he had already devoted to the case, he would just as soon "give it a shot rather than take a settlement under $90,000."[4] He concluded the conversation by telling the lawyer that he had had the case evaluated by a mock jury and that their range of figures was such that he expected a jury to return a verdict substantially in excess of $90,000. He concluded, "The potential is there for many times $90,000 . . . $90,000 is my take-it-or-leave-it number."

The next day, Brown called his client to discuss trial preparations and to review the state of the negotiations. While Brown had authority from the client to decline an offer in the $50,000 range, he wanted to be sure that the client was still of that mind. When he reached the client, he reviewed where things stood, emphasizing the opposing side's position that there was a good chance that the defendant would prevail on summary judgment. Brown told the client that his estimate was that there was a 70 percent chance of winning on liability. "It is my advice that you turn down this offer; I think there will be one more offer before trial." The client agreed to this recommendation after a brief discussion of the costs of going to trial.

Brown communicated to the opposing lawyer his client's rejection of the $56,000 offer. About five days later, the judge ruled on pending motions, ruling for Brown's client. Late in the day, the opposing lawyer faxed Brown a letter with a new settlement offer of $75,000 (the lawyer had said in an earlier conversation that the letter had been mailed two days earlier, and he was surprised that Brown had not received it before the rulings on the motions). After reviewing the offer letter, Brown speculated that the lawyer might actually have authorization to settle for $90,000 and could just be testing Brown's resolve.

The next morning, Brown called his client to tell her about the outcome of the pending motions, and the $75,000 settlement offer. They discussed telling the opposing lawyer that in light of the outcome of those motions, it would now take more than $125,000 to settle the case. In the end, Brown decided to let the other lawyer simply stew for a day or two.

The next day, the opposing lawyer called to inquire about the $75,000 offer the defendant had put on the table. Brown told the opposing lawyer that in light of the decisions on the summary judgment motions, his client was now talking about wanting $125,000. However, Brown went on to say, "I don't like backing off from a number. . . . I am telling my client that we need to stick at $90,000 but we won't settle for less than that." After some other discussion of the case, Brown told the other lawyer that the defendant needed to come up with another

$15,000: "I'm being told that I am wimping out on the case given its potential value."

At this point in the discussion the opposing lawyer raised the possibility of mediation. Brown responded that he was skeptical about the value of going to mediation because he believed that if they went to mediation with a seventy-five-to-ninety split, the mediator would simply split the difference and say $82,500. He told the lawyer that if they did go to mediation, he would start at $130,000. He reiterated that his bottom line was still $90,000, and if the opposing party needed someone else to state that figure (e.g., a mediator) to save face, that was fine, "but ninety is what I have to have." Brown went on to talk about the expenses the defendant would incur by going to trial. "I'm sorry you and your client have evaluated the case so low. . . . If it is any consolation for your client, the number on the table is a huge bath for me.[5] At this point I'd just as soon try the case; ninety is a drop-dead figure for me. If you can do something creative with the costs, I am willing to listen. At ninety, I'm not particularly proud of the result."

After the phone call, Brown told me that he did not respond to the $75,000 offer as a way of indicating that he did not take it seriously. He also speculated on needing to find some way for the opposing side to save face, commenting that his statement about "taking a bath" was partly intended to help mollify the defendant.

About half an hour later, while Brown was downstairs getting a soft drink, the opposing lawyer called back. Brown was paged and picked up a phone in the staff lounge. The lawyer offered $87,000 and agreed to cover $1,000 outstanding in witness fees. Brown suggested ways of coming up with another $2,000, such as the defendant covering some subrogation costs to a medical provider. In the course of the conversation, the opposing lawyer told Brown that the adjuster with whom the lawyer had to clear any settlement was leaving town that evening for a long scheduled vacation and would be unavailable for ten days (Brown doubted that was in fact true). After about thirty minutes of discussion the call ended with Brown saying that he would call his client and get back to the opposing lawyer.

After about an hour, during which he discussed the situation with one of his partners and his paralegal, and grumbled a bit about being nickeled-and-dimed (but not calling his client), he called the opposing lawyer back. He told the lawyer that "my client says you all have jerked us around and wants me to do the same. The client is willing to split the difference. I don't know how you want to do it. You're at eighty-eight, we are at ninety, eighty-nine will settle it." The opposing lawyer at this point informed Brown that there was in fact another outstanding witness fee in the amount of $1,900. Brown immediately responded, "This changes things. . . . If your client will cover that and the other outstanding witness fee, my client will accept $87,000 new money to settle the case." The opposing lawyer responded that he would call the adjuster and get back to Brown.

Ten minutes later, the opposing lawyer called back and accepted the settlement: $87,000 new money, and the defendant would cover outstanding witness fees, which totaled almost $3,000.

Bob Adams.   Because Bob Adams's practice is only about 20 percent contingency fee work, I saw much less negotiation activity when observing him. From what I did observe, and from extensive conversations with Adams, his pattern was generally consistent with what I saw in the other two offices, with one possible exception. Adams seemed to make quite high initial demands that the other side did not take particularly seriously, and then he backed off of those demands almost immediately to a range in which the case would settle. In one case, in which I saw only the tail end of the negotiation process, Adams sent an initial demand brochure asking for $188,000, came down almost immediately to $85,000, to which the opposing side offered $50,000, and then the two sides worked to a settlement at $60,000.[6]

Statistical Patterns

As I noted previously, my survey was not designed to collect detailed information on negotiations.[7] I did ask several negotiation-related questions:

What was your first demand and what was the defendant's first offer?

Did the initial exchange occur before filing or after filing [asked only for cases in which there was a formal case filing in court or with an administrative agency]?

In total, how many rounds of demands and offers were there (i.e., the number of times you went back and forth)?

These questions can be compared to responses concerning the amount at stake and an estimate of the amount actually recovered (see the appendix at the end of this chapter for a discussion of this latter variable).

Given the design of my sample, most cases by necessity were resolved by negotiation. However, as discussed in earlier chapters, my sample design actually understates the dominance of negotiated resolutions because it overrepresents cases that went to trial (or administrative hearing in the case of workers' compensation). For those cases that did go to trial or hearing, I asked whether there were any settlement demands or offers before the trial or hearing. For most types of cases 90 percent or more involved pretrial efforts at resolution. Two types of cases stand out as less likely to involve pretrial settlement activities: medical malpractice (22 percent of cases going to trial involved no pretrial negotiations) and workers' compensation (44 percent of cases going to administrative hearing involved no prehearing negotiations).[8]

Exchanges. In *Let's Make a Deal* (Kritzer 1991, 37), I found that court cases involved relatively few exchanges of demands and offers (see also Hyman et al. 1995, 68). Forty-one percent of the lawyers reported two exchanges, compared to only 15 percent involving three or more exchanges. In tort cases, which form the vast bulk of the cases in the current study, 45 percent involved two exchanges and 27 percent involved three or more (Hyman et al., 38). The structure of the survey asked the lawyers to report on the last exchange, then the first exchange, and finally the most important intermediate exchange; the number of exchanges was derived from the lawyers' patterns of responses to this series of questions. Information on each exchange was obtained through a series of questions patterned on the following sequence (Kritzer 1991, 31):

Now I'd like to ask about any negotiations attempting to settle the case which you may have had on behalf of your client(s). At any point did you negotiate with the opposing party(s) or (his / her / their) lawyer?
> IF YES: Can you briefly describe what happened the first time you discussed what would be necessary in order to settle the case; what did you ask them to do and / or what did you offer to do to settle the problem?

During your first discussion with the opposing party, did he / she / they make a settlement offer or demand?
> IF YES: What did they offer to do or ask your client to do to settle the problem?

The lawyers were then asked a similar sequence about the last set of exchanges (i.e., the settlement, if there actually was one) and about the "most important" intermediate round. The question about the "intermediate offer" was phrased in terms of offers or demands that "played an important role in getting to the last [exchange or settlement]"; that is, if in the lawyer's judgment there were no intermediate exchanges that played an important role in the negotiation process, no information was collected about them.

The question structure in the contingency fee survey was quite different. I simply asked the lawyers how many exchanges there were. The median response was three, with 18 percent reporting less than three, 38 percent reporting exactly three, and 44 percent reporting more than three. One of the obvious problems in comparing the patterns from the two studies is the ambiguity in what constitutes an exchange. Take, for example, case A discussed above. How many exchanges did this case involve? Did any of the intermediate exchanges play an important role in getting to the final settlement? The initial demands and offers were $6,000 and $4,000 respectively; Clarke tried to push the offer to $5,000, and they settled at $4,500. Is this two or three exchanges? Is an exchange a round of communication (that might involve several different offers or demands), or is it an individual pair of demand and offer? What if a demand or offer does not actually produce a shift by the opposing side, as was true in case C, in which Chuck Brown made a demand of $90,000 (not counting the original demand of $300,000, which produced no response and led Brown to file suit), to which the opposing side first offered $56,000, then $75,000, then $88,000 ($87,000 plus paying a witness fee of $1,000), and finally almost $90,000 ($87,000 plus the witness fees totaling almost $3,000). How many exchanges did this constitute?

Despite the ambiguity in what constitutes an exchange, it is worth asking whether there are any meaningful variations in the number of exchanges lawyers reported. Specifically, is the pattern different for lawyers who specialize in personal injury plaintiffs' work compared to general practitioners or other lawyers, and is there any meaningful variation that relates to whether the case was disposed of without filing, without trial after filing, or by, during, or after trial? The simple answer is that there is not a lot of variation. The median number of exchanges is three regardless of whether the lawyer is a personal injury specialist, a general practitioner, or in some other type of practice.[9] The median is three for cases settled without filing and cases going to trial, rising to four for cases settled after filing but before trial; the mean number of exchanges does vary in a statistically significant way ($F = 23.029$, $p < .001$) by when the case was completed: 3.64 for unfiled cases, 4.37 for filed but untried cases, and 3.13 for cases that went to trial.

A second variable that might be associated with the amount of vari-

Exchanges

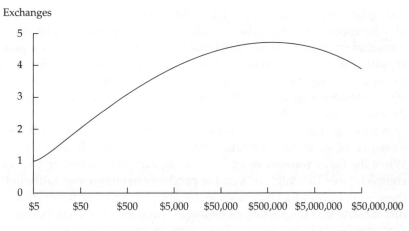

High Valuation of Stakes (Logarithmic scale)

FIGURE 5.1 Number of Exchanges by Stakes

ation is the amount at stake. In my earlier work, I argued that the relatively small number of exchanges in most ordinary cases reflected the fact that the amount at stake was such that it was very easy for the two sides to get quickly to a reasonable settlement range (Kritzer 1991, 58–66). One might hypothesize that larger cases were more likely to involve more rounds of negotiation, or alternatively, that small cases were more likely to involve few rounds of negotiations. While these two statements may look like simple restatements of the same point, that is not quite the case, as the results show.

Recall that I asked lawyers the following question: "At the time you accepted the case, or when you first valued it, what did you think was the likely range of recovery?" The lawyers provided both a high and a low value.[10] I looked at whether there was a relationship with the average of the two values, the low value, and the high value. My examination involved looking at the number of rounds for categorized versions of the valuation variables and looking at continuous relationships based on the log of the valuation variables. What I found was evidence of a modest curvilinear relationship, with the number of rounds increasing as stakes increased up to a point, and then decreasing. Figure 5.1 shows a sketch of the tendency expressed as the average number of exchanges expected depending on the value of stakes.[11] In looking at the figure it is important to keep in mind that the degree of relationship is quite modest and that the variation around the line is substantial. Nonetheless, the pattern suggests that the number of rounds rises quite rapidly from the smallest cases through cases involving about $50,000; the increase after that is much slower, with the number of rounds tending to decrease after crossing the half million dollar mark, although the decrease is quite gradual.

A final variable to consider is the area of law the case dealt with. The evidence of systematic variation based on this variable was mixed. While the mean number or exchanges did vary, from a low of 3.11 for contract cases to a high of 5.05 for products liability cases (although there were only eight such cases in the sample), and one statistical test did indicate that the variations had a low probability (6 chances out of 100) of reflecting chance sampling variation, the explanatory power of the variable was at best very weak, accounting for less than 2 percent of the variation in the number of exchanges. The largest category of cases, personal injury from auto accidents, fell in the middle of the range, at an average of 3.89 exchanges.

In summary, there is considerable variation in the number of exchanges that lawyers report in the settlement of contingency fee cases, but there is little in the way of systematic patterns to be detected in that variation using the variables I have available. One can imagine other variables that might account for the variation—case complexity comes to mind. However, the limits of my survey preclude examining such variables.

Timing of Initial Exchange. Cases varied significantly in when negotiations began. For cases filed but not tried, 54 percent involved prefiling negotiations; for cases ultimately going to trial or administrative hearing, only 40 percent involved prefiling negotiations. There are at least three factors that might explain the lack of prefiling negotiations. First, filing a formal claim or case may be the norm in some areas (e.g., workers' compensation, securities cases, etc.), and negotiations simply do not usually start until after this is completed; only 4 percent of workers' compensation cases involved prefiling negotiations. Second, the plaintiff's lawyer might believe that the opposing party will not take the claim seriously unless or until a formal case is filed. Prefiling negotiations were most likely in cases such as auto accident cases and "other" types of personal injury cases; they were much less likely in areas such as products liability. Third, the nature of injuries might be such that the recovery period pushes up to or goes beyond the statute of limitations, and the lawyer must file to protect the case even though the case is not yet ripe for settlement. As discussed in Chapter 4, the one court case that Steve Clarke filed during my month in the office was filed for precisely this reason.

Initial Demands. What do the initial exchanges look like, both in terms of how the initial demand compares to the lawyer's initial assessment of the case value and in terms of how the opposing party responds? In terms of the lawyer's initial assessment, recall that I asked the lawyers to provide a range rather than a single value. For purposes of the following discussion, I created three categories: more than 150 percent of the high valuation, between 100 percent and 150 percent of the high valuation, and less than 100 percent of the high valuation. Information on the first demand and offer is available for 806 cases; after weighting the cases to adjust for sample design, the sample is 820.[12]

Well over half (57 percent) of the initial demands fall between one and one and a half times the lawyers' initial high-end valuation of the case's worth. The remaining cases are about equally likely to fall above or below this midrange: 21 percent less than the high evaluation and 22 percent more than 150 percent of the high evaluation.[13] For purposes of discussion, I will refer to the midrange as "typical" initial demands, demands at the high end as "aggressive" demands, and demands at the low end as "soft" demands.[14] Are there any types of cases, or any characteristics of lawyers, that are associated with higher likelihood of either aggressive or soft demands? I explored this question using a combination of statistical tools, including cross-tabulations and regression analyses.

The clearest relationship involves the amount at stake. As the amount at stake goes up, as measured by the lawyers' high-end valuations, the likelihood of the lawyer making a soft demand goes up, from 20 percent or less for cases up to $60,000 in stakes to over 30 percent for cases over that amount (39 percent for cases over $100,000). Still, with the exception of the highest category, 55 percent to 62 percent of cases involve initial demands in the typical range; for the highest category, 38 percent are in the typical range.

The other variable that shows variations worth noting is area of law. Looking only at those areas of law for which I had at least twenty cases, we can take auto accident cases as the archetype: 59 percent of initial demands in the typical range, 16 percent soft, and 26 percent aggressive. Workers' compensation cases were more likely to be in the typical range, with 86 percent of the initial demands between 100 percent and

150 percent of the lawyers' high valuation; in part, this probably reflects that both sides could reasonably estimate the range of compensation given the structure created by the workers' compensation system. In contract cases, offers were much more likely to be in the soft range (51 percent), and almost all of the rest were in the typical range (47 percent). The two other areas with twenty or more cases were medical malpractice and other personal injury (excluding products liability). The former involved initial demands that were mostly in either the soft or typical range (41 percent and 46 percent respectively), with only 14 percent in the aggressive range, suggesting that contrary to what is probably the popular perception, plaintiffs' lawyers in medical malpractice cases are much more likely to make conservative rather than aggressive demands. This probably reflects the combination of high litigation costs and high levels of uncertainty in medical malpractice cases (see Sloan et al. 1993; Vidmar 1995).[15] For the category other personal injury, the pattern is somewhat similar to the auto accident archetype, but with a bit fewer in the typical range: 24 percent soft, 46 percent typical, and 31 percent aggressive; only for this category does the percentage in the aggressive range exceed that for the most common category of auto accident cases.[16]

One possibility is that each attorney has an individual negotiation style, including a preference for making initial demands of a particular type—soft, typical, or aggressive. To some degree, this is what I would hypothesize based on my observation as well as work by others suggesting the role of habitual patterns (Hyman et al. 1995, 81, 84). One of the lawyers seemed to make aggressive demands (from which he would quickly back off), while the other two seemed more likely to make demands in the typical range. One way to test this using my survey data is to take advantage of the fact that the survey asked for information on up to three cases from each lawyer. In the sample of cases, 148 lawyers provided data on an initial exchange for two cases and 166 provided data on three exchanges. Of the lawyers with two cases in the sample, 55 percent make initial demands of the same type in both cases; among those with three cases, 42 percent make demands of the same type in all three cases. If one were to assume that lawyers chose among the three types randomly rather than having a personal style of negotiation, one would expect half of the lawyers with two cases to make the same type of demand in both cases, and a third of those with three cases to make the same type in all three cases. The pattern here shows some deviation from that expectation, but not enough to make a strong case for individual negotiating styles as a good explanation for the observed variation.

In the end, it is hard to come up with strong explanations for the variation in initial demands. It may well be that the nature of the demand reflects the lawyers' judgment about the strength of the client's case and what will get the opposing side thinking along the terms the plaintiff's lawyer would like. It might also simply reflect a seat-of-the-pants decision by the lawyer as the lawyer composes the demand letter.

While there is no clear explanation for variation in the nature of initial demands, the fact that 78 percent of initial demands are in the typical or soft range is not surprising. Making "reasonable" demands facilitates settlement. A demand that is perceived by the defense as clearly excessive may be taken as a signal that the lawyer is not really interested in reaching a settlement and may encourage the defense to bring in an outside lawyer, thus raising the contingency fee lawyer's costs. In order for the contingency fee lawyer to keep control of the investment necessary to resolve a case, it is crucial to negotiate in a way that reduces the likelihood of getting into formal litigation and the costs such litigation entails for the contingency fee lawyer. At the same time, the lawyer may want at times to make higher-than-expected demands as a way of trying to signal to the opposing side that a case needs to be taken seriously; this kind of signaling, done selectively, may tend to increase the overall return from the lawyer's portfolio of cases.

Initial Offers.   Of the initial demands, 91 percent produced offers of some payment from the opposing side. Whether or not there was an offer in response to an initial demand depended very much on the type of case, ranging from a high of 97 percent in auto accident cases to a low of 33 percent in products liability and non-personal injury tort cases. In between, there were initial offers in 65 percent of medical malpractice cases, 62 percent of discrimination cases, 79 percent of workers' compensation, 87 percent of contract cases, and 91 percent of other types of personal injury cases.[17] The nature of this pattern is not surprising. It reflects in significant part the likely clarity of liability, with those cases in which the rules of fault are relatively clear and broadly understood (auto accidents) most likely to produce offers and those in which liability is less clear, less likely to produce offers. In the words of one lawyer:

Auto cases are auto cases. Companies will be cheap or tough, but the liability issues there are pretty clean, usually. Premises cases are fascinating because I could give you the same slip-and-fall in a parking lot, exactly the same case, I could take it to one company and they will treat it as a liability case and negotiate on the damages, maybe asking a little cut because these aren't a sure thing, but basically you are negotiating damages. Other companies, they are denying liability almost reflexively, and the fight is to see whether they will pay anything at all.

There is also a clear relationship between how a case was terminated and whether there is an offer in response to the initial demand: such offers came in 94 percent of cases terminated without filing, 89 percent of cases filed but not tried, and 78 percent of cases that went to trial. Interpreting the causal significance of this pattern is difficult because cases may have been filed or gone to trial because of the unwillingness of the defendant to negotiate, or it might be that the stage of termination is an indicator of the strength of the plaintiff's case on liability.

The relationship between the receipt of offers in response to initial demands and the amount at stake is somewhat curvilinear. Such offers were most common for cases in the $10,001-to-$100,000 range (measured by the plaintiff's lawyer's high-end valuation), coming in 93 percent of those cases, compared to 89 percent of cases up to $10,000 and 83 percent of cases over $100,000. Finally, there was a weak but interesting relationship between the nature of the first demand and whether that demand produced an offer. Soft demands (less than the high valuation) were *least* likely to produce an offer (89 percent), and aggressive demands were most likely to produce an offer (96 percent); typical demands fell in between, with 91 percent producing offers.[18]

More interesting is the nature of the offer. One can compare the offer to the demand, to the lawyer's high-end valuation of the case, and to the lawyer's low-end valuation. Comparing to both the high-end valuation and to the demand, the dominant pattern is that the initial offer tends to be a relatively small fraction of the comparison; the median ratio of offer to demand is .31 (i.e., the offer is 31 percent of the demand), and the median ratio of the offer to high-end valuation is only .36 (the offer is 36 percent of the high valuation). However, comparing the offer to the lawyer's low-end valuation, the median ratio of offer to valuation is .88 (the offer is 88 percent of the low valuation), and in 48 percent of the cases the offer is equal to or greater than the low valuation. In other words, in almost half the cases, if the client accepted the first offer received, that offer would meet or exceed the client's lawyer's conservative valuation of the case.

For purposes of exploring the relationship between the initial offer in more detail, I dichotomized the offer into those less than the conservative (low) valuation and those equal to or greater than the low valuation. Looking first at the area of law, a number of areas had approximately 45 to 50 percent of the offers equaling or exceeding the low valuation: auto accident cases (actually 51 percent), other personal injury (including products liability but excluding medical malpractice), workers' compensation, and contract. In medical malpractice, only 25 percent of the cases had initial offers equal to or exceeding the low valuation. In discrimination cases and non-personal injury tort cases, the percentage of initial offers equaling or exceeding the low valuation was under 20 percent.

Not surprisingly, cases ultimately going to trial were unlikely to have initial offers equaling or exceeding the lawyers' low valuation (18 percent), while such offers were quite common for cases settled short of trial (55 percent for unfiled cases and 44 percent for cases filed but not tried). Similarly, offers equaling or exceeding the low valuation were less likely as the amount at stake increased, occurring only in 26 percent of cases with high valuations over $100,000, but occurring in over 50 percent of cases under $25,000. Also not surprising is that such offers were less common when "soft" demands were made (35 percent of soft demands produced offers equaling or exceeding the low valuation); somewhat surprising is that there was no difference in the likelihood of such offers between typical and aggressive demands, with 52 percent of offers equaling or exceeding the low valuation for either typical or aggressive demands.

Finally, lawyers whose practices specialized in personal injury cases were more likely to obtain initial offers equaling or exceeding their low valuation: 55 percent. In contrast, general practice lawyers got such offers in 43 percent of their cases, and lawyers in other types of practices got them in 38 percent of cases. However, there is no way to determine whether this apparent success reflects better offers or more conservative low valuations.[19]

The frequency of initial offers that equal or exceed the lawyer's conservative valuation of the case makes it clear why most cases settle: for around half the cases, the initial offer puts the case into an acceptable settlement range. In reality, the proportion is larger, because I have not been able to take into account potential transaction costs, which form a central part of the standard analysis of settlement (Friedman 1969; Kritzer 1991, 58–64; Posner 1973) and serve to lead the plaintiff to discount the potential recovery to avoid incurring those costs.[20] Still, while lawyers in about half the cases in which the other side makes an offer in response to an initial demand know from that first exchange that the case clearly can be settled, this does not mean that the lawyer accepts the very first offer, or even the second offer. In fact, there is no relationship between whether the first offer falls in this minimally acceptable range (equaling or exceeding the low valuation) and the number of rounds of exchanges the lawyers report.

Getting to Settlement

The statistical analysis does not provide a lot of insight into the factors shaping variation in negotiation. One reason for this is that much of the variation is not particularly systematic. As another study of negotiation in routine litigation described the situation,

> We think that what we observed can best be understood as a social practice. Through this lens, lawyers' negotiation practices are explainable in terms of habit, small scale social organization, and individual psychology. We learned from lawyers that they handle settlement efforts as a kind of ordinary processing, treating cases as occasions to repeat their familiar set of moves. Their expectations are encouraged and confirmed by other lawyers and judges with whom they have to deal. (Hyman et al. 1995, 81)

In terms of systematic patterns and habits, lawyers may focus less on what they ask for than on how they ask for it. I saw this clearly in my observations. Each lawyer had his own way of producing an initial demand, and each treated that demand as taking on a somewhat different role in the ultimate resolution. One lawyer treated the initial demand as a signal to the other side that he wanted to be taken seriously; typically he did this by making demands several multiples above what he was prepared to settle for. Another lawyer used the initial demand to define clearly what he was seeking; while he typically came down from that demand, he was able to justify the demand pretty clearly and the other side took that justification seriously. The third lawyer made demands that he was prepared to stick to. He often dealt with cases in which he could make a demand for policy limits (i.e., if the opposing side's insurance had a coverage limit of $500,000, he was able to demand and justify that full amount).

Also important to note is that lawyers did not grab minimally acceptable offers or offers that their clients were willing to accept. Rather, the inclination was to push the other side to what the lawyer perceived was that side's probable settlement limit or something close to it. This runs counter to the concern that contingency fee lawyers will tend to accept settlements that are lower than otherwise might be best for their clients (Johnson 1980–81; Miller 1987; Polinsky and Rubinfeld 2001; Rosenthal 1974).

One reason lawyers make this extra push is the need to have clients go away happy. Recall the case in which Steve Clarke had an offer of $22,000 on the table in response to a $32,000 demand. He called the client to discuss the situation, telling the client that (a) the case would probably settle for between $25,000 and $27,000 and that the cash value to the client of a $25,000 settlement was about the same as the $32,000 verdict. The client authorized Clarke to settle for whatever he could get. Based on this, Clarke could have readily settled for $25,000, and the next offer from the adjuster was $25,000. However, Clarke did not stop there; he was able to push the adjuster up to $26,500. By getting the settlement toward the top of the range he had suggested to the client as likely for the settlement, he was going to increase the client's satisfaction with the outcome.

A second reason for the extra push is Clarke's own immediate incentives. The additional time it took Clarke to obtain the additional $1,500 was no more than fifteen minutes of conversation with the adjuster. For this extra time, Clarke increased his own fee by $500, a return of about $2,000 per hour. Thus, from the lawyer's perspective, the additional jawboning that produces the last marginal increase in the settlement is a very productive use of the lawyer's time.

This leaves open the question of whether Clarke might have been able to double or triple the payment from the insurer if he had pushed the case to the door of the courthouse. There is no easy way to ascertain what a case might have been worth at trial. The injury in this case, a broken vertebra in the back, is not one that is common enough that there is a significant number of Wisconsin jury verdicts to form a basis of estimate. The 1997 national survey of closed claims conducted by the Insurance Research Council (IRC) can help put the result Clarke obtained into perspective. The IRC survey (1999) did not specifically code for "broken back" or "broken vertebrae," but it does include codes for "disc injury," fracture of weight-bearing bone, and other fractures. Nationally, the median bodily injury payments for these three injuries in cases in which the claimant was represented by an attorney were $20,000, $25,000, and $20,000 respectively;[21] the corresponding seventy-fifth percentiles were $31,105, $60,000, and $30,000. Within Wisconsin, the survey does not have sufficient cases of these separate injuries for comparison; grouping them together, the median and seventy-fifth percentiles are $22,000 and $50,000. These national figures fail to take into account two elements of this particular case: the available insurance was more than $25,000 (a common liability limit), and the client made a full recovery from his injuries (i.e., there was no "permanency"). If I limit the national data to cases in which the insurance coverage exceeded $25,000 and the claimant had no permanent disability, the medians are $20,000, $30,000, and $19,000, and the seventy-fifth percentiles are $34,361, $61,100, and $35,000. The sample includes only five Wisconsin cases involving these three injuries, attorney representation, a policy limit of over $25,000, and no permanency; the median for these five cases is $15,700. One final control can be introduced, and that is for the magnitude of the medical costs the client incurred, which in this case was on the order of $5,000. Limiting the estimates to those cases with medical costs in the range of $4,000 to $6,000 (as well as attorney representation, a policy limit greater than $25,000, and no permanency), the medians for the three injuries are $17,500, $21,000, and $15,000, and the seventy-fifth percentiles are $25,000, $25,000, and $28,000.[22] Based on this, my best estimate is that the settlement Clarke obtained was considerably better than the typical range for the injury and the loss his client sustained, although it was probably not "top dollar."[23]

Negotiating with Third Parties

Discussions of settlement negotiations in the litigation context focus almost exclusively on the process between parties that are formally opposed to each other. However, there are often other parties that are relevant in the settlement process. In this section, I focus on the lawyers' negotiations with three other types of parties: parties holding subrogation interests in a claim, the claimant's own insurance company when that insurer has contractual obligations to pay for all of a claim normally the responsibility of an opposing party, and other plaintiffs who have potentially conflicting claims against the defendant.

Subrogation

The plaintiff's lawyer often has to negotiate not only with the side formally in opposition to the lawyer's client, but also with other parties who have an interest in any recovery. Most commonly, these interests are parties that have subrogation claims or other types of liens on any money going to the client. Such claimants are typically health insurers that originally paid the cost of treatment of injuries. In the case of third-party claims arising out of injury on the job, a workers' compensation insurer will be entitled to at least partial reimbursement of any payments made to the client. Rules and practices differ from state to state. In Wisconsin, insurers are very aggressive in asserting their subrogation claims, and plaintiffs' lawyers routinely deal with such claims as part of reaching a settlement. In cases where the subrogated claim is substantial, the holder of the claim may be represented by its own counsel, who will participate in, or at least be present at, discovery activities, pretrial conferences, and the trial. In other situations, particularly those arising in workers' compensation cases when a third-party claim exists, the holder of the subrogation claim may encourage and support the plaintiff's lawyer in pursuing the case.

Under Wisconsin law, an insurance carrier that has paid medical expenses for someone injured in an accident has a claim on any recovery subject to a discount for their insured's share of responsibility for the injury. Thus, in theory, if a case goes to trial and the plaintiff is found 25 percent at fault and damages are set at $30,000, $10,000 of which is specified as for past medical bills—in Wisconsin jury awards customarily list categories of damages[24]—the health insurer holding the subrogated claim is entitled to up to $7,500 of the award, depending upon how much the insurer paid and how much the plaintiff paid out of pocket for deductibles, coinsurance, and the like.[25] If health insurance is provided through a self-funded ERISA (Employee Retirement Income Security Act) plan, the provisions of the ERISA plan take precedence over the standard rules; typically this means that the health insurer has a claim that need not be adjusted for comparative negligence and which need not even necessarily be adjusted for the costs of collection (i.e., attorney's fees and the like).

The situation is somewhat different for a third-party claim when the subrogated interest arises from payment under workers' compensation. The workers' compensation carrier has a claim on a portion of any award or settlement. Specifically, after deducting the costs of collection (i.e., attorney's fees and expenses), the first third goes to the claimant, the workers' compensation carrier is then reimbursed up to the amount it has paid, and if anything is left, that amount goes to the claimant. If there is a continuing workers' compensation claim, and the workers' comp insurer did not exhaust its entitlement to reimbursement (i.e., past workers' compensation benefits were less than two-thirds of the third-party payment adjusted for costs of collection—the difference is referred to as the ("cushion"), the workers' comp insurer does not have to pay any of the future benefits until the "cushion" is exhausted. That is, assuming a one-third contingency fee on the third-party claim, the lawyer gets a third off the top, any expenses associated with the case are deducted, the claimant then gets one-third of what is left, the workers' compensation lien is then paid, and anything that is left goes to the claimant (Wis. Stat. 102.29[1]).

Workers' compensation cases without third-party claims can also produce subrogation issues between the workers' compensation carrier and the client's health insurer. Many if not most health insurance policies specifically exclude coverage for injuries arising in the work context. Health insurers may nonetheless pay medical bills in these circumstances, either because they did not realize that the injury was work-related or because there is a dispute over the question of the cause of the injury and the claimant has signed an agreement with the health insurer that if the workers' compensation claim is successful the claimant will reimburse the health insurer from the proceeds. In the latter case, the postinjury agreement constitutes an enforceable contract outside the workers' compensation proceeding; the health insurer has no standing in that proceeding, so it would need to bring a collection action to be paid if the claimant failed to abide by the agreement. Nonetheless, the lawyer has the opportunity to negotiate with the health insurer in cases that settle, making arguments (discussed below) about why the health insurer should discount its claim.

The issue of subrogation creates many opportunities and issues in the settlement negotiation process, both vis-à-vis the defendant and vis-à-vis the subrogated party. While it is most common for the plaintiff's lawyer to work out the subrogation settlement, it is possible for that to be handled by the defendant's representative. In some cases, part of the settlement is to specify that the payment to the plaintiff covers only nonmedical damages, leaving the medical damages to be resolved between the defendant and the subrogated interest. One lawyer I interviewed illustrated this approach with the following anecdote:

Lawyer Smith had a case scheduled to go to trial on Monday; the large health insurer had retained a major law firm to represent its interest at the trial. On the Friday before trial, Smith reached a settlement with the defendant in which the defendant agreed to pay $100,000 to settle everything except medical "specials" (i.e., medical bills). The defendant's lawyer, Jones, told Smith that he would take care of the subrogation claim directly. Jones then immediately called the lawyer representing the health insurer and told that lawyer that he had settled the case with Smith and would be ready to go to trial as scheduled on Monday to resolve the issue of medical specials. Not surprisingly, the lawyer representing the health insurer was totally unprepared to try the case because he expected Smith to try it. Jones then told the health insurer's lawyer that he would make a take-it-or-leave-it offer to resolve the subrogation claim, and if it was not accepted, he would "see them in court." The offer was accepted.

This kind of resolution to subrogation issues is unusual, but it illustrates that it is an issue that the lawyers must deal with.

Most often subrogation issues are resolved between the plaintiff's lawyer and an adjuster for the health insurer or workers' compensation insurer. In some cases, the lawyer's negotiation and the settlement with the defendant are designed to eliminate or reduce the subrogation claim; the mechanism here is to obtain a settlement that arguably is only partial compensation (i.e., the client has not been "made whole" by the settlement). Such a settlement allows for the assertion that the settlement does not include any compensation for past medical expenses—that is, the payment is represented as covering future medical expenses, lost income, and pain and suffering only. This is easiest when the defendant's insurer pays the full policy limits of its coverage.

More often, the goal of the lawyer is to convince the subrogated party to accept a discount on its full claim. There are three lines of argument that the lawyer uses to achieve this. First, the client is partially at fault, which means that the subrogated party is responsible for the client's share. In most types of cases, some fault can be attributed to the client, although this is less likely to be true in rear-end collisions or when the client was a passenger wearing a seat belt. Ironically, while negotiating with the defendant, the lawyer wants to minimize the client's responsibility; when it comes time to negotiate with the subrogated party, the more responsible the client is, the more it advantages the client. In the words of one lawyer, "You kind of change hats. All of a sudden you are making some of the same arguments that were made to you by the defense people."

The second argument used by the lawyer to reduce the payment to the subrogated party is to claim that even taking into account comparative negligence issues, the client has not been "made whole," either because of inadequate insurance coverage or because of discounting to take into account the risks and costs of taking the case to trial.[26] This approach seems to work best when the damages are very substantial, because it is easier to argue that the client has not been fully compensated in those situations.

The third argument is that some portion of the subrogated party's theoretical share should go to compensate the lawyer. That is, even if the defendant is fully compensated and the subrogated party has access to the full amount of its claim, it should pay a portion of its recovery as compensation to the lawyer—a third or a quarter, whatever percentage the lawyer is charging the client. In some situations, when it does not raise an issue of conflict with the client, the plaintiff's lawyer will have formally entered into an agreement to represent the subrogated interest; in these situations, there is an agreement between the lawyer and the subrogated party with regard to the lawyer's fee percentage.

These are the standard lines of argument I saw on a recurring basis. Lawyers also make case-specific arguments. For example, in one case, the lawyer explained that he was not actually taking a fee himself in order to maximize the amount to the client, who was a personal friend. Specifically, the lawyer explained that the compensation the client received for his totaled vehicle was substantially below the vehicle's actual market value, and he was trying to help cover the expense of the car. The health insurer in this case agreed to a 33 percent discount. In several cases, the lawyer justified a requested reduction in the subrogation payment as a means of getting a certain amount of cash to the client, explaining that he felt it was necessary to get the client at least that amount to accept the settlement.

Insurers with subrogated claims differ in their willingness to negotiate and in their timeliness in responding to requests to resolve subrogation issues. Medicare is reputedly a particular problem. One lawyer described a recent case she had recently settled. The client started receiving dunning notices from Medicare after receiving the settlement check. Over a period of months before the settlement, the lawyer had repeatedly tried to get Medicare to submit to her its subrogation claim so that she could try to resolve it. In the course of these efforts, the lawyer sent three letters to Medicare, and in the third letter she stated that if she did not hear from Medicare by a certain date she would go ahead and settle the case. A couple of months after settling the case, Medicare finally contacted the lawyer to discuss the subrogation claim. The lawyer essentially told them to "get lost."

Workers' compensation carriers are generally very reluctant to compromise their subrogation claims when a third-party claim is settled. The formulas discussed above—the workers' compensation insurer is entitled to up to two-thirds of any recovery net of the reasonable costs of collection (i.e., attorney's fees and expenses)—is specified in the statute governing workers' compensation. In response to the nature of negotiations over workers' compensation subrogation claims, Steve Clarke described the situation as follows:

The formula is set in stone; there is *no* reduction for anything. My strategy is to try to convince the comp carrier that if they don't make some reduction, my client may reject the third-party offer and go to trial. If liability is at all shaky, the comp carrier is occasionally willing to make some reduction to grease the settlement. An alternative strategy is to negotiate a reduction of the comp pay-back in exchange for giving a full and final compromise as to future [workers'] compensation claims. This is not uncommon.

Negotiating subrogation claims actually constitutes a substantial amount of the negotiation time in many cases. There can be a number of such claims, and each has to be dealt with separately. For example, in one case involving a substandard insurer from out of state, the lawyer had previously reached a settlement, but because of the insurer's cash flow problems the settlement was not to be paid until some months hence. The lawyer was contacted by a firm offering to "purchase" the settlement at a 3 percent discount (i.e., it would pay ninety-seven cents on the dollar); payment would be immediate after signing the document with a wire transfer to the lawyer's trust account. In addition to getting the client's approval for this "deal," the lawyer had to contact three different subrogated parties with whom he had previously reached agreements and get them to agree to accept the 3 percent discount in return for immediate payment (they all agreed).

In rare cases, subrogation claims can lead to litigation between the plaintiff and the party with the subrogated interest. While one would expect this primarily in large claims, it can happen in claims large and small. One lawyer told of a subrogation claim for $880 in a case in which the total recovery was on the order of $5,000. The lawyer offered to settle the subrogation claim for $90; the holder of the claim rejected that offer and hired a lawyer from Milwaukee, who took the case to small claims court and won a ruling that the plaintiff had to pay the subrogation claim based on the documentary evidence alone. The plaintiff's lawyer informed the lawyer for the insurer with the subrogation claim that he would appeal the case to Circuit Court, which would consider the matter de novo; when the opposing lawyer realized that he would need to bring a witness—documentary evidence would not be sufficient—at a cost of $500 to $1,000, he broached the issue of settlement, asking for $500. The plaintiff's lawyer again offered $90, and the this time the offer was accepted.

While subrogation may seem to be a problem for the plaintiff, there are times when it may work to the plaintiff's advantage when negotiating with the primary party. For example, in a workers' compensation case with a potential third-party claim, there is pressure on the workers' compensation carrier to not do anything that would jeopardize the third-party claim from which the compensation carrier might potentially recoup some or all of what it might have to pay. In other situations, there may a subrogation issue that can be resolved *first*, strengthening the plaintiff's claim. For example, Steve Clarke had a rear-end accident case in which the opposing insurer denied liability, claiming that the accident happened because Clarke's client changed lanes. Clarke suggested to the client that the client collect on the medical payments coverage of the client's own insurance and then have the insurer seek reimbursement from the tortfeasor's insurer, relying on intercompany arbitration if necessary.[27] If the client's insurer succeeded in obtaining payment for the intercompany claim, that would provide a strong basis to argue liability.

In some circumstances, a potential subrogation claim may discourage seeking certain types of compensation. For example, Chuck Brown had a workers' compensation case in which there had been very substantial medical expenses but which had resulted in a full recovery for his client. Given that the claim for noneconomic damages would be limited by the absence of continuing disability, it was not clear whether a third-party claim would be worth the cost in time and expenses that would be required to bring that claim because such a large portion of any recovery would have to be returned to the workers' compensation carrier.

Uninsured/Underinsured Coverage

A second type of third party that plaintiffs' lawyers must consider are sources of compensation other than the tortfeasor or the tortfeasor's insurer. These come in the form of the client's own insurance coverage for uninsured or underinsured motorists. The former functions essentially the same as insurance for the tortfeasor, except that if no settlement is reached the dispute is resolved through arbitration if so specified in the client's insurance policy. Several of the cases the lawyers I observed worked on during my observation involved uninsured motorist claims. I saw only one hint of difference between these negotiations and those with an opposing party or an opposing party's insurer: the insurance company *may* be more willing to let a claim under uninsured motorist coverage be resolved by arbitration than to let a regular personal injury claim go to trial. If this is the case, and I emphasize the speculative nature of the *if*, it may be that this allows the adjusters to take a somewhat tougher stand in negotiation.

Of more consequence for the negotiation process are *under*insured motorist claims. As with uninsured motorist coverage, these claims involved the client's own insurer. Such coverage supplements the amount recoverable when the opposing party has limited insurance coverage. While uninsured motorist coverage has been widely available since the mid-1950s (Long and Gregg 1965, 593; Widiss 1999, 1:10–14), underinsured motorist coverage is a more recent development as a common type of insurance, beginning in Wisconsin around 1970 and nationally by the mid-70s (see Widiss 1999, 1:538–42, 3:2–6); exactly when it became a common type of coverage that a significant percentage of car owners carried is less clear. One consequence of its relative newness is that some of the issues it raises for compensation have continued to be in flux, and the nature of the policies has been changing. Two major issues have arisen.

The first issue is whether the face amount of the coverage represents the total compensation the claimant can receive (i.e., when combined with payments from the tortfeasor) or the maximum supplemental amount over what the tortfeasor pays. This issue arose in large part because underinsured coverage was generally written jointly with uninsured coverage. Most insurers have now revised their policies to make it clear that underinsurance coverage is reduced by any third-party payment so that the total received equals the face amount of the underinsurance coverage.[28]

The second, related issue is that of policy "stacking." If a client is covered under multiple underinsurance policies (i.e., the family owns multiple vehicles so each has its own coverage), can the coverages be combined? For example, if a family has two cars, each with $100,000 of underinsured coverage, is the total amount available $100,000 or $200,000? If two people in the family are injured in the accident, can each collect $100,000, one under the first car's coverage and one under the second car's coverage?

During the time I was observing, both of these issues were in flux, with the rules applying to specific cases depending upon when an injury occurred and the specific language of the insurance policies involved.[29] While the issue of underinsured coverage came up in only a very small portion of the lawyers' cases, few cases involved damages where such coverage would kick in. The cases where it was an issue were those that had the highest profit potential; thus, this was a very important concern. Central to accessing this coverage was getting the opposing party's insurer to tender its policy limits. One lawyer indicated that he preferred to have the insurer "offer" to pay the limits rather than specifically demanding that it do so; thus the demand should be the total damages, not just the amount of the insurance. A demand for more than the policy limits has the added effect of putting the insurer on the spot for a potential "insurance bad faith" claim from its own insured if it fails to pay the policy limit, the case goes to trial, and a verdict is returned for more than the policy limit.

For cases with substantial damages, one of the most important issues the lawyer must deal with is identifying all of the insurance coverage that might be applicable. While in some cases this may involve finding additional defendants (the famous "deep pocket"), more often it involves identifying all of the underinsurance coverages that may be applicable: Who has that coverage? Does it apply to the client? How many policies are involved? Failure to identify all the sources of compensation opens the lawyer to a legal malpractice claim from the client should the missed coverages later be discovered.

Other Plaintiffs

A final type of "third party" that is sometimes relevant to the lawyer in the negotiation process is other persons making claims against the defendant from the same injurious event. This is relevant when the total potential compensation exceeds the opposing party's insurance coverage. In this case, the lawyer must be concerned about how the insurance proceeds will be divided up. If there is underinsurance coverage available to the lawyer's client that is not available to the other claimants (or such coverage available to those claimants that is not available to the lawyer's client), that may provide some solution or some way of compromising payouts. The tortfeasor's insurer will typically want to tender its policy limits and have the funds deposited with the court; the various parties with claims against the insurance can then work out the division. Most important to any one claimant is to prevent the insurer from making payments before the insurer becomes aware of the full magnitude of the set of claims it is facing. I saw only one case in which this was an issue. In that case, the lawyer I was with focused on clearly communicating to the defending insurer that the total of claims it was facing exceeded the policy limits and on trying to convince the lawyers representing other parties to fully assess the available coverage through underinsurance coverages their clients might have.

"Negotiating" with the Client

While the language of negotiation is not typically used to describe the process by which the lawyer gets a client to accept a settlement offer, in reality the lawyer is in fact essentially engaged in a kind of negotiation process.[30] In this section, I look at how the lawyers handle these negotiations, both in the preliminary stage of preparing the client for the settlement and in the stage of leading a client to accept a specific settlement.

In a study of solicitors' divorce practice in England, John Eekelaar, Mavis Maclean, and Sarat Beinart (2000, 89–91) conceptualize the problem of negotiating with the client over settlement as involving three overlapping circles which they label "client's interests," "client's instructions," and "normative standards." They use this conceptualization as a foundation for discussing both the problem of clients whose expectations are unrealistic and the problem of those whose expectations are too modest. In the divorce context, both problems are quite common. The idea of "normative standards" does not move well into most areas handled on a contingency fee basis, because the standards for setting damages are not enshrined in law as is the case for many of the contested aspects of divorce. Nonetheless, one might relabel "normative standards" something like "realistic possibilities." Similarly, the idea of "client instructions," while theoretically possible, is probably not a good fit either; perhaps better is "client's expectations." Figure 5.2 adapts Eekelaar, Maclean, and Beinart's figure to the context of American contingency fee practice and shows how client interests, client expectations, and realistic possibilities can diverge and converge in the settlement process. The problem for the lawyer is (1) to control and shape expectations as much as possible, a problem that was first discussed in Chapter 4, (2) to be aware of what outcomes work in the client's interest, a problem that can be very important when issues such

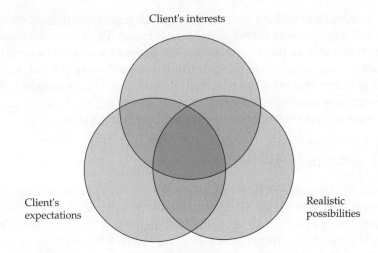

FIGURE 5.2 Moving the Client Toward Settlement

as subrogation arise, and (3) to live in the world of the possible. From the perspective of Figure 5.2, the lawyer wants to achieve an alignment of these three elements, which is the area of the figure where all elements overlap. Note that this is an area, not a single specific location.

Preparing Clients for Settlement

In Chapter 4, I discussed the strategies lawyers use to avoid creating expectations on the part of the client on what the client might ultimately receive. One of the central strategies is to avoid mentioning specific dollar amounts. However, there comes a time when the lawyer can no longer avoid mentioning actual dollar figures to the client. When a case is ripe for settlement, most lawyers will make a settlement demand that involves stating a specific amount (although some lawyers prefer to lay out the "specials" and ask the respondent to make an offer to cover both those specials and general damages[31]). As is standard in most bargaining situations, and as was described in the first part of this chapter, the lawyer typically makes a demand that is somewhat higher than the lawyer's valuation of the case. This presents the danger that the client will expect to get a settlement equal to the initial demand. The lawyers have to be extremely careful to explain to their clients that they should not expect to get anything like the amount of the demand. They want the clients to understand that the eventual settlement will almost certainly be considerably less than the initial demand. There are three primary ways that lawyers do this, beyond simply stating the fact that this is the case.

Not surprisingly, the first approach is to talk explicitly about the kind of settlement range the lawyer thinks is likely. For example, in one case I observed the lawyer explained to the client that he thought the case would settle in the range of $20,000 to $25,000 and that the client should not pay any attention to the specific amount of the demand because that was "just for negotiating purposes." In another case, the lawyer told the client (a repeater) that he hoped the instant case would *net* the client "perhaps $1,000 to $1,500." As this latter example suggests, often the emphasis to the client was not on the settlement amount but on what the client would net after fees, expenses, and the payment of subrogated claims. In fact, typically the lawyer, when presenting a settlement offer to a client, would emphasize the bottom line for the client, not the total settlement amount.[32]

Part of setting the settlement expectation may involve putting a range in the context of a likely jury verdict. Some lawyers simply put this in terms of their own experience. One or two lawyers I talked to mentioned having available copies of jury verdict reports that they could show to clients. One lawyer reported that he kept a set of clippings from the newspapers in his small local community which he could use to deflate the expectations of overly optimistic clients.

The second approach is to play on the risk aversion of the usually one-shot client by emphasizing the risk and uncertainty of going to trial (compare to Rosenthal 1974, 111). The lawyer will explain to the client that while the lawyer is convinced that the client's case is solid, and that the lawyer believes that a jury would return a verdict favorable on both liability and damages, "one simply doesn't always know what a jury will do." During my observation it was common for the lawyers to emphasize to their clients that all of the publicity about tort reform had resulted in juries that were both skeptical of plaintiffs and very reluctant to make significant damage awards, particularly in cases where the injuries were not clearly visible.[33]

The third approach I saw was for the lawyer to bad-mouth the client's case. The lawyer would talk about the weaknesses of the case and what might go wrong if the case went to trial or hearing (the latter in workers' compensation cases). This is not to say that the lawyers made up problems just to convince clients to accept a settlement.

Rather, it was a matter of emphasis; there seemed to be a clear pattern of emphasizing the weaknesses of a case when the lawyer strongly wanted to settle (which was most of the time). While one might be tempted to attribute this pattern to the incentives produced by the lawyer's own economic interest in avoiding the cost of trial, the pattern I saw was more in line with the realities of cases because it tended to happen after the lawyer had completed most of the preparation for the trial or hearing. For example, in one workers' compensation case, the lawyer had the client come in on the eve of the hearing to prepare the client for his testimony; this happened to be a case in which the client came to the lawyer relatively late. As the lawyer and client went through the client's testimony, the weaknesses in the case became increasingly clear. Early in the session the lawyer commented that it would be easy to take the case to hearing; the "hearing would be quick, so we could easily do it." As the session progressed, the lawyer became less inclined to push forward for the hearing, eventually commenting to the client that "this case wasn't set up right. . . . This is almost the kind of case that I'd say take the money and run, regardless of what they offered."

Selling a Settlement Proposal

What happens once a lawyer has a settlement proposal in hand that the lawyer would like the client to accept? As indicated by the summaries at the beginning of this chapter, the lawyers normally conferred with their clients as settlement offers were made, but typically they tried to push the opposing party to a higher settlement figure. The lawyers were inclined to stop only when in the lawyer's judgment additional efforts were not likely to produce significant movement. Only then would the lawyer either recommend that the client accept an offer or act on the client's authorization to "get as much as you can." The plaintiff's lawyer had no way of knowing the opposing party's true resistance point (except possibly in cases exceeding policy limits) and had to make judgments based largely on experience and intuition.

As suggested above, the focus for the lawyers in convincing the clients to accept a settlement was on how much the client would walk away with.[34] The lawyer would mention the total settlement value but quickly move on to the client's bottom line. Given Wisconsin's subrogation rules, it was common for the client to end up with well under the proportion of the settlement that the fee agreement suggests the client would receive. The lawyers employed three strategies to "sell" the settlement to the client, although for many (perhaps most) clients no "selling" was really necessary.

One strategy was to tell the client that the lawyer was taking a reduced fee. Most often what this meant was that the lawyer computed her fee based on the recovery net of payments to subrogated interests. For example, a settlement of $5,000 might involve medical bills totaling $2,000; the lawyer convinced the health insurer to accept $1,400 from the settlement. Based on the retainer agreement, the lawyer could claim a fee of $1,667 (one-third of $5,000); however, she took a fee of only $1,200 (one-third of $3,600). In this example, assuming $100 of miscellaneous expenses (e.g., charges for medical records, accident reports, etc.), for which the lawyer also receives reimbursement out of the settlement, the client nets $2,300 out of a total settlement of $5,000. Alternatively, the lawyer might feel that the client needs to get $2,500 in order to walk away happy, and the lawyer consequently reduces her fee to $1,000, particularly if the case was resolved quickly once the client's medical outcome was clear.

A second strategy came up when the lawyer's fee agreement involved a graduated fee based on when the case was resolved (recall case B described at the beginning of this chapter).[35] A typical graduated agreement called for a 25 percent fee until the lawyer had to begin "substantial trial preparation," at which point the fee went up to 33 percent. This arrangement allowed the lawyer to demonstrate to the client that the client was better off with a settlement considerably below what the case might bring at trial, *even ignoring the possibility of losing at trial.* This result was explicitly driven by the costs associated with going to (or even getting ready for) trial.[36] From the client's perspective, the costs of proceeding to trial included the expenses of bringing experts to testify (particularly medical experts) and the increased lawyer's fee.

It is easy to see how this works. Assume a case that the lawyer estimates would produce a $25,000 verdict. If the case goes to trial, the lawyer's fee would be one-third, or $8,333, and there would be $2,000 in additional expenses which the client would have to pay. The net to the client, before payments to subrogated interests, would be $14,667. If, on the other hand, the client accepts a $20,000 settlement with a 25 percent contingency fee, the client gets $15,000. The picture becomes even stronger when one takes into account subrogation. If the client's case succeeds at trial, the subrogated parties will normally accept discounts only from full repayment that reflect the jury's determination of their insured's degree of negligence.[37] Furthermore, given the lawyer's increased costs, the lawyer will not be inclined to take his or her fee off the verdict net of the amounts due to the subrogated parties. To make the example concrete, assume medical expenses of $5,000; the net to the client if the case produces a verdict of $25,000 will be only $9,667 (assuming zero liability on the client's part). If the lawyer can persuade the subrogated party to accept $3,500 and does not charge a fee on that part of the settlement, a $20,000 settlement will net $12,375 to the client, and a settlement of $18,000 still leaves the client ahead of going to trial with $10,875; in fact, under this scenario, the settlement equivalent of a $25,000 verdict is only $16,389. What this means is that, *even without taking into account discounts for risk preference*, any settlement over $16,389 puts more money in the client's pocket than a verdict of $25,000.

While this works most clearly with a graduated fee arrangement, even without such an arrangement, the lawyer may be able to show a client that a settlement is worth more than a trial; one lawyer described his approach this way:

I have two columns, settlement now versus trial. I will go through and say, okay, your costs and disbursements are this; if we go to trial, you are going to end up here. If your subrogation claims are this now, we can probably negotiate these [down], but if we try it, you will be deemed whole and you will have to pay every cent on the dollar. So let's assume we can get this now and this much at trial. You can show them that even with more at trial, they will get more money if they settle now.

The final strategy is to play specifically on the uncertainty of trial. This is both with regard to the likelihood of a jury verdict favorable to the client and with regard to the valuation of the injury by the jury. On the former, one lawyer told me, "We usually have some recent, less-than-exciting results. For example, at this time, the last four jury trials in Northland County were defense verdicts, and those were all in the last month." On the latter, another lawyer stated, "The headline says that a Lakeville man won his lawsuit. Yeah, well you read it, and the guy had $12,000 in damages, and the jury gave him $2,000. The paper thought it was a win, but it certainly wasn't." The lawyer might also emphasize the issue of comparative negligence and explain to the client that even if the jury finds that damages are, say $25,000, it might also determine that the client was 40 percent at fault, which would entitle the client to only $15,000 before the attorney's fee, disbursements, and subrogation claims.

Dealing with a Balky Client

What can the lawyer do if the client balks at a settlement? One of the lawyers I observed described a client who expressed in very clear terms expectations about the amount of money he would like to come out of the case with. Specifically, the client wanted to get enough to purchase a $20,000 sailboat; the client claimed to have friends who had gotten compensation on the order of that amount for similar injuries. The case involved perhaps $1,000 in medical bills (a couple of visits to the doctor plus a half dozen physical therapy sessions); the client missed no work (and hence, there was no claim for lost wages), and there was no residual impact of the injuries. The lawyer got what he viewed as a reasonable offer of settlement, $5,000. The client balked. What can the lawyer do at this point?

One solution for many lawyers is simply to withdraw from representing the client (compare to Mather, McEwen, and Maiman 2001, 104–7). The typical contingency fee retainer agreement in Wisconsin does include an "out" clause for the lawyer, and the lawyer has a great deal of leeway in exercising this option. Interestingly, when I asked the lawyers I interviewed about "firing clients," the problems that lawyers talked about had relatively little to do with clients balking at settlement. Rather, more often lawyers terminated representation because a client failed to keep appointments or was difficult to work with in some way, or the lawyer discovered that the client had lied on some critical point.[38]

So what can a lawyer do, short of firing a client, if a client balks at accepting what the lawyer views as a reasonable settlement offer? There are three approaches that I saw or heard about. First, the lawyer can tell the client that it is then necessary to move the case along in the process, including initiating suit or preparing for trial. The lawyer might emphasize that under the fee agreement the percentage will go up, and if the lawyer is not able to get a very substantially improved settlement offer, the outcome will be worse than if the client accepts the settlement now. The lawyer might also exercise the option in most retainer agreements of demanding that the client immediately pay costs such as filing fees, expert witness fees, and the like. While none of the lawyers I spoke to acknowledged that they did this as a means of encouraging acceptance of a settlement offer, one lawyer reported that at a firm where he had previously worked this was a fairly regular practice: "We used to regularly try to frighten people into taking settlements that they didn't want because they were still kind of gung ho on the whole litigation at that point. So when it was a gray area case, we used to say, yes, pay us $1,000 and we will file suit. They wouldn't have the money so that would be the end of it." It may be that simply asking the client to provide a check to cover even the relatively small fees involved in filing the court case will cause the client to pause and reconsider accepting the settlement offer.

Second, some lawyers genuinely have no problem moving cases along to trial. As discussed in the previous chapters, there are some practices in which a case will not be accepted unless from the outset the lawyer is willing to pursue it all the way through trial (with the out that if some unknown fact comes up that radically changes the case, the lawyer may reconsider). If a client declines an offer, these lawyers will proceed to prepare the case for trial. The lawyer may believe from experience that the client will have second thoughts about having declined the settlement offer as the process continues. That is, as the client experiences more of the litigation process (e.g., a deposition) and as the reality of a trial looms larger on the horizon, the client will become more reasonable.[39]

A third approach, and one that seemed to be fairly common, is to invite the client to have another lawyer evaluate the case. In the case above, in which the client was hoping to buy a sailboat with the proceeds of his case, the lawyer suggested to the client that the client find out who the lawyers were who handled the cases of the client's friends who got supposedly $20,000 to $30,000 settlements for injuries similar to the client's. If one of those lawyers anticipated being able to get substantially more than what was on offer, then the first lawyer would agree to take a fee only on the amount of the offer on the table. One of my interviewees described a case he was then handling in which he had recommended accepting a settlement offer:

[The client] doesn't want to do it. I told her that given my investigation, including reports from eyewitnesses and from other people who were involved in the accident, the impact was so minor that I don't feel that a jury is going to [come up with] an award above and beyond what the insurance company is willing to offer, nor am I going to spend resources and time pursuing the case further. I told the client, "Please reconsider the offer that the insurance company has made. If you do not want to accept it, please find another attorney to represent you, and have that attorney contact me to work out a suitable arrangement."

Conclusion

Very, very few cases handled by contingency fee lawyers are ultimately resolved by adjudication. My estimate is that the figure is something less than 1 percent, taking into account cases that never even result in a filing with an adjudicatory body. Thus, the core work of most cases is preparing for settlement. In the minds of litigation-oriented lawyers, preparing for settlement and preparing for litigation may be essentially the same. For cases in which there is a major issue of liability, this may in fact be close to accurate. However, if issues of liability are not central, then the primary issue is documenting damages and otherwise justifying a demand.

There is a clear routine to the process of settlement. The lawyer prepares a letter or brochure documenting the claim. This may involve an explanation of a theory of liability if that is unclear, although liability is often at most a peripheral issue by the time a demand is advanced. The bulk of the demand letter or brochure documents that basis for damages. The letter or brochure's elaborateness will depend upon the combination of the size of the demand and the lawyer's style. Photographs of injuries, videotapes showing disabilities, and copies of medical records and medical bills are common elements of the presentation. Most often the negotiation is conducted by a combination of written communication and telephone conversation; I observed no case of in-person, face-to-face negotiation. While undoubtedly some negotiations take place in person, I suspect that such negotiation is most common in "courthouse-door" situations or during pretrial meetings with court officials; it *may* also happen in very high-volume practices where an adjuster is resolving batches of cases with the law firm at the same session—one interview respondent hinted at this happening in his firm.

While one might be tempted to attribute the dominance of settlement to the economic incentives of contingency fee practice, the reality is that settlement is the dominant mode of case resolution regardless of the manner by which the attorneys are paid (see, e.g., Sarat and Felstiner 1995, 191; Mather, McEwen, and Maiman 2001 on divorce; Genn 1988 on personal injury litigation in England, where at the time of her study contingency fees were not permitted; and Kritzer 1998a, 151–92, on labor grievance arbitration).[40] The costs and uncertainties are an issue for whoever must bear those costs and risks. The impact of contingency fees is not to be found in the frequency of settlement versus trial, but rather in the way attorneys approach the settlement process. As discussed in the previous chapter, and as explained theoretically by the portfolio perspective, contingency fee lawyers have a strong incentive for efficiency as a means of controlling the level of investment at risk in each case. The result is an emphasis on avoiding formalized litigation procedures when possible. The lawyer has an incentive to design internal processes that facilitate the settlement process. In contrast, the hourly fee lawyer has an incentive to design internal processes that emphasize the more time-consuming litigational procedures, leaving it to the client to find ways of counteracting these incentives. The check on the contingency fee lawyer comes from the incentives created by the long-term need to maintain a profitable portfolio of cases; these incentives dictate both delivering favorable outcomes for clients (to facilitate a flow of clients) and properly preparing cases (to get good offers from opposing parties). Both of these themes will be developed in detail in Chapter 7.

Appendix

While my survey did ask whether there was any recovery in the case, I did not include a specific question about the amount of any recovery. However, I did have information on the percentage fee that was specified in the retainer agreement and what the final percentage was if it differed from what was specified in the agreement. Using this information, I estimated the amount of the recovery. For virtually all cases, this estimate was in a reasonable range, and I used it for analyses requiring a figure for recovery amount.

One interesting anomaly was that 18 percent of the recoveries exceeded the lawyer's initial high-end estimate of the value of the case.[41] My first reaction to this was that it might indicate a problem with my estimate of the recovery. However, after reviewing my field notes, particularly from Steve Clarke's practice, I realized that cases did sometimes produce results that surprised the lawyer. I specifically asked Steve Clarke what percentage of the time the recovery in a case exceeded his initial estimate of the case's value. He replied,

Every three months I prepare a summary of my active cases with projections as to case values. When I complete a case, I enter the amount and compare it to my most recent estimate. In about 75 percent of cases, I have beaten my estimate. However, it is my practice to be very conservative on my estimates. In terms of comparing the final figure with what I would have realistically (not conservatively) estimated at the time of initial intake, I would guess that about 50 percent of the cases finish higher and 50 percent lower. I caution that at the time of intake I have little info and can't accurately predict how long the client will treat and how serious the injury will be. I tell clients that I don't have a crystal ball, and I really believe that. I can ballpark a range about 90 percent of the time, but in terms of the actual final figure, it's about 50 percent higher / lower.

CHAPTER 6

Cashing Out the Investment

Introduction

Thinking of contingency fee practice as a form of investment in a portfolio of risky cases leads directly to the important question, perhaps the *key* question, of what types of returns lawyers earn on their investments. To answer this question, this chapter focuses on the fees lawyers earn in relationship to the time they invest in their contingency fee cases.

Historically, contingency fee practice developed both to fill a gap in legal services and to fill a gap in legal demand. The ordinary working person could not afford to hire a lawyer on the traditional fee-for-service basis to assist in recovering damages from someone (or that someone's insurance company) who had caused them injury. The contingency fee made it possible for such people to obtain the legal assistance they needed (Bergstrom 1992, 88–94; Karsten 1998).

During the same period that contingency fees were becoming common, large numbers of immigrants and first-generation Americans sought to rise on the economic ladder by attending night law school and opening legal practices. The contingency fee opened a market for practitioners, many of whom were struggling to earn a living because they had great difficulty finding clients able to pay standard legal fees. In this era, the question for many, if not most, lawyers offering contingency fee services was to find work that would generate fees even if those fees were less than what might be the market hourly rate for services to clients able to pay standard fees (on such struggling practitioners circa the late 1950s, see Carlin 1962). The issue for these lawyers was not that of finding the most profitable form of legal practice but that of finding any kind of legal work that would generate any fee at all (Auerbach 1976, 44–52).

By the late twentieth century, the situation had changed significantly. The demand for legal services had expanded along with the booming postwar American economy. As documented in previous chapters, contingency fee work is the province of lawyers who seek out this work as a specialty or as a way of "beating their hourly rate." While there are still some lawyers who simply offer contingency fee representation as part of a struggling general practice, most lawyers who do such work do it with an eye to the bottom line. What does this bottom line look like?

Economists would argue that the economically rational lawyer would demand to do better, on average, from contingency fees than from hourly (or flat) fees because the contingency fee lawyer is providing additional services to the client which merit compensation (see, e.g., Posner 1977, 448–49; Schwartz and Mitchell 1970, 1153–54). However, this type of economic rationality presumes an opportunity cost analysis in which the contingency fee lawyer has alternative uses of his or her time that will provide a known level of compensation. A lawyer with unused time may be willing to accept cases in which the expected compensation is less than what the lawyer would like to believe is the value of the time involved (see Carlin 1962).

Measuring the Returns from Contingency Fee Practice

The central measure I will employ to assess the economic returns of contingency fee practice is the "effective hourly rate" (EHR), the fee received by the lawyer divided by the amount of time the lawyer had to expend to obtain that fee:

$$EHR = \frac{\textit{fee received}}{\textit{hours worked}}$$

This measure captures the various elements of the contingencies facing the lawyer. The numerator, the fee received, is a function of both the amount of damages and whether the lawyer obtains any recovery for the client. The denominator is the amount of the lawyer's time the case actually took. Across a number of similar cases, the variations in the numerators and denominators reflect the risks and uncertainties of those cases.

In addition to being a good way of measuring return on investment, effective hourly rate is a useful focus because it is precisely this that some critics of contingency fees have attacked, suggesting that lawyers are frequently able to obtain "effective hourly rates of thousands and even tens of thousands of dollars" (Brickman 1996a, 269; 1996b, 1345). While there are some cases that do earn lawyers fees that translate into rates of $1,000 or more per hour, we know little or nothing about the frequency of such cases, or *more importantly*, what more typical effective hourly rates look like.

One problem with the effective hourly rate measure is that it measures return at the level of the individual investment, not at the level of the overall portfolio. Short of a complete audit of a lawyer's cases over a period of time, there is no ready way to measure the overall performance, or "yield," on a portfolio. One might be tempted to view the mean effective hourly rate, or the median effective hourly rate, as a measure of portfolio performance, but even that is somewhat flawed. Using such a measure would presume that all cases should be treated equally. It is a bit like a stock investor with $25,000 to invest putting $1,000 into a penny stock and the remaining $24,000 into three stocks ($8,000 each). If the investor sells all of the stock a year later, receiving $5,000 for the penny stock and $9,000 for each of the mainstream stocks, the total received on the $24,000 investment is $32,000 for a yield of $8,000, or 33.3 percent of the original $24,000. However, the individual returns are 400 percent on the penny stock and 12.5 percent on each of the mainstream stocks. If one were to average these returns, the average would be 109.375 percent. Clearly this final figure makes little sense as an overall indicator of the yield from the portfolio.

While I do not have the data needed to look at the portfolio return for individual lawyers, I can obtain estimates of the yield from what I will label the "metaportfolio." By this I mean returns across sets of cases using information from sets of respondents. This would be something like taking all of the stocks listed on the New York Stock Exchange, the total dividends paid out by the companies for these shares (i.e., multiplying the dividend by number of shares for each company and adding these up), computing the total capitalization of each company's listed stock (the selling price times the number of shares and adding these up), and then dividing the total dividends by the total capitalization.

The same operation can be done for definable subsets of stocks (e.g., the thirty industrial companies in the Dow Jones Index, banks, technology companies, insurance companies, etc.) as a way of getting an average return for the subset.[1]

In the case of yields for contingency fee portfolios, I compute the metaportfolio returns by adding up the fees received across the sampled cases and adding up the hours worked across the cases. I then divide the resulting total fees by the total hours to produce a "mean hourly return" (MHR), which is a measure of the yield for the metaportfolio:

$$MHR = \frac{\Sigma\, fees}{\Sigma\, hours}$$

As with the stock example, this procedure can be applied to metaportfolios defined along various dimensions (e.g., unfiled cases, filed cases, tried cases, auto accident cases, etc.). The advantage of the mean hourly return measure is that a very high return for a relatively small case will not dominate the calculation, because the computation is effectively weighted to reflect the sizes of the cases included in the portfolio.

Before turning to my data, let me first briefly describe what we can discern from earlier studies that permit the computation of effective hourly rates and mean hourly returns.

Previous Effective Hourly Rate Studies

There is surprisingly little prior research on the kinds of fees and incomes lawyers earn from contingency fee work. Some of the most successful practitioners make no effort to hide their financial success, but these lawyers, persons like John Jamail or John O'Quinn, are not typical contingency fee practitioners. And publications targeted at the profession often trumpet the names of the members of the profession with the highest incomes, usually contingency fee practitioners (McMenamin 1995). I could find only two published studies predating the data collected for this study that provide systematic information on effective hourly rates earned from contingency fee cases.

The first study is from the early 1970s and considers only medical malpractice cases (Dietz, Baird, and Berul 1973, 113–16). This study, based on a survey of 671 lawyers, reported mean effective hourly rates for plaintiffs' lawyers somewhere in the range $61 to $84;[2] this range primarily reflects uncertainty about and the treatment of cocounsel or referral fees. The authors of the study compared these figures to the mean hourly rate charged by medical malpractice defense lawyers at the time of their survey, $47, and concluded that the "'effective hourly fee' is not excessively large . . . [and that] plaintiff and defense fees are in the same general ballpark" (p. 116). It is worth noting that the use of mean hourly rates here would have tended to skew the figures upward; more typically one finds information on median rates.[3]

The second published study on effective hourly rates is from the Civil Litigation Research Project (CLRP), a large federally financed study conducted around 1980. This study focused on a sample of federal and state cases selected from courts in five federal judicial districts around the country: eastern Pennsylvania (Philadelphia), central California (Los Angeles), South Carolina, New Mexico, and eastern Wisconsin (Milwaukee). The analysis of effective hourly rates from this study is reported in my book based on the CLRP data, *The Justice Broker* (Kritzer 1990, 137–41).[4] The overall median effective hourly rate for contingency fee lawyers is $43 (the mean is $89), the first quartile is $6 (i.e., in 25 percent of the cases, contingency fee lawyers earn $6 per hour or less), the third quartile is $98 (25 percent of the lawyers earn $98 or more), and the ninetieth percentile is $200 (the maximum is $2,500).[5] These figures show that very large effective hourly rates are possible, but typical effective hourly rates are not extreme.[6] For comparison, the median hourly rate reported by hourly fee lawyers in the same study was $50 (Kritzer 1990, 138; see also, Kritzer, Sarat, et al. 1984).

The information on effective hourly rates from the CLRP study is quite rich, albeit quite dated. Table 6.1 shows information broken down a variety of ways. Two items are particularly interesting. Effective hourly rates tend to go down for small cases (under $10,000) with a median of $38, rising to $62 for cases in the $10,000–$50,000 range but dropping off slightly to $58 for cases over $50,000. Also, it appears that contingency fees in cases other than contracts and torts are very risky; in noncontract, nontort cases, the median is only $7 (38 percent of the cases yield no fee at all).

When I look at the mean hourly return (defined above), I obtain a figure of $47 across all of the contingency fee cases in the sample. Looking only at tort cases, the mean hourly return is $52, compared to $45 for contract cases, and $23 for cases involving neither tort nor contract.

TABLE 6.1

Effective Hourly Rate Estimates, Circa 1980

	Mean ($)	Median ($)	First Quartile ($)	Third Quartile ($)	90th Percentile ($)	Maximum ($)	Mean Hourly Rate ($)	N
All cases	89	43	6	98	200	2,500	47	343
By stakes								
< $10,000	59	38	12	70	155	590	29	127
$10,000–$50,000	96	62	9	114	237	614	49	118
> $50,000	203	58	6	189	332	2,167	73	29
By court								
Federal	91	40	0	99	201	2,167	51	161
State	88	45	16	99	200	2,500	40	182
By area of law								
Torts								
All	92	49	15	101	216	2,167	52	232
Federal	113	56	0	102	272	2,167	61	90
State	79	45	19	100	200	590	39	142
Contracts								
All	118	47	19	117	206	2,500	45	71
Federal	101	56	27	138	224	614	44	35
State	135	45	4	94	223	2,500	47	36
Neither torts nor contracts								
All	29	7	0	45	75	255	23	50
Federal	28	5	0	45	82	255	23	40
State	30	25	—[a]	—	—	65	20	10

SOURCE: Civil Litigation Research Project data.

Most of these figures are from table 9-2 in my earlier book *The Justice Broker: Lawyers and Ordinary Litigation* (New York: Oxford University Press, 1990), p. 139. I have added means and maximums to the information given in the book.

[a] Number of cases insufficient for meaningful statistic.

Taking only cases under $10,000, which constitute almost half of the sample, the mean hourly return is only $22, rising to $49 for cases in the $10,000 to $50,000 range and $73 for cases over $50,000.[7] Table 6.1 also shows breakdowns for state and federal cases and breakdowns by area of law, controlling for venue; it is useful to keep in mind that most cases are actually in the state courts and that the mean hourly rate for most of the state subsets shown in the table are on the order of $40 per hour.

These two existing studies do not show a large proportion of contingency fee cases yielding extremely high hourly returns for lawyers.[8] The CLRP data show that occasional high hourly returns do occur in individual cases. The situation may have changed in the twenty to thirty years since these studies were completed. It may also be that the frequent high hourly rates come not in cases that get filed in court (all of the cases in the CLRP study were filed in court, as probably were most or all of the cases in the medical malpractice study), but in those that are settled quickly before formal litigation begins.

Returns on Contingency Fee Cases

My primary source for estimating effective hourly rates and mean hourly returns is my survey of Wisconsin contingency fee practitioners. I supplement this analysis using data collected by the RAND Corporation for its evaluation of the Civil Justice Reform Act (I describe this data in more detail below). The RAND data provide a check to see whether the patterns in Wisconsin stand out as particularly high or low. From both the Wisconsin and the RAND data sets, I have core information for random samples of cases on the number of hours lawyers spent on the case and the amount of the fee that they received.[9]

Establishing an Appropriate Basis for Comparison and Other Estimation Issues

Understanding and assessing the returns lawyers earn for contingency fee work requires some base for comparison. There are many possible comparisons that one could make. For example, what types of effective hourly rates do various types of physicians earn? About the time of the data collection, I had a minor dermatological procedure carried out. The fee came to $195 for ten to fifteen minutes of the physician's time (and the clinic billed another $112 for the use of its facilities); the hourly rate, then, was something between $800 and $1,200. More recently, one of my adult children had a three-hour surgical procedure for which the surgeon billed over $12,000, or more than $4,000 per hour.

Alternatively, one might compare to the effective hourly rate charged by a good automotive service operation. The stated hourly rate for the mechanic might be $45 (as of 2002); however, the actual amounts charged are usually based on the "book time," and a good mechanic can beat the book time by 25 to 50 percent; to that, one needs to add the markup on the parts that the shop sells to its customers. Alogether, a good auto mechanic shop might generate $75 to $100 per mechanic hour including the markup on replacement parts.

Another potential comparison is to the hourly rates charged by lawyers with similar training and experience. An examination of the hourly rates reported by insurance defense lawyers in the economic surveys of state bars during the mid-1990s showed that these rates tended to be in the $80 to $100 per hour range. If anything, this is probably a low-end estimate of comparable hourly rates because insurance companies have sufficient purchasing power that they are able to keep the hourly rates paid to outside counsel at the low end of market rates. In a sense, the insurance companies are able to buy outside legal services wholesale and pay wholesale rather than retail rates (see Silver 1998).[10]

Probably the best comparison would be to the hourly rates actually charged by the lawyers who responded to my survey and the lawyers in the RAND survey who were billing by the hour. As it turns out, most of the lawyers responding to the Wisconsin survey (85 percent) had done at least some work on an hourly basis during the previous year. In that survey, I asked them what was the hourly rate quoted for the most recent matter they accepted on an hourly basis. A total of 389 lawyers provided information on that hourly rate; the median hourly rate was $125 per hour, and the mean was $124.

The RAND data set includes substantial information from lawyers who were working on an hourly fee basis. These lawyers were asked to report the hourly rate they were charging for the sampled case;[11] 42 percent and 43 percent of the respondents provided that information for the 1991 and 1992–93 surveys respectively. Based on a frequency distribution published by RAND (Kakalik et al. 1996, 283), I estimate the mean hourly rates for the two sets of cases (1991 and 1992–93) as $136 and $144; the corresponding estimated medians are $125 and $133.[12] Taking my data together with the RAND data, an hourly rate figure in the range of $125 to $140 provides a useful baseline for comparison in the discussion that follows.

In making comparisons between the contingency fee lawyers' fees and the rates charged by lawyers billing on an hourly basis, it is necessary to be careful to exclude from the fees obtained by contingency fee lawyers components that hourly fee lawyers would typically bill separately. Under both fee arrangements expenses such as copying, travel, witness fees, and filing fees are normally handled as separate billable expenses. In contrast, while most hourly fee lawyers also bill separately for paralegal time, this is an expense absorbed within the typical contingency fee. Consequently, to estimate the effective hourly rate of contingency fee lawyers, it is necessary to deduct from the gross fee the equivalent of what would be charged for any paralegal time devoted to the case.

A second issue is that many lawyers do not maintain time records for their work on contingency fee cases. Interestingly, the majority of the lawyers who responded to my survey reported that they did keep time records, but only about a quarter of the respondents actually consulted those records. Even if all of the lawyers did keep time records and did consult those records, my observations of the lawyers at work (two of whom did keep time records) made clear that the nature of contingency fee practice (i.e., constant shifting from one case to another) often makes tracking time at best an effort at approximation. This same problem may apply to many hourly fee lawyers as well. The result is that it is typically necessary to rely upon estimates; this means that a specific figure for an individual case might involve some significant error, but if the errors are essentially random, they will cancel out across a set of cases. Below I will present a supplemental analysis of returns for cases for which lawyers had kept and consulted time records; the results from that analysis indicate that the absence of time record information is probably not significantly distorting my summary results.

Contingency Fee Returns in Wisconsin

How do Wisconsin contingency fee lawyers do in terms of the effective hourly rates they earn from contingency fee legal practice? I was able to compute an effective hourly rate for 878 cases. About 4 percent of these exceeded $1,000, and 1 percent exceeded $2,000; in three of the cases, the rate exceeded $3,000, with the highest single rate at $4,473. In contrast, in about 11 percent of the cases the effective hourly rate was negative or zero. In one case, the lawyer had an effective hourly rate of −$2,617, and in another case the rate was −$1,225; these negative figures arise because of the costs of paralegal time spent on the case. A final indicator of the extreme variability is that the standard deviation for effective hourly rate is extremely high, 430, reflecting the fact that the distribution in effective hourly rates is highly skewed toward a small number of very large figures.

One problem with the figures above is that they do not adjust for the characteristics of my sample, whereby cases handled by high-volume lawyers are underrepresented, cases handled by general practitioners are underrepresented, and cases going to trial are overrepresented. If I weight my sample to approximate the population of cases in Wisconsin, the figures shift somewhat with just under 8 percent exceeding $1,000 and about 2 percent exceeding $2,000. Only about 7 percent were zero or negative. With the weighting, the variability of effective hourly rates is even greater, with a standard deviation of 631.

The variability, and the potential for "jackpots," is not surprising. That is, in one sense, the essence of the contingency fee. However, how do lawyers do in the "typical" case? How we define *typical* becomes important. The presence of a small number of very high hourly rates leads to the result that we will see very different things depending on whether we look at the median (the middle case) or the arithmetic mean (the common average). In fact, as I will argue below, the gap between the median and the mean reflects the risky nature of contingency fee practice. If I simply take all of the cases in my sample, without considering the lawyers' caseloads or the way I designed the sample (i.e., oversampling cases that went to trial, undersampling general practitioners), the median effective hourly rate is $132, which is almost the same as the mean / median hourly rate that these same lawyers report charging for their hourly fee work. Thus, in about half the cases in my sample, lawyers did better than the median hourly rate for hourly fee work, and in about half the cases they did worse.

If this were the end of the story, an economist would probably conclude that contingency fee lawyers were not pursuing an economically rational course of action, given that the economist expects the contingency fee lawyer to extract higher fees to reflect the risks the lawyer bears and the financing services the lawyer provides. These higher fees appear in the mean effective hourly rate, which is considerably higher: $242, which corresponds to the seventy-second percentile. That is, in the typical case, the contingency fee lawyer may not do better than the median hourly rate, but across a set of cases, the lawyer will do better. As an illustration of this, recall the lawyer I interviewed who had a very high-volume practice (mentioned in previous chapters) who told me that 60 to 70 percent of his gross fees came from perhaps a dozen of the cases he closes each year. Eliminating the top 10 percent of the cases from the sample leaves a mean effective hourly rate for the remaining 90 percent at $136, which is virtually the same as the overall median.[13]

Again, I need to refine the picture by looking at what happens after adjusting the results to take into account the sample structure. With the appropriate weighting, the median rises to $167, and the mean goes up to $345, reflecting the fact that it is the upper tail that is pushing the mean up. Eliminating the top 10 percent of cases reduces the weighted mean effective hourly rate to $181.

What type of overall picture emerges focusing on the "mean hourly return" (estimated by adding up all of the hours reported on the cases in the sample and all of the fees received, adjusted for the costs of paralegal time, and dividing these two figures)? The result, unadjusted for the sampling structure, is $169. As with the mean effective hourly rate, this estimate is greatly influenced by relatively small numbers of extremely profitable cases. Dropping the 10 percent most profitable cases from the sample leaves a 10 percent trimmed samplewide mean hourly return of $104; dropping only the top 5 percent most profitable cases, the mean hourly return is $137, virtually identical to the median. This pattern reemphasizes the role of a relatively small portion of cases as generating the "profits" across a portfolio of contingency fee cases. Again, the pattern is somewhat different if we rely on the weighted data. The untrimmed mean hourly return is $187, and the 10 percent trimmed samplewide mean hourly return is $147.

Variations in Effective Hourly Rates

One would expect the returns lawyers earn from contingency fee work to vary systematically based on either case or lawyer factors. Table 6.2 shows a variety of summary statistics for both measures of return (effective hourly rate and mean hourly return) broken down by the following variables: nature of disposition, amount at stake, area of law, gender of lawyer, lawyer's advertising practices, type of firm, lawyer's position, lawyer's years of experience, community population, nature of lawyer's practice, lawyer's income from the practice of law, and lawyer's caseload. Table 6.2a shows summary statistics without applying weighting to adjust for the sample structure, and Table 6.2b shows the statistics applying weights. Both weighted and unweighted results are shown because of the complexity of the weighting problem.[14] As with the overall measures, the weighted versions of most the measures are higher for the weighted results than for the unweighted results.

These tables are dense with information. In addition to the standard summary measures of mean and median, they show the mean hourly return and trimmed figures for mean effective hourly rate and mean hourly return. To give an indication of variability, they show several additional positional measures—the first and third quartiles (the twenty-fifth and seventy-fifth percentiles), and the ninetieth percentile, plus a statistic called the midspread, which is the difference between the third and first quartiles.[15] In the following discussion, I will not attempt to explicate in detail everything that the tables show. Rather, I will focus on broad patterns.

Some general patterns shown in the tables reflect the skew involved in a small number of highly profitable cases. This shows up in the much higher figures for the overall mean effective hourly rate compared to both the median effective hourly rate and the mean hourly return. It also shows up by the very sharp drop in the mean effective hourly rate and the mean hourly return when I trim the 10 percent of cases with the highest effective hourly rates.[16] For example, looking at cases involving less than $20,000, the unweighted mean effective hourly rate is $163 (weighted mean $244[17]) compared to a median of $109 ($138) and a mean hourly return of $104 ($139). Applying a 10 percent trim to the data, the mean effective hourly rate drops to $127 ($171) and the mean hourly return drops to $95 ($125). Note that the impact of "trimming" for this category of cases is relatively minor because relatively few cases get trimmed out. In contrast, if one looks at the cases involving more than $50,000, the impacts are dramatic. The mean effectively hourly rate is $392 ($739), and the mean hourly return is $199 ($261); trimming the top 10 percent leaves a mean of $136 ($196) and a mean hourly return of $108 ($162).

Given this skew, it is not surprising that the returns from contingency fee work, on a case-by-case basis, are highly variable. For the overall data, the midspread is $208 ($272). The role of skew in the midspread can be seen in the fact that the distance between the median and the third quartile is about double that between the median and the first quartile. Generally, the variability is higher with the weighted data than with the unweighted data; the average midspread shown for the

TABLE 6.2a Effective Hourly Rate Estimates, Wisconsin Data (unweighted)

	Mean EHR[a] ($)	Median EHR ($)	First Quartile EHR ($)	Third Quartile EHR ($)	EHR Mid-spread ($)	90th Percentile EHR ($)	Mean Hourly Return ($)	10% Trimmed Mean EHR ($)	10% Trimmed Mean Hourly Return ($)	N
All cases	242	132	61	269	208	552	169	137	104	878
By disposition										
Unfiled	286	166	78	333	255	600	186	163	127	304
Filed, not tried	251	144	73	383	310	549	220	153	127	343
Tried	170	89	12	181	169	363	134	81	85	231
By stakes										
< $20,000	163	109	59	193	134	378	104	127	95	348
$20,000 – $50,000	214	148	72	273	201	465	119	153	96	264
> $50,000	392	200	54	390	336	1,188	199	136	108	237
By area of law										
Auto accident	286	163	84	310	226	624	161	161	120	525
Medical malpractice	314	36	-25	368	393	1,185	316	60	134	39
Other personal injury	190	122	33	255	222	413	149	120	86	152
Workers' comp / social security	124	100	38	186	148	325	103	116	103	60
Contracts	127	64	21	170	149	410	92	103	90	33
Other	169	100	26	191	165	382	128	111	60	87

	Mean EHR[a] ($)	Median EHR ($)	First Quartile EHR ($)	Third Quartile EHR ($)	EHR Mid-spread ($)	90th Percentile EHR ($)	Mean Hourly Return ($)	10% Trimmed Mean EHR ($)	10% Trimmed Mean Hourly Return ($)	N
Gender of lawyer										
Male	252	135	63	276	213	560	184	141	115	756
Female	208	100	56	239	183	424	122	132	70	105
Lawyer's advertising practices										
Uses media or direct mail	326	182	76	272	196	683	243	157	128	185
Does not use media	220	122	60	243	183	457	158	133	102	685
Type of firm										
Plaintiffs' personal injury firm	293	153	63	333	270	723	248	141	103	336
Other type of firm	215	122	60	239	179	429	126	135	102	493
Lawyer's position										
Partner in firm	275	140	66	280	214	594	205	146	120	580
Solo practitioner	164	116	50	213	163	383	114	128	97	123
Associate or firm employee	181	105	52	255	203	533	102	106	67	163

(continued)

[a] EHR = effective hourly rate.

TABLE 6.2a (continued)

	Mean EHR[a] ($)	Median EHR ($)	First Quartile EHR ($)	Third Quartile EHR ($)	EHR Mid-spread ($)	90th Percentile EHR ($)	Mean Hourly Return ($)	10% Trimmed Mean EHR ($)	10% Trimmed Mean Hourly Return ($)	N
Years of experience										
5 or less	163	88	36	228	192	491	141	102	59	79
6 – 10	216	104	58	238	180	390	119	129	105	748
11 – 20	213	135	64	268	204	460	123	141	97	349
> 20	310	156	63	326	263	792	279	147	130	300
Community population										
Milwaukee area	246	137	58	281	223	552	255	146	121	278
Other community over 100,000	245	114	64	262	198	568	118	137	95	170
100,000 – 50,000	230	125	64	228	164	460	128	139	108	199
Under 50,000	244	148	60	291	231	625	148	125	96	221
Lawyer's practice area										
Personal injury plaintiffs	309	157	63	334	271	734	212	144	112	368
Other litigation	208	118	62	242	180	451	129	138	91	273
General practice	179	118	60	194	134	327	110	122	92	166
Other type of practice	140	114	78	154	76	298	101	115	96	37

	Mean EHR[a] ($)	Median EHR ($)	First Quartile EHR ($)	Third Quartile EHR ($)	EHR Mid-spread ($)	90th Percentile EHR ($)	Mean Hourly Return ($)	10% Trimmed Mean EHR ($)	10% Trimmed Mean Hourly Return ($)	N
Lawyer's income										
<$50,000	130	75	26	164	138	360	115	91	64	109
$50,000 – $74,999	171	107	59	213	154	375	88	134	74	172
$75,000 – $99,999	193	118	54	208	154	414	152	134	125	185
$100,000 – $199,999	312	153	74	306	232	531	134	142	90	229
$200,000 or more	405	215	106	426	320	932	360	189	161	127
Caseload										
1 – 5	186	113	59	200	141	402	108	126	80	175
6 – 10	206	112	55	206	151	410	185	127	79	173
11 – 25	198	140	62	252	190	387	157	139	133	181
26 – 100	286	155	64	329	265	657	212	147	126	274
> 100	397	155	58	455	397	1,078	294	145	142	75

[a] EHR = effective hourly rate.

TABLE 6.2b Effective Hourly Rate Estimates, Wisconsin Data (weighted)

	Mean EHR[a] ($)	Median EHR ($)	First Quartile EHR ($)	Third Quartile EHR ($)	EHR Mid-spread ($)	90th Percentile EHR ($)	Mean Hourly Return ($)	10% Trimmed Mean EHR ($)	10% Trimmed Mean Hourly Return ($)	Weighted N
All cases	365	167	84	356	272	728	207	184	147	852
By disposition										
Unfiled	387	180	80	356	276	600	189	174	130	287
Filed, not tried	296	155	86	387	301	549	239	176	149	335
Tried	148	104	41	167	126	363	113	98	82	224
By stakes										
<$20,000	244	138	76	303	227	462	139	171	125	433
$20,000 – $50,000	230	175	85	295	210	432	150	187	133	208
>$50,000	739	285	103	922	819	2,026	261	196	162	177
By area of law										
Auto accident	417	200	102	375	273	1,004	221	204	155	553
Medical malpractice	132	-12	-19	154	173	616	260	76	156	31
Other personal injury	281	160	58	381	323	705	216	174	166	135
Workers' comp / social security	133	103	63	210	147	353	110	133	110	49
Contracts	188	64	42	417	375	417	96	186	95	48
Other	185	155	94	208	114	478	102	138	96	46

	Mean EHR[a] ($)	Median EHR ($)	First Quartile EHR ($)	Third Quartile EHR ($)	EHR Mid-spread ($)	90th Percentile EHR ($)	Mean Hourly Return ($)	10% Trimmed Mean EHR ($)	10% Trimmed Mean Hourly Return ($)	Weighted N
Gender of lawyer										
Male	378	160	84	334	250	791	226	181	155	722
Female	317	203	104	394	290	728	132	201	121	87
Lawyer's advertising practices										
Uses media or direct mail	513	182	124	423	299	1,611	284	218	201	265
Does not use media	269	165	70	314	244	645	184	170	137	583
Type of firm										
Plaintiffs' personal injury firm	446	192	109	394	285	1,200	277	201	167	433
Other type of firm	251	155	65	303	238	428	156	171	136	377
Lawyer's position										
Partner in firm	395	171	100	314	214	987	226	179	158	568
Solo practitioner	188	118	42	334	292	417	129	175	109	129
Associate or firm employee	290	192	77	400	323	757	168	205	119	149

(continued)

[a] EHR = effective hourly rate.

TABLE 6.2b *(continued)*

	Mean EHR[a] ($)	Median EHR ($)	First Quartile EHR ($)	Third Quartile EHR ($)	EHR Mid-spread ($)	90th Percentile EHR ($)	Mean Hourly Return ($)	10% Trimmed Mean EHR ($)	10% Trimmed Mean Hourly Return ($)	Weighted N
Years of experience										
5 or less	201	195	81	297	216	491	106	194	104	63
6 – 10	672	189	77	668	591	1,250	253	178	160	139
11 – 20	230	153	84	303	219	417	162	179	136	341
> 20	356	181	85	394	309	1,008	273	190	169	309
Community popula-tion										
Milwaukee area	291	168	91	327	236	652	234	202	164	283
Other community over 100,000	230	154	62	313	251	420	153	174	123	173
100,000 – 50,000	559	194	100	394	294	1,275	242	186	160	185
Under 50,000	324	167	69	400	331	1,076	199	163	141	207
Lawyer's practice area										
Personal injury plain-tiffs	309	202	109	394	285	1,157	263	212	195	515
Other litigation	208	155	63	370	307	800	143	201	129	134
General practice	179	149	64	275	211	417	134	161	111	66
Other type of practice	140	128	86	155	69	155	84	120	84	38

	Mean EHR[a] ($)	Median EHR ($)	First Quartile EHR ($)	Third Quartile EHR ($)	EHR Mid-spread ($)	90th Percentile EHR ($)	Mean Hourly Return ($)	10% Trimmed Mean EHR ($)	10% Trimmed Mean Hourly Return ($)	Weighted N
Lawyer's income										
< $50,000	236	131	34	241	207	827	93	114	84	60
$50,000 – $74,999	215	188	88	303	215	482	170	197	159	160
$75,000 – $99,999	252	132	64	383	319	677	157	173	121	161
$100,000 – $199,999	480	155	76	357	281	1,275	195	176	121	246
$200,000 or more	424	232	138	394	256	1,289	370	229	250	183
Caseload										
1 – 5	149	100	40	180	140	327	106	109	84	186
6 – 10	204	128	61	205	144	377	129	131	77	213
11 – 25	197	115	67	216	149	385	146	102	122	205
26 – 100	269	175	64	314	250	590	203	137	119	146
> 100	366	164	56	420	364	994	293	104	75	32

[a] EHR = effective hourly rate.

unweighted data is $209 compared to $266 for the weighted data (the respective medians of the midspreads are $197 and $262).

Let me now turn to some of the specific variations shown in Tables 6.2a and 6.2b.

Disposition: Returns tend to be lowest for cases that go to trial. This is not surprising given that cases that go to trial take more time on the part of the lawyer and are more likely to produce a zero return. The pattern between unfiled and filed-untried cases is less clear. Overall, unfiled cases seem to produce a slightly better return, but this is not true when the 10 percent trimmed statistics are examined.

Stakes: Overall returns tend to improve as stakes go up, and this is true regardless of whether one looks at the mean effective hourly rate, the median effective hourly rate, or the mean hourly return. However, this is clearly a function of the results from the highest-return cases; the 10 percent trimmed statistics show less variation based on stakes.

Area of law: There is a lot of inconsistency in the patterns when controlling for area of law. There is some indication that returns for tort cases are higher than for nontort cases. Perhaps of most interest is medical malpractice, where the mean actually goes down with the weighted data; this may reflect the relatively small number of medical malpractice cases in the data set, but it may also be reflective of the higher level of uncertainty in these cases and the higher costs that arise owing to the need for expensive experts.[18] Leaving aside medical malpractice, auto injury cases appear to produce the best typical returns.

Type of practice: Personal injury plaintiffs specialists tend to do somewhat better than other lawyers. This probably reflects a combination of expertise and efficiencies that these lawyers are able to obtain.

Type of law firm: Consistent with type of practice, lawyers in firms specializing in personal injury plaintiffs' work produce higher returns. It may also be the case that lawyers in specialized personal injury firms get better cases.

Advertising practices: Lawyers in firms that employ media or direct mail advertising produce higher returns. This reflects, at least in part, that those employing this type of advertising tend to be in firms that specialize in personal injury work.

Community population size: There is no clear relationship between typical returns and the kind of community where the law firm is based.

Lawyer's position in the firm: Somewhat different patterns appear depending on whether one looks at the weighted or unweighted data. With the unweighted data, the ordering of returns consistently puts partners first, then solo practitioners, and finally nonpartners in firms (associates and employees). With the weighted data, the ordering of solo practitioners and nonpartners reverses.

Years of experience: Looking at the unweighted data, there is a consistent pattern that more experienced lawyers produce better returns. However, with the weighted data, the pattern is more ambiguous.

Lawyer's caseload: Looking at the overall results, higher caseloads are associated with better returns. However, looking at the 10 percent trimmed results, the pattern is less clear. Undoubtedly this reflects that those with larger caseloads are more likely to get some of the highly profitable cases.

Lawyer's income: Not surprisingly, lawyers with higher incomes produce higher returns; perhaps it would be better to say that those lawyers who produce higher returns have higher incomes.

Lawyer's gender: The evidence on the impact of gender is ambiguous. Looking at the unweighted data, males appear to produce higher returns than females; however, looking at the weighted data, the pattern is reversed.

The patterns described above are somewhat inconsistent, and some of the apparent differences may reflect confounding between variables rather than effects of the specific variables (i.e., the apparent effect of position in the law firm may reflect the characteristics of cases that are assigned to nonpartners). To sort out which variables are and are not related to the lawyer's return, I turned to multivariate methods. One advantage of this method is that it helps avoid some of the problems arising from the sample design; including as predictors the variables along which the sample was stratified (i.e., caseload, type of practice, how cases terminated) eliminates the need to weight the data to reflect these variables.

However, applying multivariate estimation techniques to these data raises some problems that necessitate doing something more than standard multiple regression. The first problem is that the dependent variable, effective hourly rate, is highly skewed, and this gives undue influence to observations with very high effective hourly rates.[19] A standard solution for this type of skew is to apply a logarithmic transformation to the dependent variable before estimating the regression equation.[20] Applying a logarithmic transformation produces a second problem: in about 10 percent of the observations, the effective hourly rate is zero or negative, and one cannot take logarithms of negative numbers or zero. To solve this problem, I employ an estimation technique that essentially estimates two equations simultaneously; one equation is a probit model for whether an effective hourly rate greater than zero is observed (the "selection" equation), and the second is a normal regression equation predicting the log of the effective hourly rate for those cases where the effective hourly rate is greater than zero (the "rate" equation).[21] As predictor variables, I use all of the variables shown in Table 6.2 except community population. I set up all predictors as one or more dummy variables because I have no reason to assume that the impact of variables such as years of experience or caseload would be neatly linear. I use the same predictors for both of the equations in the statistical model.

The results of this analysis are shown in Tables 6.3 and 6.4. Table 6.3 presents the estimates of the coefficients for the two equations. What is most relevant in this table are the variables that do and do not show significant relationships with the two equations predicting effective hourly rates. Those that show no significant relationships include type of firm, lawyer's position in firm, lawyer's practice area, and lawyer's years of experience. Several variables show ambiguous or possibly weak relationships:

> *Gender*: No relationship with the rate itself, but possibly a relationship with whether a positive return is obtained (men slightly less likely to obtain a positive return than women)
>
> *Advertising practice*: No relationship with the rate itself, but a weak relationship with whether a positive return is obtained (users of media advertising less likely to obtain a positive return)
>
> *Caseload*: Some indication that the effective hourly rate itself may decrease as caseload decreases

There are clear relationships with the following:

> *Disposition*: Higher rates for unfiled cases; higher likelihood of positive return for cases not tried
>
> *Stakes*: Effective hourly rate increases with stakes, but likelihood of a positive return is not related to stakes
>
> *Area of law*: Effective hourly rate higher for personal injury cases, particularly for medical malpractice cases; likelihood of a positive return higher for auto accident cases, but lower for other personal injury cases, particularly medical malpractice cases
>
> *Income*: Effective hourly rate and likelihood of a positive return both increase as income increases.[22]

In Table 6.4 I present results that try to put these effects into clearer perspective. Combining the results for the selection and rate equations, I obtained estimates of the change in the effective hourly rate associated with each of the variables, controlling for the other variables. Because both the selection and rate equations use transformed variables (the "probit" for the selection equation and the natural logarithm for the rate equation), these effects vary depending upon what values one selects as the base. The results shown in Table 6.4 employ a constant base for each equation: the probit transformation of the unweighted proportion (.901) of cases that produced positive, nonzero effective hourly rates and the mean of the natural logarithm of the effective hourly rate for the cases with a positive nonzero effective hourly rate.[23] The value of interest in the table is in the column labeled "impact." This is the estimate of how much the effective hourly rate will change for a case that was otherwise average in terms of the likelihood of producing a positive return and average in terms of what that return would be. For example, compared to a tried case, an untried case would produce an average effective hourly rate $93 higher; a case involving less than $20,000 would produce an average effective hourly $76 lower. A particular interesting example is medical malpractice, which has an increased average effective hourly rate only $23 higher than the "other" category and $26 lower than auto accident cases; however, this reflects a combination of a low "win" rate and a high effective hourly rate for those cases that are successful ($151 higher than "other" cases and $114 higher than auto accident cases).

The Record-Keeping Issue.   One of the possible problems with the estimates above is that, even though many of the attorneys in the sample did keep time records, only a small fraction of those who had such records referred to their records in responding to the survey. One might expect that attorneys overestimate their time, either remembering it incorrectly or responding strategically in order to make their per-hour return look more acceptable.

When I was first thinking about doing the current study, I had the impression that virtually no lawyers working on a contingency fee basis maintained time records. In conversations with several local attorneys, I became aware that there were at least some lawyers who did keep track of their time while doing work on a contingency fee basis. Drawing upon a list of attorneys who were likely to be in practices where this was true (provided to me by several local persons knowledgeable about various practices), I conducted a nonscientific survey in which I asked these attorneys to provide me with information on contingency fee cases closed over a recent time period.[24] These lawyers provided me with information on a total of ninety-two cases, with gross fees received ranging from $0 to $910,000 and lawyer effort ranging from 3 hours to 7,000 hours.[25] Dividing net fee by lawyer hours

TABLE 6.3 Multivariate Analysis of Effective Hourly Rates

	Rate Equation				"Selection" Equation			
	b	se / df	z / Wald	p-value	b	se / df	z / Wald	p-value
By disposition		2	14.87	0.001		2	32.30	<0.001
Unfiled	0.428	0.120	3.57	<0.001	0.619	0.193	3.21	0.001
Filed, not tried	0.168	0.123	1.37	0.170	1.264	0.215	5.89	<0.001
Tried	base				base			
By stakes		2	54.51	<0.001		2	0.79	0.680
<$20,000	-0.782	0.106	-7.38	<0.001	0.101	0.218	0.46	0.643
$20,000 – $50,000	-0.481	0.108	-4.46	<0.001	-0.076	0.225	-0.34	0.734
>$50,000	base				base			
By area of law		5	12.08	0.034		5	52.99	<0.001
Auto accident	0.213	0.153	1.39	0.165	0.734	0.268	2.74	0.006
Medical malpractice	0.673	0.283	2.38	0.017	-1.198	0.353	-3.39	0.001
Other personal injury	0.204	0.170	1.21	0.228	-0.469	0.268	-1.75	0.080
Workers' comp / social security	-0.183	0.220	-0.83	0.405	0.506	0.381	1.33	0.184
Contracts	-0.132	0.256	-0.52	0.606	-0.451	0.359	-1.26	0.209
Other	base				base			
Gender of lawyer								
Male	0.160	0.127	1.26	0.207	-0.471	0.264	-1.79	0.074
Female	base				base			

	Rate Equation				"Selection" Equation			
	b	se / df	z / Wald	p-value	b	se / df	z / Wald	p-value
Advertising practices								
Uses media or direct mail	0.191	0.118	1.62	0.105	-0.427	0.225	-1.90	0.058
Does not use media	base				base			
Type of firm								
Plaintiffs' personal injury	-0.033	0.109	-0.31	0.758	0.030	0.211	0.14	0.888
Other type of firm	base				base			
Lawyer's position		2	0.53	0.768		2	0.45	0.797
Partner in firm	-0.069	0.122	-0.57	0.569	0.071	0.234	0.30	0.762
Solo practitioner	-0.118	0.172	-0.68	0.495	0.245	0.364	0.67	0.500
Associate or employee	base				base			
Years of experience		3	4.62	0.202		3	2.22	0.528
5 or less	0.063	0.188	0.34	0.736	-0.122	0.350	-0.35	0.727
6 – 10	-0.146	0.131	-1.11	0.265	0.302	0.271	0.52	0.605
11 – 20	-0.174	0.096	-1.81	0.070	0.102	0.196	1.12	0.264
> 20	base				base			
Lawyer's practice area		3	2.11	0.550		3	1.50	0.683
Personal injury plaintiffs	-0.162	0.214	-0.76	0.449	0.218	0.420	0.52	0.604
Other litigation	-0.102	0.207	-0.49	0.623	0.013	0.392	0.03	0.974
General practice	-0.247	0.217	-1.14	0.255	-0.124	0.422	-0.30	0.768
Other type of practice	base				base			

(continued)

TABLE 6.3 (*continued*)

	Rate Equation				"Selection" Equation			
	b	se / df	z / Wald	p-value	b	se / df	z / Wald	p-value
Lawyer's income		4	13.65	0.009		4	10.96	0.027
< $50,000	-0.644	0.184	-3.49	< 0.001	-1.024	0.373	-2.75	0.006
$50,000 – $74,999	-0.424	0.151	-2.80	0.005	-0.739	0.355	-2.08	0.038
$75,000 – $99,999	-0.292	0.143	-2.04	0.042	-0.761	0.320	-2.38	0.018
$100,000 – $199,999	-0.185	0.126	-1.47	0.143	-0.231	0.295	-0.78	0.434
$200,000 or more	base				base			
Caseload		4	7.01	0.135		4	3.74	0.442
1 – 5	-0.470	0.195	-2.40	0.016	0.425	0.378	1.13	0.261
6 – 10	-0.459	0.187	-2.45	0.014	0.591	0.370	1.60	0.111
11 – 25	-0.304	0.179	-1.70	0.089	0.329	0.339	0.97	0.331
26 – 100	-0.244	0.157	-1.56	0.120	0.516	0.305	1.69	0.091
> 100	base				base			
Constant	5.962	0.346	17.24	< 0.001	1.058	0.626	1.69	0.091

TABLE 6.4 Estimated Differences from the Multivariate Analysis of Effective Hourly Rates

	Rate Equation		"Selection" Equation		Combined	
	b	Est. Rate ($)	b	Est. Probability	Estimate ($)	Impact ($)
By disposition						
Unfiled	0.428	241	0.619	0.972	234	93
Filed, not tried	0.168	186	1.264	0.995	185	43
Tried	0.000	157	0.000	0.901	142	0
By stakes						
< $20,000	-0.782	72	0.101	0.917	66	-76
$20,000 – $50,000	-0.481	97	-0.076	0.887	86	-55
> $50,000	0.000	157	0.000	0.901	142	0
By area of law						
Auto accident	0.213	195	0.734	0.978	190	49
Medical malpractice	0.673	308	-1.198	0.535	165	23
Other personal injury	0.204	193	-0.469	0.793	153	11
Workers' comp / social security	-0.183	131	0.506	0.963	126	-16
Contracts	-0.132	138	-0.451	0.798	110	-32
Other	0.000	157	0.000	0.901	142	0
Gender of lawyer						
Male	0.160	184	-0.471	0.793	146	5
Female	0.000	157	0.000	0.901	142	0

(continued)

TABLE 6.4 (continued)

	Rate Equation			"Selection" Equation		Combined	
	b	Est. Rate ($)	b	Est. Probability	Estimate ($)	Impact ($)
Lawyer's advertising practices							
Uses media or direct mail	0.191	190	-0.427	0.805	153	12
Does not use media	0.000	157	0.000	0.901	142	0
Type of firm							
Plaintiffs' personal injury firm	-0.033	152	0.030	0.906	138	-4
Other type of firm	0.000	157	0.000	0.901	142	0
Lawyer's position							
Partner in firm	-0.069	147	0.071	0.913	134	-8
Solo practitioner	-0.118	140	0.245	0.937	131	-11
Associate or firm employee	0.000	157	0.000	0.901	142	0
Years of experience							
5 or less	0.063	168	-0.122	0.878	147	5
6 – 10	-0.146	136	0.302	0.944	128	-13
11 – 20	-0.174	132	0.102	0.917	121	-20
> 20	0.000	157	0.000	0.901	142	0

	Rate Equation		"Selection" Equation		Combined	
	b	Est. Rate ($)	b	Est. Probability	Estimate ($)	Impact ($)
Lawyer's practice area						
Personal injury plaintiffs	-0.162	134	0.218	0.934	125	-17
Other litigation	-0.102	142	0.013	0.903	128	-13
General practice	-0.247	123	-0.124	0.877	108	-34
Other type of practice	0.000	157	0.000	0.901	142	0
Lawyer's income						
< $50,000	-0.644	83	-1.024	0.603	50	-92
$50,000 – $74,999	-0.424	103	-0.739	0.708	73	-69
$75,000 – $99,999	-0.292	117	-0.761	0.700	82	-59
$100,000 – $199,999	-0.185	131	-0.231	0.854	112	-30
$200,000 or more	0.000	157	0.000	0.901	142	0
Caseload						
1 – 5	-0.470	98	0.425	0.957	94	-48
6 – 10	-0.459	99	0.591	0.970	96	-45
11 – 25	-0.304	116	0.329	0.947	110	-32
26 – 100	-0.244	123	0.516	0.964	119	-23
> 100	0.000	157	0.000	0.901	142	0
Base	5.058	157	1.286	0.901	142	0

produced an estimate of the effective hourly rate. The median was $125; the mean effective hourly rate was $189.[26]

In the sample from the systematic Wisconsin survey, there were 151 cases with information on effective hourly rate for which the lawyers reported having consulted case files containing time records;[27] this is only 17 percent of the entire sample, and consequently the data need to be treated with caution. For these 151 cases, the median effective hourly rate was $111 and the mean was $170. Looking separately at the un-filed, filed, and tried cases, the respective medians/means are $146/$224 ($n = 51$), $109/$170 ($n = 61$), and $95/$99 ($n = 39$).

Taken together, both the earlier nonscientific sample and the sub-sample from the 1995 survey show that, if anything, the absence of time records may have led to an overestimation of the effective hourly rates that lawyers are earning from contingency fee work.

Returns on Contingency Fee Cases in the Federal Courts

One obvious question from the analysis above is whether the patterns I report are peculiar to Wisconsin and Wisconsin practitioners. Ideally, one would like to have closely comparable data drawn from a nation-wide sample. I do not have such data, but I do have data beyond Wis-consin for cases handled in the federal district courts in the early 1990s.

The RAND-CJRA Data.   These data come from an evaluation of the impact of the Civil Justice Reform Act (CJRA) carried out by the RAND Corporation under contract with the Administrative Office of the U.S. Courts. For my purposes, I have employed data from two separate samples drawn by RAND.[28] The first sample is from cases terminated during 1991 (up until December 15); the second is from cases filed in 1992 (and in some situations 1993). RAND sampled cases from twenty federal districts around the country, some of which were involved in pi-lot projects under the CJRA and some which served as comparison dis-tricts. Samples were stratified to include adequate numbers of cases for each of the types of case-processing interventions adopted in response to the CJRA and to include adequate numbers in three categories of work burdens placed on federal judges; asbestos cases were specifically omitted from the study. RAND constructed sample weights to allow more comparisons to take into account variations in sampling rates. Each of the two samples (1991 terminations and 1992–93 filings) contained approximately 5,000 cases. Surveys of the lawyers involved in each case were then carried out (omitting the 7 percent of cases from the 1992–93 sample that were still pending as of January 1996, when the final surveys were sent out); the response rate from lawyers was around 50 percent.[29] Of the respondents from the 1991 sample, 742 reported being paid on a contingency fee basis, as did 603 respondents for the 1992–93 sample.

RAND's lawyer survey captured information on the following variables relevant for analysis of effective hourly rates: amount of time spent by lawyers on the case; legal fees paid by the lawyer's client, excluding expenses; the amount at stake ("the best likely monetary outcome"); the number of years the lawyer had been practicing law; the percentage of the lawyer's practice devoted to federal district court litigation during the previous five years; and the size of the lawyer's firm.[30] The wording of some of the questions would tend to produce underestimates of the amount of lawyer effort involved. Specifically, some respondents could not provide estimates of the hours worked by *all* attorneys for their client and hence provided only partial estimates of lawyer effort. More importantly, lawyers were instructed to exclude the number of hours devoted to proceedings before administrative agencies or in state courts involving the dispute in the federal court case. The question design also may have led to overestimates of the fees the lawyers received (the fee question asked for the fees paid for all lawyers for their client). The result is that effective hourly rates and mean hourly returns may be *over*estimated in the analysis I report below. The information on hours and fees required for analysis was available for 392 (weighted) respondents from the 1991 sample and 297 (weighted) respondents for the 1992–93 sample.[31]

In addition to the data from the lawyer survey, I was able to draw on data coded from the court records. The key variables from the court records are the type of case as indicated by the plaintiffs' lawyer at the time of filing and the stage of processing when the case was terminated.

There are two key differences between the cases represented in the CJRA data and the Wisconsin cases discussed above. First, all of the cases in the CJRA sample were filed in court; unlike the Wisconsin data, there are no cases that were resolved prior to court filing. Second, the federal cases on average have substantially more money at stake. Specifically, according to the lawyer respondents, slightly less than 30 percent of the CJRA cases involved a potential recovery of $50,000 or less compared to 73 percent of the Wisconsin cases; only 17 percent of

the Wisconsin cases involved potential recoveries of over $100,000 com-
pared to more than 50 percent of the CJRA cases; and only 5 percent of
the Wisconsin cases involved potential recoveries of over $300,000 com-
pared to over 20 percent of the CJRA cases.

Results from the RAND-CJRA Data. Table 6.5 shows the returns contingency fee lawyers report for cases in the CJRA sample for the 1991
(Table 6.5a) and 1992–93 (Table 6.5b) samples. One striking feature of
these results is the generally much higher values shown for 1991 compared to 1992–93. Recall that the 1991 sample is of cases terminated in
1991, while the 1992–93 sample is of cases filed in 1992 or 1993 and terminated by January 1996; approximately 7 percent of the cases originally included in the 1992–93 sample had not terminated by January
1996 and were excluded from the final surveys. One possible explanation for the difference between the two samples is that the high-return
cases are those that are in the last 7 percent of cases terminated. However, this does not explain the difference in results for the two samples:
excluding the slowest 7 percent of cases from the 1991 sample does not
bring the figures for that sample into line with the figures for the 1992–
93 sample. In the following discussion I will reference both figures,
showing the lower 1992–93 figures in parentheses.

Overall, I assess the patterns for the CJRA data as quite consistent
with the Wisconsin data. In terms of overall level, the median effective
hourly rate, mean effective hourly rate, and mean hourly return for the
CJRA data are $127 ($108), $425 ($236), and $215 ($157). If one compares
these to the overall (weighted) figures for Wisconsin—$167, $365, and
$207 for the three statistics respectively (from the top line of Table
6.2b)—the differences cut both ways, with Wisconsin higher for some
and the CJRA data (from the 1991 sample) higher for others. If one limits the comparison to the Wisconsin cases with $50,000 or more at
stake—$285, $739, and $261—the Wisconsin data show considerably
higher returns than do the federal cases from around the country. Limiting the Wisconsin cases to those that were filed in court, the median
effective hourly rate, mean effective hourly rate, and mean hourly return for Wisconsin are $155, $281, and $218. Further limiting the Wis-
consin data to only those cases filed in court that involved stakes of
$50,000 or more, the comparable figures are $310, $497, and $274 respectively.

The general conclusion from this overall analysis is that the figures from the Wisconsin survey are not significantly out of line with patterns that one would expect to find from national studies.

Table 6.5 also shows that some of the general patterns discussed for Wisconsin hold up with the national CJRA data. The returns lawyers receive are highly skewed. Median effective hourly rates are much, much lower than mean effective hourly rates, as are mean hourly returns; applying a 10 percent trim to the upper tail of effective hourly rates greatly reduces both the mean effective hourly rate and the mean hourly return. Other patterns that appear again here include the following:

Stakes: Returns tend to go up with the size of case, with larger cases yielding better returns for the lawyer.

Stage of resolution: Returns tend to be higher when cases are resolved early in the litigation process.

Area of law: Tort cases tend to produce better returns than other types of cases (e.g., contract, civil rights).

Type of practice: Solo practitioners tend to get somewhat lower returns than lawyers in firms (although whether that is a function of the types of cases solo practitioners get or something else about solo practice, I cannot say).

The patterns relating returns to years of experience and concentration on federal court practice are not consistent between the two sample years; the 1991 sample produces a pattern indicating that there are relationships (with returns going up with experience and concentration on federal court work), while the 1992–93 sample does not show such patterns.

Finally, there are some hints in Table 6.5 as to why the returns for the 1991 sample appear to be much higher than those for the 1992–93 sample. The large differences appear for tort cases, with much higher returns in 1991 for auto cases and "other torts" (the 1992–93 sample actually has higher figures for products liability cases). Perhaps more important are the comparisons controlling for stakes: the 1991 sample shows a mean effective hourly rate of over $1,000 for cases with more than $300,000 at stake, compared to only $283 for the 1992–93 samples, and the other summary statistics for this group of cases show figures on the order of 50 percent higher for 1991 than for 1992–93. Moreover, only 20 percent of the 1992–93 sample is in the over $300,000 category, compared to 27 percent of the 1991 sample.

TABLE 6.5a Effective Hourly Rate Estimates, 1991 CJRA Data

	Mean EHR[a] ($)	Median EHR ($)	First Quartile EHR ($)	Third Quartile EHR ($)	EHR Mid-spread ($)	90th Percentile EHR ($)	Mean Hourly Return ($)	10% Trimmed Mean EHR ($)	10% Trimmed Mean Hourly Return ($)	N
All cases	425	127	20	348	328	907	215	209	160	392
By area of law										
Auto	1,031	345	103	686	583	2,071	480	313	259	64
Product liability	371	156	62	369	307	884	245	203	235	42
Other tort	484	165	32	415	383	1,109	240	181	155	83
Contract	276	92	23	211	188	1,106	160	117	111	65
Civil rights	143	49	0	143	143	522	118	103	95	52
Social security	95	0	0	92	92	488	55	95	55	21
Other	257	153	18	330	312	697	107	173	100	60
By nature of disposition										
Before court action	589	138	54	369	315	835	288	206	188	97
Court action, before pretrial	422	122	18	363	345	1,106	204	165	163	186
After pretrial	342	155	55	380	325	1,125	231	191	158	77
During / after trial	141	0	0	147	147	645	137	102	123	27

[a] EHR = effective hourly rate.

	Mean EHR[a] ($)	Median EHR ($)	First Quartile EHR ($)	Third Quartile EHR ($)	EHR Mid-spread ($)	90th Percentile EHR ($)	Mean Hourly Return ($)	10% Trimmed Mean EHR ($)	10% Trimmed Mean Hourly Return ($)	N
By stakes										
$50,000 or less	161	79	25	209	184	461	80	139	79	93
$50,001 – $100,000	226	138	27	208	181	692	113	169	105	60
$100,001 – $300,000	265	119	10	354	344	605	161	175	140	87
> $300,000	1,021	265	58	829	771	1,697	271	257	195	89
By years of experience										
< 10	318	74	17	254	237	715	127	150	118	66
10 – 19 years	337	155	26	539	513	1,297	233	217	181	21
20 or more	639	171	69	543	474	1,577	300	199	187	120
By % federal practice										
< 10%	353	96	35	544	509	1,106	181	163	142	69
10% – 24%	392	166	26	404	378	1,001	200	189	157	74
25% or more	541	162	66	379	313	1,588	245	174	171	64
By size of firm										
Solo	202	98	48	231	183	703	149	159	130	41
2 – 4 lawyers	336	156	40	500	460	1,444	236	200	183	85
5 – 9 lawyers	901	173	54	645	591	7,829	285	148	172	40
10 or more	297	157	28	415	387	1,106	169	176	140	40

TABLE 6.5b Effective Hourly Rate Estimates, 1992–93 CJRA Data

	Mean EHR[a] ($)	Median EHR ($)	First Quartile EHR ($)	Third Quartile EHR ($)	EHR Mid-spread ($)	90th Percentile EHR ($)	Mean Hourly Return ($)	10% Trimmed Mean EHR ($)	10% Trimmed Mean Hourly Return ($)	N
All cases	236	108	11	253	242	531	157	125	110	297
By area of law										
Auto	288	181	107	341	234	708	226	178	201	32
Product liability	516	233	40	668	628	1,159	232	149	138	25
Other tort	230	92	0	299	299	816	215	100	104	47
Contract	332	113	24	267	243	528	205	145	122	51
Civil rights	104	58	0	143	143	282	80	83	67	69
Social security	150	174	0	228	228	368	116	150	116	15
Other	174	123	13	296	283	432	103	138	99	48
By nature of disposition										
Before court action	258	144	51	301	250	767	271	138	122	93
Court action, before pretrial	214	106	0	253	253	491	113	129	91	60
After pretrial	340	126	40	270	230	594	195	126	134	87
During / after trial	105	10	0	148	148	534	144	68	110	89

[a] EHR = effective hourly rate.

	Mean EHR[a] ($)	Median EHR ($)	First Quartile EHR ($)	Third Quartile EHR ($)	EHR Mid-spread ($)	90th Percentile EHR ($)	Mean Hourly Return ($)	10% Trimmed Mean EHR ($)	10% Trimmed Mean Hourly Return ($)	N
By stakes										
$50,000 or less	158	105	13	228	215	366	66	129	63	74
$50,001 – $100,000	179	107	42	249	207	672	113	115	90	48
$100,001 – $300,000	355	120	0	271	271	703	132	124	87	79
> $300,000	283	164	13	342	329	817	167	135	122	51
By years of experience										
< 10	248	84	0	267	267	502	179	118	136	61
10 – 19 years	220	105	49	398	348	708	150	141	132	16
20 or more	235	89	1	229	228	455	104	114	94	115
By % federal practice										
< 10%	203	111	0	302	302	560	160	129	103	68
10% – 24%	287	106	39	248	209	650	150	149	108	47
25% or more	236	66	0	192	192	385	160	107	114	76
By size of firm										
Solo	172	81	31	220	189	259	126	113	87	40
2 – 4 lawyers	275	86	0	253	253	425	138	120	118	74
5 – 9 lawyers	201	87	6	255	249	708	204	117	82	38
10 or more	272	120	29	267	238	821	166	159	128	40

The Profits of Contingency Fee Work

As the investment framework would dictate, there clearly are profits to be made from contingency fee work. For most lawyers handling cases on a contingency fee basis, it is a small subset of cases, typically the top 10 percent, that produce the largest profits. However, the typical contingency fee practitioner can expect even the remaining 90 percent of cases as a portfolio to produce a fee premium on the order of 25 to 30 percent of what market-rate hourly fee work generates.

Contingency fee work can be very lucrative, particularly for those lawyers who develop expertise and processes for handling large numbers of cases. The high profitability comes from locating a small segment of the cases that produce extremely good returns on the lawyers' investment of time. Some lawyers are able to cherry-pick the good cases; others handle large volumes of cases in order to find the occasional very profitable case. Relatively few lawyers ever see "the really big one." One of the lawyers I observed had been doing plaintiffs' contingent fee work for twenty years, had a very successful practice, and had never collected a fee of over $100,000 on a case.[32]

One important implication of the portfolio framework is the need to look not at results of individual cases but at the portfolio of cases. Any single case can be a big loser or a big winner when measured in terms of effective hourly rate. That will depend on the quality of the case in terms of questions of liability, causality, and damages; the stand the opposing party takes with regard to the case; and the amount of effort the lawyer must devote to it. These elements are all matters of uncertainty and risk, although the degree of uncertainty for any one element may be relatively low in a particular case. As I have discussed in previous chapters, successful contingency fee lawyers routinely construct diversified portfolios of cases, with the diversification along dimensions such as potential return, amount of uncertainty about liability and causation, and the likely level of effort required. Unlike Jan Schlichtman, the lawyer who bankrupts himself in *A Civil Action* (Harr 1995), most contingency fee lawyers are attentive to the need to maintain a portfolio rather than essentially putting all of their money into what might be likened to a lottery. Just as those who invest in a portfolio of stocks seek to have their money do better than it would in a certificate of deposit, the goal of most contingency fee lawyers is to do better than they could do handling cases on an hourly fee basis.

CHAPTER 7

The Role of Reputation in Contingency Fee Practice

Introduction

Jeffrey Wischler was a construction worker in Milwaukee, Wisconsin. In the summer of 1999, he was working on the new baseball stadium under construction in Milwaukee. On a windy July day, he was in a basket suspended by a crane 250 feet above ground while a larger crane lifted a 450-ton piece of what was to be part of the stadium's retractable roof. The wind caught the roof piece, stressing the lifting crane, which collapsed into the smaller crane suspending the basket containing Wischler and two coworkers. All three men died in the resulting fall. Some days before his death, in a premonition of what was to happen, Wischler had told his wife, "If anything ever happens to me, I want you to call Bob Habush." Within twenty-four hours of the accident, his wife had called Habush and set in motion what would end in a jury verdict totaling $99.25 million to be shared by the families of the three dead men (*National Law Journal*, July 16, 2001, C9).[1]

Why did Wischler tell his wife to call Bob Habush? Simply put, Bob Habush and his firm—Habush Habush & Rottier—have a reputation for winning large jury verdicts and large settlements for their clients.[2] As discussed in Chapter 3, this firm works hard to put that reputation in front of the public. A significant portion of the citizens of Wisconsin will spontaneously name the Habush firm as the one they would call if they needed a lawyer to represent them in a personal injury case.

The Habush firm's reputation does not just draw clients; it also elicits settlements. A lawyer who does a lot of defense work (and a little plaintiffs' work) once told me informally that the Habush firm prepares its cases so well that it effectively covers its fee; that is, in a typical case handled by the firm, the lawyer will get a settlement sufficiently larger than what could be obtained by most other lawyers that it is like paying no fee (i.e., assuming a one-third fee, Habush will get a settlement 50 percent higher than would most lawyers). I have no way of assessing whether this lawyer's view of the results achieved by Habush is correct, although it does accord with a description of Habush's style as "relentless." What *is* important is the reputation it reflects.

The idea that lawyers care about their reputations is no surprise, and this concern is by no means limited to lawyers handling contingency fee cases. Lawyers rely on reputational capital both for attracting clients and for how their representation of clients is evaluated by opponents and decision makers. This concern is manifest from lawyers who handle cases before the Supreme Court (Coyle 1997; McGuire 1993, 1999, 127–30) to those who handle the most routine cases before administrative tribunals (Kritzer 1998a, 143–48) or in divorce court (Mather, McEwen, and Maiman 2001, 127–30).

Reputations are important in settings where actors engage in repeated interactions (Bailey 1971; Bromley 1993; Gilson and Mnookin 1994; Klein 1997b; Mercer 1996). It is not necessary that any specific dyad of players interact repeatedly, only that there is some formal or informal mechanism for sharing reputational information. One widespread formal system for disseminating reputations when actors engage in repeated interactions but not with one another is the credit bureau. The credit record disseminated by the credit bureau is a form of reputation (Klein 1992; Newman 1997). As with all forms of reputation, the credit record is a compilation of past behavior which an actor in a new interaction can use to predict future behavior. At the other end of formality in modes of disseminating reputations is word of mouth (increasingly in the Internet age, "word of mouse") or gossip (Beiley 1971; Merry 1984).

Reputations, however disseminated, have potential importance for contingency fee practitioners in their interactions with a variety of different players, including potential clients, opponents and opponents' lawyers, judges and other adjudicators, expert witnesses, and other supporting actors. In thinking about the role of reputations, there are two general questions to consider: (1) how do reputations come about, and (2) what difference do reputations make? In this chapter, my focus is primarily on the second of these questions because I do not have the kind of overtime information that would be needed to analyze how reputations are formed.[3] The analysis in this chapter is based entirely on my observational and interview data. In part, this is because it is difficult for an individual to gauge either the nature or the impact of his or her reputation, and hence it would have been difficult to design questions related to reputations to include on my mail survey. The larger part of the reason that I have no survey data on reputation is that I did not anticipate the role I found it to play during my observation; that is, while my theoretical frame did not completely neglect reputation, my grasp on its role was at best weak when the research began.

From the viewpoint of portfolio theory, reputation is important as a form of correlation among investments. In the formal version of portfolio theory, the measure of risk is the variability of return on the individual investments in a portfolio. However, to assess the overall level of risk in the portfolio, one must aggregate this variability, and that aggregation must take into account whether there are correlations among the returns of the individual investments. In the case of the contingency fee lawyer's investments—the contingency fee cases the lawyer is handling—correlation arises both from the kinds of cases the lawyer is able to put into the portfolio and from the amount of time the lawyer has to invest in those cases to obtain a return. Both of these factors are related to the lawyer's reputation. As discussed in some detail in Chapter 3, most lawyers obtain most of their cases either through referrals from other lawyers and prior clients or from broader community contacts. Obtaining cases from these sources relies upon the lawyer's reputation. As discussed in the previous chapter, the effective hourly rate lawyers obtain on their cases is a measure of the return on investment; this effective hourly rate is significantly a function of the lawyer's efficiency in handling cases, and that efficiency can be affected by the lawyer's reputation for both vigorously pursuing cases when necessary and for being willing to cooperate to reduce potential inefficiencies that litigation can easily produce.

As suggested in Chapter 5, reputation has a second important role in understanding contingency fee practice, and that is as a form of constraint on lawyer incentives in individual cases. The standard economic analysis of contingency fees shows that, looking at the individual case, the incentive for the lawyer is to settle many, perhaps even most, cases relatively early for amounts that are not in the client's best interest (Clermont and Currivan 1978; Hay 1997b; Johnson 1980–81; but see Kritzer et al. 1985; Miller 1987; Rosenthal 1974). While professional norms may well mitigate the incentives for a lawyer to make decisions in the lawyer's own interest rather than in the client's interest, the lawyer's concern for his or her reputation among future sources of cases functions as an economic control on the potential for "self-dealing" by the lawyer in settling cases.

Reputation and Portfolio Development

In Chapter 3, I discussed in detail how contingency fee lawyers obtain their cases. While much public discussion has centered on media advertising and direct client solicitation, I presented detailed evidence that most lawyers obtain most of their cases in ways that rely primarily on reputation. Clearly, the anecdotal example of Jeffrey Wischler's instruction to his wife to "call Bob Habush" is a dramatic instance of how reputation links clients to lawyers. As previously discussed, the lawyers I observed were very cognizant of their reputations in their dealings with potential and actual clients. In handling queries and cases, the lawyers considered not only what was best vis-à-vis the instant matter, but also how what they did might be related to future potential clients.

Recall Steve Clarke's exit procedure described in Chapter 3: as he handed the settlement check to the client, he also handed the client a copy of his card and commented, "Hopefully you won't need me again . . . [but] if you know someone who does, please send them in." Another example was the extensive time Chuck Brown spent on the telephone with potential clients even after he had concluded he was not interested in handling the case the potential client had called about; this was particularly true when the caller was from one of the union groups that Brown was trying to cultivate as a source of clients. Similarly, Steve Clarke often took on workers' compensation cases with an eye to a potential claim for loss of earnings, but where he knew that it would not be clear for some time whether there was in fact such a claim; he would monitor those cases over a period of months and not infrequently find in the end that the client had found alternative employment that did result in a loss of earnings. Clarke explained his willingness to invest in such cases as partly a means of encouraging the client to think of him in the future, either in the case of injury to client or in the case of injury to a friend or family member.

In Chapter 3, I observed that lawyers want clients (and even potential clients whose cases they have declined) to go away happy and stay happy because they perceive that a disgruntled former client will not refer future cases to the lawyer or return should the occasion arise. Similarly, if another lawyer refers a case to a lawyer and later hears of a result that does not seem to the referring lawyer to represent effective representation, that lawyer will be lost as a future source of referrals. Stated in terms of the portfolio image, the lawyers' reputations are the key source of their future investment opportunities. Unlike the traditional investor who can simply look in the market and choose from among a vast array of investment options, the contingency fee lawyer must have potential investments come to him or her.[4]

Theoretical Frames for Understanding Reputations

To understand the role played by reputations for contingency fee practitioners' problem of obtaining cases, we can turn to theoretical analyses of reputations in other settings. A useful place to start is with the example of credit and the role of credit bureaus.

Through the vehicle of game theory, Daniel Klein (1992, 1997a) has analyzed the problem of granting credit. His initial analysis is in the form of a two-move sequential game. One starts with the situation of a single business confronted with the issue of whether to offer credit to a single consumer and what the consumer does if credit is extended. The first move is that of the business; the second move is that of the consumer, but it occurs only if on the first move the business extends credit. Figure 7.1 shows the game schematically with the payoff matrix at the bottom.

According to this game, if the business fails to extend credit, the consumer makes a cash purchase, with each side receiving a payoff of 0. If the business does extend credit, then the consumer must decide whether to pay off the credit or to default. If the consumer pays the bill, the business payoff is 1 and the consumer payoff is 1; the consumer gains slightly by spreading payments over time and having the benefit of the purchase before paying the full price, and the business benefits by charging a small fee for the extension of credit. If the consumer defaults, the consumer payoff is 6 and the business payoff is –4. The specific values here are not particularly important. So long as the consumer is better off receiving credit regardless of whether he or she decides to

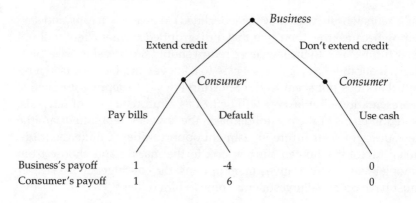

FIGURE 7.1 The Credit Game
SOURCE: Daniel B. Klein, "Promise Keeping in the Great Society: A Model of Credit Information Sharing," *Economics and Politics* 4 (1992): 118.

default, and the business is best off if credit is extended and the consumer pays the debt and worst off if credit is extended but the consumer defaults (i.e., not extending credit is a better situation than if the consumer defaults).

Assuming a single play of the game, the analysis is clear: no economically rational consumer would ever pay the debt, and hence no economically rational business would extend credit. The only way this could be mitigated on a one-shot basis would be if the consumer felt some moral imperative to pay the bill. Stated another way, the consumer would pay the debt only if the consumer's utility was a function of something more than the specific transaction such that the consumer's payoff from defaulting was not 6 but less than or equal to 1.

Of course we know that businesses routinely extend credit, and the reason they extend credit is that consumers and businesses are not engaged in a single transaction but a series of transactions. While each transaction does not necessarily involve the same dyad of consumer and business, the consumer is nonetheless concerned about maintaining a positive credit record (i.e., a positive *reputation* as paying bills incurred) because businesses share credit information through credit bureaus. In other words, in the real world the credit game is iterated, and the consumer's reputation (credit record) is a key factor in the decisions of businesses to extend credit. Klein's analysis of the credit game extends to the businesses' decisions to join a credit bureau and the costs the business incurs in doing so. We need not consider that here.

However, it is useful to modify the game before adapting it to specify the Hire-a-Lawyer Game. Let us complicate the consumer's decision by adding a stochastic element to what the consumer does if no credit is extended.[5] Let us say that the consumer draws a random variable from a uniform distribution between 0 and 1, and if the random variable is equal to or greater than p, the consumer goes ahead and makes the purchase; in other words, there is a p probability of the consumer who is declined credit making the cash purchase, and a $1 - p$ probability of not making the cash purchase. Assuming that the consumer's utility in the goods purchased is equal to the cash purchase price, then the payoff to the consumer who is denied credit stays 0 regardless of what draw comes from the uniform distribution. On the other hand, the business's payoff will be Q, which will be greater than 0 and possibly greater than 1; where exactly that payoff falls will depend on whether the business essentially charges a fee for extending credit and the additional costs it incurs in extending credit. Since the business knows only that the consumer who is denied credit has some probability p of making a cash purchase, the merchant's expected payoff from not giving credit is equal to $p * Q$. This modified game is shown in Figure 7.2. In fact, it does not change the analysis of the game vis-à-vis one-shot encounters, except perhaps to increase the business's incentive to deny credit, particularly if credit is costly.

With regard to a repeated game, one can add a multiplier for the

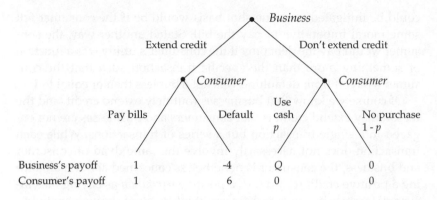

FIGURE 7.2 The Revised Credit Game

payoff matrix so that the within-game relative values of the payoffs are constant from game to game, but the magnitudes vary from game to game. If one also adds to this an assumption that someone who has defaulted once will not necessarily always default in the future (an assumption implicit in Klein's analysis of the repeated play version of the Credit Game), a business could want to establish a relationship with a consumer with a prior record of defaults by taking risks for initial small purchases in hopes of eventually getting large purchases, even if it might insist on cash later on.

Let us now transform the Revised Credit game into the Hire-a-Lawyer game. To do this, we need to add a third player, a defendant, whom I will call the Insurer. Here is how the game works. The potential Client makes a decision whether to hire a Lawyer. I assume that the Lawyer will always be able to obtain a settlement from the Insurer, so that if the Lawyer is hired, the Insurer is not actually a player. The Lawyer can decide to make a settlement that maximizes the Lawyer's own interest or a settlement that maximizes the represented Client's interest (we will eventually see that in some cases the Lawyer's and the Client's interests may coincide). We will call the payoffs maximizing the Lawyer's interest L_L and C_L for the Lawyer's and the Client's payoffs respectively; the corresponding payoffs maximizing the represented Client's interest are L_C and C_C. For the client, the payoff is net of the lawyer's fee (and expenses). If the Client opts not to hire the Lawyer, the Insurer makes a draw from a uniform random distribution ranging from 0 to 1 to decide whether to settle with the Client; if the draw is greater than or equal to p, the insurer settles, and if it is less than p, it declines to settle. In other words, the unrepresented Client's probability of obtaining a settlement is p, and the probability of receiving no settlement is $1 - p$. Regardless of what the Insurer does, the Lawyer's payoff is 0; for the unrepresented Client, the payoff is 0 if the Insurer does not settle, and C_I if the Insurer does settle. Figure 7.3 shows the structure of the game.

What the rational potential Client and Lawyer will do in a one-off Hire-a-Lawyer game will depend on the relative values of the payoff. Let us first consider the relatively modest, routine case. In such cases, it is typically not in the lawyer's interest to devote substantial resources to the case if the lawyer's payoff is to be evaluated in terms of the effective hourly rate that the case will generate. In this situation, the relative payoffs if the Client does hire the Lawyer are

$C_C > C_L > 0$

and

$L_C < L_L$

Given that the lawyer always gets something for the client, the risk-neutral client's decision will turn on whether $p \times C_I$ is greater than C_L; if the client is risk-averse, that will make hiring the lawyer more attractive. For the lawyer, the decision on a one-shot basis is clear-cut from

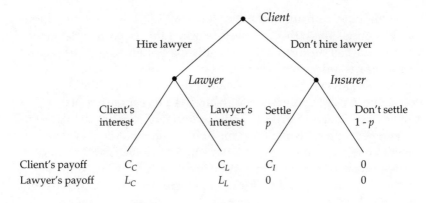

FIGURE 7.3 The Hire-a-Lawyer Game

the perspective of economic rationality: the lawyer should pursue his or her own interest.

Given that the assessment of the lawyer's payoff is in terms of effective hourly rate, it need not be the case that $L_C < L_L$. In larger cases, the marginal gain in the lawyer's own payoff from additional effort by the lawyer may be positive across the range of alternatives the lawyer can use to increase the payoff to the client. As long as the lawyer's marginal gain is positive, $L_C = L_L$. In "large" cases this is almost certainly the case. Somewhere in the middle range of cases, the inequality will apply rather than the equality, and at that point the lawyer's incentive is to neglect the client's interest if all we consider is the one-shot situation.

One caveat before turning to the role of reputation: in the iterated version of the game, I have assumed that the lawyer is always able to obtain a settlement. Let us assume that the settlement is a discounted payment of what the lawyer *might* win at trial (i.e., a settlement is assumed, but a trial outcome is uncertain). Let us further assume that the repeat-player lawyer is risk-neutral and the one-shot client is risk-averse (Galanter 1974). In this case, the lawyer may want to go to trial, but the client would prefer to settle if provided with full information about the risk of trial. This is because the preferred payoffs from the lawyer's perspective are now expected payoffs which are equal to the probability of success times the payoff discounted by any risk aversion. In this case,

$$C_C > E\{C_L\}$$

and

$$L_C < E\{L_L\}$$

Here again, the rational lawyer will want to pursue his or her own interest. That is, a rational lawyer may want to take a case to trial if the settlement discount demanded by the defendant is too great. On the other hand, the client, after discounting for the possibility of losing, risk aversion, and perhaps also for the trauma of the trial experience, will prefer to accept the highly discounted settlement offered by the defendant.

Let us now add to the game several elements. First, lawyers must play this game again and again and again; most of the time the clients are new, although in a nontrivial number of instances, a past client returns. Second, lawyers have reputations for whether they pursue their clients' interests or their own interests. Third, lawyers believe that these reputations are disseminated through the community by past clients and other lawyers. Fourth, lawyers believe that potential clients make decisions about hiring a lawyer based upon reputation for doing a good job for their clients. Note here the importance of the lawyer's belief about his or her reputation; unlike the Credit Game, there is no institutionalized mechanism like the credit bureau for sharing reputation. However, in terms of motivating the lawyer, it is the lawyer's belief about the impact of reputation that is crucial.

In the iterated Hire-a-Lawyer game, the analysis of what lawyers will do vis-à-vis the interests of their clients will depend very much on the mix of cases lawyers get. A lawyer who only got cases in the range $L_C < L_L$ would be in a very difficult situation. If the lawyer only pursues the client's interest, the lawyer's return will be relatively low. However, if the lawyer only pursues his or her own interest, the lawyer's return will become zero because over time no client will hire the lawyer to handle cases on a contingency fee basis. What this lawyer will do will depend on opportunities for work that is not on a contingency fee basis. That is, if the lawyer can make seventy-five dollars per hour writing routine wills but gets contingency fee cases that produce only twenty-five dollars per hour if handled in the clients' best interest, the lawyer should abandon contingency fee work. If, on the other hand, this lawyer can get only thirty hours per week of will writing, the lawyer might as well go ahead and handle the small contingency cases producing only twenty-five dollars per hour, presuming the lawyer's marginal overhead cost is less than twenty-five dollars per hour.

For the lawyer who gets a mix of cases, some in the $L_C < L_L$ category and some in the $L_C = L_L$, it is the relationship between the two sets of cases that is important. From my research, it appears that many lawyers treat the former category of cases as something akin to loss leaders; that is, they take these cases as a way of attracting clients who will then disseminate the lawyer's reputation in the community. Certainly, this was how Steve Clarke saw many of the small cases he handled. His belief in the importance of his reputation for doing well for his clients was reinforced by comments such as that which occurred at the end of an initial meeting with a potential workers' compensation client who had a case that could generate a fee in the $10,000 range. When Clarke specifically asked the potential client whether he would like to retain Clarke, the potential client replied, "We checked you out. . . . You've got a good reputation." Not surprisingly, the potential client signed the retainer agreement.

What about the lawyer whose practice is primarily such that the lawyer's and client's interests coincide ($L_C = L_L$), at least before taking into account risk preference issues? One might expect that in this situation the lawyer has it made and need not worry particularly about the client's interests because the lawyer's own incentives will lead to the best resolution for the client. In certain kinds of cases, this may be true to some degree. One such situation may be in social security disability cases which lawyers handle on a contingency basis (typically 25 percent of back benefits up to a maximum of $4,000). In these cases there is very seldom an issue of a compromise settlement;[6] either the client is found to be disabled and receives benefits or the client is determined not to be disabled and gets no benefits. The basic result is that for most social security cases $L_C = L_L$. This does not mean that social security lawyers have no concerns about their reputations. Quite the contrary, they are very concerned about their reputations. However, their reputations turn not on how much they get for their clients but rather on their likelihood of winning for their clients, plus subsidiary issues such as how they interact generally with their clients. However, reputations do not function as a control on a conflict of interest between lawyer and client (Kritzer 1998a, 146–48).

When the lawyer's and client's interests coincide, there can still be issues related to the client's risk aversion and general fears about going to trial. Some analyses of the contingency fee point to situations in which the lawyer wants to go to trial while the client would prefer to accept a settlement involving a substantial compromise. The lawyer's preference for trial might be the simple economic calculation of a risk-neutral actor; an opponent might offer a $500,000 settlement, when in the lawyer's estimation there is an 80 percent chance of winning at trial, and the minimum verdict would be $1 million. With a one-third contingency fee, the lawyer is comparing a $166,667 fee from settling to an *expected* fee of $266,667 if the case goes to trial. If the lawyer expects preparation and trial to require 100 hours of time, the expected effective hourly rate for the marginal time investment is $1,000 per hour. To the lawyer who is genuinely risk-neutral, trial will look advantageous. On the other hand, for the risk-averse client, a certain payment of $333,333 from the $500,000 settlement may look very attractive when compared to an 80 percent chance of $666,667 (which means there is a 20 percent chance of $0), even though the expected value is $533,334. And beyond risk preference vis-à-vis outcomes, a client may prefer settlement simply to avoid the trauma of the trial experience.

The lawyer may also prefer to go to trial for reputational reasons. The case might be such that it is likely to garner some media attention and get the lawyer's name before the public. Alternatively, as discussed later in this chapter, the lawyer may feel the need to demonstrate to the opposing party (and hence to future opposing parties) that the lawyer is perfectly willing to take cases to trial, even if that involves "rolling the dice." Even if a lawyer already has a reputation, both among potential clients and among opposing parties, the lawyer may feel a need to take some percentage of cases to trial to maintain a reputation (Kessler, Meites, and Miller 1996, 247). Thus, the lawyer may have goals beyond the instant case that have nothing at all to do with the client's interest.

What this analysis suggests is that lawyers must be cognizant not only of their reputations for what they get for the client but for the reputation for how they get it. Having a reputation of taking every case to trial may actually turn off a significant number of potentially lucrative clients. Moreover, these clients may have some of the best cases from the viewpoint of the lawyer: cases for which liability and damages are so clear that defendants will want to settle the case quickly. In the course of my interviews, one lawyer remarked that the Habush firm had actually changed its advertising strategy. For many years, Habush emphasized its success in winning trials, and the firm garnered a reputation as an aggressive, highly successful plaintiffs' litigation firm. At some point, Habush shifted its advertising strategy to emphasize that its litigation success meant that its lawyers were able to get good *settlements* for most of their clients. Respondents attributed this change to a realization by Habush that it was losing potential clients who were afraid of having to go through a trial. This was not lost on other contingency fee lawyers: Habush was "afraid that everyone in the public thought that if you hired the Habush firm you were going to be in a trial. When we sit down with our clients, I don't have one client who wants to go to trial. They want to settle their case, and some of them we end up having to go to trial because we are so far apart, but none of them want a trial. So, the Habush firm has even changed its ad to say that 'we achieve more settlements because of our reputation.'"

Finally, as discussed in Chapter 3, lawyers whose practices rely heavily or primarily on paid referrals from other lawyers must be very cognizant of their reputation with their referral sources. These sources are likely to have very accurate information on past performance of the lawyers, much like that provided by a Dunn & Bradstreet operation vis-à-vis the creditworthiness of businesses. One lawyer I interviewed who worked in such a firm was very clear about the firm's concern about its reputation with its referral sources: "We bring in business by developing relations with other lawyers and developing a reputation. So our client development is through other lawyers." This goes to the extent that if a past client contacts the firm directly with a new case, the client is redirected to the original referring lawyer:

Let's say a past client's sister got into a bad accident, and then he [the past client] calls me and says, "My sister got hurt. Will you take her case?" I will tell him, "I really liked working with you, and I'm really sorry to hear your sister's hurt, but you were referred to me by Joe Smith, and you are Joe Smith's client, and I cannot steal you from him. You must go see him. If he wants to send your sister's case to me, that's his business." And I will then call Joe Smith, the referring lawyer, and say, "Guess who just called me. . . . Steve so-and-so's sister was in a bad accident. I wanted you to know that he called me. I told him to call you." We do this sort of thing routinely.

While traditionally the idea of paid referrals has been controversial, particularly from an ethical perspective (see Gibson 1994), it is now formally permitted in many states (including Wisconsin[7]). One of the clear advantages of paid referrals from the client's perspective is that the lawyer receiving the referral should have a heightened concern about reputation because the referring lawyer (1) is more likely to be able to assess the quality of the result from the client's perspective (which closely coincides with the referring lawyer's interest), and (2) the referring lawyer has a high probability of being a source of future cases. Thus, one of the major effects of a system of referral is to provide a system of monitoring and constraint on the lawyer actually handling the case.[8]

Reputations bring in clients, and lawyers want to maintain reputations that will keep clients coming. Just as consumers want to maintain a good credit rating by paying debts so that they can obtain credit in the future, lawyers want to be seen by their clients as working for what is in the client's best interest, because present happy clients will bring future happy clients. Most lawyers are very cognizant that most clients come by word of mouth, and they want the word of mouth to be positive. Without the positive word of mouth, without the positive reputation, contingency fee lawyers believe that they will have a difficult time generating new cases for their portfolios. Thus, while looking at cases on a one-off basis, lawyers would appear to have substantial incentives to reach settlements not in their clients' best interests—just as on a one-off basis, no economically rational debtor would be economically motivated to pay the debt, lawyers' long-term interest is served by maintaining a reputation for getting good results for clients.

While previous analyses of the contingency fee have identified what might be labeled "shirking" by the lawyers as a major problem, the implication of this analysis is that shirking should be much less prevalent. Thus, where the primary solution for shirking would be greater client oversight of what the lawyer is doing on behalf of the client (as suggested in Rosenthal 1974), taking the portfolio view of contingency fee practice reduces the need for oversight. Given that oversight is extremely difficult for the typical client who relies on a contingency fee arrangement, this provides a much more efficacious solution to the agency problem

Reputation and Managing Cases in the Portfolio

In addition to the incentive effects produced by their need to maintain a long-term flow of cases, contingency fee lawyers have strong incentives to obtain results that serve their clients well in as efficient a manner as possible. Simply put, the more efficiently a lawyer can handle cases, the more cases the lawyer can handle.

To this end, many contingency fee lawyers emphasize the importance of cooperativeness. They see cooperativeness not as necessarily inconsistent with obtaining good results for their clients, but rather as an approach that involves not doing things simply as a way of making it more difficult for the other side. As one lawyer described it, "Obviously I'm not going to try and give away my case, but if they're asking for something within the bounds of the law, I would not make them go through all kinds of expensive procedures. And also, if I know I might have a good chance of settling the case, I'll be more cooperative." Some lawyers described this not so much as "cooperation" but as "accommodation": "By and large it is mostly accommodating, because it is a matter of getting along. You hope people will accommodate you for [things like] scheduling."

We can understand the impetus for cooperation by again turning to game theory as a framework. In a fundamental sense, the two sides involved in resolving disputes, including the cases handled by contingency fee lawyers, face a "prisoner's dilemma" situation (Gilson and Mnookin 1994, 514–22). The classic prisoner's dilemma involves two persons suspected of committing a crime together who are interrogated separately. If neither confesses (which would also implicate the other), they both are subject to a minor fine on some minor related charge; if only one confesses, implicating the other and agreeing to testify against the other, the confessor goes free without sanction and the other gets a long jail sentence; if both confess, they both get a shorter jail sentence. The best solution for both suspects is to not confess, but the worst situation is if the other confesses; the tendency, on a single play, is for both to confess to avoid the worst situation. It is easy to see how this works in the context of our interest here. If side A could be assured that side B would be cooperative, side A would be advantaged to be noncooperative. However, if both sides have to make a decision whether to be cooperative, there is an impetus to be noncooperative out of fear of being taken for a "sucker."

The prisoner's dilemma has been subjected to extensive analysis, and one of the most important results is that if the game is played in an iterated fashion rather than on a single-shot basis, there is a motivation to be cooperative (Luce and Raiffa 1957). The "best" overall strategy turns out to be "tit-for-tat" (Axelrod 1984), where the initial strategy is to cooperate, and then to continue to play cooperatively until the opponent is uncooperative, and then to play uncooperatively until the opponent reverts to cooperation. It is easy to see that once the game is further extended to involve plays with differing opponents, reputations become a substitute for a prior interaction with a new opponent. The result is that, in spite of the one-off prisoner's dilemma, the dominant norm should be one of cooperation. Gordon Tullock (1985) shows how this extends specifically to economic relationships; Ronald Gilson and Robert Mnookin (1994, 520–22) discuss how this applies generally to litigation.

With regard to interactions involving contingency fee lawyers, this analysis readily explains why one would expect to see cooperation. Laurence Ross's study (1980, 59) of insurance claim adjusters found that a primary motivation for adjusters was to clear cases, and to do so in as efficient a manner as possible. Adjusters were evaluated based in significant part on how efficiently they handled claims. Thus, for interactions between contingency fee lawyers and insurance adjusters, there should be a norm to avoid making each other's work more difficult than necessary. In terms of theoretical analyses of reputation, what is happening here is that lawyers are seeking to elicit "good behavior" from an opponent, and they do that in significant part by good behavior on their own part (Klein 1997a). The recognition of the importance of trust flowing from reputation in economic relationships can be traced at least back to Adam Smith's idea of the "discipline of continuous dealing" as described in his "Lecture on the Influence of Commerce on Manners" (reprinted in Klein 1997b; see also Shearmur and Klein 1997).

However, what about when the defense is represented by a private practice attorney being paid on an hourly fee basis? In that situation, the apparent motivation of the hourly fee lawyer is not to minimize time but to maximize it (see Johnson 1980–81). Recall the discussion in Chapter 4 about the contingency fee lawyers' expectation that defense lawyers need to work cases to generate hours. In some situations, the contingency fee lawyers believed that certain members of the defense bar "churned" their files to build hours.

However, there are limits on the ability of defense lawyers to engage in this kind of behavior. Specifically, if one considers the relationship between the defense lawyer and that lawyer's client as involving an ongoing relationship rather than a one-off representation, the defense lawyer has to be cognizant of the client's likely evaluation of whether the lawyer's bill is excessive. In fact, one area of controversy in recent years has been on rigorous auditing of outside counsels' bills by insurance companies (see Brennan 1998; Conley 2001; Van Duch 1999). The result of this is that because of their own needs to maintain relationships (and reputations) with their own sources of cases, hourly fee defense lawyers also have a motivation to be cooperative, at least to a significant degree (see Gilson and Mnookin 1994, 525–27).

Thus, it should not be surprising that the importance of cooperative working styles came up again and again in the observation and interviews. One lawyer commented that the legal community was not that large and that it was common to work opposite the same lawyers and adjusters again and again. Being cooperative and engendering cooperative behavior did not necessarily mean that opposing representatives needed to like one another. For example, in talking to his client about working out a schedule for an independent medical examination in a workers' compensation case, one of the lawyers I observed commented about the opposing lawyer: "He is a good lawyer. He can at times have a losing personality, but I've worked with him. He can be strident, but he isn't an asshole like some other lawyers." It was not uncommon for a contingency fee lawyer dealing with a defense lawyer for the first time to talk to other lawyers in the office or to call other plaintiffs' lawyers to get a "read" on the defense lawyer.

Lawyers will shape their own behavior based on what the opposing lawyer does. In the words of one attorney, "If someone jerks me around, I will jerk them back. I usually like to try and stay friendly with the people I am working against. I like to have fun while I am working. But if somebody jerks me off and says that you can't have an extra week to answer the interrogatories or something, then they are not going to get any breaks coming back at them." Another lawyer observed, "I have a partner who is tough, tough aggressive, at all times, who plays more of a hardball type of litigator. And he will tend to draw that kind of response, although with certain defense lawyers he will get along famously." In the minds of many of the lawyers I observed and interviewed, the reputation of being fair and reasonable in the day-in and day-out dealings with opposing lawyers and adjusters tended to lead to a norm of cooperation and reciprocity. One point of comparison that cropped up in the interviews was a perception that lawyers from Milwaukee were less likely to adhere to this norm than were lawyers from elsewhere in the state, and this was true on both the plaintiff and the defense side. Whether norms of cooperation are generally less evident in large urban bars is not clear from my research; other research (e.g., Ross 1980) did not find evidence of major differences in behavioral patterns of claims settlement based on the size of the community.

When the opposing side violates the cooperation and reciprocity norm, most lawyers indicated that they would respond in kind; "what goes around, comes around" was a phrase that was used by some. Many gave examples of relying on what amounts to the "tit-for-tat" approach predicted by the iterated prisoner's dilemma analysis:

I just went through a case with Smith and Jones, and they were absolute, utter jerks. And at the beginning I was giving them everything in the world, and then all of a sudden when I wanted something it was, "Uh . . . I'm sorry." They set a motion for when they knew I would be out of town. Frankly, towards the end I did not give them any breaks that I would normally give with another firm that I know if I called up and said, "Hey, I need a break. Give me some extra time on this, or give me this without a formal request," they'll do it. I really don't like to do it that way. If I run up against these same guys again in the next six months, I will not give them the benefit of the doubt because they've screwed me and almost screwed my client. So, I will not give them the benefit of the doubt.

However, even here the emphasis was on trying to do things in a somewhat reasonable way or to resist being vindictive:

I just do everything by the book, I make sure that I'm not late on anything, I don't ask for any favors, but on the other hand, I don't give them any, and if they are not in line, I file motions.

I try not to [jerk back]. I really resist that. I really live by the motto in this business that what goes around comes around, and that, if somebody is jerking my chain in this particular case, I am still going to do my job, I am going to resist. There will be an opportunity when I can jerk it, and I don't forget.

While the typical stance was akin to tit-for-tat, some lawyers rejected that in favor of, in one lawyer's words, turning the other cheek:

I am not a believer in [jerking back]. My mentor taught me to turn the other cheek on that kind of thing, when it comes to jerking each other around. He says that he thought that was the answer, because what goes around comes around in our business, and I typically, if I feel like I'm getting jerked around, I'll call up the other lawyer and say, hey, what is going on here? We are decent human beings; we're just trying to solve a problem here. If they still are jerking me around, then I will just ignore them. Then I will do everything the hard way. Go through court, do the motions; all the discovery will be very formal.

Others simply said that they tried to avoid getting into a tit-for-tat situation:

If somebody needs a time limit or a time extension, if it's not going to compromise your client's position, you give it. But you do get those situations where somebody's out of line. I think in my younger days I was probably a little more feisty and would just get all upset. The position I take now basically is I'll try to be reasonable at all costs, because when the thing does get into court, on some type of discovery dispute, which it probably will, it'd be nice to have one of you to appear reasonable for the judge.

To some degree, we [will jerk back]. I prefer just getting an understanding, you know, let's find out, what are the rules going to be. It's fun—you can play that way—it's just that it is counterproductive and people would be hurt around here if you did it. So, you just get an understanding.

As the above comments suggest, most of the contingency fee lawyers I spoke with wanted to present themselves as reasonable people. Defense lawyers generally expressed a preference for cooperative styles as well:

I think most defense lawyers would rather deal with, what I guess, we would call the more established plaintiffs' lawyers, because you get to the bottom line relatively quickly. In contrast to some of the people that enter into the personal injury, bodily injury world, maybe a couple of times a year, who flounder. For example, I recently had a call from a lawyer representing a guest passenger. He sent out some requests to admit. It is kind of a waste of time, no discovery has been taken, and he is trying to look for a deep pocket, because there is very little coverage on the accident vehicle. And so he has sort of a specious position that involves an argument against two other parties. . . . I've seen another attorney who doesn't do this [personal injury work] very much. He will send out a request to admit that the defendant was 100 percent at fault; next question, admit that the defendant was 90 percent at fault. . . . Some lawyers will file a request to admit for limited medical bills and specials and stuff like that. But most of the time, with the more experienced defense lawyers and plaintiffs' lawyers, it is a phone call . . . do you have any problems stipulating to the medical bills, etc.? And it is taken care of in a few minutes on the phone.

Related to reciprocity is honesty. Lawyers want to be able to trust what the other side tells them. When a lawyer develops a reputation for lack of truthfulness, the lawyer generates more work both for those on the other side and for him- or herself. Recall the lawyer discussed in Chapter 4 (p. 130) who described the problem of an opposing lawyer whose settlement offers could not be trusted, resulting in the need to continue preparing a case involving that opponent even after a verbal agreement on settlement had been reached. While most lawyers can undoubtedly relate examples of dealing with an untrustworthy opponent, the day-to-day working world is one that tries to foster reputations for trustworthiness because this increases the efficiency which is so crucial to contingency fee practice.

Lawyers emphasized that cooperation and reciprocity did not mean neglecting the interests of their clients. Sometimes clients will perceive the lawyers' interaction with the opposing lawyer as being too friendly, and the lawyer must explain to the client that good relationships do not equate to less than zealous representation: "I've had clients that kind of get mad at you. 'What were you doing out in the hallway? You seemed kind of friendly to Joe Defense Attorney. What's that about?' And I tell people that if acting like an asshole is going to get my client ahead, then I will act like an asshole, but I haven't quite yet figured out how that is going to get my client ahead. So, figure it out and let me know and I'll try to do it." In a study of lawyers in a rural Missouri, Donald Landon (1985, 95) quoted one lawyer who routinely told clients at the first meeting, "You can hire me to fight your case, but you can't hire me to hate the opposing attorney." The client's perception of tension between representation of the client and continuing relations the lawyer has with others involved in the system is emblematic of the tension between the short-run perspective of the client and the long-run perspective of the lawyer. It is another indication of the importance of thinking not about individual cases but about the lawyer's portfolio of cases, both those cases currently in the portfolio and the future cases the lawyer wants to have in the portfolio.

The defense-side actors seemed to recognize that the plaintiffs' lawyers had incentives for efficient handling of cases. One of the defense lawyers I interviewed observed:

When there is a contingent fee basis, if the case can be settled, the other lawyer's motivation is to settle it early. He has no incentive to keep the thing going forever. As a matter of fact, the key to a good [personal injury] practice is to turn the cases over. You don't make any money until you turn them over. And knowing that, if you can get in there and figure out where you stand, your chances of settling are a little better, I think, early in the litigation, or at least more so with a contingent fee. [In] the hourly cases that I have seen, the lawyer has no motivation whatsoever to settle the case.

While the defense bar sees some contingency fee lawyers as "in-your-face" and all stops off, full ahead, this perception was limited to a relatively few lawyers.

As noted in previous chapters, for contingency fee lawyers, efficiency means profit. To achieve efficiency, not only must lawyers create good internal processes, but they need cooperation from opponents. Everyone recognizes that certain things must be done. Everyone also recognizes that the rules make it possible to force opponents to put in a lot of time and effort that is essentially nonproductive to the eventual result. Contingency fee lawyers seek to create reputations for cooperation in the expectation that will be reciprocated. At the same time, they must tread the line that separates zealous representation of a client's interest and reciprocity with opposing interest.

Even so, there are situations when cooperation breaks down and when contingency fee lawyers generally expect a noncooperative response from opposing counsel. Typically this comes when the defense side has decided to make a stand over some class of cases. Medical malpractice was one example where experienced contingency fee practitioners expected to meet resistance from the defense at virtually every point of a case. In these cases, defense insurers and lawyers knew that the risks of trial for plaintiffs were great and the amount at stake meant that going to trial frequently represented a good risk from the viewpoint of the defense (see Vidmar 1995). However, insurers may decide to adopt a resistant, noncooperative policy vis-à-vis other types of cases, including those with typically modest values. Chuck Brown commented during my observation about a cyclical pattern he had observed with some of the insurers he dealt with. "For a while XXX was giving only low-ball offers. At one point, I started just putting all XXX cases into suit and I told the other [personal injury] lawyers in the firm to do the same. At some point, I got a call from one XXX adjuster asking why I was doing that, and I explained that I didn't like the offers I was getting. After that the offers seemed to get better, but things may have shifted back toward low ball again." One of the defense lawyers I interviewed commented on the same pattern:

It is kind of a cyclical thing, you know. The insurance companies go in cycles. Sometimes they go on a real "let's get these things paid off without involving litigation and lawyers." And then after they realize that they are getting pounded on settlements, then they go back to the lawyers, and "let's fight everything," you know, the thousands for defense and not a penny for tribute, that kind of thing. Yes, there are lawyers in town who they would be less likely to want to tangle with, if that is a good way to put it.

In a conversation with Steve Clarke several years after the observation, he reported that one national insurer had adopted a very hard-line policy on settlement of "low-impact" auto accident cases (see Hechler 2001). The insurer routinely took the position that it would pay $1,000 in such cases, and if that was not acceptable, it would take the case to trial. As Clarke described it, the insurer would bring in experts to testify that the impact, as evidenced by the damage to the vehicle, could not have produced the claimed injury. Juries, according to Clarke, were inclined to return defendant's verdicts, and if the plaintiff did not request a jury trial, the defense would. The result was that Clarke no longer accepted low-impact cases without clearly visible injuries.

Reputation and Portfolio Redemption

For contingency fee practice to be profitable for most lawyers, cases must be resolved short of trial. One defense lawyer in fact referred to plaintiffs' lawyers as "liquidating" suits. While a small percentage of cases can produce a profitable result for the lawyer even if they end in trial, many—probably most—cases will not. Everyone knows that most of the time a contingency fee lawyer would prefer a good settlement to the costs and uncertainty of trial. The situation is somewhat akin to a deterrence problem: the contingency fee lawyer wants the other side to believe that he or she has both the resources and the will to go to trial if necessary, even if the result would not be rational if viewed from a simple, immediate cost-benefit calculation. The contingency fee lawyer deters the opponent from forcing a case to trial because the opponent will also incur costs that are not rational from an immediate cost-benefit calculation.

From a game-theoretic perspective, the best metaphor may be the game of "chicken": two opponents are driving toward each other down the center of a highway; each player must decide whether to swerve (play the *weak* strategy) or go straight (play the *strong* strategy). If neither swerves, the result is a disaster for both; if only one swerves, the other wins the game; if both swerve it is a tie, although each loses face (Rapoport 1969, 116–18). In the game of chicken, one or both players can announce in advance the strategy that player will play; however, this by no means binds the player to that strategy, particularly if it is to play the strong strategy. This is where reputation comes in: if player A announces strong, should player B believe A or not? This is the problem of credibility so thoroughly debated by nuclear deterrence theorists (Kahn 1960) and deterrence theorists more generally (Mercer 1996, 14–43; Schelling 1960). Credibility is enhanced by (1) past behavior, (2) the degree to which the player has the resources to play the game, and (3) an assessment of the likelihood of winning.

With this framework in mind, it is easy to see why the quality of settlements that contingency fee lawyers can achieve depends heavily on reputation. Several key dimensions of reputation link directly to the factors related to achieving credibility: taking cases that are strong (winnability); having the resources necessary to properly prepare a significant case (resources); making demands that are well prepared and well documented, and hence justifiable (demonstrating winnability); and going to trial without hesitation if necessary (past behavior). Note that the issue is not one of getting a settlement. Everyone recognizes that most cases settle, and they settle even if (1) they are not strong, (2) the plaintiff's lawyer submits a poorly documented demand, and (3) the plaintiff's lawyer has a reputation of never taking cases to trial. Nonetheless, the lawyer's ability, which most of the lawyers I spoke with viewed as well reflected in a lawyer's reputation, does matter in terms of the kind of settlement that eventually results. It is not necessarily the case that a very good lawyer will get a significantly better result in a modest case, but a bad lawyer can hurt the client's recovery. In the words of one lawyer, "I don't know that a good lawyer or a great lawyer is going to get any more for your case than it's worth. But a bad lawyer can always screw a case up." In the worst-case situation, a lawyer could "screw up" a case so badly that a deserving plaintiff has to "walk away" from a claim. While a plaintiff might have a potential malpractice claim against the lawyer who screwed up the case, short of something obvious such as missing a statute of limitation deadline, few clients are likely to realize that they could bring such a claim.

Initial Evaluation

Many defense lawyers I interviewed cited the identity of the plaintiff's lawyer as a factor in their initial evaluation of a case, both in terms of value and quality vis-à-vis liability:

I will make an assessment of the case just on the lawyer that is bringing it. There are some people where you just sort of roll your eyes and say, "another one from him."

One of the first things that I ask when someone tells me that there is a new case and what is it worth, I say, "Who is the lawyer on the other side?" And the reason for that is that I can tell a lot from who the plaintiffs' lawyer is. I know who is who, and I know that one guy will handle generally kind of marginal claims and questionable matters, and there may well be a lot of defenses to them. Another guy will be very, very selective in terms of the cases that he takes, and he won't take a case unless he thinks he can make money at it. I can almost tell you, and quite frankly, that the guy who has the marginal cases, if he does get a good case, the first thing he does is refer it to somebody who handles good cases.

You will find that it is the marginal player who ends up with the marginal claims; even if they have big damage cases, there is always some huge problem and that they are trying overreach with the claim, or they want way too much even for a good claim, or there is some obvious liability problem that they refuse to recognize. The failure to recognize problems is probably the thing that I notice more than anything else about the plaintiffs' bar. The good firms, they know when they have a good case, and they know where problems are, and they steer clear of problem cases, because they are in the business of making money, and they don't want problems. To them, if they never leave their office, they have done a good job, because they haven't had to come to court and try anything. . . . Firms that are more marginal will take anything.

Everybody in the business knows that so-and-so has a lot of these marginal claims and this other person has a lot of fairly legitimate claims. . . .

One line of distinction has to do with the type of firm. Some firms, typically those that process a high volume of cases, have reputations as "mills," or "factories." Defense lawyers view these firms as nonselective in the cases they take, as less competent in a general sense, and as primarily interested in turnover rather than seeking to get top dollar for their cases.

There are what we call the factory attorneys. Those are the people who are taking claims no matter what they are, and they are going to turn them over quickly. . . . You have to conduct your dealings with those attorneys accordingly. You also know the attorneys who are going to try a lot of cases, so again, you have to conduct your handling of those cases in that regard.

I have plenty of experience with mill-type firms, and I would say that on the whole I would evaluate them as less competent.

There are some [firms] that are volume dealers, and all they are looking for is the quick, easy-buck settlement. They generally get the lower run-of-the-mill types of claims that don't have a great deal of value, and they don't do a lot of work in preparing their cases.

My experience is that a firm that operates on [a volume basis], the degree of competency that they display in court is lacking. . . . They can talk the talk, but they don't have to walk the walk. And the vast majority of these volume firms simply cannot afford to have top-notch trial attorneys on their staff, because a top-notch trial attorney could never keep up with the volume. . . . While they sue cases an awful lot as a leverage thing, the actual trials when they occur are at best minimally successful.

In contrast, there are firms that are recognized as very selective in the cases they take. These firms want to be sure that their cases have what one defense lawyer termed the "blessed trinity": "There are three things first of all you have to have. You have to have what we call the 'blessed trinity.' You have to have liability; you have to have injury; and you have to have coverage. If you've got all three of those, the question then is, how much is the coverage?" In part, the top firms and top lawyers want cases that will enhance, or at least not damage, their reputations: Good lawyers "want, first of all, only cases that they know they will get something—they don't like to take a case where their reputation might be smeared by losing." These firms do not hesitate to play hardball if they perceive that is necessary: "It may be a situation where, and this happens to some people, I think, where the insurance company that is involved in defending against the claim may have the reputation of not paying or jerking people around. When you get the high-caliber personal injury lawyer on those claims, then the jerking around tends to stop." Interestingly, for cases from these firms, the defense lawyers paid close attention to who in the firm was actually handling the case:

I can almost tell you what a case is worth just by knowing who [within a firm] signed the pleadings. The further the case goes down the letterhead, the more inherent weaknesses there are, and that is like a statement that they are making as to the value of the claim.

As I understand the way XXX works, it is kind of a filter-down, or trickle-down, system. The big ones are swiped at the top, and as they get further and further down, you can expect that the value of the case will be lesser and lesser dollars, frankly. So that if you get their low-level associate, who is very competent, for his age, you can expect that the size of the case is not valued that highly there.

While the lawyer bringing the case is often a signal to the defense on the quality of the case, it is only a signal, not a determinant:

We always look at the other lawyer as one of the factors in trying to decide what a case is worth. . . . A good lawyer, or a great lawyer, isn't going to turn a sow's ear into a silk purse, but a bad lawyer can take a case that has a basic, reasonable value, and turn it into nothing. . . . Let's say we're talking a $10,000 to $20,000 case, and you wind up with somebody who I know to be incapable on the other side. I might tell my client, number one, hold tough on settlement because he isn't going to get what it's worth, and he probably doesn't want to try it, or he shouldn't try it. So maybe that case, instead of paying $15,000 to settle it, maybe it will be more like $7,500. On the other hand, if you are talking a case that could be worth $2.5 to $3.5 million, and you have somebody on the other side who gets the top dollars that case can bring, now instead of trying to settle and holding tough at $2.0 or $2.25 million, you might pay $3 million.

Recall my observation earlier in this chapter about the Habush firm's reputation that it prepares its cases so well that it effectively covers its fee.

Resources and Expertise

For cases involving complex issues (e.g., medical malpractice) or severe injuries (e.g., quadriplegia), a reputation for being able to handle such cases was closely tied to whether the lawyer and the law firm had the resources necessary to bring in appropriate experts and fully prepare the case. Many lawyers who were otherwise well regarded, and very willing to take cases to trial if necessary, were not seen as having the resources necessary to stay the course and prepare the top-end cases. Firms such as Habush, Habush & Rottier were well known to be able to put whatever was necessary into a case to maximize the chances of getting the best result:

I would say that a firm like the Habush firm, with the resources that it can bring to bear on a case, is much more likely to get the top value for that case, or maybe take a case that has big damages, but weak liability, and bring home the liability case than is a firm like XXX [a well-regarded personal injury firm]. The resources that they [Habush] have, number one, they have all the money that they need to go get experts anywhere around the world. Number two, they have people on staff who are engineers and nurses. They bring so many large contingent fees in the course of a year that they can devote much more time to any one case. For a firm like XXX, the bread and butter of their craft is the $15,000 to $50,000 case, so they have to have a high volume of cases, a high volume of relatively small cases, which is very time-intensive. But the big case in their office simply isn't going to get the resources, either in terms of dollars or manpower, that the other firm is going to have.

[For large cases] it's a combination of reputation and ability. As you know, the smaller firms just don't have the financial wherewithal to maintain a case like this.

[Habush] has the money to fund a case right off the bat. These, you take a quadriplegic plaintiff or someone who has had a very serious medical complication; by and large these people are on the verge of bankruptcy because of the personal disaster that has occurred to them, and they can't afford the costs, the out-of-pocket costs of running the malpractice case. You take a bad baby case; so you have to hire OB-GYN experts, you need neonatology experts, you need pediatric neurologists, you need pediatric neuro-radiologists. It gets obscenely expensive, and the small shops can't bear those expenses, sometimes don't even know that you need all of that stuff, whereas the Habush type firm can spend that money without blinking, and that affects the way the case is going to be run.

I think some of your more prominent plaintiff attorneys probably would be able to do a little better job, and probably would, if you needed some expert testimony, would have the knowledge, would know who to go to . . . the more prominent plaintiffs' attorneys have experts almost on a retainer fee—they know who, and they can get them—they know pretty much in advance what the doctor will testify to.

The firms that are well endowed with resources almost invariably also have the expertise to handle complex or difficult cases. Some of this expertise is substantive: medical knowledge related to issues in a case. For example, Chuck Brown had reviewed extensive medical literature in connection with a "bad baby" case he was handling; on his shelves were multiple binders of relevant articles from medical journals, and he could talk knowledgeably about this material. One of the defense lawyers I interviewed commented, "I have a case where the issue is the development of something called XXXX, which is a brain injury. You could ask fifteen family practitioners what that is, and they couldn't tell you. But the lawyers involved with the case could lecture on the topic. That is the same with any bizarre medical issue." Other types of knowledge are also extremely important. One defense lawyer emphasized the centrality of insurance coverage law, followed by the law related to subrogation.[9]

Someone who knows insurance coverage law, that is the biggest mistake that I see. . . . So the first thing for a good plaintiff's lawyer is to understand how much money there is and what are the potential sources of that money. The people I generally deal with, they all know it. Jones [a respected plaintiffs' lawyer] says that he will regularly get phone calls from plaintiffs' lawyers trying to figure out underinsured and uninsured—I mean, it does change, daily. . . . The second thing a good plaintiffs' lawyer has to understand is the subrogation rights.

While this can be fairly technical, identifying sources of compensation is one of the most important things a good plaintiffs' lawyer will do. The same defense lawyer went on to relate the following anecdote:

A year ago or so, maybe it was two years ago, I went over to the Edgewater Hotel for a WATL [Wisconsin Academy of Trial Lawyers—the Wisconsin affiliate of the Association of Trial Lawyers of America] seminar. One of the speakers was known for his work on stacking [combining underinsured / uninsured motorist coverage for multiple vehicles]. The speaker started talking about stacking under certain policies in light of a recent Wisconsin Supreme Court decision.[10]

   The guy sitting next to me leaned over and said, "I'm really confused about this; they've only got one insurance policy. How do you stack, what are they talking about, two or more policies?"

   I turned to him and I said, "Well, how many vehicles were on the policy?"

   "Three, I think."

   "So we have three policies."

   He said, "That doesn't make any sense; there is only one physical policy."

   This is a guy who does plaintiffs' work. I commented on this to a well-regarded Madison plaintiffs' lawyer, and he said, "You'd be surprised how many people don't understand the basics of insurance coverage."

All three of the lawyers I observed were highly attuned to the issue of insurance coverages. In fact, with any significant injury case, virtually the first question was the nature of the insurance coverage that would be available.

Dispositional or Litigational Style

In Chapter 4, I described two broad styles of contingency fee practice: the litigational style, where the lawyer approaches all cases as if they are potential trials, and the dispositional style, where the lawyer approaches cases primarily in terms of processing and preparing for settlement. This distinction, as reflected in a lawyer's reputation, becomes very important in the settlement process. The most common reputational comment among defense lawyers vis-à-vis contingency fee lawyers had to do with willingness to take cases to trial.[11]

A plaintiffs' attorney has to be able to convince the defense that we will take this case to trial; we are not going to fold at the last minute. If the attorney is not a good trial lawyer, he better be associated with somebody who is.

I think that certain firms command a better settlement value than others. This is largely because of their reputations for willingness to try the case.

If you know that your opponent is not willing to go to trial, then your position is a little stronger in the bargaining

There are some lawyers in town who are known to never try a case, and that makes a difference. A lot of the insurance companies that we represent more recently have become very tight with their settlement money, and if they know that the attorney is one not likely to try the case, they are likely to stay tighter.

There's one firm down here which has as good a reputation as anybody, and I've never tried a case against them. And my sense is—and this is a sentiment that has been shared among defense lawyers—my sense is that all of their cases are good, that they don't want it to go to trial. They don't . . . they aren't going to increase their overall profitability by trying a case. So that I may settle a surgical back case with them for $60,000 where someone else may have gotten $75,000.

If I had practiced against an attorney, and I've seen him a few times, and I know that he or she isn't going to go to trial and is likely to settle a claim real cheap, I am certainly going to get it at the lowest price.

The reputation for taking cases to trial is important not just because of the deterrent value it represents, but also because it is an indicator of the lawyer's reputation for preparing cases. As one respondent stated very simply, "The good lawyers tend to put together a better case."

Finally, having a reputation for winning cases at trial can lead a lawyer to have a very strong motivation to avoid trial in some cases. Having a reputation for winning at trial can be damaged by losing cases. What this means is that a lawyer who relies heavily on a trial reputation may be reluctant to take cases to trial when there is some heightened uncertainty or risk. If a lawyer perceives that trying a case may actually be harmful to his or her reputation, the lawyer might choose to settle, even settle for more of a discount than would otherwise be the case, rather than risk reputational damage (Kessler, Meites, and Miller 1996, 247); a lawyer who was less concerned about a reputation for winning cases at trial might actually be *more* willing to try a case in that situation.

Negotiation Strategies

While many defense lawyers indicated they would vary their negotiating strategy based on the reputation of the opposing lawyer for being willing to go to trial, the plaintiff's lawyer's reputation for negotiation itself was also important. At the extreme of cynicism was the observation about one unnamed law firm: "When they feel the need for some cash, they settle a case." The more common comment had to do with reputations for making demands that were realistic and defensible.

You get to know attorneys after a while, and there are some attorneys who are going to make what we would consider to be a ridiculous demand.

When you are dealing with somebody who makes off-the-wall demands, you make off-the-wall low offers. When you are dealing with somebody who has their feet on the ground and usually has a pretty good sense of what the case is worth, it is just a whole different ball game. You deal with them straight on.

While a few of the people I interviewed on the defense side insisted that their own negotiating behavior was keyed primarily to their own evaluation of what the case was worth, most indicated that their responses to demands were significantly affected by the nature of the plaintiff's demands:

If a demand is within reason, you have a dialogue and you make more frequent contact to bridge the difference. But if it is totally outrageous, it puts a pretty quick end to the talking, and there is no point in attempting negotiations.

By and large, people have a fairly good idea of what cases are worth. To give you an example, I had a broken leg case—a bad broken leg a year ago. And there's a firm in Waukesha that notoriously overevaluates their cases. And when the demand came in, it was $175,000. A broken leg, even with some hardware in it, isn't even worth $75,000. When we get demands like this, typically we'll start lower than if the demand was realistic.

At one extreme, one could argue that the defense bar would prefer that the plaintiff's lawyer make unreasonable demands, given that for the defense lawyer being paid by the hour, there is no disincentive to take a case to trial. From the viewpoint of the defense lawyer, having an unreasonable contingency fee lawyer to deal with allows the defense lawyer to justify expending significant billable hours on a case that the client would like to resolve through a reasonable settlement: "I think making a large demand makes my job a lot easier. Because then there is no pressure on us to settle the case at all." While none of the contingency fee lawyers I observed or spoke to suggested that they might gear their offers to avoid giving a defense lawyer a reason for stretching out a case, it is clear that this would be a factor that would reinforce a contingency fee lawyer's motivation to avoid making demands that might put an eminently settleable case into a litigation mode.

It should come as no surprise that reputations are an important part of negotiation. This is by no means limited to the context of litigation. It is important in any situation where either there is repeated interaction between players or there is some vehicle for disseminating information on reputations. Scholars of international negotiation have long understood the importance of reputation in bargaining (see Young 1968; Schelling 1960). While one can imagine bargaining situations in which reputations do not play a role, the archetypical tourist in the archetypical local market, those situations are far from that confronted by contingency fee lawyers. Perhaps what is surprising in the context of contingency fee practice is the breadth of the range of relevant reputations that exist among lawyers doing this work. This allows the players on the defense side to structure their responses to demands from contingency fee in accordance with the reputations the defense side is able to discern.

Reputational Capital

In this chapter I have laid out three different but interrelated ways in which reputation is important in the work of contingency fee lawyers. Using the terminology of investment, reputation is important for acquiring the initial investment opportunity, it is important for managing and controlling the amount actually invested in the opportunity, and it is important for the return that can be realized on an investment. From both observation and interviews, the concerns expressed by the lawyers about their reputations were prominent and very often explicitly mentioned with a lawyer referring directly to some aspect of his or her reputation.

In this chapter, I have said very little about how the reputations come to be formed and maintained. Some of the formation process is fairly obvious. Some lawyers handle cases that generate significant amounts of coverage in the press, and actors in the system see the same players again and again and take note of what they do and how they do it. In a sense, reputation is nothing more than expected behavior. The single best predictor of future behavior is past behavior, and the players in the system are attentive to the behavior of their opponents. Within a community, even a fairly large professional community, the actors know (or can readily find out) who does and does not take cases to trial. They know who gets the better cases. They know who prepares cases carefully and who turns them over for a quick settlement. If Jones does not know about Smith, Jones will know someone who does know about Smith, unless Smith is an entirely new player in the system. Alternatively, Smith may work within a firm that has a reputation, and Jones will attribute the firm's reputation to Smith until experience suggests some modification.

Behavioral expectations that function as a kind of reputation can be formed during an individual case. In the words of one defense lawyer,

There is sort of a feeling-out process through the course of discovery. To give you an example, I got a case today where the lawyer sends me, three weeks into the suit, this barrage, wanting me to admit that Dr. Smith said this in his report, and that is what Dr. Smith would say in trial. Well, I know that no experienced attorney would want to waste the paper of getting me to admit that medical report says what it says, because they are going to call the doctor to testify at the trial anyway. If I am being chased around like that, it indicates to me that we are probably not dealing with somebody who has a lot of experience. . . . You can tell from some of the questions that are asked at depositions and the responses that are given whether a person has done a lot of this work or not. If they start out like they are deposing the defense doctor, and they ask to depose him, and then they come in and first, they spend an hour asking how many medical exams he has done in the last year, that tells me, again, this is probably not a real experienced player in the whole business. On the other hand, if they bring out five transcripts and say, "Well, here is what you testified to last month," that leads me to think that maybe this fellow has done a little bit more of this work than I would have thought.

If a lawyer has a preformed judgment of what the opposing counsel will do, or if the lawyer forms a judgment from interaction early in the litigation, that will typically influence how the lawyer proceeds with the case.

One difficulty for a lawyer may arise if the lawyer wants to change his or her reputation. Erasing a negative reputation can be costly. For example, the Gallo Wine Company has for years sought to establish an image of producing high-quality wines, and it may be the case that it does. However, for someone who came of age when Gallo was known largely as a producer of jug wines, it is very difficult to accept this. I reached drinking age at a time when Gallo and other California producers were involved in conflict with the farm workers, leading to boycotts of their wines. One joke that circulated was that Gallo should not be affected by the boycott because there were no grapes involved in making its wine. Gallo has yet to succeed in convincing me to buy any of its wines.

From a game-theoretic perspective, imagine the problem faced by a player in a repeated game of chicken. Once a player has developed a reputation for playing the weak strategy (swerving), the other players will expect that behavior. The cost of changing the expectation is high because it can be done only by action, not by words (Mercer 1996, 40–41). There might be the possibility of disguising the player's identity in some way. Gallo produces wines on many labels (usually identifiable by coming from Modesto, California), and one interpretation of this is an effort to escape its older reputation. Similarly, after a major disaster that led to ValuJet Airline's being grounded by the Federal Aviation Administration in 1996, the airline resumed flying under a new name, Air-Tran; the change of name was an effort to escape the image or reputation that had become associated with ValuJet. I know of no instances of a lawyer changing his or her name as part of an effort to build a new reputation. A lawyer can relocate to a new market and try to build a different type of reputation. Short of that, the lawyer has to confront the "game of chicken" problem and win.

The classic quote from Publilius Syrus advises us that "a good reputation is more valuable than money." For the contingency fee lawyer, a good reputation *is* money, because having a "good" reputation along the right dimensions is central to a profitable contingency fee practice.

Praying for Justice or Preying on Justice?

Providing Access or Promoting Abuse?

Historically, the contingency fee developed both as a means of providing access to legal services to injured persons who otherwise would not have been able to pay a lawyer and as a means of obtaining clients (and income) by struggling segments of the bar. By the last third of the twentieth century, contingency fee legal practice had evolved to emerge from the margins of the practitioner community. While some contingency fee work continues to be done by the struggling practitioners described forty years ago by Jerome Carlin (1962), today's top contingency fee specialists are very visible and very wealthy. The focus in this book has been on the vast majority of lawyers offering services on a contingency fee basis who fall between these two extremes. In the preceding chapters, I have examined a variety of aspects of contemporary contingency fee legal practice in the United States. The central theme drawing together this discussion is that understanding the way that contingency fees work requires a framework that focuses on the practices of lawyers rather than on single cases. I have drawn from the literature on portfolio theory to provide that needed framework.

As discussed in Chapter 1, supporters of contingency fees describe them as the average person's "key to the courthouse" (Corboy 1976). In contrast, critics of contingency fees see such fees as at least partly responsible for many of the evils and excesses of the American legal system (Brickman 1992; Kagan 2001; O'Connell 1979; Rein and Barry 1999) and as unjustly enriching and empowering members of the legal profession (Brickman 1989, 1996a; Olson 2003). Nonetheless, from the perspective of the average citizen, contingency fees *are* about "access to justice" through the mechanism of civil litigation, or the threat of civil litigation.

Does the availability of contingency fees increase the resort to litigation? It seems that the obvious answer must be "yes, of course." However, that answer is too simplistic, because one must go on to ask, "compared to what"? While Americans like to claim, with a kind of perverse pride, that we are the most litigious people in the world, that may not in fact be the case; a comparative study of litigation rates by the late German scholar Christian Wollschläger (1998) shows several countries as having higher litigation rates than those of the United States, and none of those countries employ contingency fees. Moreover, the United States is by no means alone in employing contingency fees (as I discuss in the next section), and several countries which allow contingency fees, most notably Japan, have much lower litigation rates than those of the United States, according to the data assembled by Wollschläger. Thus, while contingency fees may facilitate access to justice (and hence increase the use of litigation), contingency fees are neither a necessary nor a sufficient condition for high reliance on litigation. That is, contingency fees can provide a means of access to justice, but there are other ways of accomplishing this (e.g., legal aid, legal expense insurance), and there are ways of negating the access role of contingency fees through mechanisms such as fee shifting. Furthermore, it is also possible to reduce or eliminate the need for access to legal remedies in many types of cases by providing strong social welfare policies and first-party insurance systems.

As the preceding chapters should make clear, I am generally supportive of contingency fees as a means of funding litigation. At the same time, I do not presume that there are never situations in which lawyers take advantage of clients to obtain fees that raise equity and ethical issues. However, abuses of this type are confined neither to lawyers working on contingency fees (see Lerman 1999) nor to members of the legal profession generally, as indicated by the spate of corporate accounting fiascos that came to light in 2001–2. Likewise, while litigation provides a vehicle for compensation, deterrence, and reallocation of social costs, it is by no means the *only* way to accomplish such goals, although likely alternatives are not particularly palatable in the political climate of the early-twenty-first-century United States. There may be very good *political* reasons for relying on litigation to serve the important social purposes (see Burke 2002), at least in the relatively short term.

Can the existing contingency fee system be improved? Are there mechanisms that would reduce the incidence of the abuses that do occur despite the self-regulating effects that the portfolio perspective brings to the fore? Possibly, but to develop good reforms, it is imperative for us to understand not just the situations of abuse and malfunction, but also the routine ways in which systems operate day-to-day (see Feeley 1983). There is a long history of reforms of the court system being adopted in the wake of newsworthy and usual cases on the assumption that such cases indicated that the system is out of whack. Often, careful examination, usually post hoc, reveals that the day-to-day operation differed sharply from the perceived problems. One of my favorite examples of this involved a perception of rampant abuse of continuances in Ohio. As a result of this perception, Ohio adopted a set of rules, the Ohio Rules of Superintendence, designed to discourage judges from granting such continuances. The goal was to reduce court delay. An evaluation of the impact of these rules found that before the rules were introduced, the average case had one-half of one continuance. That is, the modal case had *no* continuances, most cases that had any continuances had only one, and only a very small number of cases had multiple continuances (Grau and Sheskin 1980, 1982).

A second area that regularly is flogged as a problem is discovery. To deal with problems related to perceived discovery abuse, Arizona adopted rules to provide for sanctions for lawyers who engaged in abusive discovery activities. As in Ohio, after the rules were introduced, an evaluation was commissioned. After taking a sample of cases from Maricopa County, the evaluation team concluded that it was virtually impossible to identify cases in which abusive discovery did occur (Chapper and Hanson 1983; Mullenix 1994a; see also Mullenix 1994b). More generally, while discovery abuse is a frequent target of civil justice reform (Brazil 1978; Ebersole and Burke 1980; Keilitz, Hanson, and Daley 1993; Lacy 1978; Lundquist 1980), research has repeatedly shown that very few cases involve the level of discovery that might be deemed to rise to being abusive (Connolly, Holleman, and Kuhlman 1978; McKenna and Wiggins 1998; Mullenix 1994a). This does not mean that discovery abuse does not occur (most judges and litigators can undoubtedly provide war stories), but rather it is a particular kind of problem in particular kinds of cases. Blanket reforms probably create more problems than they solve. To deal with a whole host of perceived problems of cost and delay in federal civil litigation, Congress passed the Civil Justice Reform Act (CJRA) in 1990 as a means of improving and streamlining the way that the federal courts handle civil cases, despite the lack of evidence that a large proportion of cases in the federal courts suffered from the kinds of problems the reforms supposedly addressed (see Sanders and Joyce 1990). Not surprisingly, an extensive after-the-act evaluation found little evidence that the reforms changed significantly either the cost or the time required to process civil cases through the federal courts (Kakalik et al. 1996).[1]

Those who would reform the contingency fee system (e.g., Brickman, Horowitz, and O'Connell 1994) fall into the same trap as have previous reformers. They presume to know how the system works, but that presumption is based largely on the atypical cases that capture media and public attention. Not surprisingly, those interests that believe that they would benefit by reforming or limiting contingency fees rush to support supposed reforms that they like (Haltom and McCann 2004).

Contingency Fees Around the World

Underlying many of the proposals to modify contingency fees is the common assumption that contingency fees are unique to the United States, and consequently contingency fees must account, at least in significant part, for many of the supposed problems in our civil justice system. The belief that only the United States permits contingency fees is widespread, even among people who should know better.[2] As suggested earlier in this chapter, contingency fees are not peculiar to the United States. As Table 8.1 shows, a surprising number of countries permit "no win, no pay" fee arrangements, some of which look quite similar to the American percentage fee.[3] Clearly, the United States is by no means unique in permitting contingency fees. Even as contingency fees have come under attack in the United States, other countries—England is a prominent example—have looked to the *percentage fee* system as a model that might solve problems created by existing systems of funding litigation (Zander 2002a, 2002b).[4] Nor is the percentage principle unique to the United States. As shown in Table 8.1, several of the Canadian provinces permit contingency fees to be computed as a percentage of recovery, as do Greece and the Dominican Republic.

While the specific analyses I have presented in the preceding chapters are built in part upon the specific characteristics of the American contingency fee—in particular, the percentage nature of the fee calculation—the portfolio framework is relevant for any type of "no win, no pay" fee, given the combination of investment and risk inherent in legal services provided on this basis. In particular, for any "no win, no pay" structure, it is crucial to look not just at the economic incentives at the case level but also at the economic incentives at the practice or portfolio level (see, as an example, Kritzer 2001a, 239–41).

While the portfolio framework is readily applicable to systems employing contingency fees outside the United States, caution is in order in making the assumption that the results I have described directly apply in other countries, even countries using the percentage form of the contingency fee. There are two major differences that are relevant. First, no other country makes as much use of juries in civil cases as does the United States, although juries are used in some civil cases in some provinces of Canada and in Australia (Vidmar 2002, 802).[5] The result is that outside the United States, damage awards are set by judges, and at least in common law countries, the judges typically rely upon a set of precedential cases (Kritzer 1996, 145–46). One result of this is that damage amounts may be less variable than in the United States, and while a significant element of uncertainty may remain (see Genn 1988, 75), defendants may have less fear of being hit with an extreme verdict. The impact is to modify some elements of the risks involved in contingency fee cases.

The second key difference is fee shifting. In the United States, the general rule is that each side pays its own lawyer. In most other countries, including those having some form of contingency fee, the general rule is that the loser is responsible for some or all of the winner's legal expenses. While there is a danger in accepting simplistic descriptions of how these systems operate in practice (see Kritzer 1992), or the nature of their impacts on such things as litigiousness or settlement (see Kritzer 2002b, 1948–60), there are undoubtedly some significant interactions between fee shifting and the operation of "no win, no pay" fees. These relationships may be further complicated by the development of "after-the-event" insurance systems that protect clients from the risks of fee shifting (see Moorhead 2000).

TABLE 8.1

Contingency Fees Around the World

Country	Contingency Fee Arrangements Allowed
Canada	All provinces now permit contingency fees (Skordaki and Walker 1994, 36), as some have for over 100 years (Minish 1979, 69); the last holdout was the province of Ontario, where contingency fees became generally available through a combination of court decisions (see *Raphael Partners v Lam*, 2002, O.J. no.3605, as well as *McIntyre Estate v. Ontario [Attorney General]*, 2001, 53 O.R. [3d] 137, docket no. 00-CV-195898) and legislative action (Justice State Law Amendment Act 2002, available at http://www.e-laws.gov.on.ca/DBLaws/Source/Statutes/English/2002/S02024_e.htm, visited June 26, 2003). In some provinces, the amount charged is based on the same factors as a noncontingency fee (see Watson et al. 1991, 474), while in others it is based on a percentage (see *McIntyre Estate v. Ontario [Attorney General]*, 2001, 53 O.R. [3d] 137, docket no. 00-CV-195898, appendix).
England	Since 1995, English solicitors could charge clients on a "conditional fee" basis in which the client pays nothing if no recovery is obtained and pays an "uplift" of up to 100 percent over the normal fee if there is a recovery (Yarrow 1998; Maurer, Thomas, and DeBooth 1999, 307–16).[a] In 1999, the government moved to greatly expand the use of conditional fees in order to reduce the cost of legal aid (Lord Chancellor's Department 1998; Zander 1998), and under provisions of the Access to Justice Act 1999, successful plaintiffs can recover the "uplift" from the defendant (Underwood 1999, 1033; Robins 1999).[b] Furthermore, in a 1998 decision, the Court of Appeal in England ruled that it was not contrary to law for English solicitors to act on a contingency basis whereby the solicitor would forgo some or all of his or her normal fee if the case was not successful (*Thai Trading Company v. Taylor*, 1998, Q.B 781).
Scotland	Lawyers have long been permitted to act on a "speculative" basis. If the plaintiff wins, he or she pays the lawyer the normal fee, but pays nothing if he or she loses (Skordaki and Walker 1994, 26).
Northern Ireland	"Speculative fee arrangements have operated unofficially . . . for many years" (Skordaki and Walker 1994, 29).
Irish Republic	Barristers take cases on a "no goal–no fee" basis, in which the barrister receives his or her normal fee unless no recovery is obtained (Skordaki and Walker 1994, 43).

Country	Contingency Fee Arrangements Allowed
New Zealand	Both barristers and solicitors may charge on a "speculative basis" (Skordaki and Walker 1994, 33).
Australia	Courts began to recognize the appropriateness of no-win, no-pay fee arrangements in 1960, although it was not until 1994 that such fee arrangements started to be available for potential litigants in certain types of cases (e.g., product disputes) in any type of routine way (Cannon 1998, 105–6; Bolt 1999).
Dominican Republic	Percentage fees, called *cuota litis,* much like those in the United States, are permitted but are limited to no more than 30 percent of the recovery (Pastor and Vargas 2000, 17).
Greece	Percentage fees, but with a limit of 20 percent of the amount recovered, are permitted (Skordaki and Walker 1994, 57); lawyers may also consider the result achieved in setting a fee (Sheridan and Cameron 1992, Greece-10; Kerameus and Koussoulis 1999, 376).
France	Major Paris law firms are using contingency fees increasingly (Skordaki and Walker 1994, 61) as well as being permitted to base fees in part on results achieved (Sheridan and Cameron 1992, France-15).
Brazil	Fees that include a contingency / percentage element are permitted (Bermudes 1999, 353).
Japan	While few auto accident cases lead to lawsuits, in those cases that do go to court, the lawyers (*bengoshi*) representing the claimant normally charge on a contingency (no-win, no-fee) basis (Tanase 1990, 659).

[a] While until 1995 England forbade the contingency fee for personal injury cases, it has long permitted solicitors to charge their commercial clients on a commission basis for work such as debt cases (Law Society 1970, 8–9).

[b] There has been substantial litigation over how much of the uplift (and how much of a premium for after-the-event insurance for the potential of having to pay an opposing side's costs in an unsuccessful case) can be recovered from the opposing party. See *Callery v. Gray,* 2002, UKHL 28; *Halloran v. Delaney,* 2002, EWCA Civ 1258, and *Sharratt v. London Central Bus Co Ltd,* 2003, 1 All ER 353.

Who Benefits from Contingency Fees?

Contingency fee legal practice can produce very good financial rewards for some of the lawyers who do such work. However, what the analyses presented in earlier chapters show is that the typical lawyer who takes a typical case on a contingency fee basis can expect to do only somewhat better than he or she would do if the case were billed on an hourly fee basis. The occasional very good case will yield some significant "profits" over and above the balancing out of the typical better-than-average cases and the worse-than-average cases. There is a small group of lawyers who are able to cherry-pick cases and do much better from contingency fee work than most lawyers do from hourly fee work; however, even these lawyers will have the occasional case that "goes south," producing either no return or a return substantially below what the lawyer invested in the case.

What about the client's perspective? Are the lawyers "doing well by doing good," or are they "preying" on the misfortunes of others? As with any type of moneymaking situation, greed can be a dominant factor, at least for some actors. Lawyers (and clients) are as susceptible to temptation as others are. The fact that some people make a lot of money does not mean that the system fails to benefit injured persons.

In one sense, contingency fees are a form of cross-subsidy among clients. The client who turns out to have a very good case subsidizes the client whose case turns out to be a dog. Is that good or bad? In challenging contingency fees, one might argue that any cross-subsidy constitutes a violation of professional ethics because, according to this argument, the lawyer is failing to fulfill his or her duty to the clients effectively providing the subsidy to other clients. I am not a legal ethicist, but this line of argument would also seem to preclude any form of pro bono practice (i.e., lawyers providing free or reduced-price services to needy clients or worthy clients), because those clients who are paying full rates are subsidizing those receiving free or discount services. The central difference between the two cross-subsidies lies primarily in the lawyers' motivation with one, pro bono, ostensibly involving altruism and contingency fees involving profit. Many contingency fee lawyers would assert that there is not necessarily a difference between the two; one lawyer I interviewed described his decision to go into personal injury practice as a way of doing some good for the average person while being able to make a decent living to support his young family. Moreover, highly visible pro bono work can serve as a form of advertising which will attract paying clients in the future.

Again, what about the client's perspective? Probably if a client whose case had turned out to be good knew for certain that the case was good up front, that client would not have chosen to pay the contingency fee lawyer on a percentage basis. The problem is that clients generally have no way of knowing how good a case they have. This reflects both the general uncertainty about cases and the client's lack of information. To the degree it is the latter, one can certainly argue that a lawyer's duty is to advise the client as to what is in the client's interest. The problem, of course, is that "very few cases are clear winners when they come in the door" (Parikh 2001, 76). Cases typically involve a variety of uncertainties: How will the other side respond to a demand? What will the damages be? What are the ambiguities in the factual situation? What will the costs be in obtaining redress? Some lawyers who do not rely primarily on contingency fee cases may in fact be inclined to advise potential clients that a case would be better handled on an hourly basis.

This suggests that there are cases in which the risks are minimal. However, what would a lawyer do who had advised a client to rely upon an hourly fee arrangement only to see the case turn sour, or end up costing much more to handle than originally anticipated? I suspect that this has not happened to the lawyers who have had clients use an hourly arrangement on the lawyer's advice. Most of the lawyers who told me that they had recommended to a client that a matter be handled on an hourly basis found that clients almost always opted for the contingency fee when advised of even the slight possibility of a downside risk or uncertainty over what the fees might ultimately amount to. Occasionally potential clients would themselves raise the possibility of an hourly fee; however, most of these were in fact seeking a contingent hourly fee, not a straight hourly fee.

My conversations with lawyers who depend mostly or exclusively on contingency fee cases indicated that they find the idea of handling cases on a traditional hourly basis much more problematic. First, they need the lucrative cases to balance off the unprofitable ones. Recommending to clients with the best cases that they use an hourly fee changes the overall practice equation in ways that are unattractive. Second, some of them are not set up to bill by the hour, and as the opening chapter's narrative of a day with lawyer Steve Clarke shows, the practicality of keeping an accurate track of hours can be problematic (an issue not considered by some of the proponents of contingency fee reform). Third, they view the big profits yielded by some cases as compensation for their willingness to fund cases and take risks.

One lawyer told me about a case which came to him on an hourly fee basis. The client had originally retained a lawyer on a contingency basis but came to the decision that an hourly fee would be a better deal. The original lawyer worked only on a contingency fee basis and refused to renegotiate the fee. That lawyer and client agreed to part ways, and the lawyer I was speaking to accepted the case on an hourly basis. As it turned out, the client was not in a good position to assess the risks involved in his case. The case had some significant problems that greatly reduced its settlement value, and whether he came out better in the end with the hourly fee arrangement was not at all clear.

One certainly hears about clients who are unhappy about how much they had to pay their lawyers. However, there is no extant evidence showing that those who pay their lawyers on a contingency basis are more likely to be unhappy than those who pay their lawyer on some other basis (e.g., fixed fee, hourly, etc.).[6] In recent years, many corporations have tried to move toward contingency arrangements with their attorneys (Kritzer 1994; Litan and Salop 1994). The fact that some of the most successful contingency fee attorneys are those, such as Joe Jamail, who handle very large cases on behalf of major corporations indicates that the most knowledgeable consumers of legal services are not unwilling to pay purely on a "results-achieved" basis even if that means astronomical hourly rates.[7] Being unhappy about the costs of legal services is neither a new issue nor an issue limited to clients who paid lawyers on a contingency fee basis.

In some ways, the bottom-line question, and probably the most difficult question to answer, is whether clients are ultimately better off or worse off given the contingency fee as opposed to alternative mechanisms of paying for legal services. Many clients probably do pay more for legal services than they might if they paid by the hour, but many of those same clients would probably never seek redress if it were not for the insurance function provided by the contingency fee. In a sense, clients pay a premium for eased access to the civil justice system. Furthermore, many, perhaps most, clients are able to have access precisely because of the availability of a system like the contingency fee. In a fundamental sense there is a trade-off between access and cost, where here the access issue is a combination of risk shifting from the client to the attorney and the availability of funds up front to purchase a needed service.

Could one design a system which would permit access but reduce the fees contingency fee clients pay? In the mid-1990s, proposals were advanced to strictly control the percentages that could be charged in cases where the client receives an early offer (Brickman, Horowitz, and O'Connell 1994) or to otherwise cap contingency fees (Burke 2002, 113).[8] As I reported in Chapter 2, in Wisconsin many attorneys already charge lower percentages for cases resolved earlier in the process, and in some proportion of cases, they charge fees that are less than what the retainer agreement calls for. In a sense, the market has, at least in Wisconsin, already reduced fees for early resolution. Critics might view even these lower fees as too high. Even if in some cases the fees are too high according to some criterion, designing a mechanistic system which would allow attorneys and clients to determine which cases are generating excessive fees and which are not would be very difficult. The "reform" proposals that were advanced during and since the 1990s fail to take into account the uncertainties that typically exist regarding damages, liability, and sources of compensation at the time a potential client first contacts an attorney. Those proposals also fail to recognize that their image of an "early" offer incorporates a view of the work involved in processing personal injury cases that does not apply to a significant portion, perhaps even a majority, of such cases.

None of the proposals for change envision any type of post hoc review of fees (something which technically is already available under inherent judicial authority). Post hoc review is potentially time-consuming and costly, particularly in the absence of well-established standards, but relying upon such a system would probably serve to avoid the problems of the mechanistic systems others have proposed.[9]

One of the ironies of many of the proposals to reform or limit contingency fees is that they come from quarters one would expect to be most likely to support market solutions to pricing. One could imagine a number of market-related alternatives that might serve to bring down existing fees. The first would be to find ways to get more information about fees to potential clients so that clients could make better-informed choices. The obvious mechanism for this would be what amounts to price advertising.[10] There is, of course, the problem that cheapest is not necessarily best; however, most consumers are fully aware that there is a trade-off between price and quality. However, simply making consumers aware that there are alternatives in pricing will put some market pressures on the providers of the service.[11]

Competition could also be opened up by permitting nonlawyer specialists to handle cases within some defined specialties. For example, why shouldn't I, as a knowledgeable consumer, have the option of retaining a private insurance adjuster to negotiate on my behalf with an insurer? Particularly in those types of cases where the concern about excessive charges by lawyers is greatest (i.e., the clear liability, policy limits case), someone who knows the insurance claims system should be able to represent a claimant's interests effectively. If Kritzer's Claims Service will do the case for 15 percent, while Kritzer & Kritzer, S.C. would charge 33 percent, why shouldn't the consumer have that choice?[12]

Lastly, one could imagine a system in which claims were actually sold to lawyers in an auctionlike setting (see, e.g., Shukaitis 1987).[13] Lawyers would bid for claims: the better and more certain the claim, the more the lawyer would offer (i.e., the less the lawyer would discount the projected recovery).[14] Obviously, there is the problem that the full value of a claim is not necessarily known at the time a potential client might first want to retain a lawyer. This might be handled by a system of lawyer or claims brokers, where the broker would sign up the client for a small percentage of the ultimate recovery (e.g., 5 or 10 percent) and provide the initial "front-end" legal assistance (e.g., doing the things necessary to preserve the claim, collect initial evidence, etc.). Once the claim had matured, the broker would put the claim up for bid. To avoid the problem that the client would simply walk away once the auction was completed, the amount of the payment could be put into escrow, to be collected only when the claim was actually paid or the case was otherwise resolved. If the claim was potentially lucrative but very risky, clients would have the option of selling the claim at a steep discount or entering into something that looked like a traditional contingency fee arrangement. It is important to note that I am not advocating that an auction system should be adopted; undoubtedly there are many issues that I have not identified or discussed. My point here is simply that this represents one possible "market" alternative to the current system that needs to be examined in detail before making major changes to the existing system.

The goal should be to find ways of increasing the options in the existing system and making potential clients aware of those options. Legislative limitations on fees are likely to have more negative than positive consequences. In contrast, while deregulation has risks, competition among service providers is more likely to have long-run payoffs than is increased regulation.[15] Typically, limitations on legal fees have served to reduce the availability of legal representation. The extreme example is veterans' benefits claims (see Legal Services Corporation 1979), but this is also evident in unemployment compensation cases, where there are often strict limits on the fees attorneys can charge claimants (see Kritzer 1998a, 25). In contrast, creating competitive mechanisms has the potential of not only lowering fees but also making services available in cases where previously legal representation was not affordable.

Contingency Fees, Access to Justice, and the Ills of the American Legal System

From its founding, the United States has emphasized the importance of the "rule of law," and in the last half century, the rule of law has taken on increasing global significance. Importantly, any system based on a rule of law heightens the role of those who are expert in the law. Having access to those experts, whom we typically think of as lawyers, requires that there be some way to compensate the experts. There are four general approaches to dealing with the compensation issue: (1) government funding of legal services for those who cannot otherwise pay for it; (2) private charitable funding of legal services for those who cannot otherwise pay for it; (3) pro bono legal services whereby lawyers donate time to serve the needs of those who cannot otherwise pay them (effectively cross-subsidizing from their clients who can pay); and (4) in monetary claims situations, paying the lawyer out of the recovery. The latter is, of course, a contingency fee system.

Given the growing emphasis on the rule of law and access to justice around the democratic world, it is not surprising that country after country has struggled with the issue of how to provide access to legal expertise. In many countries, the solution of choice in the second half of the twentieth century was government-funded legal aid (see Ryan et al. 1999). However, as the costs of such programs began to mount, and in the face of a growing emphasis on liberalist, market-based approaches to social needs, governments have looked to reduce the reliance on government-funded legal aid. One alternative, at least for claims involving monetary compensation, is contingency fee funding. Thus, it is not surprising that jurisdictions where contingency fees were traditionally viewed as an anathema (e.g., England, Australia, Ontario) have in recent years adopted such fees in various forms.

One advantage of contingency fee funding is that it is available to everyone with a monetary damage case that has the prospect of producing a reasonable recovery from which a fee can be taken. While legal aid was available only to the relatively poor, leaving the middle class to struggle with paying legal fees for an uncertain outcome, the middle class can just as easily turn to contingency fees as can the relatively poor. The attractiveness of contingency fees extends even to those with substantial resources, as indicated by their growing use by corporations, and by the fact that even individuals who could afford the risks of having to pay a fee out of pocket choose contingency fees over hourly fees.

The middle-class alternative to contingency fees is some form of legal expense insurance, a practice that is most common in Germany (Blankenburg 1982–83, 1994). The problem with legal expense insurance is that one must be able to pay for it, unless it is provided as a benefit through an employer or a union. Thus, while legal aid leaves the middle class to face the vagaries of litigation cost, legal expense insurance leaves the poor to face those dilemmas. Obviously, some combination of legal aid and legal expense insurance would be possible, but that brings us back to the growing unwillingness of governments to foot the bill for legal aid.

Critics of the current American system come from both the right (e.g., Olson 2003; Howard 1994) and the left (e.g., Bogart 2002; Kagan 2001). For these critics, the contingency fee is but one element of a larger complex of issues that are harming American citizens and businesses. This is not the place to take on the full extent of the critics' arguments. However, it is important to recognize that the critics have radically different images of what a less litigious, less adversarial, less lawyer-dominated society would look like. For the critics on the right, that society would be market-based, welcoming to the entrepreneurial spirit, and once again reliant on the ethic of individualism that they see as the basis for America's greatness. For the critics on the left, the alternatives come in the form of greater reliance on social welfare policies (e.g., generous universal health insurance, generous support for those unable to work owing to disability, etc.) and on governmental regulation built on expert consensus rather than the rough-and-tumble of pluralist politics. For those on the left, the freewheeling entrepreneurial individualistic image is an anathema. For those on the right, the image of the social welfare state, particularly when combined with extensive government regulation, is an anathema.

The reality is that any system produces positive and negative effects. The existing system in the United States produces lawyers with incentives to seek out and exploit opportunities that serve both their own interests and the interests of clients. In some situations, the economic payoffs to the lawyers are huge, but it was the potential of those payoffs that encouraged lawyers to pursue what often, in the beginning, appeared to be highly risky and costly cases.[16] There will be occasions when lawyers pursue issues that prove unworthy of attack and which produce perverse results. However, there are also cases where, in the absence of legal attack, dangerous products and practices would have gone unabated. There may be other systems that serve the clients' interests better, but those systems rely upon other sets of incentives which will undoubtedly produce a combination of positive and negative benefits. Moreover, predicting exactly what changes will come as a result of any specific change are at best difficult (Bogart 2002).

Does this mean that we should reject change and just live with what we have? Certainly not. What the analysis in this book shows, and what motivated the research in the first place, is that considerations of change must start from a good understanding of the status quo. For example, one simple change regarding contingency fees that has sometimes been advocated is that lawyers should be required to provide their contingency fee clients with an accounting of the time that the lawyer devoted to the case. The argument underlying this is that clients will (1) come to know that lawyers are charging excessive fees and (2) have a basis to file formal complaints about such fees. This proposal has an image of the working world of a lawyer that sees the lawyer as devoting concentrated time on individual cases. What this research shows, as exemplified by our visit with Steve Clarke in Chapter 1, is that time accounting in a fast-moving law practice is difficult and at best very approximate.[17] Individual-level time accounting is likely to be of relatively little value.

However, even if we have good information on the empirical phenomenon we wish to change, we need to undertake change with some caution. We need to consider how the phenomenon we propose to change interacts more broadly with the system. Getting a good understanding of these interactions is more difficult than the research I have carried out here. In significant part this is because within a given setting the phenomenon is relatively constant. We do not know how a system exactly like ours, except for contingency fees, works because those systems without contingency fees differ in other important ways. We can look to systems adopting contingency fees, or combining contingency fees with other variations, to begin to understand how these interactions do work. However, to date there is little such research available. Despite the fact that some provinces of Canada have allowed contingency fees for over 100 years, there is virtually no empirical research available on the operation of contingency fees in any province in Canada.[18]

It is possible to discern the hoped-for impact of change by looking at the interests supporting those changes. It is noteworthy that backing for limitations on contingency fees comes from corporate interests, not from groups such as labor organizations and consumer groups. One might ask why labor and consumer groups fail to back alternatives that would mitigate the need for contingency fee representatives. Actually, they do support at least one such system, universal health care! The single change that would have the most impact on the need for contingency fee representation would be the development of such a health care system (particularly one that did not impose copays or deductibles for some or all accidental injuries). Still, why is there not large-scale support for no-fault auto insurance, or for some alternative such as a compensation system based on a "pay-at-the-pump" tax system with compensation through administrative procedures similar to those used for workers' compensation? In concert with a system of universal health care, such a system could provide compensation for lost income and other types of out-of-pocket expenses. One reason that there is not more support for such systems is that the existing models typically provide compensation that is actually far from adequate. No-fault auto insurance and workers' compensation fail to come close to replacing lost earnings for a large percentage of those who are entitled to such compensation. Some such systems impose limitations as low as $250 per week in the amount of compensation that will be paid; for a full-time worker, this is barely above minimum wage! Even those systems that are substantially more generous have limits that would mean substantial income loss for many people.

In considering change, the central questions ultimately are who benefits and who bears the costs. Limitations on contingency fees, as well as many other changes to the civil justice system, will certainly harm lawyers who depend on them (see Daniels and Martin 2002), and it is not surprising that organizations of such lawyers have been strong defenders of the current system. While contingency fee lawyers act in their own self-interest, they also claim to act in the interest of future victims of injury, discrimination, and other compensable wrongs. Are there ways to reform the system that do protect those latter interests? There probably are. Ironically, such changes, like introducing more competition into the market for representational services by allowing representation by nonlawyers, would probably come under attack both from the lawyers defending the current system and from the corporate interests seeking to reel in the plaintiffs' bar, the former fearing a loss of income and the latter fearing an increase in claims.

The Future of American Contingency Fee Practice

While some advocates of reform would change the rules governing contingency fees, the nature of contingency fee practice is evolving in its own natural way, as is American legal practice generally (Kritzer 1999, 2002a). As I noted in the beginning of this chapter, most contemporary contingency fee practitioners are neither the marginal practitioners of the early twentieth century nor the highly successful, very rich lawyers associated with large-scale mass tort litigation such as tobacco, asbestos, or silicone breast implants.

The dramatic success of a small group of contingency fee practitioners in high-profile, very lucrative cases is changing the dynamics of relationships among lawyers competing for contingency fee clients. The result is increasing stratification within what is customarily called the plaintiffs' bar, with the interests of those who handle high-value cases diverging significantly from those who handle the run-of-the-mill cases. The former group stands to lose significantly from changes such as damage caps, restrictions on punitive damages, and mandated sliding scales for contingency fees; the latter would be largely unaffected by such changes (Kritzer 2001b). Likewise, for the practitioner handling routine cases, growing evidence suggests that damages that can be obtained from a judge differ little from what might be obtained from a jury (Clermont and Eisenberg 1992; DeFrances and Litras 1999; Eisenberg et al. 2002). The highly visible success of the top contingency fee practitioners, and the tendency of some of those practitioners to revel in the wealth they have achieved, is fueling the calls for broad change in the contingency fee (Brickman 1992, 1999; Olson 2003), some of which will dramatically affect those working in the trenches of contingency fee legal practice.

The growing availability of self-help tools may also come to cut into the client base for contingency fee practitioners even if the hypothetical Kritzer Claims Service does not come into being. One could image a service that helped unrepresented claimants value their claim and provide guidance on how to present the claim to an insurance adjuster. There are now online services for assisting in the settlement of damage claims, and over time such services will build up databases on what various injuries are "worth"; a potential line of future business will be to provide valuation information, perhaps using a Web site which solicits information—such as medical expenses, medical treatment, lost days of work, restriction on activities, numbers of days of pain experienced, and level of pain—and converts that into a damage estimate, all for a modest fee.

What exactly will contingency fee legal practice look like in the middle of the twenty-first century? It will be different, but exactly what those differences will be I do not know. Some changes will come as a result of the United States finally resolving the issue of universal health insurance. Other changes will come as the legal profession loses its grip on providing law-related services. And still others will reflect an increasingly educated population with access to information and self-help tools unthinkable a hundred years earlier. Is it possible that contingency fee practice will wither and disappear? It is certainly possible, but the move *toward* various forms of contingency fees around the world suggests that some form of contingency fee will be an important element in providing access to justice for many years to come.

Weighting for Case Processing

Estimating what percentage of cases accepted by lawyers get filed as court cases is not easy, because there is no systematic record keeping of unfiled cases. Different sources of information produce varying estimates. A study conducted in five federal judicial districts in the late 1970s estimated that the cases of just under half of those disputants who retained a lawyer resulted in a court filing; in tort cases, the figure was 33 percent (Miller and Sarat 1980–81, 544). A national study of compensation for injury conducted in the late 1980s by the RAND Corporation's Institute for Civil Justice reports both the percentage of cases in which lawsuits were filed and the percentage of claimants who hired lawyers (Hensler et al. 1991, 20–22). From RAND's published data, I estimate that 42 percent of the cases handled by lawyers resulted in a suit being filed. An insurance industry study of auto personnel injury liability claims resolved in 1992 found figures as high as 42 percent in California and Tennessee, but only 17 percent in Wisconsin (Insurance Research Council 1994, 53). The Texas Department of Insurance (TDI) puts out an annual report regarding commercial liability claims. For 1994, TDI reported that in cases leading to payments of $10,000 or more, with attorney representation of the claimant, 61 percent involved the filing of a lawsuit (Texas Department of Insurance 1995, 58).[1]

For my purposes, I could try to estimate the percentage of cases in each of the categories based on data collected in the Wisconsin Contingency Fee Survey (I asked the lawyers how many cases they terminated during the year in each of the three dispositional categories). If I do this, I get estimates of 10 percent tried, 37 percent filed but not tried, and 52 percent not filed.[2] This would mean that 21 percent of filed cases went to trial, but this seems much too high. If one assumes that only about 10 percent of filed cases go to trial, then we can adjust the above figures to reflect that ratio. Based on this logic, I arrived at estimates that 4 percent of cases are tried, 40 percent are filed but not tried, and 56 percent are not filed. These estimates may still overestimate the proportion tried, but once the proportion is down to 4 percent, further reductions have little effect on the values I get for the mean or median effective hourly rates. Using this distribution, I developed a set of weights to adjust my sample to these proportions.

Survey Instrument

University of Wisconsin
Institute for Legal Studies

Contingent Fee Study

Please return this questionnaire within ten days in the envelope provided to:

Contingent Fee Study
Institute for Legal Studies
University of Wisconsin-Madison
2418 Social Science Building
1180 Observatory Drive
Madison, WI 53706-1393

Instructions: This survey concerns plaintiffs' contingent fee practice. In the questions that follow, please answer in terms of work done on behalf of plaintiffs (or potential plaintiffs) where your fee is dependent upon the outcome. Please **do not** include work done on behalf of defendants (or potential defendants) where your fee included a contingent element, such as subrogation issues.

1. Do you do any plaintiff's work on a contingent fee basis?

    ☐ yes   ☐ no ⟶   PLEASE COMPLETE AND RETURN THE ENCLOSED POSTCARD
                                      TO US TODAY. DO NOT COMPLETE THIS QUESTIONNAIRE.

GO TO QUESTION 2 ON PAGE 2

2. If you had to characterize the primary nature of your practice over the last three years, which of the following would be the **best** description: *Check one box.*

    ☐ personal injury plaintiffs   ☐ personal injury defense   ☐ business litigation
    ☐ other or general litigation   ☐ general practice   ☐ other:_____

3. During that time, what percentage of the **contingent fee cases** which you closed and for which you had primary responsibility involved each of the following: *Percentages should total 100%.*

    ____% INJURY/ILLNESS/DEATH   ____% OTHER

Please provide more detailed percentages for your injury/illness/death cases below. *Percentages should total the % INJURY/ILLNESS/DEATH specified above.*	Please provide more detailed percentages for your other cases below. *Percentages should total the % OTHER specified above.*
____% auto injury ____% product liability ____% medical malpractice ____% other personal injury ____% workers compensation ____% social security ____% other, specify _____	____% discrimination ____% other employment ____% securities ____% non-personal injury torts ____% contract & other business ____% other professional malpractice ____% other, specify _____

4. What percentage of those contingent fee cases were: *Percentages should total 100%.*

    ____% filed in court

    ____% filed with an administrative agency

    ____% closed without being filed with a court or agency

5. Over the **last 12 months** (or for your last accounting year if that is easier), approximately what percentage of the gross fees that you generated were from plaintiffs' contingent fee work?
    _____%

6. During that same 12 month period, what percentage of your time practicing law was devoted to:

    a. Tasks not related to a specific client (e.g. office management, etc.)   _____%

    b. Time spent screening cases of potential contingent fee clients   _____%

    c. Work for clients paying on a contingent fee basis   _____%

    d. Work for clients paying on some basis other than contingent fee   _____%

7. During that period, approximately how much time did you devote to work for clients, including screening potential contingent fee clients (i.e., what would be considered "billable hours" if all of your time attributable to clients involved hourly-fee clients)?   _____ hours

SCREENING POTENTIAL CLIENTS:

8. If you work in a firm, is the screening of potential contingent fee clients handled primarily on a firm-wide basis or does each individual lawyer do his or her own screening? *Check one box.*

   ☐ firm-wide   ☐ by individual lawyers   ☐ solo practice

9. **In answering the parts of this question, please answer for your firm as a whole if screening is done on a firm-wide basis, or just for yourself if you handle your own screening of potential contingent fee clients.**

   a. During the past 12 months, approximately how many potential contingent fee clients made initial contacts with you/your firm?
   _____ *clients*

   b. How many of those clients did you/your firm accept?
   _____ *clients*

   c. How many were declined based on information obtained solely from one or more telephone conversations?
   _____ *clients*

   d. How many were declined as a result of failing to appear for a scheduled in-person meeting?
   _____ *clients*

   e. How many were declined as a result of what was learned at an initial in-person meeting?
   _____ *clients*

   f. How many were declined after additional investigation?
   _____ *clients*

10a. Who handles the initial telephone contacts?   ☐ nonlawyers   ☐ lawyers   ☐ both

10b. Who makes the decision whether or not to pursue a case? *Check one box.*

   ☐ I do   ☐ I do, subject to review   ☐ a more senior lawyer   ☐ a committee

11. Of those that were declined what percentage was due to each of the following:
   Percentages should total 100%.

   _____% no liability or no basis for a claim

   _____% inadequate damages or inadequate fee potential

   _____% both lack of liability and inadequate damages

   _____% case was outside my/our area of practice

   _____% other reasons (e.g., statute of limitations, credibility of the client, etc.)

12. What percent of the potential contingent fee clients who contact you do you refer to other lawyers?

   _____% to lawyers more specialized than me

   _____% to lawyers less specialized than me

   _____% due to conflicts of interest

TRIED LAWSUITS:

13a. During the last 12 months, approximately how many contingent fee files did you close after the case went to trial?

with recovery: _____ *# of files*   *without recovery:* _____ *# of files*

IF BOTH ARE ZERO, GO TO QUESTION 14a ON PAGE 6

13b. Thinking about the case you closed most recently, did you obtain any recovery for your client?

☐ yes   ☐ no

13c. Approximately, what date was that case closed?   _____ *MM/YY*

13d. Approximately, when was the retainer signed?   _____ *MM/YY*

13e. Where was the case filed?

☐ state court   ☐ federal court   ☐ other, specify _____

13f. What kind of case was it? *Check all that apply.*

☐ auto-related injury   ☐ product liability   ☐ medical malpractice
☐ other personal injury   ☐ workers compensation   ☐ social security
☐ discrimination   ☐ other employment   ☐ securities
☐ non-personal injury torts ☐ contract & other business ☐ other professional malpractice
                                                          ☐ other, specify _____

13g. If the case involved personal injury, what was the nature of the injury or injuries? *Check all that apply.*

☐ death   ☐ concussion   ☐ other head injury
☐ neck (whiplash)   ☐ back injury   ☐ other soft tissue
☐ limb or joint injury   ☐ multiple fractures   ☐ other fracture
☐ burns   ☐ laceration   ☐ scarring
☐ loss of sight   ☐ loss of mental capacity   ☐ paralysis
☐ other permanent disability   ☐ other, specify _____

13h. At the time you accepted the case, or when you first valued it, what did you think was the likely range of recovery?

$_____ *low* $_____ *high*

13i. What fee arrangement was specified in the retainer agreement for that case? *Check one box.*

☐ flat percentage (____%)

☐ variable percentage:

____% if no suit filed   ____% if case does not go to trial

____% if there is a trial but no appeal   ____% if there is an appeal

☐ other, specify _____

13j.   Did the final fee differ from this?   ☐ yes (final fee was ____%) ☐ no

13k.   Who bore the risk of disbursements?   ☐ me/my firm   ☐ client

13l.   How much time did you (and other lawyers in your firm, if any were involved) devote to the case? _____ *hours*

13m.   How much paralegal time did the case use?   _____ *hours*

13n.   Approximately how much did you or your firm advance to the client in expenses (witness fees, filing fees, etc.)? $_____

13o.   What fee did you receive for this case? $_____

13p1. Were any settlement demands or offers made before trial?

   ☐ yes ⟶   13p2.   What was your first demand and what was the defendant's first offer?
   ☐ no
                        demand $_____   *offer* $_____

              13p3.   Did this exchange occur: ☐ before filing   ☐ after filing

              13p4.   In total, how many rounds of demands and offers were there (i.e. number of times you went back and forth)?   _____ *rounds*

13q.   Was the case tried to: ☐ a jury   ☐ the court?

13r1. Was a verdict returned in the case?

   ☐ yes ⟶   13r2.   Was it in favor of:
   ☐ no
                        ☐ your client   ☐ the defendant ⟶   GO TO QUESTION 14a ON PAGE 6

              13r3.   What were the total damages? $_____

              13r4.   What were the specials? $_____

              13r5.   If applicable, what if any negligence was attributed to your client? _____ %

GO TO QUESTION 14a ON PAGE 6

UNTRIED LAWSUITS:

14a.   During the last 12 months, approximately how many contingent fee files did you close after filing a lawsuit but before starting trial?

with recovery: _____ *# of files*   *without recovery:* _____ *# of files*

IF BOTH ARE ZERO, GO TO QUESTION 15a ON PAGE 8

14b.   Thinking about the case you closed most recently, did you obtain any recovery for your client?

☐ yes   ☐ no

14c.   Approximately, what date was that case closed?   _____ *MM/YY*

14d.   Approximately, when was the retainer signed?   _____ *MM/YY*

14e.   Where was the case filed?

☐ state court   ☐ federal court   ☐ other, specify _____

14f.   What kind of case was it? *Check all that apply.*

☐ auto-related injury   ☐ product liability   ☐ medical malpractice
☐ other personal injury   ☐ workers compensation   ☐ social security
☐ discrimination   ☐ other employment   ☐ securities
☐ non-personal injury torts   ☐ contract & other business   ☐ other professional malpractice
                                                            ☐ other, specify _____

14g.   If the case involved personal injury, what was the nature of the injury or injuries? *Check all that apply.*

☐ death   ☐ concussion   ☐ other head injury
☐ neck (whiplash)   ☐ back injury   ☐ other soft tissue
☐ limb or joint injury   ☐ multiple fractures   ☐ other fracture
☐ burns   ☐ laceration   ☐ scarring
☐ loss of sight   ☐ loss of mental capacity ☐ paralysis
☐ other permanent disability   ☐ other, specify _____

14h. At the time you accepted the case, or when you first valued it, what did you think was the likely range of recovery?

$_____ *low* $_____ *high*

14i. What fee arrangement was specified in the retainer agreement for that case? *Check one box.*

☐ flat percentage (_____%)

☐ variable percentage:

____% if no suit filed   ____% if case does not go to trial

____% if there is a trial but no appeal   ____% if there is an appeal

☐ other, specify _____

14j. Did the final fee differ from this?   ☐ yes (final fee was _____%) ☐ no

14k. Who bore the risk of disbursements?   ☐ me/my firm   ☐ client

14l. How much time did you (and other lawyers in your firm, if any were involved) devote to the case?   _____ *hours*

14m. How much paralegal time did the case use?   _____ *hours*

14n. Approximately how much did you or your firm advance to the client in expenses (witness fees, filing fees, etc.)? $_____

14o. What fee did you receive for this case? $_____

14p. What was your first demand and what was the defendant's first offer?

demand $_____   *offer* $_____

14q. Did this exchange occur: ☐ before filing   ☐ after filing

14r. In total, how many rounds of demands and offers were there (i.e. number of times you went back and forth)?   _____ *rounds*

UNFILED CASES:

15a.   During the last 12 months, approximately how many contingent fee files for which you had a retainer did you close without filing a lawsuit or an administrative case?

with recovery: _____ *# of files*   *without recovery:* _____ *# of files*

IF BOTH ARE ZERO, GO TO QUESTION 16 ON PAGE 10

15b.   Thinking about the case you closed most recently, did you obtain any recovery for your client?

☐ yes   ☐ no

15c.   Approximately, what date was that case closed?   _____ *MM/YY*

15d.   Approximately, when was the retainer signed?   _____ *MM/YY*

15e.   What kind of case was it? *Check all that apply.*

☐ auto-related injury   ☐ product liability   ☐ medical malpractice
☐ other personal injury   ☐ workers compensation   ☐ social security
☐ discrimination   ☐ other employment   ☐ securities
☐ non-personal injury torts ☐ contract & other business ☐ other professional malpractice
                                                         ☐ other, specify_____

15f.   If the case involved personal injury, what was the nature of the injury or injuries? *Check all that apply.*

☐ death   ☐ concussion   ☐ other head injury
☐ neck (whiplash)   ☐ back injury   ☐ other soft tissue
☐ limb or joint injury   ☐ multiple fractures   ☐ other fracture
☐ burns   ☐ laceration   ☐ scarring
☐ loss of sight   ☐ loss of mental capacity ☐ paralysis
☐ other permanent disability   ☐ other, specify_____

15g.   At the time you accepted the case, or when you first valued it, what did you think was the likely range of recovery?

$_____ *low* $_____ *high*

15h. What fee arrangement was specified in the retainer agreement for that case? *Check one box.*

☐ flat percentage (_____%)
☐ variable percentage:

_____% if no suit filed   _____% if case does not go to trial
_____% if there is a trial but no appeal   _____% if there is an appeal

☐ other, specify_____

15i. Did the final fee differ from this arrangement?   ☐ yes (final fee was _____%) ☐ no

15j. Who bore the risk of disbursements? *Check one box.*   ☐ me/my firm   ☐ client

15k. How much time did you (and other lawyers in your firm, if any were involved) devote to the case? _____ *hours*

15l. How much paralegal time did the case use? _____ *hours*

15m. Approximately how much did you or your firm advance to the client in expenses (witness fees, filing fees, etc.)? $_____

15n. What fee did you receive for this case? $_____

15o. What was your first demand and what was the defendant's first offer?

demand $_____   *offer* $_____

15p. In total, how many rounds of demands and offers were there (i.e. number of times you went back and forth)? _____ *rounds*

YOUR PRACTICE:

16. For each of the following types of cases, please indicate whether there is there a minimum damage figure before you will consider taking the case. If yes, please indicate amount.

auto   ☐ yes ($_____) ☐ no
medical malpractice   ☐ yes ($_____) ☐ no
product liability   ☐ yes ($_____) ☐ no

17. When do you **normally** ask a potential client to sign a retainer agreement? *Check one box.*

☐ at first in-person meeting
☐ after the first meeting but before any independent investigation
☐ after some minimal independent investigation
☐ after more than minimal independent investigation
☐ other, specify _____

18a. In the last year, did you do any work on an hourly fee basis?

☐ yes   ☐ no ⟶ GO TO QUESTION 19a BELOW
  ↓

    18b. What hourly rate are you charging for the most recent case you took in on an hourly basis? $_____ *per hour*

19a. Do you ever advise a client that an hourly fee would be better?

☐ yes   ☐ no

19b. During the past 12 months did any clients choose to pay you on an hourly fee basis rather than on a contingency basis?

☐ yes   ☐ no

20. What percentage of the potential contingent fee clients you talk to have "lawyer shopped" by contacting other lawyers in addition to you?   _____%

21. What percentage of your contingent fee clients come from each of the following? *Percentages should total 100%.*

____% referrals from other lawyers   ____% referrals from other clients

____% yellow pages   ____% other advertising (TV, etc.)

____% already a client   ____% community contacts, word of mouth

____% direct mailings   ____% other, specify _____

                            ____% unknown

22. If you regularly refer contingent fee clients to other lawyers, please name the lawyers (or firms) to whom you referred the last two such cases:

1. _____   2. _____

23. What is the largest amount of disbursements that you have ever had at risk in a contingent fee case? $_____   *Largest amount that you have written off?* $_____

GENERAL INFORMATION

24. How long have you been practicing law? _____ *years*

25. Which law school did you attend?
    - ☐ UW-Madison ☐ Marquette ☐ other, specify _____

26. Are you male or female? ☐ male ☐ female

27. Where is your practice primarily located? *Check one box.*
    - ☐ city of Milwaukee
    - ☐ suburban Milwaukee
    - ☐ community of less than 2,500
    - ☐ community of 2,500-9,999
    - ☐ community of 10,000-24,999
    - ☐ community of 25,000-49,999
    - ☐ community of 50,000-99,999
    - ☐ community of 100,000 or more
    - ☐ other, specify _____

28. What is your position? *Check one box.*
    - ☐ partner ☐ associate ☐ solo practitioner
    - ☐ of counsel ☐ employee ☐ other, specify _____

29. If you are in a firm, what is the size of the firm in terms of the number of:
    - ____ partners   ____ other lawyers   ____ paralegals   ____ other staff

30a. Does the *firm* specialize in plaintiffs' work? ☐ yes ☐ no

30b. Does the *firm* specialize in a particular type of case? ☐ yes, specify _____ ☐ no

31. Approximately what percentage of your gross practice revenue goes to cover overhead?
    _____%

32a. Is paralegal time treated as overhead, or is it treated as a billable item?
    - ☐ no paralegals
    - ☐ overhead
    - ☐ billable ⟶ 32b. What is the cost of paralegal time, including overhead?
      $_____ *per hour*

33a. In answering the questions on pages 4-9 regarding specific cases, did you consult your files?
    - ☐ yes ⟶ 33b. Did the files contain time records? ☐ yes ☐ no
    - ☐ no ⟶ 33c. Did you keep time records for these cases? ☐ yes ☐ no

34.   What was your before tax income in 1994 from the practice of law? *Check one box.*

☐ under $25,000   ☐ $150,000-$199,999
☐ $25,000-$49,999   ☐ $200,000-$249,999
☐ $50,000-$74,999   ☐ $250,000-$349,999
☐ $75,000-$99,999   ☐ $350,000-$499,999
☐ $100,000-$124,999   ☐ $500,000-$749,999
☐ $125,000-$149,999   ☐ $750,000 or more

These last two questions are not related to the contingent fee study. As part of other projects, we are trying to locate lawyers who have had experience with particular types of cases or court procedures. The responses to the questions that follow will be segregated from the rest of the survey data. This will be done to allow researchers to make contact with you regarding these other projects without knowing anything about the information you provided in this questionnaire.

35.   Have you ever had a potential client contact you regarding tobacco-related injury or illness?

☐ yes   ☐ no

36.   Have you ever been involved in a jury trial where the issues of liability and damages were handled through a bifurcated procedure?

☐ yes   ☐ no

CONCLUDING COMMENTS

Please feel free to provide any additional comments you may have about the information you described in the questionnaire. If the space below is not sufficient, please attach a separate sheet of paper.

_____

_____

_____

_____

If you have standard forms that you use for case intake and evaluation, it would be helpful if you would enclose a copy (or copies) along with your completed questionnaire.

THANK YOU FOR YOUR COOPERATION AND ASSISTANCE IN THIS STUDY.

Notes

1. Attacks on the contingency fee have been a prominent part of the broader attack on tort litigation advanced by conservative interests. For a thorough discussion of this broader campaign, see Haltom and McCann 2004; an earlier discussion, focused more on juries, can be found in Daniels and Martin 1995.

2. See Galanter 1998, 731–33 for one of many articles and reports debunking the myths that have arisen around this case.

3. This case settled for $35,000, with Steve taking a fee of $10,000 rather than the one-third that the contingency fee retainer called for; the client did decide to file for bankruptcy.

4. Subrogation claims refer to claims by another party against any settlement or judgment a claimant obtains. Typically they involve reimbursing a health insurer that originally paid the medical bills arising from an accident; such claims also arise in worker-related accidents where a workers' compensation claim is paid and the claimant later obtains payments under a tort claim against a party other than the employer.

5. The case did settle the following week; Steve was able to move the adjuster up only $500 to $63,000. He did succeed in getting the subrogation claim reduced to $11,000, which was a considerably larger reduction than he had expected to be possible. (I discuss the role of subrogation claims in the settlement process in Chapter 5.)

6. Cross-subsidization is not limited to contingency fee work. An element of cross-subsidization also occurs in fixed-fee work, where some cases take more time than the fixed fee might compensate for, while other cases take less time.

7. In Chapter 6, where I explore in detail the actual returns from contingency fees, I use a simplified version of this formula that uses not distributions but the

actual values of the fee received and the hours worked as known once a case is concluded.

CHAPTER 2

1. These other data on lawyers practicing in Wisconsin come largely from surveys conducted by the State Bar of Wisconsin of its membership. These data were generously made available by the State Bar; I would particularly like to thank George Brown and Rebecca Murray for their assistance.

2. I looked only at lawyers reporting more than 400 hours of time across the list of "areas of practice." Those labeled plaintiffs' personal injury were lawyers who obtained at least 70 percent of their income from contingency fee work and who devoted at least 70 percent of their hours to some combination of "personal injury / torts" and "workers' compensation." If I limit the definition to those who obtained 70 percent or more of their income from "personal injury / torts," I have only twenty-nine respondents.

3. I again looked only at lawyers reporting more than 400 hours of time across the list of areas of practice. I labeled as "general practice" those who reported 10 percent or more of their time in at least three of the following areas: criminal, estate planning / wills and trusts, family, general practice, personal injury / torts, probate, real estate / real property, traffic, workers' compensation.

4. This may be changing for some types of high-profile contingency fee work (see Kritzer 2001b).

5. As a comparison, a survey of lawyers who did litigation in New Jersey around 1990 found that 19 percent were in solo practice (Hyman et al. 1995, 20).

6. A recent study of the plaintiffs' personal injury bar in Chicago found roughly similar patterns: firms are small (typically with fewer than ten lawyers), and solo practice is underrepresented (20–25 percent), although less so than in my survey (Parikh 2001, 78).

7. A 1990 survey of New Jersey litigators found that the mean number of years of practice was seventeen (Hyman et al. 1995, 19); a study of personal injury specialists in Indiana found that "the path from law school to a plaintiffs' personal career is not linear or well-defined" (Van Hoy 1999, 352).

8. The underrepresentation of women in the plaintiffs' bar is not unique to Wisconsin; Sara Parikh (2001, 91) found that about 90 percent of the personal injury plaintiffs' lawyers in Chicago were male.

9. A single sample difference of proportions test yields a Z of 3.91, p < .001.

10. I also asked the lawyers how many cases they had terminated in the prior twelve months in each of the three categories.

11. Parikh (2001, 57) reports that the median case value for personal injury cases in Chicago is somewhere between $5,000 and $20,000.

12. The results discussed here have been obtained applying weights for case volume and practice type. They differ somewhat from previously reported figures (see Kritzer 1998b) because of the refinement in the weighting scheme to include practice type.

13. One might question why the lawyer charged even this much; would not the insurer tender its limits directly to the injury victim? During my observation and interviews I was told of several cases in which insurers had talked unrepresented claimants down from a limits payment on the grounds that if the claimant went to a lawyer to get the entire payment, the claimant would have to pay a sizable fee to a lawyer. This is generally supported by an analysis I did of data on closed auto accident claims using data collected by the Insurance Research Council (IRC) (1999). The claims in the IRC study were closed in 1997. Overall, 8 percent of the represented claims led to payment of the policy limit compared to only 1 percent in claims without attorney representation. In only three kinds of injuries were limits payments made with essentially equal frequency: those involving fatality, loss of a body part, a disc injury. This pattern holds up if I look separately at claims in which the policy limit is under $100,000, exactly $100,000, and over $100,000. In some kinds of cases the likelihood of a limits payment is much greater with an attorney than without an attorney: scarring or permanent disfigurement, knee injuries, fractures of non-weight-bearing bones, internal organ injury, permanent brain injury, loss of one of the senses, or paralysis (91 percent paid limits with a lawyer versus only 33 percent without).

14. In my sample, in a bit over 1 percent of the cases in which some recovery was obtained, the lawyer collected no fee.

15. If I correlate the fee percentage (using the lowest percentage quoted when the fee involved a variable percentage) with the lawyer's income, I get a correlation of .12. This is statistically significant but not indicative of a meaningful relationship.

16. Some summary data from these reports are presented in reports published by the Alaska Judicial Council.

17. Teresa W. Carns, senior staff associate of the Alaska Judicial Council, made available to me a frequency distribution for this data item.

18. Further evidence on this point is provided by a 1991 national survey of Association of Trial Lawyers of America (ATLA) members, which found that only 54.3 percent of respondents reported that they always stated fees as a fixed percentage of recovery (see Stock 1992, appendix B, question 12).

19. These breakdowns are from the unweighted frequencies. The RAND researchers developed an elaborate weighting scheme to take into account a number of issues. I reran the frequencies applying the various weights, and they did not change the relative frequencies.

20. One area where the one-third fee may not be dominant is medical malpractice. In Wisconsin, contingency fees in medical malpractice are limited to a sliding scale based on recovery, with one-third being charged for the $1 million recovered (unless liability is stipulated within 180 days of the commencement of the suit, in which case the first $1 million is subject to a 25 percent fee), and 20 percent for amounts in excess of $1 million (Wis. Stat. 655.013). Several other states (California, Illinois, Maine, Massachusetts, New Hampshire, and New York) impose limits on fees in medical malpractice cases. A survey of Florida

medical malpractice plaintiffs found that 80 percent were charged a fixed percentage, and of that 80 percent only 30 percent reported paying a fee of one-third; the majority paid fees exceeding one-third, with the most common (46 percent) fixed fee being 40 percent (Sloan et al. 1993, 77).

CHAPTER 3

1. William Felstiner has observed that concerns about maintaining what he calls an "inventory" of cases often leads lawyers to accept many more cases than they can actually handle; the resulting overcommitment leads to problems in service quality and lawyer-client relations (Felstiner 1998, 66–67).

2. The first section of this chapter draws heavily on a paper I coauthored with Jayanth Krishnan (Kritzer and Krishnan 1999); the minor discrepancies between some of the figures reported in the earlier paper and this chapter reflect further data cleaning.

3. Included in "other" would be newspaper advertising. Very few lawyers in Wisconsin advertise regularly in the newspaper, although doing so is not unknown, and it may be becoming more common, both in Wisconsin and elsewhere. In fact, not a single respondent listed "newspaper advertisements" in the space provided for "other."

4. The pattern for my respondents differs sharply from that reported by Jerry Van Hoy in his study of franchise law firms (1997a, 12–14); franchise law firms rely much more heavily on modern advertising methods.

5. I use the term *included* here because a significant number of lawyers reported two or more sources tied as producing the largest proportion (the 471 respondents produced 639 responses).

6. Of PI specialists, 29 percent get none of their contingency fee clients from advertising, compared to 48 percent of general practitioners and 66 percent of other lawyers.

7. Sara Parikh (2001, 124) found that in Chicago "low-end" practitioners obtained a median of 15 percent of cases through lawyer referrals, while "high-end" and "elite" practitioners obtained 70 to 72 percent of their cases through lawyer referrals. Parikh (2001, 117–69) explores in detail "referral networks" among plaintiffs' personal injury lawyers in Chicago.

8. Direct mail, or other types of solicitations, by business lawyers of business clients is an accepted practice. Direct mail and similar solicitations of individual clients is less controversial or noncontroversial in other areas in which potential client names can be distilled from court or other public records: bankruptcy (sending advertising to persons against whom foreclosure proceedings have been initiated), recent home buyers (sending information about legal recourse for undisclosed defects), new car buyers (sending information on lemon law recourse options), persons arrested for drunk driving (offering general defense services), persons cited for traffic violations (offering services to help reduce "points" toward license suspension or revocation). It is only in the area of personal injury claims that the practice appears to raise par-

ticular controversy, no doubt in part because of the interest against whom claims are brought.

9. Since the data collection phase of this research was carried out, BAPR has been renamed the Office of Lawyer Regulation.

10. Interestingly, even though only 5 percent of those receiving letters eventually hired an attorney who sent a letter, 10 percent of the respondents who read the letter reported that the letter was in some way helpful.

11. It is worth noting, however, that in the world of direct mail more generally, a 2 percent success rate is quite good.

12. For an analysis of the factors influencing lawyers' decisions to advertise, see Bowen 1995b.

13. While this advertising is primarily television and radio, it also includes classified advertisements, billboards, and other print advertising.

14. This was in response to an open-ended question. Compare these figures to those from a 1996 survey in Florida which found that only 3 percent of the respondents who had retained a lawyer had learned of that lawyer from electronic (i.e., television or radio) advertising (Magid 1997, 2).

15. In his study of franchise law firms, Van Hoy (1997a, 54) found that the firms that rely heavily on advertising had to spend time sorting out significant numbers of "undesirable" clients.

16. In smaller communities, local cable channels provide a medium somewhere between radio (less audience specific) and television (more geographically targeted).

17. Van Hoy (1999) and Stephen Daniels and Joanne Martin (1999) found that media advertising was dominated by a small number of firms in both Indiana and a number of cities in Texas.

18. Habush has bought time during radio broadcasts of Green Bay Packer football games ("you need a winning team of lawyers").

19. This and several other questions were included in a statewide omnibus survey called Wisconsin Opinions, which was conducted periodically by the Wisconsin Survey Research Laboratory, part of the University of Wisconsin Extension.

20. Habush was one of three firms that represented the state of Wisconsin in the health cost tobacco case; the case yielded tens of millions of dollars to the firm.

21. The punitive damage portion of this award, $94 million, was eventually thrown out by a state appeals court (Pommer 2003).

22. This is also true of radio. In one firm involved in the observational part of the research, the lawyers were negotiating with a radio station for a series of ads; one of the problems they encountered was the question of "how much is enough?" For advertising to create visibility, it takes a sustained advertising program, and it can be very difficult to accurately gauge the payoffs (compare to Van Hoy 1997a, 12–13).

23. See Van Hoy 1999 and Daniels and Martin 1999, 389–90, for descriptions of generally similar patterns in Indiana and Texas.

24. The 1996 Florida survey found that 15 percent of the respondents who had used a lawyer had "learned about their lawyer from the telephone book or Yellow Pages" (Magid 1997, 2).

25. Of the twenty cases described during the semistructured interviews, three (15 percent) came as referrals from lawyers in other firms.

26. Looking at whether the lawyer obtains *any* clients as referrals from other lawyers follows a slightly different pattern. Only 61 percent of general practitioners get at least some of their contingency fee clients as professional referrals, compared to 88 percent of personal injury specialists and 78 percent of other practitioners.

27. Only about 4 percent of the respondents in the practitioner survey indicated that they referred no potential contingency fee cases to other lawyers.

28. Whether referrals are paid or unpaid undoubtedly depends on the size and types of cases involved; lawyers handling large cases referred from other personal injury lawyers are probably most likely to pay for the referral (see Parikh 2001, 155–69).

29. This appears to contrast somewhat to the situations described by Van Hoy (1999) and Daniels and Martin (1999) for Indiana and Texas respectively. The apparent absence of paid referrals in Wisconsin cannot be attributed to formal restrictions; the Wisconsin Supreme Court rules governing attorney fees explicitly permits sharing of fees provided either that the division is proportional to the services performed *or* that it is by "written agreement with the client and each lawyer assumes joint responsibility for the representation" (SCR 20:15:5[e]).

30. Daniels and Martin (1999, 385–88) describe the phenomenon of lawyers who advertise cases and then broker them to other lawyers. I could not find evidence that this was a significant source of clients for Wisconsin lawyers, but some lawyers do receive at least some cases through this mechanism.

31. One of these repeat clients was, if one counts other members of his immediate family, a multiple repeater; the case observed was at least the fourth involving this client or other immediate members of his family.

32. Three of the twenty cases (15 percent) discussed in the interviews came from friends in the community; another two cases were referred by medical providers, which is a community source that was not explicitly included in the survey.

33. Philip Jessup (1938) also quotes Root as saying "a lawyer's chief business is to keep his clients out of litigation."

34. Twelve respondents who provided information on screening are omitted from the totals reported above because their information was for firm-level patterns and I had multiple respondents from their firm. Including them would have meant double counting.

35. The midspread is the distance from the first quartile to the third quartile: 25 percent of the lawyers reported accepting 23 percent or fewer of the potential clients and 25 percent reported accepting 67 percent or more. The corre-

sponding figures for the unweighted data are mean 46 percent, median 45 percent, midspread 24 percent to 67 percent.

36. Using the unweighted data, the aggregate acceptance rate is 31 percent.

37. While the client was in his office, the lawyer did a bit of quick legal research and consulted a couple of cases and determined that the case was doubtful on liability; he also determined that the only monetary claim was for medical damages—this was a workers' compensation case—and hence there was no fee potential.

38. In line with the previously reported patterns, I used three categories of contact volume: low (seventy-five or fewer contacts over the year), medium (76 to 1,000 contacts), and high (over 1,000 contacts).

39. For a discussion of case screening among Chicago plaintiffs' lawyers, see Parikh (2001, 75–77).

40. This difference must be approached cautiously because of the small number of respondents in high-volume firms (twelve); the difference does not achieve statistical significance.

41. As discussed in the first half of this chapter, a very small number of lawyers or firms initiate the contact by a postincident mailing. Only eight of the lawyers who responded to the survey indicated that any of their clients were obtained as a result of direct mail contacts.

42. Included here, at least implicitly, would be cases where there were significant damages, but where there was no insurance coverage or other ready source of compensation. I did not systematically pursue with my respondents the possibility of obtaining compensation directly from individuals who were either uninsured or who had low coverage levels, what Tom Baker (2001) has described as being referred to as "blood money," a term I never heard during my research in the field.

43. The four high-volume lawyers report declining a total of 7,145 cases, 68 percent solely on liability grounds, 7 percent owing to low damages, 5 percent owing to a combination of low damages and lack of liability, 12 percent because they were outside the lawyer's areas of practice, and 8 percent for other reasons.

44. Mather, McEwen, and Maiman 2001, 92–96, describes a similar concern among lawyers handling divorce cases.

45. In one case, the lawyer found an angle unrelated to the medical malpractice issue and did accept the case to pursue the nonmalpractice claim.

46. I also looked to see if practice setting might be obscuring the impact of years of experience. I split the sample into three groups depending on size of firm (one to three, three to nine, and more than nine lawyers). The only significant pattern that showed up at all when I did this was that lawyers in the larger firms who had less than ten years of experience were less likely to obtain clients as referrals from prior clients.

47. The four categories are Milwaukee and its suburbs, other communities with populations of 100,000 or more, communities between 25,000 and 99,999, and communities with fewer than 25,000 residents.

48. F = 3.072 (df = 3,208), p = .029
49. F = 4.612 (df = 3,147), p = .004.
50. In their studies in Texas and Indiana, Daniels and Martin (1999, 2002) and Van Hoy (1999) place emphasis on substantive specialties. My study found much less substantive emphasis (and this was true regardless of whether I looked at all respondents or only at those who identified themselves as personal injury plaintiffs' lawyers). For example, in the survey only four respondents reported that more than 75 percent of their practice consisted of products liability cases (only two said their practices were 100 percent products liability), and only six said that they devoted 75 percent or more of their time to medical malpractice (three reported 100 percent medical malpractice). While it may be that specialization falling along some other dimension (e.g., type of injury) is more common, I found no evidence of that from any of my data sources (none of the lawyers participating in the semistructured interviews reported specializations consuming the bulk of their practices). Whether the differences in Wisconsin reflect sampling strategies used in the research or differences among the states in the organization of legal practice is not clear.
51. Even after taking into account the higher likelihood of general practice in the smaller communities, lawyers in those communities were much less likely to be insurance defense specialists than were lawyers in large communities (10 percent versus 20 to 25 percent).
52. The percentage of women did not vary significantly by type of practice (13 percent personal injury plaintiff, 10 percent general practice, 14 percent other).
53. The differences in means between men and women for the latter two sources are statistically significant, while for the former two the statistical tests are borderline.
54. Because of the small number of women, only three of the fifteen statistical tests achieved significance after adding controls.
55. T-tests show that all of these differences are statistically significant.
56. As an initial comparison, I did a t-test between the acceptance rates for low- and medium-volume lawyers; the test was significant (t = 3.72, p < .0001).

CHAPTER 4

1. In their study of divorce lawyers, Lynn Mather, Craig McEwen, and Richard Maiman (2001, 110–31) describe two styles of advocacy that parallel my distinction between "dispositional" and "litigational" styles. In the latter, the lawyer relies more heavily on the formal tools of litigation, such as formal interrogatories, while in the latter the emphasis is on finding less formal ways of sharing information and getting the case resolved.
2. Typically the literature, both scholarly and popular, on such cases portrays an intensive litigational style (see, e.g., Mintz 1985; Sanders 1998; Stern 1976; Vidmar 1995).
3. Clearly the lawyer was deceiving the person he called. Deception can raise

ethical questions (see Hazard 2000), but the harmless deception here almost certainly did not rise to that level.

4. In fact, in an accident case involving a member of my immediate family, I accompanied the lawyer we retained on a visit to the site of the accident.

5. Here I focus only on contingency fee cases. In the firm where the lawyer had a general trial practice, I did observe instances where the lawyer instructed a law clerk / investigator to handle specific investigative tasks such as obtaining maintenance records on an intoxilizer involved in a drunk driving case he was defending.

6. This lawyer told me that he also spoke at length on a number of occasions with medical experts about the medical issues in the case (i.e., standards of care, normal procedures, etc.).

7. Vocational assessments can also be done as part of social security disability appeals handled on a contingency fee basis.

8. In this latter case, there was a second deposition, the spouse of the first deponent, but I had a scheduling conflict and could not stay for that deposition.

9. Workers' compensation cases do not involve issues of fault, further mitigating the need for discovery; in some cases there is a dispute over whether the incident allegedly causing injury actually occurred, and in others there is a dispute over whether there is any permanent disability.

10. Once a lawsuit is initiated, the insurance policy is "discoverable"; before formal court action is initiated, the insurer is not obligated to provide a copy of the policy, although most insurers will do so.

11. The pattern of limited face-to-face contact is by no means specific to American personal injury practice; Boon (1995, 258) describes a similar pattern for at least an important part of personal injury practice in England.

12. At least one of the lawyers I interviewed who does primarily insurance defense along with an occasional plaintiff's case specifically commented that he did not see cases that he felt were particularly abusive, even if there was some overtreating.

13. In Wisconsin, strictly speaking, the employer need only come up with a position that pays 85 percent of the original wage rate.

14. See "Surveillance Tape Crucial in McDonald's Defense Win," *National Law Journal*, June 18, 2001, p. A12.

15. See Mather, McEwen, and Maiman 2001, 96–98, for a description of this same process in the divorce context.

16. A good source of information on the size of claims is data collected by the Insurance Research Council (IRC). I reanalyzed data collected for the IRC's 1992 and 1997 (see Insurance Research Council 1994, 1999) studies of closed automobile injury claims and found that 99.5 percent (1992) and 99.8 percent (1997) of claimants represented by lawyers receive bodily injury compensation of less than $250,000; if one includes all claims regardless of legal representation, 99.9 percent received payments of less than $250,000 (only one unrepresented claimant in either study received a payment exceeding $250,000). Among the 582 Wisconsin claims in the studies (n = 582 for 1992 and n = 695 for 1997), there

was not a single one that involved a payment of $250,000 or more. The absence of significant numbers of large payments reflects a combination of the modest nature of most claims and the absence of large numbers of auto insurance policies with limits of $250,000 or more. However, even where there is a source that can pay a large amount of compensation, such payments are rare. For example, the Texas Department of Insurance (TDI) collects, or at least at one time collected, data annually on closed commercial liability claims. For calendar year 1994, TDI reported a total of 53,437 paid claims, of which only 2.5 percent involved payments of $250,000 or more (computed from information in Texas Department of Insurance 1995 and reanalysis of the TDI data).

17. Subrogation refers to the claims that other parties might have to part of a recovery. For example, medical bills from an accident may be paid by the injured person's health insurer. If that person then collects damages from the tortfeasor, the medical insurer will want to be reimbursed for some or all of what it paid to medical providers. In Wisconsin, subrogation is taken very seriously. The insurance companies' claims systems kick out subrogation liens almost automatically in many situations. As I will discuss in the next chapter, part of the work of the plaintiff's lawyer in a personal injury case is to negotiate with the medical insurer to satisfy the subrogation claim.

18. Filing probably has more significance for the contingency fee lawyer than for the client; as I discuss below, the filing of a case will bring in a lawyer on the defense side who is being paid by the hour, and that lawyer will have an incentive to spend time on the case which will require the contingency fee lawyer to spend time. While there are some circumstances when the defendant may hold back on preparing a case even after a court filing (i.e., as I discuss below, the filing is simply to deal with a statutes of limitations problem), contingency fee lawyers tend to view the defense lawyers' "running the clock" as the dominant pattern.

19. It is certainly possible that the relative lack of "law talk" I find in contingency practice reflects differences in data collection methods. I observed fulltime in lawyers' practices while Sarat and Felstiner specifically observed, and tape-recorded for analysis (I did not tape-record during my observation), lawyer-client meetings. I am convinced that there is little evidence of law talk in my field notes or the transcripts of my interviews; as a check, I had a research assistant read the Sarat and Felstiner article and then read all of the notes and transcripts to see if he could identify significant and widespread examples of law talk. He came up with essentially the same examples that I found in my own analysis.

20. I include in this group risk managers who function essentially as adjusters but are employed directly by a defendant such as a government agency or large corporation

21. Parikh 2001, 172–95, explores in detail "advice networks" among personal injury plaintiffs' lawyers in Chicago.

CHAPTER 5

1. Susan Shapiro (2002, 242–46) discusses the various ways fee arrangement creates conflicts of interest between lawyers and clients.

2. Wis. Stat. 807.01(3) and 807.01(4). Technically, this is called a "written offer of settlement," but attorneys commonly refer to it as a "statutory demand."

3. This was by no means an idle threat. As mentioned previously, one of the cases Brown was working on while I was in his office did result in a trial court ruling against Brown's client on a key issue, and Brown did appeal that decision.

4. Brown told me that he had about 300 hours invested in the case.

5. This was in fact true. After deducting various costs that Brown covered, the net fee on a $90,000 settlement would be about $12,500. For the 325 hours he ultimately put into the case, this worked out to an effective hourly rate of less than forty dollars per hour.

6. In another case, for a repeat client, which Adams was handling on an hourly basis, he made an initial demand of $5,000. Then, when the adjuster responded, "We are so far apart I'm not sure there's anything to talk about. . . . We usually do meds [medical expenses] plus something like $500 in cases like this," Adams replied that if the adjuster was offering meds plus $500, he thought they could settle the case. The adjuster offered to toss in other specials (lost luggage, costs of alternative transportation, etc.) if Adams could document them.

7. I omit from the following analyses the small number of social security cases in my sample because it is unclear exactly what negotiations in such cases would involve, since there really is no opposing party in the usual litigation sense.

8. Products liability and other professional malpractice had figures similar to medical malpractice, but the number of cases (eight and four) make inference very difficult.

9. Looking at the mean number of rounds, there is a weak statistical relationship with type of practice ($F = 4.288$, $p < .05$), with means of 3.77, 3.86, and 4.28 for personal injury specialists, general practitioners, and other types of practitioners respectively.

10. While the lawyers' valuations undoubtedly do change in the course of handling a case—I saw substantial evidence of that during my observations—those changes do not appear to be the result of the negotiation process itself or information learned during that process (see Hyman et al. 1995, 89).

11. Figure 5.1 is based on a Poisson regression predicting the number of rounds of negotiation from the log of the high valuation and the square of the log of the high valuation.

12. My analysis was not limited to the simple three categories above. In addition, I explored relationships between the first demand and other variables using the natural logarithm of the ratio of the demand to the high evaluation, the natural logarithm of the ratio of the demand to the low evaluation, and a

grouped categorical variable with six categories (one at least twice the high valuation, two between the 151 percent and 199 percent of the high valuation, three between 101 percent and 150 percent of the high valuation, four exactly 100 percent of the high valuation, five equal to or greater than 150 percent of the low valuation but less than 100 percent of the high valuation, and six less than 150 percent of the low valuation).

13. This distribution is very similar to what I found in my study of negotiation in ordinary litigation; based on the data collected for that study, 15 percent of the initial demands were in the "soft" range, 62 percent in the "typical" range, and 23 percent in the aggressive range.

14. Using this categorization, 78 percent of the initial demands are in the soft or typical range. While there may be an image that contingency fee lawyers, particularly those handling personal injury cases, typically make demands that are "highly inflated" (Mather, McEwen, and Maiman 2001, 117), these data do not indicate that is in fact the case. Contingency fee lawyers seem to pursue strategies generally similar to those pursued by divorce lawyers as described in Mather, McEwen, and Maiman 2001.

15. Some of the movement into the soft range may reflect that medical malpractice cases tend to be at the higher end of the stakes range; in fact, in multivariate regressions where I included controls for stakes, medical malpractice as an area of law did not evidence statistically significant differences.

16. I also explored possible relationships with the gender of the lawyer, the type of legal practice, and at what stage the case was terminated. I found several hints of possible relationships, but the patterns were either inconsistent or disappeared when I added for other variables such as stakes or area-of-law controls. The most intriguing of the possible patterns was with gender, where I found some suggestion that women might be more aggressive in initial demands than were men (compare to Mather, McEwen, and Maiman 2001, 125–27). However, I suggest this only as an issue for possible future research; my results were too inconsistent to draw firm conclusions.

17. In his study of medical malpractice litigation, Neil Vidmar (1995, 80–81) reports that "if insurers decide that the defendant is liable, they will attempt to settle the case for as little as possible and as quickly as they can. However, if they make the assessment that there is no defendant liability or that the plaintiff demands about the settlement amount are unreasonable, they will move for trial as quickly as they can."

18. Logistic regression analyses including the variables discussed above and other variables such as gender and practice type show that the relationships described hold up when controls are introduced.

19. I again conducted a logistic regression analysis to determine whether the pattern of relationships described above held up. By and large they did; the possible exception is the area of law in which neither the set of coefficients nor individual coefficients were statistically significant; however, the values of the parameter estimates for the areas of law were generally consistent with the bivariate analysis.

20. It is possible that the lawyers' valuations, particularly the low valuation, incorporate a discount for transaction costs. There is no straightforward way to determine whether this is the case given my survey data. One could design valuation questions that ask lawyers to value the case both in terms of a range of likely verdicts if the case went to trial and in terms of the case's settlement value. My survey did not do this.

21. The figures I report here are based on my own analysis of the data the Insurance Research Council collected.

22. There is only one case in the sample from Wisconsin that meets all of these criteria.

23. The ninetieth percentiles for the three injuries were $37,200, $64,050, and $42,000.

24. It is often the case that the parties will stipulate to the amount of past medical costs and that amount is filled in on the jury verdict form by the judge before deliberation even begins.

25. This presumes that the jury verdict is deemed to "make whole" the plaintiff, after discounting for the plaintiff's own negligence. Even with a jury verdict, a plaintiff's lawyer could at least advance the argument that the verdict did not constitute full compensation; how often lawyers advance such arguments, I have no way of knowing.

26. See *Rimes v. State Farm Mutual*, 106 Wis. 2d 263, 316 N.W.2d 348 (1982).

27. There is a massive program of intercompany arbitration in the insurance industry to resolve these kinds of disputes; the arbitration process is cheap and quick and is used for claims large and small (see Hines 1982). The dominant provider of these services is Arbitration Forums, Inc. (see http://www.arbfile.org, visited July 5, 2002).

28. Even with such limits, it may be possible to obtain a payment over the limit; one lawyer related that he was able to get total compensation of $110,000 for a client where the limit of the underinsurance coverage was $100,000 (as a total amount of compensation when combined with third-party payments). He was able to get the client's insurer to toss in an additional $10,000 to avoid costs associated with litigation and appeals. At least in Wisconsin, there are some specific exceptions to these limitation clauses. The 1995 tort reforms in Wisconsin made it possible for the companies to have reduction clauses in their policies.

29. Since my research time, insurers have been able to add "antistacking" clauses to their Wisconsin policies.

30. In their book on the relationship between divorce lawyers and divorce clients, Austin Sarat and William Felstiner (1995) develop the argument that there is an ongoing negotiation process between the lawyers and clients. However, their emphasis is on the relationship between lawyer and client and how it evolves in the course of the representation.

31. This is the common procedure in England (see Genn 1988).

32. As discussed in Chapter 2, in almost 20 percent of cases the lawyer took a fee lower than what the retainer agreement called for; most often this was be-

cause the lawyer felt that he or she needed to get a certain amount to the client in order for the client to be satisfied with the settlement. In some of these cases it might have been the situation that the lawyer had raised a client's expectations and felt that it would be easiest just to take a fee cut rather than to try to explain why the result fell below that expectation.

33. This strategy was not entirely rhetorical on the part of lawyers; the lawyers I observed and interviewed were strongly of the view that juries had become less favorable in their treatment of plaintiffs. Several lawyers indicated that for certain types of routine soft-tissue injuries it was now the defendants who wanted to go before a jury, not the plaintiffs (one lawyer told me that he normally did not request a jury in soft-tissue cases because he knew that if he didn't the defendant would, which meant that the defendant would have to pay the court fee associated with requesting a jury trial!). Nor, as Stephen Daniels and Joanne Martin (2001) have documented, is this change unique to Wisconsin.

34. I have no systematic data on how frequently lawyers encountered resistance from clients when the lawyer recommended accepting a proposed settlement. A study of medical malpractice cases found that clients seldom rejected a settlement that a lawyer favored accepting (less than 5 percent); similarly, clients seldom (5 percent) accepted a settlement that the lawyer favored rejecting (Sloan et al. 1993, 85).

35. Recall from Chapter 2 that my survey of practitioners found that, excluding those types of cases in which fees were explicitly limited or regulated by law, 39 percent of the cases described by the practitioners involved a graduated fee; only 53 percent of the cases involved the supposed standard one-third contingency fee.

36. Interestingly, one of the impacts of a flat percentage contingency fee is that it removes a substantial portion of the costs of going to trial from the client's settlement calculation. The biggest trial cost is the lawyer's time, which for a flat percentage contingency fee is irrelevant to the client.

37. An exception to this occurs when the tortfeasor's insurance coverage is less than the amount of the verdict, and hence part of the award may be uncollectible.

38. In several of the cases I observed in process, the lawyer had a clear understanding with the client that the case would never go to trial (or possibly even to suit); that is, the lawyer had accepted the case for purposes only of securing a settlement offer. It may well be the case that under these circumstances it is common for the lawyer to terminate representation if the client declines a settlement offer.

39. I suspect that when a lawyer has had to proceed with a case after the client rejected a reasonable settlement offer, the lawyer is very unlikely to be inclined to reduce the fee (although I can also imagine that if the lawyer thinks an offer is close to acceptable, the lawyer might reduce the fee to make the offer "go").

40. An exception to this is in types of cases, such as social security disability

appeals (Kritzer 1998a, 111–49), where a negotiated settlement is not really an option.

41. Recall that I asked the lawyer, "At the time you accepted the case, or when you first valued it, what did you think was the likely range of recovery?"

CHAPTER 6

1. In fact, there is an investment trust, DIAMONDS, traded on the American Stock Exchange, that is intended to produce a yield that mirrors the Dow Jones 30 Industrials. See http://www.amex.com/?href = /etf/prodInf/EtPi-Overview.jsp?Product_Symbol = DIA, visited July 8, 2002.

2. The sample design for this study combined a national mail survey of lawyers selected from Martindale-Hubbell with a "selective" mail and in-person survey of lawyers known to do medical malpractice cases (Dietz, Baird, and Berul 1973, 89–91). In the original sample, about two-thirds of the targeted respondents were from the national sample, with the remaining from the selective sample, but in the final sample only 23 percent were from the selective survey; however, if one eliminates from the national survey those who had had no contact with medical malpractice cases during the time frame covered in the questionnaire, 59 percent were from the selective survey. Most of the respondents, 80–90 percent, were plaintiffs' lawyers.

3. In a telephone conversation (September 22, 1994), one of the authors of this study, Stephen Dietz, told me that he could not remember the exact reason they had used the mean rather than the median. He did say, however, that he recalled that even using the mean, the effective hourly rate of contingency fee lawyers was only about 20 percent above what the typical hourly fee defense lawyer charged; this is correct if one uses the lowest of the various figures (after adjusting for cocounsel and referral fees). Dietz also informed me that the data from the 1973 study were no longer available, making it impossible to reanalyze those data to obtain the median figure.

4. The numbers reported in Table 6.1 differ slightly from those in my earlier book because here I have used somewhat more refined information on fee arrangement and different rounding procedures.

5. The mean is not reported; I have computed that from the original data.

6. It would be nice to be able to compare these figures to those from Dietz, Baird, and Berul 1973; however, data from only six contingency fee lawyers handling medical malpractice cases were available. Interestingly, the mean was $52; for three cases the effective hourly rate was $0, and the other three were $47, $77, and $267. One thing my data do show is that Dietz, Baird, and Berul's use of means most likely overstated the difference between hourly and contingency fee lawyers; there is a significant possibility that the median hourly rate in the earlier study was actually less than the median hourly rate charged by defense lawyers.

7. The only reason these smaller cases do not constitute much more of the sample is because the study was designed to have equal numbers of state and

federal cases; the median case in state court involved only $4,500 in stakes (see Kritzer 1990, 31).

8. It is possible to try to estimate typical effective hourly rates using aggregate income data from economic surveys of lawyers. When I do that, I obtain results consistent with the patterns I will report below from the Wisconsin contingency fee survey; if anything, the aggregate data yield lower estimates of the hourly returns than what I find from my survey data (see Kritzer 1998b, 276–83).

9. There are certain kinds of state-to-state variations that may be important but which I have no way to sort out. Specifically, states that employ a no-fault regime for auto accident injuries may have different patterns for the roughly half of contingency fee cases that arise as a result of such injuries.

10. The above figures may be less comparable than they first appear. Insurance defense lawyers bill for everything at the full rate, including things that they might be inclined to discount for clients paying "retail" rather than "wholesale" rates. As one defense lawyer described this to me, for a "retail" client he might decide to discount his charges for a trip to take a deposition out of town, particularly if the deposition proved to be unproductive; however, he would not discount this for an insurance company client paying "wholesale" rates. This same lawyer pointed out that with insurance defense work, time is more productive in that relatively little effort needs to be devoted to acquiring business, unlike other areas of practice (particularly plaintiffs' work).

11. For cases extending over a period of years, the hourly rates may have changed over the course of the case. If more than one lawyer worked on the case, the respondent was directed to provide the average rate.

12. The RAND survey used a closed-ended question in which the respondents were asked to choose from among the following categories: $75 or less, $76–$125, $126–$175, $176–$250, and more than $250. I estimated the means and medians using standard methods (see Blalock 1979, 61–66).

13. The median for this "right-trimmed" sample is $113. Because the medians are not generally affected greatly by the "trimming," I will not report trimmed medians in the tables or discussion.

14. Some of the variables listed above are the factors involved in the sample design (type of disposition, type of practice, and caseload), necessitating application of modified weights to the breakdowns for those categories.

15. I employ the midspread as a measure of variability because the more common measure, the standard deviation, is greatly inflated when the data are highly skewed, as is the case here.

16. In computing the trimmed figures for the weighted data, I used differing cut points depending on the specific weight employed.

17. In the remainder of this section I will show weighted figures in parentheses.

18. One of the lawyers I observed was working on a large medical malpractice case, and at one point I worked through with him the likely outcomes of the case and their probabilities (these ranged from a 50 percent chance of getting

nothing to a 10 percent chance of getting $8 million). We estimated that his "expected" fee was $500,000 (although his actual fee could range as high as $1.7 million under the rules governing legal fees in medical malpractice cases in Wisconsin); given the amount of time the lawyer had devoted to the case, and what was yet to come, I estimated that while he might end up making as much as $1,100 per hour, his expected effective hourly rate was $330. When I later examined the medical malpractice cases in the sample from my survey; I had information on thirty-nine cases. The median effective hourly rate was only thirty-six dollars, which is what is shown in Table 6.2a. However, this reflected in part that 45 percent resulted in no payment at all. The maximum effective hourly rate reported was $2,900, and 10 percent of the cases had effective hourly rates of $1,000 or more. The mean effective hourly rate was $314, and the mean hourly return across the thirty-nine cases was $316 per hour.

19. The skew also violates the normality assumption, although normality is not all that important for large samples when least squares methods are used.

20. The log transformation will also often produce a distribution of residuals that is approximately normal.

21. The estimation was done using the Heckman procedure in STATA 6.0; I used the maximum likelihood estimator rather than the original two-step Heckman model. Note that this procedure requires an assumption that the disturbance term for the normal regression model be normally distributed; examining the residuals shows that they do nicely approximate a normal distribution.

22. The absence of relationships with measures of experience or position may be somewhat surprising. Is this because these variables are confounded with income? To test this, I reestimated the model omitting the income variable. With this change, years of experience shows a significant relationship with the effective hourly rate, but not with the likelihood of a positive return. *However*, the largest negative coefficient is for those with six to ten years of experience, not for those with the least experience.

23. This mean is 5.058, which when transformed back to the linear scale is $157.

24. The time frame varied from lawyer to lawyer depending upon case volume.

25. In addition to attorney hours, I asked each respondent to provide information on paralegal hours. Many cases involved no paralegal time, but others consumed substantial quantities. To adjust for this, I subtracted an estimate of the cost of paralegal time (I assumed that the gross cost was $30 per hour). With this adjustment, two of the cases actually yielded negative net fees; the median adjusted fee was $6,550, with the first and third quartiles at $2,600 and $15,000.

26. The first and third quartiles are $61 to $250, yielding a midspread of $189. The mean hourly return, obtained in the usual way—by summing all of the hours reported, summing all of the fees (after adjusting for paralegal time), and dividing these two sums to get the per hour fee—was $160.

27. The questionnaire did not specifically ask the lawyers if they consulted

their time records, only if they consulted their case files and if those files contained time records.

28. For details on the complex design employed by RAND, see Kakalik et al. 1996, 95–128.

29. There are differing ways to compute the response rate, hence the somewhat ambiguous figure provided above (see Kakalik et al. 1996, 117).

30. The full questionnaire can be found in Kakalik et al. 1996, 281–85.

31. The results reported in this section all employ the sampling weights prepared by the RAND staff (see Kakalik et al. 1996, 95–128).

32. A conversation with this lawyer more than five years after I had observed in his practice revealed that the "big one" had finally come in, and he had settled a case that generated a fee in excess $250,000.

CHAPTER 7

1. The punitive damage portion of this award, $94 million, was eventually thrown out by a state appeals court (Pommer 2003).

2. At the time this research was carried out, the name of the firm was Habush, Habush, Davis & Rottier.

3. While there are many analyses of the impact of reputation, there is very little work on how reputations are actually formed (Mercer 1996, 3).

4. There may be certain types of exceptions, such as in the area of securities, where the case is effectively initiated by lawyers who monitor the stock market for events that constitute potential lawsuits.

5. In this modification, and in the Hire-a-Lawyer game to follow, I have used game-theoretic elements for purely heuristic purposes; I have not attempted to structure games with an eye to formally deriving equilibria.

6. In an earlier study that included social security cases as a particular focus (Kritzer 1998a), I saw only one social security case in which the issue of a compromise came up; in that case, an administrative law judge suggested to the lawyer finding that the claimant was disabled but that the onset of the disability was a later date than in the original application. In this situation, the proposed compromise probably had more negative impact for the lawyer's fee than for the client, whose concern included both back benefits and a stream for future benefits.

7. According to the Wisconsin Rules of Professional Conduct 1.5(e),

A division of fee between lawyers who are not in the same firm [i.e., a referral fee] may be made only if:

(1) the division is in proportion to the services performed by each lawyer or, by written agreement with the client, each lawyer assumes joint responsibility for the representation;

(2) the client is advised of and does not object to the participation of all the lawyers involved and is informed if the fee will increase as a result of their involvement; and

(3) the total fee is reasonable.

This same provision, which is taken from the Model Code, appears in the professional conduct codes of many states.

8. For a theoretical analyses of the economics of lawyer referrals, see Hay 1996b and Spurr 1988, 1990; Stephen Spurr also provides some empirical analysis based on data covering 1974 through 1984 from New York. A less extensive analysis of New York data from 1957 can be found in a study by Maurice Rosenberg and Michael Sovern (1959, 1139–41).

9. The issue of subrogation was discussed in some detail in Chapter 5..

10. See Chapter 5 for a discussion of the "stacking" issue.

11. A reputation for going to trial can potentially work both ways. The defense can also have such a reputation. In a study of settlement of personal injury cases in New Jersey, one judge commented to the researcher that a particular defendant's lawyer "had a reputation of never trying cases" (Hyman et al. 1995, 131).

CHAPTER 8

1. Not only do reformers typically presume that they know what the problem is, rather than systematically assessing the situation before acting, they also tend to ignore any research that might call into question their favored reforms. For example, one of the cornerstones of the Civil Justice Reform Act was oversight of cases by judges. One of the more intriguing findings from a study comparing state and federal cases circa 1980 was that, even after controlling for factors such as stakes and complexity, cases handled in the federal courts required more time than did cases handled in the state courts. The authors' best explanation for this pattern was that federal judges, by monitoring cases more closely than do their state counterparts, actually increased the demand on lawyers, thus raising the costs of litigation. That is, judicial case management, rather than making litigation less costly for the litigants, actually increases the costs (see Kritzer, Grossman, et al. 1984).

2. I have attended a number of academic conferences where prominent, knowledgeable scholars have stated this supposed fact. For example, at a session of the 2001 Clifford Symposium held at the DePaul Law School, one of the participants, a prominent faculty member from one of the top law schools, stated that "only the United States has contingency fees." Even when this was challenged from the floor, the speaker maintained that contingency fees were unique to the United States.

3. Even where contingency fees are banned, informal contingency arrangements, where the lawyer does not seek payment of fees in unsuccessful actions, are common (Genn 1988, 109–10; Kritzer 1984, 130).

4. Starting in 2003, solicitors' fees in modest cases (up to £10,000) could be based on a fixed cost plus percentage: £800 plus 20 percent of the first £5,000 and 15 percent of the next £5,000 (see Rose 2003).

5. In England (and Wales), Ireland, Scotland, and New Zealand, civil juries are used in cases of defamation, malicious prosecution, and some other rare

causes of action (Vidmar 2002, 802). Civil juries are not generally used outside the common law world.

6. I found one survey of persons who had used a lawyer within the previous five years (Miethe 1993) that permits a crude assessment of this question. While the survey does not ask about the fee arrangement, it seems reasonable to assume that virtually all of the personal injury clients paid their lawyers on a contingency fee basis, while few if any of the users of lawyers' services for other types of cases (property deed / wills / inheritance, divorce and child custody, property damage and real estate dispute, traffic violation, criminal violation, other dispute) did. One of the questions on the survey asked how satisfied the respondent was with "the amount of money you had to pay for legal services" (not satisfied, somewhat satisfied, or very satisfied). Regardless of whether I look across all seven case categories or at a simple dichotomy between the personal injury cases and other types of cases, there is no support in these data for an argument that personal injury (i.e., contingency fee) clients are more dissatisfied than other clients with the cost of the legal services.

7. Brigid McMenamin (1995, 160) notes that Joe Jamail is reported to have earned $90 million during 1994, with most of his income coming from corporate clients. Jamail has an office with five associates, no partners (see "The Forbes Four Hundred," *Forbes*, October 16, 1995, 190); if one makes the generous assumption that Jamail works 4,000 hours per year and has responsibility for the cases producing half of that $90 million, he is earning at the rate of $11,250 per hour; if one assumes he works "only" 3,000 hours per year, and generates the full $90 million, this goes up to $30,000 per hour. His corporate clients don't seem to complain.

8. These proposals resurfaced as late as 2003 in the form of petitions to at least thirteen state supreme courts to impose limits on the contingency fees in certain circumstances (Liptak 2003).

9. Such post hoc systems of review are common in most other civil law countries such as England and Canada. The process is referred to as "taxation of costs" and typically relies upon a specialized court official (the "costs judge," the "taxing master," or "taxing officer") to do the actual review of fees. See Brickman 1996b for a critique of post hoc case-by-case review of contingency fees.

10. Jeffrey O'Connell, a proponent of limitations on contingency fees, has asserted that part of the problem arises because of the lack of price advertising; he describes a study that found that "only 7 of more than 1,400 advertisements by lawyers in the Yellow Pages of the telephone directories in 12 big cities stated the percentage to be charged" (reported in Liptak 2003). While this may be true, it needs to be put into the perspective that few, if any, lawyers advertise hourly rates or fixed-fee rates in the Yellow Pages; nor is there much price advertising in the Yellow Pages by other professionals such as accountants, dentists, or doctors.

11. In England, opening the market for conveyancing work, long held as a monopoly by solicitors, during the 1980s to nonlawyer "licensed conveyancers"

led to a sharp decline in the fees charged for conveyancing, even though solicitors continued to be the dominant provider of such services (see Domberger and Sherr 1989).

12. My own research (Kritzer 1998a) comparing lawyer and nonlawyer advocates shows clearly that specialized, nonlawyer advocates can provide very effective legal representation. A review of such nonlawyer providers in England, where they are called "loss assessors" (Blackwell 2000), produced no evidence that they produced results that differed significantly from those produced by solicitors, despite the legal profession's long-standing opposition and critique of such providers (Law Society 1970).

13. It is now possible to sell some or all of a pending tort claim to a nonlawyer. Two companies that make such purchases are Interim Settlement Funding Corporation and Future Settlement Funding Corporation (see *Rancman v. Interim Settlement Funding Corp.*, 99 Ohio St.3d 121, 2003-Ohio-2721; http://www.oswegolaw.com/fsfny.htm, visited June 30, 2003).

14. One might ask here whether poorer-quality or less experienced lawyers would bid more to get business. This might happen, but it would not concern the seller of the claim because the amount the seller would receive would be assured because it would be placed into escrow when the claim was sold.

15. The uncertainties created in the short term by deregulation would be substantial, and it would take a period of time for the system to achieve an equilibrium. The problems of transitioning from a long-established system of litigation funding to a radically different system are evident in England, where at least two major players in personal injury compensation (Claims Direct and The Accident Group) have risen rapidly and crashed and burned (see Robins 2003).

16. A good example is the current whipping boy of excessive contingency fees, the fees received by lawyers in the tobacco litigation (Olson 2003, 25–71). However, what most critics fail to consider is the uncertainty that existed at the outset of the litigation: "The tort lawyers were . . . no strangers to legal contests with the tobacco companies, but always before they had been on the losing side. The combination of industry money, legal talent, and legal tactics, along with supportive juries when the cases got that far, had been overpowering" (Derthick 2002, 72).

17. What does this point mean for my analysis of effective hourly rates? It means that any one value is likely to involve some significant error. However, assuming the errors are essentially random, the kinds of summary figures I present should be reasonably accurate because the errors will cancel out across cases.

18. The only published work I have been able to locate is a study by Douglas Cumming (2001).

APPENDIX A

1. This high figure does not simply mean that cases in Texas are more likely to result in suits. Only 12 percent of Texas auto injury cases involving lawyers

result in lawsuits. Part of the 61 percent figure reflects that the Texas Department of Insurance reports only those cases in which a payment is made, and only those involving payments of at least $10,000. A national study of commercial liability claims closed in 1993 with payments of $75,000 or more found that 92 percent of the claims involved a lawsuit (Insurance Services Office 1994, 6).

2. In this calculation, I discounted the responses of six lawyers who claimed to have tried between 72 and 300 cases during the year. I arbitrarily reduced each of these responses to 30, which still seems high but not totally out of sight. Some of these "trials" were in fact administrative hearings in social security and workers' compensation tribunals. Lawyers handling those cases do have higher volumes of hearings, but not that high.

Bibliography

Abel, Richard L. 1987. "The Real Tort Crisis—Too Few Claims." *Ohio State Law Journal* 48: 443–67.

Abrahamse, Allan F., and Stephen J. Carroll. 1999. "The Frequency of Excess Claims for Automobile Personal Injuries." In *Automobile Insurance: Road Safety, New Drivers, Risks, Insurance Fraud, and Regulation*, ed. Georges Dionne and Claire Laberge-Nadeau, 131–49. Norwell, MA: Kluwer Academic Publishers.

Association of Trial Lawyers of America. 1994. "Keys to the Courthouse: Quick Facts on the Contingent Fee System." Washington, DC: Association of Trial Lawyers of America. http://www.civiljustice.org/Pages/05-Contingent-FeeSystem.html.

Auerbach, Jerold S. 1976. *Unequal Justice: Lawyers and Social Change in Modern America*. New York: Oxford University Press.

Axelrod, Robert. 1984. *The Evolution of Cooperation*. New York: Basic Books.

Babcock, Linda, and Greg Pogarsky. 1999. "Damage Caps and Settlement: A Behavioral Approach." *Journal of Legal Studies* 28: 341–70.

Bailey, F. G., ed. 1971. *Gifts and Poison: The Politics of Reputation*. Oxford: Basil Blackwell.

Bailis, Daniel S., and Robert J. MacCoun. 1996. "Estimating Liability Risks with the Media as Your Guide." *Judicature* 80: 64–67.

Baker, Tom. 2001. "Blood Money, New Money, and the Moral Economy of Tort Law in Action." *Law & Society Review* 33: 275–319.

Balen, Paul. 1995. "Conditional Fees: Investing in the Future." *Solicitors' Journal* (July 14): 678–780.

Barber, James David. 1965. *The Lawmakers: Recruitment and Adaptation to Legislative Life*. New Haven, CT: Yale University Press.

Bergstrom, Randolph E. 1992. *Courting Danger: Injury and Law in New York City, 1870–1910*. Ithaca, NY: Cornell University Press.

Bermudes, Sergio. 1999. "Administration of Civil Justice in Brazil." In *Civil Justice in Crisis: Comparative Perspectives of Civil Procedure*, ed. Adrian A. S. Zuckerman, 347–62. Oxford: Oxford University Press.

Bhattacharya, Sudipto, and Dilip Mookherjee 1986. "Portfolio Choice in Research and Development." *RAND Journal of Economics* 17: 594–605.

Biederman, Christine. 1996. "Families of Valujet Crash Victims Find Lawyers Ignore Solicitation Ban." *New York Times*, June 4, p. A13.

Blackwell, Brian (chairman). 2000. "The Report of the Lord Chancellor's Committee to Investigate the Activities of Non-Legally Qualified Claims Assessors and Employment Advisors." London: Lord Chancellor's Department. http://www.lcd.gov.uk/civil/blackwell/indbod.htm.

Blalock, Hubert M., Jr. 1979. *Social Statistics*. New York: McGraw-Hill.

Blankenburg, Erhard. 1982–83. "Legal Insurance, Litigant Decisions, and the Rising Caseloads of Courts: A West German Study." *Law & Society Review* 16: 601–24.

———. 1994. "The Infrastructure for Avoiding Civil Litigation: Comparing Cultures of Legal Behavior in the Netherlands and West Germany." *Law & Society Review* 28: 789–808.

Blum, Andrew. 1987. "Deaths in the Snow Lead to Suits." *National Law Journal* (November 30): 3.

Blumberg, Abraham. 1967. "The Practice of Law as a Confidence Game: Organizational Cooptation of the Profession." *Law & Society Review* 1: 15–39.

Bogart, W. A. 2002. *Consequences: The Impact of Law and Its Complexity*. Toronto: University of Toronto Press.

Bok, Derek C. 1983. "A Flawed System." *Harvard Magazine* 85: 38–45, 70–71.

Bolt, Cathy. 1999. "WA Canola Farmers in Class Action over Seeds." *Australian Financial Review* (January 21): 2.

Boon, A. 1995. "Client Decision-Making in Personal Injury Schemes." *International Journal of the Sociology of Law* 23: 253–72.

Bourdieu, Pierre. 1987. "The Force of Law: Toward Sociology of the Juridical Field." *Hastings Law Journal* 38: 805–53.

Bowen, Lauren. 1995a. "Advertising and the Legal Profession." *Justice System Journal* 18: 43–54.

———. 1995b. "Attorney Advertising in the Wake of *Bates v. State Bar of Arizona* 1977." *American Politics Quarterly* 23: 461–84.

Brainard, William C., and James Tobin. 1968. "Pitfalls in Financial Model Building." *American Economic Review [Papers and Proceedings of the Eightieth Annual Meeting of the American Economic Association]* 58: 99–122.

Brazil, Wayne D. 1978. "The Adversary Character of Civil Discovery: A Critique and Proposals for Change." *Vanderbilt Law Review* 31: 1295–1361.

Brennan, Lisa. 1998. "Outside Fee Audits Draw Bar Dissent." *National Law Journal* (August 3): A6.

Brickman, Lester. 1989. "Contingent Fees Without Contingencies: Hamlet Without the Prince of Denmark?" *UCLA Law Review* 37: 29–137.

———. 1992. "The Asbestos Litigation Crisis: Is There a Need for an Administrative Alternative?" *Cardozo Law Review* 13: 1819–89.

———. 1996a. "ABA Regulation of Contingency Fees: Money Talks, Ethics Walks." *Fordham Law Review* 65: 247–335.

———. 1996b. "Contingency Fee Abuses, Ethical Mandates, and the Disciplinary System: The Case Against Case-By-Case Enforcement." *Washington and Lee Law Review* 53: 1340–73.

———. 1999. "The Tobacco Litigation and Attorneys' Fees." *Fordham Law Review* 67: 2827–58.

Brickman, Lester, Michael Horowitz, and Jeffrey O'Connell. 1994. *Rethinking Contingency Fees*. New York: Manhattan Institute.

Bromley, D. B. 1993. *Reputation, Image, and Impression Management*. New York: John Wiley & Sons.

Burke, Thomas F. 2002. *Lawyers, Lawsuits, and Legal Rights: The Battle over Litigation in American Society*. Berkeley: University of California Press.

Cain, Maureen. 1979. "The General Practice Lawyer and the Client: Towards a Radical Conception." *International Journal of the Sociology of Law* 7: 331–54.

Cannon, Michael. 1998. *That Disreputable Firm: The Inside Story of Slater and Gordon*. Carlton, Victoria: Melbourne University Press.

Carlin, Jerome E. 1962. *Lawyers on Their Own: A Study of Individual Practitioners in Chicago*. New Brunswick, NJ: Rutgers University Press.

Carroll, Stephen, Allan Abrahamse, and Mary Vaiana. 1995. "The Costs of Excess Medical Claims for Automobile Personal Injuries." Documented Briefing, RAND Corporation, Santa Monica, California.

Carson, Clara. 1999. *The 1995 Lawyer Statistical Report*. Chicago: American Bar Foundation.

Casper, Jonathan D. 1972. *American Criminal Justice: The Defendant's Perspective*. Englewood Cliffs, NJ: Prentice-Hall.

Chapper, Joy, and Roger Hanson. 1983. "Cost Shifting in Maricopa County Superior Court: An Exploratory Study of Rule 37 (A) (4)." *Justice System Journal* 8: 325–37.

Chase, Oscar G. 1995. "Helping Jurors Determine Pain and Suffering Awards." *Hofstra Law Review* 23: 763–90.

Clermont, Kevin M., and J. D. Currivan. 1978. "Improving on the Contingent Fee." *Cornell Law Review* 63: 529–639.

Clermont, Kevin M., and Theodore Eisenberg. 1992. "Trial by Jury or Judge: Transcending Empiricism." *Cornell Law Review* 77: 1124–77.

Coffee, John C., Jr. 1986. "Understanding the Plaintiff's Attorney: The Implications of Economic Theory for Private Enforcement of Law Through Class and Derivative Actions." *Columbia Law Review* 86: 669–727.

Common Good. 2003. "Memorandum in Support of Petition for Rulemaking to Revise the Ethical Standards Relating to Contingency Fees" (filed with the Supreme Court of the State of Virginia).

Conley, Janet. 2001. "Fight over Auditing Coming to an End." *National Law Journal* (April 23): A1.

Connolly, Paul R., Edith A. Holleman, and Michael J. Kuhlman. 1978. "Judicial Controls and the Civil Litigative Process: Discovery." Washington, DC: Federal Judicial Center.

Corboy, Philip H. 1976. "Contingency Fees: The Individual's Key to the Courthouse Door." *Litigation* 2(4): 27–36.

Coyle, Marcia. 1997. "Hat Tricks for These Two High Court Lawyers." *National Law Journal* (August 11): A10.

Crane, Mark. 1988. "Lawyers Don't Take *Every* Case." *National Law Journal* (January 25): 1, 34.

Cumming, Douglas. 2001. "Settlement Disputes: Evidence from a Legal Practice Perspective." *European Journal of Law and Economics* 11: 249–80.

Daniels, Stephen. 1989. "The Question of Jury Competence and the Politics of Civil Justice Reform: Symbols, Rhetoric and Agenda-Building." *Law and Contemporary Problems* 52: 269–310.

Daniels, Stephen, and Joanne Martin. 1995. *Civil Juries and the Politics of Reform.* Evanston, IL: Northwestern University Press.

———. 1999. "'It's Darwinism—Survival of the Fittest': How Markets and Reputations Shape the Way in Which Plaintiffs' Lawyers Obtain Clients." *Law and Policy* 21: 377–99.

———. 2001. "'We Live on the Edge of Extinction All the Time': Entrepreneurs, Innovation, and the Plaintiffs' Bar in the Wake of Tort Reform." In *Legal Professions: Work, Structure and Organization,* ed. Jerry Van Hoy, 149–80. New York: JAI/Elsevier Science Ltd.

———. 2002. "It Was the Best of Times, It Was the Worst of Times: The Precarious Nature of Plaintiff's Practice in Texas." *Texas Law Review* 80: 1781–828.

Danzon, Patricia M. 1983. "Contingent Fees for Personal Injury Litigation." *Bell Journal of Economics* 14: 213–24.

Davis, Ann. 1995. "The Earth Breathes Fire, Scorches Lawyers." *National Law Journal* (April 10): A10.

DeFrances, Carol J., and Marika F. X. Litras. 1999. "Civil Trial Cases and Verdicts in Large Counties, 1996." Washington, DC: Bureau of Justice Statistics, U.S. Department of Justice. http://www.ojp.usdoj.gov/bjs/pub/pdf/ctcvlc96.pdf.

Derthick, Martha A. 2002. *Up in Smoke: From Legislation to Litigation in Tobacco Politics.* Washington, DC: CQ Press.

Dietz, Stephen, C. Bruce Baird, and Lawrence Berul. 1973. "The Medical Malpractice Legal System." In *Appendix: Report of the Secretary's Commission on Medical Malpractice,* 87–167. Washington, DC: Department of Health, Education, and Welfare [OS 73–89].

Domberger, Simon, and Avrom Sherr. 1989. "The Impact of Competition on Pricing and Quality of Legal Services." *International Review of Law and Economics* 9: 41–56.

Dover, Michael A. 1986. "Contingent Percentage Fees: An Economic Analysis." *Journal of Air Law and Commerce* 51: 531–66.

Ebersole, Joseph L., and Barlow Burke. 1980. *Discovery Problems in Civil Cases.* Washington, DC: Federal Judicial Center.

Eekelaar, John, Mavis Maclean, and Sarah Beinart. 2000. *Family Lawyers: The Divorce Work of Solicitors.* Oxford: Hart Publishing.

Eisenberg, Theodore, Neil LaFountain, Brian Ostrom, David Rottman, and Martin T. Wells. 2002. "Juries, Judges, and Punitive Damages: An Empirical Study." *Cornell Law Review* 87: 743–82.

Eisenstein, James, Roy B. Flemming, and Peter F. Nardulli. 1988. *The Contours of Justice: Communities and Their Courts*. Boston: Little Brown.

Eisenstein, James, and Herbert Jacob. 1977. *Felony Justice: An Organizational Analysis of Criminal Courts*. Boston: Little, Brown & Company.

Feeley, Malcolm M. 1983. *Court Reform on Trial: Why Simple Solutions Fail*. New York: Basic Books.

Felstiner, William L. F. 1998. "Justice, Power, and Lawyers." In *Justice and Power in Sociolegal Studies*, ed. Bryant G. Garth and Austin Sarat, 55–79. Evanston, IL: Northwestern University Press.

———. 2001. "Synthesizing Socio-Legal Research: Lawyer-Client Relations as an Example." *International Journal of the Legal Profession* 8: 191–201.

Felstiner, William L. F., and Austin Sarat. 1992. "Enactments of Power: Negotiating Reality and Responsibility in Lawyer-Client Interactions." *Cornell Law Review* 77: 1447–98.

Flemming, Roy B. 1986. "The Client Game: Defense Attorney Perspectives on Their Relations with Criminal Clients." *American Bar Foundation Research Journal* 1986: 253–77.

Flemming, Roy B., Peter F. Nardulli, and James Eisenstein. 1992. *The Craft of Justice: Politics and Work in Criminal Court Communities*. Philadelphia: University of Pennsylvania Press.

Flood, John. 1987. "Anatomy of Lawyering: An Ethnography of a Corporate Law Firm." Ph.D. diss., Northwestern University.

Friedman, Alan E. 1969. "An Analysis of Settlement." *Stanford Law Review* 22: 67–100.

Galanter, Marc. 1974. "Why the 'Haves' Come Out Ahead: Speculations on the Limits of Legal Change." *Law & Society Review* 9: 95–160.

———. 1990. "Case Congregations and Their Careers." *Law & Society Review* 14: 371–95.

———. 1993. "News from Nowhere: The Debased Debate on Civil Justice." *Denver University Law Review* 71: 77–113.

———. 1998. "An Oil Strike in Hell: Contemporary Legends about the Civil Justice System." *Arizona Law Review* 40: 717–52.

Galanter, Marc, and Thomas M. Palay. 1991. *Tournament of Lawyers: The Transformation of the Big Law Firm*. Chicago: University of Chicago Press.

Gene Kroupa & Associates. 1999. "1999 Economics of Practice Survey: Report." Madison, WI: State Bar of Wisconsin.

Genn, Hazel. 1988. *Hard Bargaining: Out of Court Settlement in Personal Injury Actions*. Oxford: Oxford University Press.

Gibson, Murray H., Jr. 1994. "Attorney-Brokering: An Ethical Analysis of the Model Rules of Professional Conduct and Individual State Rules Which Allow This Practice." *Journal of the Legal Profession* 19: 323–35.

Gilson, Ronald J., and Robert H. Mnookin. 1994. "Disputing Through Agents:

Cooperation and Conflict Between Lawyers in Litigation." *Columbia Law Review* 94: 509–66.

Glendon, Mary Ann. 1994. *A Nation Under Lawyers: How the Crisis in the Legal Profession is Transforming American Society*. New York: Farrar, Straus and Giroux.

Grady, John. 1976. "Some Ethical Questions About Percentage Fees." *Litigation* 2: 20–26.

Grau, Charles W., and Arlene Sheskin. 1980. *Ruling Out Delay: Impact of Ohio's Rules of Superintendence Upon the Administration of Justice*. Chicago: American Judicature Society.

———. 1982. "Ruling Out Delay: The Impact of Ohio's Rules of Superintendence." *Judicature* 66: 108–21.

Gravelle, Hugh, and Michael Waterson. 1993. "No Win, No Fee: Some Economics of Contingent Legal Fees." *Economic Journal* 103: 1205–20.

Gross, Samuel R., and Kent D. Syverud. 1991. "Getting to No: A Study of Settlement Negotiations and the Selection of Cases for Trial." *Michigan Law Review* 90: 319–93.

Guthrie, Chris, Jeffrey J. Rachlingski, and Andrew J. Wistrich. 2001. "Inside the Judicial Mind." *Cornell Law Review* 86: 777–830.

Hadfield, Gillian. 2000. "The Price of Law: How the Market for Lawyers Distorts the Justice System." *Michigan Law Review* 98: 953–1006.

Hagin, Robert. 1979. *The Dow Jones-Irwin Guide to Modern Portfolio Theory*. Homewood, IL: Dow-Jones-Irwin.

Haltom, William, and Michael McCann. 2004. *Distorting the Law: Reform Politics, Mass Media, and the Litigation Crisis*. Chicago: University of Chicago Press.

Harr, Jonathan. 1995. *A Civil Action*. New York: Random House.

Hastie, Reid, David A. Schkade, and John W. Payne. 1999. "Juror Judgments in Civil Cases: Effects of Plaintiff's Requests and Plaintiff's Identity on Punitive Damage Awards." *Law and Human Behavior* 23: 445–70.

Hay, Bruce L. 1996a. "Contingent Fees and Agency Costs." *Journal of Legal Studies* 25: 503–33.

———. 1996b. "The Economics of Lawyer Referrals." Discussion paper no. 203, Center for Law, Economics, and Business, Harvard University.

———. 1997a. "Contingent Fees, Principal-Agent Problems, and the Settlement of Litigation." *William Mitchell Law Review* 23: 43–79.

———. 1997b. "Optimal Contingent Fees in a World of Settlement." *Journal of Legal Studies* 26: 259–78.

Hazard, Geoffrey C., Jr. 2000. "Lawyers Not Private Eyes." *National Law Journal* (April 10): A23.

Hechler, David. 2001. "Allstate Found Liable for Abuse of Process." *National Law Journal* (October 22): A15.

Heinz, John P., and Edward O. Laumann. 1982. *Chicago Lawyers: The Social Structure of the Bar*. New York: Russell Sage Foundation.

Hensler, Deborah R., M. Susan Marquis, Allan F. Abrahamse, Sandra H. Berry, Patricia A. Ebener, Elizabeth Lewis, E. Allan Lind, Robert J. MacCoun,

Willard G. Manning, Jeannette A. Rogowski, and Mary E. Vaiana. 1991. *Compensation for Accidental Injuries in the United States*. Santa Monica, CA: RAND Corporation.

Hensler, Deborah R., et al. 2001. "RAND Survey of Compensation for Accidental Injuries in the United States, 1988–89 [Computer File and Documentation]." Ann Arbor, MI: Interuniversity Consortium for Political and Social Research [distributor].

Hines, Bernard. 1982. "Insurance Arbitration Forums." In *The Pace of Litigation: Conference Proceedings*, ed. William L. F. Felstiner, Jane W. Adler, Deborah R. Hensler, and Mark A. Peterson, 109–11. Santa Monica, CA: RAND Corporation.

Hinsz, Verlin D., and Kristin E. Indahl. 1995. "Assimilation to Anchors for Damage Awards in a Mock Civil Trial." *Journal of Applied Social Psychology* 25: 991–1026.

Holmes, Steven A. 1991. "Workers Find It Tough Going Filing Lawsuits Over Job Bias." *New York Times*, July 24, p. A1.

Horowitz, Michael. 1995. "Making Ethics Real, Making Ethics Work: A Proposal for Contingency Fee Reform." *Emory Law Journal* 44: 173–211.

Hosticka, Carl J. 1979. "We Don't Care About What Happened, We Only Care About What Is Going to Happen: Lawyer-Client Negotiations of Reality." *Social Problems* 26: 599–610.

Howard, Philip K. 1994. *The Death of Common Sense: How Law Is Suffocating America*. New York: Random House.

Hunting, Roger Bryant, and Gloria S. Neuwirth. 1962. *Who Sues in New York City? A Study of Automobile Accident Claims*. New York: Columbia University Press.

Hyman, Jonathan M., Milton Heumann, Kenneth J. Dautrich, and Harold L. Rubenstein. 1995. *Civil Settlement: Styles of Negotiation in Dispute Resolution*. New Brunswick: New Jersey Administrative Office of the Courts.

Insurance Research Council (IRC). 1994. *Auto Injuries: Claiming Behavior and Its Impact on Insurance Costs*. Oak Brook, IL: Insurance Research Council.

———. 1996. *Fraud and Buildup in Auto Injury Claims*. Malvern, PA: Insurance Research Council.

———. 1999. *Injuries in Auto Accidents: An Analysis of Auto Insurance Claims*. Malvern, PA: Insurance Research Council.

Insurance Services Office. 1994. *Closed Claim Survey for Commercial General Liability: Survey Results*. New York: ISO Data.

Jessup, Philip C. 1938. *Elihu Root*. Vol. 1, *1845–1909*. New York: Dodd, Mead & Company.

Johnson, Earl, Jr. 1980–81. "Lawyer's Choice: A Theoretical Appraisal of Litigation Investment and Decisions." *Law & Society Review* 15: 567–610.

Kagan, Robert A. 2001. *Adversarial Legalism: The American Way of Law*. Cambridge: Harvard University Press.

Kahn, Herman. 1960. *On Thermonuclear War*. Princeton, NJ: Princeton University Press.

Kahneman, Daniel, Paul Slovic, and Amos Tversky, eds. 1982. *Judgment Under Uncertainty: Heuristics and Biases.* Vol. 185. New York: Cambridge University Press.

Kakalik, James S., Terence Dunworth, Laural A. Hill, Daniel McCaffrey, Marian Oshiro, Nicholas M. Pace, and Mary E. Vaiana. 1996. *An Evaluation of Judicial Case Management Under the Civil Justice Reform Act.* Santa Monica, CA: RAND Corporation.

Kakalik, James S., Elizabeth R. King, Michael Traynor, Patricia A. Ebener, and Larry Picus. 1988. *Costs and Compensation Paid in Aviation Accident Litigation.* Santa Monica, CA: RAND Corporation.

Karsten, Peter. 1998. "Enabling the Poor to Have Their Day in Court: The Sanctioning of Contingency Fee Contracts, a History to 1940." *DePaul Law Review* 47: 231–60.

Keen, Lisa, and Suzanne B. Goldberg. 1998. *Strangers to the Law: Gay People on Trial.* Ann Arbor: University of Michigan Press.

Keilitz, Susan, Roger Hanson, and Henry W. K. Daley. 1993. "Is Civil Discovery in State Trial Courts Out of Control?" *State Court Journal* 17: 8–17.

Kerameus, K. D., and S. Koussoulis. 1999. "Civil Justice Reform: Access, Costs, and Delay. A Greek Perspective." In *Civil Justice in Crisis: Comparative Perspectives of Civil Procedure,* ed. Adrian A. S. Zuckerman, 363–84. Oxford: Oxford University Press.

Kessler, Daniel, Thomas Meites, and Geoffrey Miller. 1996. "Explaining Deviations from the Fifty-Percent Rule: A Multimodal Approach to the Selection of Cases for Litigation." *Journal of Legal Studies* 25: 233–59.

Klein, Daniel B. 1992. "Promise Keeping in the Great Society: A Model of Credit Information Sharing." *Economics and Politics* 4: 117–36.

———. 1997a. "Knowledge, Reputation, and Trust, by Voluntary Means." In *Reputations: Studies in the Voluntary Elicitation of Good Conduct,* ed. Daniel B. Klein, 1–14. Ann Arbor: University of Michigan Press.

———. 1997b. *Reputations: Studies in the Voluntary Elicitation of Good Conduct.* Ann Arbor: University of Michigan Press.

Kritzer, Herbert M. 1984. "Fee Arrangements and Fee Shifting: Lessons from the Experience in Ontario." *Law and Contemporary Problems* 47: 125–38.

———. 1986. "Adjudication to Settlement: Shading in the Gray." *Judicature* 70: 161–65.

———. 1987. "Fee Arrangements and Negotiation: A Research Note." *Law & Society Review* 21: 341–48.

———. 1990. *The Justice Broker: Lawyers and Ordinary Litigation.* New York: Oxford University Press.

———. 1991. *Let's Make a Deal: Negotiations and Settlement in Ordinary Litigation.* Madison, WI: University of Wisconsin Press.

———. 1992. "The English Rule: Searching for Winners in a Loser Pays System." *ABA Journal* 78: 54–58.

———. 1994. "Lawyer's Fees and the Holy Grail: Where Should Clients Search for Value?" *Judicature* 77: 186–90.

———. 1996. "Courts, Justice, and Politics in England." In *Courts, Law, and Politics in Comparative Perspective,* by Herbert Jacob, Erhard Blankenburg, Herbert M. Kritzer, Doris Marie Provine, and Joseph Sanders, 81–176. New Haven, CT: Yale University Press.

———. 1998a. *Legal Advocacy: Lawyers and Nonlawyers at Work.* Ann Arbor: University of Michigan Press.

———. 1998b. "The Wages of Risk: The Returns of Contingency Fee Legal Practice." *DePaul Law Review* 47: 267–319.

———. 1999. "The Professions Are Dead, Long Live the Professions: Legal Practice in a Post-Professional World." *Law & Society Review* 33: 713–59.

———. 2001a. "The Fracturing Legal Profession: The Case of Plaintiffs' Personal Injury Lawyers." *International Journal of the Legal Profession* 8: 225–50.

———. 2001b. "From Litigators of Ordinary Cases to Litigators of Extraordinary Cases: Stratification of the Plaintiffs' Bar in the Twenty-first Century." *DePaul Law Review* 51: 219–40.

———. 2001c. "Public Perceptions of Civil Trial Verdicts." *Judicature* 85: 78–82.

———. 2002a. "The Future Role of 'Law Workers': Rethinking the Forms of Legal Practice and the Scope of Legal Education." *Arizona Law Review* 44: 917–38.

———. 2002b. "Lawyer Fees and Lawyer Behavior in Litigation: What Does the Empirical Literature Really Say?" *Texas Law Review* 80: 1943–83.

Kritzer, Herbert M., William L. F. Felstiner, Austin Sarat, and David M. Trubek. 1985. "The Impact of Fee Arrangement on Lawyer Effort." *Law & Society Review* 19: 251–78.

Kritzer, Herbert M., Joel B. Grossman, Elizabeth McNichol, David M. Trubek, and Austin Sarat. 1984. "Courts and Litigation Investment: Why Do Lawyers Spend More Time in Federal Cases?" *Justice System Journal* 9: 7–22.

Kritzer, Herbert M., and Jayanth Krishnan. 1999. "Lawyers Seeking Clients, Clients Seeking Lawyers: Sources of Contingency Fee Cases and Their Implications for Case Handling." *Law and Policy* 20: 347–75.

Kritzer, Herbert M., Austin Sarat, David M. Trubek, Kristin Bumiller, and Elizabeth McNichol. 1984. "Understanding the Costs of Litigation: The Case of the Hourly Fee Lawyer." *American Bar Foundation Research Journal* 1984: 559–604.

Lacy, F. R. 1978. "Discovery Costs in State Court Litigation." *Oregon Law Review* 57: 289–308.

Landon, Donald D. 1985. "Clients, Colleagues, and Community: The Shaping of Zealous Advocacy in Country Law Practice." *American Bar Foundation Research Journal* 1985: 81–112.

———. 1988. "LaSalle Street and Main Street: The Role of Context in Structuring Law Practice." *Law & Society Review* 22: 213–36.

———. 1990. *Country Lawyers: The Impact of Context on Professional Practice.* Westport, CT: Praeger.

Law Society. 1970. *Memorandum on Maintenance and Champerty: Claims Assessors and Contingency Fees.* London: Law Society.

Legal Services Corporation. 1979. "Special Legal Problems and Problems of Access to Legal Services." Washington, DC: Legal Services Corporation.

Lerman, Lisa. 1999. "Blue-Chip Bilking: Regulation of Billing Expense Fraud by Lawyers." *Georgetown Journal of Legal Ethics* 12: 205–365.

Liptak, Adam. 2003. "In 13 States, a United Push to Limit Fees of Lawyers." *New York Times*, May 26, p. 10.

Litan, Robert E., and Steven C. Salop. 1994. "Reforming the Lawyer-Client Relationship Through Alternative Billing Methods." *Judicature* 77: 191–97.

Long, John D., and Davis W. Gregg. 1965. *Property and Liability Insurance Handbook*. Homewood, IL: R. D. Irwin.

Lord Chancellor's Department. 1998. "Access to Justice with Conditional Fees." London: Lord Chancellor's Department.

Luce, R. Duncan, and Howard Raiffa. 1957. *Games and Decisions: Introduction and Critical Survey*. New York: John Wiley & Sons.

Lundquist, Weyman I. 1980. "In Search of Discovery Reform." *ABA Journal* 66: 1071–73.

Lyons, David, and Andrew Blum. 1996. "Were ValuJet Families Solicited? Two Lawyers Accused." *National Law Journal* (June 3): A4.

MacLachlan, Claudia. 1993. "Mobile Response to Amtrak Crash." *National Law Journal* (October 11): 1.

Magid, Frank N., Associates. 1997. "Attitudes and Perceptions of Lawyer Advertising: An Executive Summary of Phase I Results." Tallahassee: Florida Bar Ethics Department.

Mann, Kenneth. 1985. *Defending White-Collar Crime: A Portrait of Attorneys At Work*. New Haven, CT: Yale University Press.

Manning, Bayless. 1977. "Hyperlexis: Our National Disease." *Northwestern University Law Review* 71: 767–82.

Markowitz, Harry. 1952. "Portfolio Selection." *Journal of Finance* 7: 77–91.

———. 1959. *Portfolio Selection: Efficient Diversification of Investments*. New York: John Wiley & Sons.

———. 1991. "Foundations of Portfolio Theory." *Journal of Finance* 46: 469–77.

Mather, Lynn, Richard J. Maiman, and Craig A. McEwen. 1995. "'The Passenger Decides on the Destination and I Decide on the Route': Are Divorce Lawyers 'Expensive Cab Drivers?'" *International Journal of Law and the Family* 9: 286–310.

Mather, Lynn, Craig A. McEwen, and Richard J. Maiman. 2001. *Divorce Lawyers at Work: Varieties of Professionalism in Practice*. New York: Oxford University Press.

Maurer, Virginia G., Robert E. Thomas, and Pamela A. DeBooth. 1999. "Attorney Fee Arrangements: The U.S. and Western European Perspectives." *Northwestern Journal of International Law and Business* 19: 272–329.

McConville, Mike, Jacqueline Hodgson, Lee Bridges, and Anita Pavlovic. 1994. *Standing Accused: The Organisation and Practices of Criminal Defence Lawyers in Britain*. Oxford: Clarendon Press.

McGuire, Kevin T. 1993. *The Supreme Court Bar: Legal Elites in the Washington Community*. Charlottesville: University of Virginia Press.

———. 1999. "The Supreme Court Bar and Institutional Relationships." In *The Supreme Court in American Politics: New Institutionalist Interpretations*, ed. Howard Gillman and Cornell W. Clayton, 115–32. Lawrence: University Press of Kansas.

McIntyre, Lisa. 1987. *The Public Defender: The Practice of Law in the Shadows of Repute*. Chicago: University of Chicago Press.

McKenna, Judith A., and Elizabeth C. Wiggins. 1998. "Empirical Research on Civil Discovery." *Boston College Law Review* 39: 785–807.

McMenamin, Brigid. 1995. "The Best-Paid Lawyers." *Forbes*, November 6, pp. 145–46+.

Meier, Barry. 1997. "Lawyer's Foundation Awash in Questions." *New York Times*, February 7, p. 2D.

Menkel-Meadow, Carrie. 1984. "Toward Another View of Legal Negotiation: The Structure of Problem Solving." *UCLA Law Review* 31: 754–842.

Mercer, Jonathan. 1996. *Reputation and International Politics*. Ithaca, NY: Cornell University Press.

Merry, Sally Engle. 1984. "Rethinking Gossip and Scandal." In *Toward a General Theory of Social Control*, ed. Donald Black, 271–302. New York: Academic Press.

Micelli, Thomas J., and Kathleen Segerson. 1991. "Contingent Fees for Lawyers: The Impact on Litigation and Accident Prevention." *Journal of Legal Studies* 20: 381–400.

Miethe, Terance D. 1993. "Public Attitudes Toward Lawyers and Legal Disputes, 1993" [Computer file]. ICPSR ed. Ann Arbor, MI: Inter-university Consortium for Political and Social Research [producer and distributor].

Miller, Geoffrey P. 1987. "Some Agency Problems in Settlement." *Journal of Legal Studies* 16: 189–215.

Miller, Richard E., and Austin Sarat. 1980–81. "Grievances, Claims, and Disputes: Assessing the Adversary Culture." *Law & Society Review* 15: 525–65.

Minish, L. 1979. "The Contingency Fee: A Re-Examination." *Manitoba Law Journal* 10: 65.

Mintz, Morton. 1985. *At Any Cost: Corporate Greed, Women, and the Dalkon Shield*. New York: Pantheon.

Moorhead, Richard. 2000. "Conditional Fee Agreements, Legal Aid, and Access to Justice." *University of British Columbia Law Review* 33: 471–90.

Mullenix, Linda. 1994a. "Discovery in Disarray: The Pervasive Myth of Pervasive Discovery Abuse and the Consequences of Unfounded Rulemaking." *Stanford Law Review* 46: 1393–445.

———. 1994b. "The Pervasive Myth of Pervasive Discovery Abuse: The Sequel." *Boston College Law Review* 39: 683–89.

Nardulli, Peter F. 1986. "Insider Justice: Defense Attorneys and the Handling of Felony Cases." *Journal of Criminal Law and Criminology* 77: 379–417.

National Employment Lawyers Association. 1991. *Unprotected Rights: The Increasing Barriers Preventing Victims of Employment Discrimination from Obtaining Legal Representation*. Cincinnati, OH: National Employment Lawyers Association.

Nelson, Robert L. 1988. *Partners with Power: Social Transformation of the Large Law Firm*. Berkeley: University of California Press.

Neustadter, Gary. 1986. "When Lawyer and Client Meet: Observations of Interviewing and Counseling Behavior in the Consumer Bankruptcy Law Office." *Buffalo Law Review* 35: 177–284.

Newman, J. Wilson. 1997. "Dun & Bradstreet: For the Promotion and Protection of Trade." In *Reputation: Studies in the Voluntary Elicitation of Good Conduct*, ed. Daniel B. Klein, 85–95. Ann Arbor: University of Michigan Press.

O'Connell, Jeffrey. 1979. *The Lawsuit Lottery: Only the Lawyers Win*. New York: Free Press.

O'Connell, Jeffrey, and C. Brian Kelly. 1987. *The Blame Game: Injuries, Insurance, and Injustice*. Cambridge, MA: Lexington Books.

Olson, Walter. 2003. *The Rule of Lawyers: How the New Litigation Elite Threatens America's Rule of Law*. New York: St. Martin's Press.

Packer, Herbert L. 1964. "Two Models of the Criminal Process." *University of Pennsylvania Law Review* 113: 1–68.

Parikh, Sara. 2001. "Professionalism and Its Discontents: A Study of Social Networks in the Plaintiff's Personal Injury Bar." Ph.D. diss., Sociology, University of Illinois at Chicago.

Pastor, Santos, and Carmen Vargas. 2000. *La Justicia Civil en la República Dominicana*. Washington, DC: World Bank (Banco Mundial).

Plous, Scott. 1993. *The Psychology of Judgment and Decision Making*. Philadelphia: Temple University Press.

Pogarsky, Greg, and Linda Babcock. 2001. "Damage Caps, Motivated Anchoring, and Bargaining Impasse." *Journal of Legal Studies* 30: 143–59.

Polinsky, A. Mitchell, and Daniel L. Rubinfeld. 2001. "Aligning the Interests of Lawyers and Clients," Stanford Law and Economics Olin Working Paper no. 223. http://papers.ssrn.com/paper.taf?abstract_id = 281628.

Pommer, Matt. 2003. "No Punitive Award in Crane Collapse: $94M Judgment Overturned," *Capital Times* (Madison, WI), September 30, p. 10C.

Posner, Richard A. 1973. "An Economic Approach to Legal Procedure and Judicial Administration." *Journal of Legal Studies* 2: 399–455.

———. 1977. *Economic Analysis of Law*. Boston: Little, Brown.

Raiffa, Howard. 1982. *The Art and Science of Negotiation*. Cambridge: Belknap Press of Harvard University Press.

Rapoport, Anatol. 1969. *Strategy and Conscience*. New York: Schocken Books.

Reed, John P. 1969. "The Lawyer-Client: A Managed Relationship?" *Academy of Management Journal* 12: 67–80.

Rein, Bert W., and John Barry. 1999. "The Case for Abolishing Contingent Fee Arrangements," Critical Legal Issues, Washington Legal Foundation, Working Papers Series, No. 91.

Reinbach, Andrew. 1993. "Modern Portfolio Theory Takes Root." *Buildings* 87: 64–66.

Richert, David, ed. 1994. "Legal Billing: Seeking Alternatives to the Hourly Rate [Symposium]." *Judicature* 77: 186–202.

Robbennolt, Jennifer K., and Christina A. Studebaker. 1999. "Anchoring in the Courtroom: The Effects of Caps on Punitive Damages." *Law and Human Behavior* 23: 353–73.

Robins, Jon. 1999. "The Price of Success." *Gazette*, January 7, pp. 14–15.

———. 2003. "Law: An Accident Waiting to Happen." *The Independent* (London), June 10.

Rohde, David. 2000. "Cochran TV Ads Sell His Firm's Legal Stardom." *New York Times*, January 28, p. B3.

Rose, Neal. 2003. "October Date Set for PI Fixed Fees Scheme." *Law Society's Gazette*, June 26.

Rosenberg, Maurice, and Michael I. Sovern. 1959. "Delay and the Dynamics of Personal Injury Litigation." *Columbia Law Review* 59: 1115–70.

Rosenthal, Douglas E. 1974. *Lawyer and Client: Who's in Charge?* New York: Russell Sage Foundation.

Ross, H. Laurence. 1980. *Settled Out of Court: The Social Process of Insurance Claims Adjustment*. New York: Aldine.

Rubinfeld, Daniel L., and Suzanne Scotchmer. 1993. "Contingent Fees for Attorneys: An Economic Analysis." *RAND Journal of Economics* 24: 343–56.

Ryan, Francis, Alan Paterson, Tamara Goriely, and Don Fleming, eds. 1999. *The Transformation of Legal Aid: Comparative and Historical Studies*. New York: Oxford University Press.

Sanders, Joseph. 1998. *Bendectin on Trial: A Study of Mass Tort Litigation*. Ann Arbor: University of Michigan Press.

Sanders, Joseph, and Craig Joyce. 1990. "'Off to the Races': The 1980s Tort Crisis and the Law Reform Process." *Houston Law Review* 27: 207–95.

Sarat, Austin, and William L. F. Felstiner. 1989. "Lawyers and Legal Consciousness: Law Talk in the Divorce Lawyer's Office." *Yale Law Journal* 98: 1663–88.

———. 1995. *Divorce Lawyers and Their Clients: Power and Meaning in the Legal Process*. New York: Oxford University Press.

Schelling, Thomas. 1960. *The Strategy of Conflict*. Cambridge: Harvard University Press.

Schwartz, Murray K., and Daniel J. B. Mitchell. 1970. "An Economic Analysis of the Contingent Fee in Personal Injury Litigation." *Stanford Law Review* 22: 1125–62.

Seron, Caroll. 1996. *The Business of Practicing Law: The Work Lives of Solo and Small-Firm Attorneys*. Philadelphia: Temple University Press.

Shapiro, Susan P. 2002. *Tangled Loyalties: Conflict of Interest in Legal Practice*. Ann Arbor: University of Michigan Press.

Shearmur, Jeremy, and Daniel B. Klein. 1997. "Good Conduct in the Great Society: Adam Smith and the Role of Reputation." In *Reputations: Studies in the Voluntary Elicitation of Good Conduct*, ed. Daniel B. Klein, 29–45. Ann Arbor: University of Michigan Press.

Sheridan, Maurice, and James Cameron. 1992. *EC Legal Systems: An Introductory Guide*. London: Butterworths.

Shukaitis, Marc J. 1987. "A Market in Personal Injury Tort Claims." *Journal of Legal Studies* 16: 329–49.

Silver, Charles. 1998. "Flat Fees and Staff Attorneys: Unnecessary Casualties in the Battle over the Law Governing Insurance Defense Lawyers." *Connecticut Insurance Law Journal* 4: 205–57.

Simon, William H. 1991. "Lawyer Advice and Client Autonomy: Mrs. Jones's Case." *Maryland Law Review* 50: 213–26.

Skordaki, Eleni, and Danielle Walker. 1994. *Regulating and Charging for Legal Services: An International Comparison*. London: The Law Society.

Sloan, Frank A., Penny B. Githens, Ellen Wright Clayton, Gerald B. Hickson, Douglas A. Gentile, and David F. Partlett. 1993. *Suing for Medical Malpractice*. Chicago: University of Chicago Press.

Slovak, Jeffrey S. 1980. "Giving and Getting Respect: Prestige and Stratification in a Legal Elite." *American Bar Foundation Research Journal* 1980: 31–68.

Smigel, Erwin O. 1964. *The Wall Street Lawyer: Professional Organization Man?* Bloomington: Indiana University Press.

Southworth, Ann. 1996. "Lawyer-Client Decisionmaking in Civil Rights and Poverty Practice: An Empirical Study of Lawyers' Norms." *Georgetown Journal of Legal Ethics* 9: 1101–55.

Spurr, Stephen J. 1988. "Referral Practices Among Lawyers: A Theoretical and Empirical Analysis." *Law and Social Inquiry* 13: 87–109.

———. 1990. "The Impact of Advertising and Other Factors on Referral Practices, with Special Reference to Lawyers." *RAND Journal of Economics* 21: 235–46.

Stanley, Alessandra. 1991. "Bronx Crash, Then Contest of Lawyers." *New York Times*, June 17, p. B1.

State Bar of Wisconsin. 1999. "1998 Economics of Practice Survey: Executive Summary." Madison: State Bar of Wisconsin. http://www.wisbar.org/bar/reports/econ98.pdf.

Stern, Gerald M. 1976. *The Buffalo Creek Disaster: How Survivors of One of the Worst Disasters in Coal-Mining History Brought Suit Against the Coal Company—and Won*. New York: Random House.

Stock, James H. 1992. "Compensation for Nonpayment Risk in Legal Cases Taken on Contingency: Economic Framework and Empirical Results." Unpublished report, Kennedy School of Government.

Sweet, James A. 1997. "Report on Survey of Accident Victims [Conducted for the Wisconsin Board of Attorneys Professional Responsibility]." Madison: University of Wisconsin Survey Center.

Tanase, Takao. 1990. "The Management of Automobile Accident Compensation in Japan." *Law & Society Review* 24: 651–92.

Taylor, Gary. 1986. "Army, Lawyers Feud Over Crash: Allegations of Solicitation." *National Law Journal* (June 2): 3.

Texas Department of Insurance. 1995. "The 1994 Texas Liability Closed Claim Annual Report." Austin: Texas Department of Insurance.

Tobin, James. 1965. "The Theory of Portfolio Selection." In *The Theory of Interest Rates*, ed. F. H. Hahn and F. P. R. Brechling, 3–51. New York: Macmillan.

Trine, William, and Paul Luvera. 1994. "Pros and Cons of Accepting a Case." *Trial* (May): 16.

Trubek, David M., Austin Sarat, William L. F. Felstiner, Herbert M. Kritzer, and Joel B. Grossman. 1983. "The Costs of Ordinary Litigation." *UCLA Law Review* 31: 72–127.

Tullock, Gordon. 1985. "Adam Smith and the Prisoners' Dilemma." *Quarterly Journal of Economics* 100: 1073–81.

Turow, Scott. 1999. *Personal Injuries.* New York: Farrar, Straus, Giroux.

Tversky, Amos, and Daniel Kahneman. 1974. "Judgment Under Uncertainty: Heuristics and Biases." *Science* 185: 1124–30.

Underwood, Kerry. 1999. "Conditional Fees in Practice." *Solicitors Journal* 143: 1000–1001, 1032–33, 1066–67, 1092–93.

Van Duch, Darryl. 1999. "Test Case for Insurers' Billing Rules: Ethics at Issue." *National Law Journal* (January 24): A1.

Van Hoy, Jerry. 1995. "Selling and Processing Law: Legal Work at Franchise Law Firms." *Law & Society Review* 29: 703–29.

———. 1997a. *Franchise Law Firms and the Transformation of Personal Legal Services.* Westport, CT: Quorum Books.

———. 1997b. "Getting Clients: Supply and Demand Among Plaintiff's Personal Injury Attorneys in Indiana." Paper presented at meeting of Law and Society Association, St. Louis, MO, May 26–June 2, 1997.

———. 1999. "Markets and Contingency: How Client Markets Influence the Work of Plaintiffs' Personal Injury Lawyers." *International Journal of the Legal Profession* 6: 345–66.

Vidmar, Neil. 1995. *Medical Malpractice and the American Jury: Confronting the Myths About Jury Incompetence, Deep Pockets, and Outrageous Damage Awards.* Ann Arbor: University of Michigan Press.

———. 2002. "Juries." In *Legal Systems of the World*, ed. Herbert M. Kritzer, 800–803. Santa Barbara, CA: ABC-CLIO.

Watson, Garry D., W. A. Bogart, Allan C. Hutchinson, Janet Mosher, and Kent Roach. 1991. *Civil Litigation: Cases and Materials.* Toronto: Emond Montgomery.

Weiner, Becky. 1993. "1992 Economics of Practice Survey Report." Madison: State Bar of Wisconsin.

Widiss, Alan I. 1999. *Uninsured and Underinsured Motorist Insurance.* Cincinnati: Anderson.

Willging, Thomas E., Donna Stienstra, John Shapard, and Dean Miletich. 1998. "An Empirical Study of Discovery and Disclosure Practice Under the 1993 Federal Rules Amendments." *Boston College Law Review* 39: 525–96.

Williams, Gerald R. 1983. *Legal Negotiation and Settlement.* St. Paul, MN: West Publishing.

Wolfram, Charles. 1986. *Modern Legal Ethics.* St. Paul, MN: West Publishing.

Wollschläger, Christian. 1998. "Exploring Global Landscapes of Litigation Rates." In *Soziologie des Rechts: Festschrift für Erhard Blankenburg zum 60 Geburtstag,* ed. J. Brand and D. Strempel, 577–88. Baden Baden: Nomos.

Yarrow, Stella. 1998. *The Price of Success: Lawyers, Clients, and Conditional Fees.* London: Policy Studies Institute.

Young, Oran C. 1968. *The Politics of Force: Bargaining During International Crises.* Princeton, NJ: Princeton University Press.

Zander, Michael. 1998. "The Government's Plans on Legal Aid and Conditional Fees." *Modern Law Review* 61: 538–50.

———. 2002a. "If Conditional Fees, Why Not Contingency Fees?" *New Law Journal* (May 24): 797.

———. 2002b. "Will the Revolution in the Funding of Civil Litigation in England Lead to Contingency Fees?" *DePaul Law Review* 52: 259–97.

Index

reputation, 221–22; selling to clients,
172–75. *See also* negotiation
Shapard, John, 106
Shapiro, Susan P., 297n1
Sharratt v. London Central Bus Co Ltd., 259
Shearmur, Jeremy, 235
Sheridan, Maurice, 235
Sherr, Avrom, 307n11
Sheskin, Arlene, 255
shirking, 227–34. *See also* agency
Shukaitis, Marc J.
Silver, Charles, 187
Simon, William H., 125
Skordaki, Eleni, 258–59
Sloan, Frank A., 154, 290n20, 300n34
Slovak, Jeffrey S., 29
Slovic, Paul, 122
Smigel, Erwin O., 26
Smith, Adam, 235
social security cases, 230–31, 297n7,
300n40, 304n6
solicitation (of potential clients): *See* direct
mail
solo practice, 29–30, 32, 44, 288n5. *See also*
practice setting
Southworth, Ann, 126
Sovern, Michael I., 305n8
special damages, 115
specialization, 27–30, 294n50; and effective hourly rates, 200–203
Spurr, Stephen J., 61, 305n8
stacking (underinsured / uninsured motorist policies), 167–68, 299n29
stakes, 37–38, 301n41; and effective
hourly rates, 200–203, 211–13; and initial demand, 153–55; and initial offer,
156–57; and negotiation, 151–52. *See
also* case value
standard fee, 38–43
Stanley, Alessandra, 45
State Bar of Wisconsin, 27
Stern, Gerald M., 26, 98, 294n2
Stienstra, Donna, 106
stock market: comparison to, 182, 301n1
Stock, James H., 289n18
Studebaker, Christina A., 122
subrogation, 124, 287n4, 296n17; and selling settlement to client, 172–73; settling
subrogation claims, 160–66, 170

suits, filing: *See* filing suit
surveillance (of clients), 119, 295n14
Sweet, James A., 22, 54–55, 57
Syverud, Kent D., 14

Tanase, Takao, 259
taxation of costs, 306n9
Taylor, Gary, 45
telephone, 112–13; screening cases, 81–82;
use of for research, 99–100
Texas, 52, 291n17, 291n23, 294n40; selectivity in taking cases, 76–77
Texas Department of Insurance (TDI), 271,
296n16
Thai Trading Company v. Taylor, 258
third parties: *See* subrogation
Thomas, Robert E., 258
time records, 267; 303n27; absence of, 188,
203, 210; difficulty of keeping, 262
tit-for-tat, 235, 237–38
tobacco litigation, 291n20, 307n16
Tobin, James, 11–12
tort reform, 1, 2, 253–56, 263–69, 287n1
Traynor, Michael, 38
trial: avoiding, 241–42; decision to go to,
231–32, 300n35; fear of losing, 248; and
reputation, 248
Trine, William, 68
Trubek, David M., 106, 221, 305n3
trustworthiness (of opposing lawyers),
130, 239
Tullock, Gordon, 235
Turow, Scott, 26, 45
Tversky, Amos, 122

uncertainty, 17; about damages, 124; about
legal process, 128; of trial, 174. *See also*
risk
underinsured motorist claims: settling,
166–68, 299n28; stacking, 167–68,
299n29
Underwood, Kerry, 258
uninsured motorist claims 7, 299n28; settling, 166–68; stacking, 167–68, 299n29

Vaiana, Mary E., 53, 76, 115, 187, 256, 271,
304n31
Valujet, 252
Van Duch, Darryl, 236